Litigation Support

Litigation Support

Third edition

Coopers & Lybrand

Butterworths
London, Dublin and Edinburgh
1995

United Kingdom	Butterworths, a Division of Reed Elsevier (UK) Ltd, Halsbury House, 35 Chancery Lane, LONDON WC2A 1EL and 4 Hill Street, EDINBURGH EH2 3JZ
Australia	Butterworths Pty Ltd, SYDNEY, MELBOURNE, BRISBANE, ADELAIDE, PERTH, CANBERRA and HOBART
Canada	Butterworth Canada Ltd, TORONTO and VANCOUVER
Ireland	Butterworth (Ireland) Ltd, DUBLIN
Malaysia	Malayan Law Journal Sdn Bhd, KUALA LUMPUR
New Zealand	Butterworths of New Zealand Ltd, WELLINGTON and AUCKLAND
Puerto Rico	Butterworths of Puerto Rico Inc, SAN JUAN
Singapore	Malayan Law Journal Pte Ltd, SINGAPORE
South Africa	Butterworth Publishers (PTY) Ltd, DURBAN
USA	Butterworth Legal Publishers, CARLSBAD, California and SALEM, New Hampshire

A CIP Catalogue record for this book is available from the British Library.

First edition 1988
Second edition 1991

ISBN 0 406 04994 7

Typeset by Phoenix Photosetting, Chatham, Kent.
Printed in Great Britain by Ashford Colour Press, Gosport, Hampshire

Preface

In writing this book, we have had two main purposes in mind. Specifically, we have sought not merely to describe how an expert witness with an accounting background should go about his task, but also to offer practical guidance to those engaging such an expert (or thinking of doing so) on how they can make the best use of the help he can offer them.

This book has also been written to fill a perceived gap in the UK literature of both accountancy and law and, as such, we hope it will be of relevance and interest to practitioners of both disciplines. We recognise, though, that such a work needs to be fairly succinct in order to remain both practical and approachable to professionals of either class. Thus, whilst seeking to cover the topics we feel to be of most importance, we have not attempted encyclopaedic coverage. In particular, we make no apologies for simplifying some matters (though not, we hope, so much as to drain them of their relevance) and eliminating many of the case histories and statutory references which might have been included if we had either a dozen volumes, or as many years, at our disposal.

The book is divided into two sections: the first dealing with the professional and technical aspects of what is known variously as 'litigation support' or 'forensic accountancy', the second with certain procedural aspects of legal and court administration. We hope that each part will have something to offer both lawyers and accountants. Whether this will be as an introduction to subjects outside the basic armoury of his professional training or as a practical aide-memoire to matters with which he is familiar will, of course, depend upon the standpoint of the individual. However, it may be helpful to set out briefly our own ideas on the respective benefits which might be derived from each part.

The first section is largely technical in its content. For the lawyer, it should serve to help summarise the aspects he may wish to consider when framing the terms of reference of his accounting expert, particularly on matters of quantum. Equally, we aim to give practical guidance to the accountant on bridging the gap between possession of conventional expertise in his discipline and the harnessing of that knowledge to provide a valuable aid, not just to those instructing him, but to the court itself.

The second section will be of assistance primarily to the accountant – and, potentially, to experts in other fields, especially those concerned with quantum – by providing background reading on various topics which may not have been covered in the individual's academic training or professional experience to date. Although the expert witness is neither advocate nor judge – a truth he forgets or ignores at his peril – the likelihood of his executing his own role effectively will be significantly diminished if he lacks an adequate appreciation of the perspectives of those with whom he aims to communicate. We doubt many would seriously take issue with the maxim that the most successful persuaders are often those who show the greatest insight into the viewpoint of whoever they hope to convince; this is especially true when applied to an expert witness, whose aim will often be to persuade the judge that his own view should be accepted in preference to that of someone else.

An expert works in the public gaze and in the face of criticism by others. Qualities of both independence and imagination are therefore important. When we first wrote this book our attention was drawn to an extract from the 1971 Report of the then Mr Justice Ormrod's Committee on Legal Education (Cmnd 4595) which dealt with the desirable qualities of practising lawyers; so much of this seems applicable, mutatis mutandis, to the role of the expert that we feel it worth quoting in full:

> 'The raw material of every practising lawyer is facts and a great deal of his time will be spent, whether he is a judge or a barrister or a solicitor, in finding the facts. The law cannot be properly applied until they are ascertained. If the facts are wrong, the advice of the most learned lawyer will be, at best, worthless – and may be dangerous. Facts, therefore, are of crucial importance to the practising lawyer at all levels, and his ability to handle facts, and then investigate and scrutinise them for accuracy. Analysis of all the available data, to separate the relevant from the irrelevant and to perceive the relation between one set of facts and another and so to check reliability or expose errors, is an essential process in every case. In every case, also, he must synthesise his facts in order to present them lucidly and cogently, whether as an advocate or as a pleader, or as a draftsman, or negotiator, or even as a letter writer. All stages of these processes will of course be controlled and informed by his knowledge of the relevant law, without which the exercise would be futile.' [Paragraph 91 at p 38.]

Others have characterised the desirable qualities of the expert as including an enquiring and open mind, the ability to render complex technical matters accessible to non-experts, a respect for the complexity of disputes and their underlying causes, and the willingness to work hard and conscientiously. A sound basis of knowledge and experience in one's professed field of expertise is to be taken as axiomatic.

Our endorsement of these comments is whole-hearted and grows daily!

All those concerned with litigation will be aware of the major changes which are occurring or in the offing. Among the factors these reflect are the plethora of litigation by Names against Lloyd's agents and syndicate auditors, the growth in actions against the accounting profession and merchant banks in the corporate finance field, and the review of civil court procedures which the Lord Chancellor has recently entrusted to Lord Woolf.

The litigation activity surrounding Lloyd's is reaching a peak as this third edition goes to press. Environmental and asbestosis claims in the US courts have already brought down dozens of syndicates at Lloyd's of London and there are many action groups amongst the Names who are seeking to prove negligence on the part of the underwriters who insured such risks, or on the part of the accountants and auditors who allegedly failed in their respective duties to acquaint names of the gathering financial disasters which were engulfing their syndicates. We have introduced a new chapter on this subject. The case law which is evolving will be significant both for insurance cases and, we would guess, for professional negligence cases generally.

The rapid advances in information technology continue to have a wide-ranging impact on the commercial world as a whole and on the legal profession in particular. To survey the implications of technology for the law would deserve a volume of its own, much of which would fall outside the scope of the present work. However, we ought to mention two specific areas where microcomputers have become especially relevant to litigation in general, and to the accountant's role in particular. The first of these involves the use of databases which, among a wide variety of potential investigative applications, can be used to catalogue documents, to produce chronologies and to permit ready identification and matching of related documents. Another important area involves the use of so-called 'spreadsheet' software. This has become a virtually essential tool for much of the analytical work of the contemporary expert accountant. It enables even complex calculations to be speedily and inexpensively reworked under various alternative scenarios; this may assist the judge in evaluating the financial consequences of various alternative judgments he might be contemplating and, by the same token, it can be an invaluable aid to lawyers when negotiating settlements.

The decision in the Autumn of 1994 to entrust the review of civil court procedures to Lord Woolf is likely to have far-reaching effects. Lord Woolf is expected to exhort judges and advocates alike to fashion an ideology of civil justice more in tune with the needs of a modern society and economy. As Sir Thomas Bingham, Master of the Rolls (and thus head of the country's civil courts), said: 'It is no use having the best jurisprudence in the world if those who need it cannot afford to tap into it'. Lord Woolf has indicated that he would like civil courts to be 'judge-driven' and to end the existing pattern of litigation led by lawyers, which soaks up a disconcerting amount of professional time, effort and money. A shift towards 'procedural judges' would mean that judges would control timetables and impose cost limits at the outset. The appointment of experts by judges themselves (as we have experienced on the continent of Europe) rather than by the parties to the case, might well follow. Alternative dispute resolution, such as conciliation and mediation, would also be encouraged by the judiciary. The cumulative effect of these reforms will be slow and some reforms will meet much opposition. However, it can be predicted that when the next edition of this book comes to be prepared there will be new dimensions for the accounting expert to be catered for.

Having said earlier that experts should not stray into areas which lie outside their remit, we recognise that it is not for us to propose radical changes in the operation of the legal system; however, there is one particular area recurring both in this book and in our own day-to-day experience where we have seen the opportunity for economy in the litigation arena. Where the chief dispute is over quantum rather than liability, there is a strong argument for referring immediately to experts in the hope of avoiding the costs associated with adversarial litigation. When counsel's opinion is first sought, he will usually deal with the law rather than with quantum, probably on the basis that there can be no quantum without liability. Often, though, there will be advantages in commissioning at least an initial study of quantum before firm positions are taken; sometimes it may even be desirable for the judge or arbitrator to order this. A particularly good example of the type of situation we have in mind was provided by Mr Justice Scott Baker (who was, at the time of quoting, a leading silk) who told us:

'I once had a case that was going to last nine months to a year. The quantum of damage reports were not exchanged until a few days before the trial was due to start. When they were, it quickly became apparent that the gap between the two sides on quantum made the litigation uneconomic. The case was settled. But it could have been done months before with a great saving of cost, if quantification of damage had been given much higher priority in preparation.'

This is a book about litigation written by non-lawyers. We are therefore more than commonly indebted to our many friends in the legal community who have given us help and advice. In particular, we would like to acknowledge the valuable review of the first edition by partners of Turner Kenneth Brown, commercial lawyers; Mr Justice Scott Baker, for his thorough review of the whole book in its first and second editions; Lord Alexander of Weedon QC for his general encouragement and, in particular, for contributing the Foreword; and George Staple, from whom we have drawn some observations on the nature of fraud. We also express our thanks to Rebecca Collinson for her work in compiling this latest edition.

This third edition has come some seven years after the first. In that period the world has moved on and some changes have had to be made to the original text to reflect more recent court decisions. Lloyd's disputes have been given a separate chapter and a new chapter has been written concerning the reconstruction of capital, a matter which has come to the fore following the industrial depression of recent years. We have also expanded certain chapters, notably those concerned with valuations, auditor's negligence, commercial fraud, taxation of damages, personal injuries and regulatory work, and have updated the appendices where necessary.

Christopher Lemar
Donald Chilvers
Andrew Mainz
Timothy Lawrence
Jeff Hunt
Ian Trumper

Plumtree Court
London EC4
April 1995

Foreword to the first edition

Accounts and accountancy techniques have become increasingly important in litigation. The first part of this book indicates the areas of law in which financial evidence may play an important role. Whether it be a calculation of loss of profits in a claim for breach of contract, or working out net loss of earnings in a personal injuries action, or in the fiscal considerations which apply in matrimonial proceedings, expert evidence has a part to play. It used to be thought that the courts were not always particularly keen on detailed assessment but would see to 'do the best they can' on a somewhat rough and ready basis which emphasised a preference for an instinctive rather than statistical approach. These days have gone, and modern judges are most willing to look rigorously at financial calculations.

So this book by Donald Chilvers and his co-author Chris Lemar, who bring great experience to their task, is most timely and welcome. It is said to be aimed particularly at the expert witness. It is full of practical advice, such as the importance of relating the evidence to the issue and setting it out in a way which bears in mind that the giving of such evidence is part of the exercise in advocacy. As such it should have great value. For example, those who are most expert in their fields may, when it comes to giving evidence, find themselves entering a novel situation in which careful guidance has to be given by the lawyers as to preparation and the giving of evidence in court. Chapter 16 [now 19], with its hints for cross-examination, illustrates how thoroughly and sensitively the authors have studied court procedures.

Tales are told of the repartee of some expert witnesses. There was a most distinguished doctor, who regularly gave evidence, and on one occasion fell to be cross-examined by counsel on whose side he had in another case once appeared. Counsel began his cross-examination sternly:

'Is it right you consider you are the greatest living expert on this topic?'
Answer: 'I don't, but that is how you described me last time I was your expert witness.'

While repartee can be dangerous, and wisely it has not been highlighted here, this book does contain all the basic armoury which a witness needs for what is rightly described by the authors as a daunting task.

But this book is not only for the expert witness. It will, I think, be of the greatest value to lawyers. The summary of the law in the first part of the book is an invaluable reminder of basic principles. Even more importantly, the advice to experts is of itself advice to lawyers as to the problems facing the experts, how their minds may work, and how to approach the task of getting the best out of them. I would not be surprised if the hints on the giving of evidence were not almost as useful to the lawyers as they will be to the experts themselves.

There is another reason why this book is so welcome. It stresses the great importance of preparation which is vital to the successful conduct of litigation. It also highlights the need for there to be early, open disclosure of expert evidence so that there can be the earliest sensible settlement of a dispute. Settlements at the door of the court are costly. The stakes are made higher because somebody has to pay the costs which by then have grown large. The courts are searching for procedures which enable issues to be identified early in a dispute and to come to trial in a way which enables them to be conducted as efficiently and economically as possible. The new commercial court procedures are an excellent example.

We value our adversarial approach to litigation and the role which oral argument plays as a way of resolving disputes. But we must keep to a minimum the time which is necessary for the fair resolution of cases. We have to seek, wherever possible, sensible forms of alternative dispute resolution. We, as lawyers, have to be alert to the need to try to settle cases in the interests of clients as early as we sensibly can. The fact that the authors stress this in their advice is a valuable reminder to us all that litigation is not an end in itself, and it is a very practical and morally responsible contribution which they have made in their most admirable book. I am glad to have been given the opportunity to commend it to both the accounting and legal professions.

Alexander of Weedon QC, 1988
1 Brick Court
Temple
London EC4

Contents

Preface   v
Foreword to the first edition   ix
List of cases   xiii
Bibliography   xvii

Introduction: The accountant as expert witness   1

PART I : TECHNICAL ASPECTS

Chapter 1   A general discussion of damages   11

Chapter 2   Loss of profits: how to calculate them   26

Chapter 3   Breach of warranty claims   36

Chapter 4   Valuations for court purposes   46

Chapter 5   Construction contract claims   60

Chapter 6   Personal injuries   78

Chapter 7   Divorce   97

Chapter 8   Professional negligence: accountants   109

Chapter 9   Commercial fraud   127

Chapter 10   Intellectual property disputes   145

Chapter 11   Reinsurance contract disputes   151

Chapter 12   Lloyd's disputes   159

Chapter 13   Security for costs   173

Chapter 14   Interest and foreign currency: their effect on damages   178

Chapter 15   Taxation of damages   188

Chapter 16   Regulatory work   199

Chapter 17   Balance sheet: capital reorganisations   211

PART II : LEGAL PROCEDURE AND PRACTICE ADMINISTRATION

Chapter 18   High Court procedures   221

Chapter 19   Hints for cross-examination   233

Chapter 20   Arbitration and other forms of alternative dispute resolution   242

Chapter 21   Day-to-day practice notes   255

APPENDICES

Appendix A   A legal lexicon   269
Appendix B   An accounting lexicon   276
Appendix C   Some examples of claims settled   282
Appendix D   Valuation of businesses   284
Appendix E   Building contract disputes: overheads formulae   293
Appendix F   Auditing standards   295
Appendix G   An example of an affidavit used in a security for costs
              application   311
Appendix H   Do's and don'ts in cross-examination   315
Appendix I   Rules for the ICC Court of Arbitration   317
Appendix J   An example of a letter of instruction   334
Appendix K   An example of terms of reference and fee arrangements   336
Appendix L   Expert accountant's report on consequential loss claim:
              example   339
Appendix M   Expert accountant's report on compensation claim:
              example   358
Appendix N   Visual presentation of evidence   373
Appendix O   A Director's affidavit in connection with a capital
              reorganisation: example   390

Index   397

List of cases

PARA

Al Saudi Banque v Clarke Pixley (1990) 819
Anangel Atlas Compania Naviera SA v Ishikawajima-Harima Heavy Industries
   Co Ltd (No 2) (1990)... 464
Arpad, The (1934) 134
Arrows (No 4), Re (1993) 952
Auty v National Coal Board (1985) 643
Axa Equity & Law Home Loans Ltd v Goldsack & Freeman (1994) 419
B v B (1989) 717, 730
Banque Bruxelles Lambert SA v Eagle Star Insurance Co Ltd (1994) 469, 470
Beoco Ltd v Alfa Laval Co Ltd (1994) 138
Biggin & Co Ltd v Permanite Ltd (1951) 142
British Transport Commission v Gourley (1956) 152, 620
Bushwall Properties Ltd v Vortex Properties Ltd (1975) 1405, 1421
Candler v Crane Christmas & Co (1951) 817
Caparo Industries plc v Dickman (1990)......................... 802, 805, 812,
                                                813–821, 873
Carnell Computer Technology Ltd v Unipart Group Ltd (1988) 2170
Carter v Boehm (1766)..................................... Introduction
Cassel v Hammersmith and Fulham Health Authority (1992) 640
Champion v London Fire and Civil Defence Authority (1990) 646
Chaplin v Hicks (1911) 142
Chorzow Factory case (1928) 171
Crosby (J) & Sons Ltd v Portland (1967) 549
Cullinane v British Rema Manufacturing Co Ltd (1954) 242
Deeny v Gooda Walker Ltd (1994) 1223, 1230–1234,
                                              1243, 1250, 1253
Department of the Environment v Thomas Bates & Sons Ltd (1990) 456
Derby & Co Ltd v Weldon (No 10) (1991) 2134
Dexter v Courtaulds (1984) 1414
Donoghue v Stevenson. See M'Alister (or Donoghue) v Steveson
Duxbury v Duxbury (1987) 742
Evans v Evans (1990) 709
Fairweather (H) & Co Ltd v Wandsworth London Borough Council (1987) 548
Federal Commerce and Navigation Co Ltd v Tradax Export SA, The Maratha
   Envoy (1978) 1430
Firbank's Executors v Humphreys (1886) 336
Folias, The. See Services Europe Atlantique Sud (SEAS) v Stockholms
   Rederiaktiebolag SVEA, The Folias
Fomento (Sterling Area) Ltd v Selsdon Fountain Pen Co Ltd (1958) 971
Franksten and Hartings Corpn v Cohen (1959) 969
Galoo Ltd v Bright Grahame Murray (1995) 802, 843–846,
                                                 972, 1248
Guinness plc v Saunders (1990) 948
Hadley v Baxendale (1854) 133, 136, 547

Hallam-Eames (William) v Merrett Syndicates Ltd (1995) 1205
Harbutt's Plasticine Ltd v Wayne Tank and Pump Co Ltd (1970) 122
Hedley Byrne & Co Ltd v Heller & Partners Ltd (1964) 817
Hodgson v Trapp (1989) 625
Hunt v RM Douglas (Roofing) Ltd (1988) 1424
Ikarian Reefer, The. See National Justice Cia Naviera SA v Prudential Assurance
    Co Ltd, The Ikarian Reefer
International Laboratories v Dewar (1933) 829, 971
James McNaughton Paper Group Ltd v Hicks Anderson & Co (1991) 822
Kelly v Dawes (1990) 657
Kingston Cotton Mill Co (No 2), Re (1896) 824, 954, 968
Lim Poh Choo v Camden and Islington Area Health Authority (1980) 629
Livingstone v Rawyards Coal Co (1880) 106
Lloyd Cheyham & Co Ltd v Littlejohn & Co (1987) 826
London and General Bank, Re (1895) 832, 877
London Oil Storage Co Ltd v Seear Hasluck & Co (1904) 968
London, Chatham and Dover Rly Co v South Eastern Rly Co (1893) 1410
Loveday v Renton (1990) 1930
M'Alister (or Donoghue) v Stevenson (1932) 811, 812
Maratha Envoy, The. See Federal Commerce and Navigation Co Ltd v Tradax
    Export SA, The Maratha Envoy
Miliangos v George Frank (Textiles) Ltd (1976) 166, 1426,
                                                    1429–1430, 1436
Miliangos v George Frank (Textiles) Ltd (No 2) (1977) 1413
Minter (FG) Ltd and Drake & Scull Ltd v Welsh Health Technical Services
    Organisation (1980) 551
Mitchell v Mulholland (No 2) (1972) 160
Morgan Crucible Co Ltd v Hill Samuel & Co Ltd (1991) 820, 821, 822
Murphy v Brentwood District Council (1990) 456
National Bank of Greece SA v Pinios Shipping Co No1 (1989) 1422
National Justice Cia Naviera SA v Prudential Assurance Co Ltd, The Ikarian
    Reefer (1993) .... Introduction
Nelson Guarantee Corpn Ltd v Hodgson (1958) 848
Norjarl K/S A/S v Hyundai Heavy Industries Co Ltd (1991) 2035
Overseas Tankship (UK) Ltd v Morts Dock and Engineering Co Ltd, The Wagon
    Mound (1961) 840
Pacific Acceptance Corpn Ltd v Forsyth (1970) 828, 831,
                                                                970
Panchand Frères SA v Pagnam and Fratelli (1974) 1404
Parry v Cleaver (1970) 628
Pennine Raceway Ltd v Kirklees Metropolitan Council (No 2) (1989) 1531
Pergamon Press Ltd, Re (1970) 1614
Polish Upper Silesia case (1926) 168
Porzelack KG v Porzelack (UK) Ltd (1987) 1309–1311
Private Bank & Trust Co Ltd v S (UK) Ltd (1993) 419
Prokop v DHSS (1985) 1414
Ratcliffe v Evans (1892) 142
Ratner's Group plc, Re (1988) 1707
Roberts (Richard) Holdings Ltd v Douglas Smith Partnership (1990) 2619
Sachs v Miklos (1948) 159
Saif Ali v Sidney Mitchell & Co (1980) 1234
Services Europe Atlantique Sud (SEAS) v Stockholms Rederiaktiebolag SVEA,
    The Folias (1979) 1432–1433
Simonius Vischer & Co v Holt & Thompson (1979) 848
Smith v Manchester Corpn (1974) 645
Smoker v London Fire and Civil Defence Authority (1991) 628
Spencer (James) & Co v IRC (1950) 1540

Tate & Lyle Industries Ltd v Greater London Council (1981) 237, 1417
Thomas v Bunn (1991) 1419
Victoria Laundry (Windsor) Ltd v Newman Industries Ltd (1949) 136
Wagon Mound, The. See Overseas Tankship (UK) Ltd v Morts Dock and
 Engineering Co Ltd, The Wagon Mound
Ward v Chief Constable for Avon and Somerset (1985) 1411
Whitehouse v Jordan (1981) . . . . Introduction
Wood v British Coal Corpn (1991) 628
Zim Properties Ltd v Procter (Inspector of Taxes) (1985) 156, 1518, 1526

Bibliography

Bellerose, R P	*Reinsurance for the Beginner* (3rd edn, 1988) Witherby
Bernstein, R	*Handbook of Arbitration Practice* (1987) Sweet & Maxwell
Curzon, P	*Dictionary of Law* (3rd edn, 1988) Pitman
Carter, R L	*Reinsurance* (1979) Kluwer
Eastaway, N, Booth, H and Eamer, K	*Practical Share Valuation* (3nd edn, 1994) Butterworths
Glover, C G	*Valuation of Unquoted Securities* (1986) Gee
Goode, R	*Commercial Law* (1985) Pelican
Gurney, R	*Share Valuation* (1987) Gower
Hibberd, P R	*Variations in Construction Contracts* (1986) Blackwells
Hodgkinson, T	*Expert Evidence – Law and Practice* (1990) Sweet & Maxwell
Huntington, I K	*Fraud – Prevention and Detection* (1992) Butterworths
Jackson, J, and Davies, DTA	*Matrimonial Finance and Taxation* (5th edn, 1992) Butterworths
Kemp, D	*Damages for Personal Injury and Death* (4th edn, 1990) Longman Professional
McGregor, H	*McGregor on Damages* (15th edn, 1988) Sweet & Maxwell
Macve, Professor	*A survey of Lloyd's syndicate accounts* (2nd edn, 1993) Institute of Chartered Accountants in England & Wales
Mustill, Lord Justice, and Boyd, S	*Commercial Arbitration* (2nd edn, 1989) Butterworths
Parris, J	*Standard Form of Building Contract JCT 1980* (2nd edn, 1985) Blackwells
Powell-Smith, V and Sims, J	*Building Contract Claims* (2nd edn, 1988) Blackwells
Pratt, S	*Valuing a Business* (1981) Dow Jones-Irwin

Smith and Keenan   *English Law* (8th edn, 1986) Pitman

Various   *The Parliament House Book* Greens

Wood, R D   *Building and Civil Engineering Claims* (3rd edn, 1985)
                      Estates Gazette

Introduction: the accountant as expert witness

How disputes come to court – The legal process – The barrister's viewpoint – Damages – The uses and attributes of expert witnesses – Urgency and commitment – The ability to communicate with a lay audience – Independence and authority

In recent years, the scope of an accountant's training and experience has been expanding rapidly. Yet few accountants will have gone into a court and fewer still have had training in how to perform as an expert witness. Until an accountant has grasped what is involved in the assessment of damages, he[1] is unlikely to carry much weight if called upon to give evidence.

So one of our objectives in writing this book is to provide professional guidance to the forensic accountant and others who work on a litigation team. It will not make the reader an expert, but it will make it easier for him to perform without embarrassment if called to give his opinion at a court or at an arbitration hearing.

'Knowing your stuff' is, however, only one of the two main skills needed by the expert witness. The other is an appreciation of the role and requirements of the lawyers and other main participants in the case.

The world of the lawyer, especially if he is engaged in litigation, is quite different from that of the rest of the commercial community. It is the lawyer who runs the case on behalf of his client. He decides strategy and acts as Master of Ceremonies. If he meets an accountant who does not appreciate his problems, he will be at something of a loss. He will not think it part of his job to try to understand the world of the accountant, nor will he take kindly to having to start from scratch and educate the accountant about court procedures and requirements. The second objective of this book is therefore to describe the legal framework within which the forensic accountant will operate, and the administrative requirements that it entails.

HOW DISPUTES COME TO COURT

It is axiomatic that a businessman should never get involved in litigation except as a last resort. Even then, he must carefully weigh the pros and cons of litigation. He may win his case, but litigation will almost certainly terminate any future business relationship.

The vast majority of transactions between individuals are of course harmonious; there is no reason for anyone to believe that he has been 'done down'. But a small number of transactions, through contractual or other causes, give one or both parties the sense of being unfairly treated; these are the seeds of a court case.

The legal process

Most commercial disputes begin with an exchange of letters, with one side claiming that the other side is to blame and should make recompense. If this does not do the trick a writ is issued, followed by claims, counterclaims, responses to claims and all the other paraphernalia laid down in High Court Rules. If these steps are unsuccessful, the process will culminate in the court action itself.

Major commercial disputes in England and Wales are heard before a judge in the High Court; juries are not used in the UK for civil cases, except where libel is involved. Arbitration is a private, but legally binding, procedure for resolving disputes, held before a tribunal or independent arbiter, who need not have a qualification in law.

In a legal case, both the lawyers and the experts are serving the interests of the client. The client's solicitors deal with the preliminary stages of litigation, and they engage the barrister (also known as counsel) who handles the formal advocacy in court. The expert witnesses may be engaged by the solicitors or directly by the client.

The expert witness needs to understand the legal process, and so we have described the structure of the courts and of the legal profession, and the steps in litigation and arbitration, in some detail in Part II. Appendix A contains a glossary of some common legal terms that the accountant is likely to come across. Appendix B contains a similar glossary of accountancy terms that lawyers and others might find useful.

At what point does the expert witness become involved in the litigation? All too often, unfortunately, the case is well developed before the accountant is approached. The battle lines are generally well drawn and both sides have established entrenched positions. A good case can be made for involving the expert accountant early in the dispute, as he can make a valuable contribution at many stages:

- giving preliminary advice on quantum,[2] following examination of pleadings and preliminary evidence;

- advising on additional evidence ('discovery') to be requested from the other side;

- briefing counsel on accounting and financial aspects of the case, prior to the trial;

- preparing a detailed expert's report following the review of all available evidence;

- meeting with the other side's expert to narrow areas of disagreement;

- reviewing expert accounting or other financial reports submitted by the other side;

- advising on payments into court;

- advising instructing solicitors and counsel during the trial;

- giving oral evidence at the trial; and

- assisting with negotiations to settle the case.

This is the mainstream of the forensic process. There are also many tributaries through which the forensic accountant may be asked to assist in navigating. He might be asked to negotiate a particular item of the dispute, for example, the interest element; or to reach agreement on the quantum of items of claim where liability is no longer contentious; or to advise, neutrally, on tax questions.

The barrister's viewpoint

If the accountant is to be successful in his role as expert witness, he needs to understand the ethics of advocacy. The first thing to understand is that advocates take on cases which are not always easy to win. Part of the system of establishing justice is that points should be decided in an adversarial atmosphere. There will be strong points which the barrister will want to emphasise; there will be weaknesses which he will not want to dwell on in court. The experienced expert accountant will form a private opinion about matters which are to be decided on a point of law; he may even be privately convinced that the balance of legal argument goes against the client for whom he is acting as an expert. But that is not his business. We have met accountants, and indeed other experts, who think that they have to enter into judgment on matters which are not strictly within their terms of reference. Whereas an accountant in a normal report may cover a wide field, and feel obliged to take a view on all sorts of subjects, he is ill-advised to stray away from his brief or expertise when assisting the court. Furthermore, it is amazing how often an initial impression, formed after reading a claim or a defence document, can be badly wrong, particularly in matters of quantum.

Damages

One of the most common remedies in civil actions for breach of contract or tort is 'damages'. Damages are awarded in money terms and are, therefore, in some way or other an expression of financial settlement. To award damages, the judge has to evaluate the financial evidence concerning the loss suffered by the plaintiff. Sometimes this is simple evidence of fact. Alternatively, the contract may make it abundantly clear what damages should be awarded for breach. However, in an increasing number of cases today, the extent of financial loss is not laid down in black and white. Rather, the court must decide between various shades of grey.

When people make claims in court they almost invariably exaggerate the damage suffered. The experienced expert will develop a sixth sense about what is likely to be the final figure for a fair settlement, once the liability questions have been sorted out. We have maintained general records of all the major claims and settlements with which we have been concerned. Extracts from these records are in Appendix C. Typically, commercial claims are settled at around 10–20% of the original claim; in some cases claims have been settled at even lower levels. No conclusion can be drawn from this observation, since the overriding factor in assessing damages is that of liability; we mention it simply to indicate the scepticism required on the part of anyone asked to assist in disputes of this type.

When a lawyer is consulted on a dispute, his first task is to assess the liability factor. There is a tendency for quantum to be treated rather casually at the initial stages, and sometimes left almost until the steps of the court are reached. The itemisation and calculation of claim sums will tend to be done on the principle: 'If it is over the top, we can sort it out later.' But this approach can be disastrous: when, for instance, by exaggerating the quantum the lawyer and his client mislead themselves into fighting a case which will not stand up to expert validation. We recommend lawyers and their clients to seek the views of an expert forensic accountant on quantum issues at the earliest stage.

THE USES AND ATTRIBUTES OF EXPERT WITNESSES

The law determines that the judge must make his decision in relation to evidence put before him. The law on evidence is thus a matter of great significance in putting a case to court. In the British legal system, evidence is put before the judge by the barrister or advocate. However, the lawyer must draw his evidence from either documents or exhibits, or witnesses. Witnesses fall into two categories: witnesses as to fact and expert witnesses.

The term 'witnesses as to fact' is self-explanatory and does not need any amplification. The subject of expert witnesses is, however, central to this book.

Under British law, all facts must be established and it is for the judge or jury to draw the appropriate inferences from them. Where the matter in question is specialised, a judge or jury may not be equipped to draw the appropriate inferences; he or they will need to listen to a witness – an expert in the field – who can provide an opinion on issues and thereby assist the court in coming to a conclusion. 'Mere opinion' is not enough. It must be based on the expert's experience.[3] In expressing an opinion, the expert must also make clear those facts which are agreed by the parties and those facts which have to be proved to the court by reference to documents or witnesses of fact.

Although the court has limited power to appoint a court expert, in practice each party usually calls its own expert.[4] The use of expert witnesses is restricted by rules that are designed to prevent surprises at the trial. Indeed, except with the leave of the court, or unless all the parties agree, no expert evidence can be adduced at the trial. In most cases, although not all, the parties exchange expert reports before the trial.

The expert witness is a servant of the court. In the English judicial system he assists the court to establish the objective truth. In this adversarial system the expert is likely to be appointed by one of the parties. Nevertheless, the expert should avoid becoming an advocate for his side. He should stick to areas within his expertise. He should avoid anything that would make him clearly appear as partisan. When an expert witness is giving evidence, he should avoid creating a bad impression by sticking dogmatically to an unimportant or, worse still, bad point.

Does the expert have a duty to cover the weak points in his side's case? This is somewhat of a dilemma. Under the adversarial system it is not the responsibility of each party automatically to make clear all its weaknesses to the other. However, the expert must bear in mind that in giving his evidence in court he will be under oath to give the truth, the whole truth and nothing but the truth.

The courts have long recognised the contribution which accountants can make as expert accounting witnesses. In 1974 Whitford J said:

> 'I do think it is advisable in all cases, even where estimates are necessarily made by internal staff, that petitioners should seek advice from some independent accountant who may be able to question them as to the basis upon which they are making their estimates and, having done so, by swearing an affidavit give to the court a rather more complete picture of the financial position that does emerge in this particular case'.

In that case, the practitioner had not sought help from an independent accountant.

The accountant acting as an expert witness in court is usually there to express opinions on the circumstances relating to damages and how these damages should be quantified. From time to time the accountant may also be asked to give the court evidence on the responsibilities of accountants, for example, in cases concerning allegations of negligence against a practising accountant.

There is a wider sphere in which an accountant's report, properly prepared, can assist in the settlement of a dispute. One of the problems of litigation is the considerable volume of paper it generates. Another is the huge span of argument concerning liability issues which, until narrowed either in argument or by court decision, leaves the parties far apart in their understanding of their respective strengths or weaknesses. The preparation of an accountant's report can sometimes provide the bridge between the conflicting views and itself contribute something to the final settlement.

Some accountants think that years of experience and knowing one's subject inside out is all that they need to be an expert witness. This is a dangerous misconception. Experience and knowledge are not enough. To succeed in the litigation field the accountant needs three other attributes:

- a sense of urgency and commitment to the case;
- an ability to communicate with a lay audience; and
- an ability to convey a sense of independence and authority.

Urgency and commitment

In the public's mind, civil litigation can seem very long drawn out, lacking any sense of urgency. But there is urgency throughout the legal process, not just in relation to the trial. Strict timetables are set down for the pleadings, the production of documentary evidence and the exchange of expert reports. If these deadlines are not met, the case may be thrown out or the experts' reports may be refused acceptance by the court. (Havoc can sometimes be caused by a party who is well prepared and insists on keeping the unprepared opposition to a strict timetable.) No one should think that litigation work can somehow be fitted in to a busy schedule.

Lawyers often instruct expert witnesses extremely late in the process. On occasions we have been telephoned by solicitors looking for help in a court case only a week or so before the trial is due to start. The proceedings may have been going for two years or more, generating mountains of paper. It is all too easy to think: 'How can I possibly help in this case in such a short time?' The answer is that an expert committed to his work can make much of even a few hours. The secret is to start by identifying the key issues rather than rushing quickly into print. The expert needs to be dedicated to the task and he requires access to good resources: a support team and a good database. It is surprising what can be done in a day once the adrenalin starts to flow.

Of course, to respond promptly to an urgent request from instructing solicitors, the expert needs some flexibility in his business diary. The accountant who has numerous audit commitments or business clients demanding his attention will find it difficult to be available at a moment's notice to assist with a case, let alone to set aside perhaps several weeks to attend a trial.

The ability to communicate with a lay audience

Lawyers are not the only professional group who use a language of their own. Accountants do the same. Many spend much of their working lives talking to and writing to other accountants; they get into the habit of using accounting shorthand and jargon. We find it better to avoid this language and to communicate accounting and economic concepts in a manner free from jargon, both orally and in writing. Judges are suspicious, rightly so in our view, of experts who fail to put across even complex economic and accounting arguments in layman's terms.

Independence and authority

Lord Salisbury once said:

'No lesson seems to be so deeply inculcated by the experience of life as that you never should trust experts. They all require to have their strong wine diluted by a very large admixture of insipid common sense'.

Lord Salisbury was not speaking as a judge, but many judges and arbitrators would probably echo his sentiments. The key requirement of a professional expert, if he is to earn the respect of the court, is objectivity combined with authority. While he is retained to make the best case he can for his client, it must be within the confines of the truth and he must follow standard accounting practice and principle.

In some cases, the expert accountant will be unable to act because of a conflict of interest. The accountant may also feel unable to act because he cannot agree with the opinions which the client wants to put forward. Such conflict is more likely to occur where he is being asked to deal, not with quantum, but with liability and where accounting principle and practice are not the matter on which his opinion is sought. We were once asked to appear in support of a Sunday news-paper which was being sued for a defamatory statement made in an article reviewing the merits of a new issue of shares. After reading the article, we decided that the comments were both defamatory and unjustified. Therefore we declined to act.

Another type of case which we sometimes hesitate to accept is where there are allegations of professional negligence on the part of an auditor, combined with allegations of misrepresentation concerning, say, the veracity of the balance sheet of a company which had been acquired. On looking at all the facts and circumstances, we sometimes conclude that there is not a clear-cut case for saying that the auditor of the other side has fallen short of acceptable standards when putting forward the balance sheet on which the offer has been based. There can be plenty of reasons to regret the purchase of a business; the fault does not always lie with the auditor.

Even when he has accepted a case, the accountant must actively defend his independence. His role is to define and simplify the issues of the case, not to intensify adversarial attitudes by introducing a bias into his evidence. He should not be persuaded by lawyers to pursue matters in his report which are irrelevant to his remit. This was made clear by Lord Wilberforce in the case of *Whitehouse v Jordan*[5]:

'While some degree of consultation between experts and legal advisers is entirely proper, it is necessary that expert evidence presented to the court should be, and be seen to be, the independent product of the expert, uninfluenced as to form or content by the exigencies of litigation.'

In this case, certain expert evidence was discounted by the court because, in addition to containing several serious inaccuracies, it was not felt to be impartial, having been unduly influenced by counsel.

The duties and responsibilities of an expert witness in civil cases were well summarised, as shown below, by Cresswell J in his judgment in the case of *The Ikarian Reefer*[6] in 1993.

- Expert evidence presented to the court should be, and should be seen to be, the independent product of the expert, uninfluenced as to formal content by the exigencies of litigation (this is an echo of *Whitehouse v Jordan*[7]).

- Independent assistance should be provided to the court by way of objective, unbiased opinion regarding matters within the expertise of the expert witness. An expert witness in the High Court should never assume the role of advocate.

- Facts or assumptions upon which the opinion is based, should be stated together with material facts which could detract from the concluded opinion.

- An expert witness should make it clear when a question or issue falls outside his expertise.

- If the opinion is not properly researched, because it is considered that insufficient data is available, then that has to be stated with an indication that the opinion is provisional. If the witness cannot assert that the report contains the truth, the whole truth and nothing but the truth, then that qualification should be stated on the report.

- If, after exchange of reports, an expert witness changes his mind on a material matter, the change of view should be communicated to the other side through legal representatives without delay and, when appropriate, to the court.

Generally, we find that barristers will look through an expert's report with great care to ensure that the written evidence can be relied upon, and that the accounting expert is not going to put forward a point of view which is in conflict with judgments made by other experts, or by other witnesses as to fact. If he feels that the expert's opinion, or indeed his character, is ill-suited to the case, the barrister will with all due courtesy, decline to make use of his services.

Clients sometimes think that it will be cheaper and more effective to use an in-house accountant than to engage an independent professional. This rarely pays off, since an employee cannot be described as independent. This is particularly true in matrimonial cases when a husband's business is being investigated. Furthermore, an independent witness has another important advantage over an in-house accounting witness: his knowledge of the client's affairs will be restricted to matters relevant to the case. Therefore, if cross-examined, he can refuse to answer wider questions, on the grounds that his knowledge is limited. In contrast, the Finance Director of a company cannot say that he does not know the answers to accounting questions concerning his company, and he could hardly refuse to answer such questions without giving an unfavourable impression.

NOTES

1 Or she: we are of course writing for readers of both sexes.
2 Meaning how much, a quantity; ie of damages or compensation.
3 *Carter v Boehm* (1766) 3 Burr 1905 at 1918.
4 RSC Ord 38 Rule 4.
5 [1981] 1 All ER 267, HL.
6 *National Justice Cia Naviera SA v Prudential Assurance Co Ltd, The Ikarian Reefer* [1993] 2 Lloyd's Rep 68.
7 See footnote 5.

Part I

Technical aspects

Chapter 1

A general discussion of damages

What are damages? – Contractual damages – Damages in tort – Damages arising from misrepresentation – Some underlying concepts – Non-pecuniary losses – New for old – Limitation to damages – Contributory negligence – Remoteness as to cause – Remoteness as to extent of protection – Mitigation – Certainty – An illustration – Issues affecting quantum – Taxation – Interest – Inflation – Insurance – Foreign currency – Expropriation – Costs of preparing claims – Postscript

101 'Exactly how much can we claim in damages?' is a question quickly posed by people who have suffered loss through the fault of someone else. Their immediate thought might be to instruct an accountant to get to work on the calculations. But they should not be too hasty. At this point they probably need a lawyer's advice.

102 The law relating to damages, or compensation, is both immense and complicated. Legal textbooks on the subject are full of contradiction and mistiness. An accountant faced with the task of computing damages or critically assessing others' calculations, obviously needs a broad understanding of this fascinating and sometimes curious subject.

103 In this chapter we introduce the legal concept of damages. The chapter covers a great deal of ground. Necessarily, some matters have been greatly oversimplified. It is important for the accountant that the lawyer explains how the law approaches damages in the case in question and points out and discusses problem areas. Close liaison and discussion of the best approach to difficult areas is essential. Many other sources of reference exist for those needing to understand damages in detail. There is no substitute for the advice of lawyers or counsel where doubt arises as to specific legal issues on damages. For those who become involved regularly as experts on damage claims we strongly recommend the acquisition of a copy of *McGregor on Damages* (see our bibliography).

WHAT ARE DAMAGES?

104 Damages have been described as pecuniary compensation, obtainable though success in an action for a wrong which is either a breach of contract or a tort, the compensation being in the form of a lump sum which is awarded unconditionally and which is generally, but not necessarily, expressed in English currency. In the next few paragraphs we explain what the legal terms in this rather daunting definition mean.

105 Before any damages can be awarded by the court, the judge must be satisfied that a wrong has been committed. This wrong, often referred to as 'the liability', can arise either by way of breach of contract, or in tort (which is a civil wrong, independent of contract).

106 The measure of damages, which is often referred to as the quantum of the claim, was defined as long ago as 1880 by Lord Blackburn in *Livingstone v Rawyards Coal Co*[1] as:

> 'that sum of money which will put the party that has been injured, or who has suffered, in the same position as he would have been in if he had not sustained the wrong for which he is now getting his compensation or reparation'.

107 This definition appears to be common sense, and indeed it is. But the accountant should realise that the precise nature of 'the same position' depends on whether the wrong is 'in contract' or 'in tort'. It is therefore necessary to understand the difference between these two circumstances, because they may affect the way quantum is calculated.

108 In some cases, a claim will partly arise under contract and partly be founded in tort. Such is the richness of life's pleasures.

Contractual damages

109 The basic rule in claims for damages for breach of contract, is that the 'plaintiff' or claimant is entitled to be placed, so far as money can do it, in the same position as he would have been if the contract had been performed in accordance with its terms.

110 If one party fails to carry out his side of the contract, the basic loss to the other party is the market value of the benefit of which he has been deprived through the breach. This damage is said to be 'compensation for loss of bargain'. In summary: to calculate the damages it is necessary to compare the plaintiff's financial position as a result of the breach of contract, with what it would have been if the contract had not been breached by the defendant.

111 It is essential for the expert accountant to consider a contractual dispute in terms of what was contractually agreed. The terms of the contract may well limit the claim for damages. For instance, there may be a provision that says that, while a defect should be made good, there can be no claim for loss of profit while that defect exists. This can be a significant limitation. Consider, for example, the situation where production is reduced by a defective installation; or, more subtly, where to avoid loss of production and revenue, the repair or replacement is delayed or in other ways complicated. Both these circumstances could give rise to complications as to when and in what way the defect should be made good.

112   The following two important principles should be noted in ascertaining the quantum of damages.

(a) If, as a result of no longer having to perform his side of the contract, the plaintiff has saved or avoided certain expenditure, these savings should be deducted when computing his net loss.

For example, if a plaintiff contracts to make and sell some furniture for £1,000 to the defendant, but the defendant is in breach of contract before the wood and other raw materials are acquired by the plaintiff, the cost of these materials will have to be deducted from the £1,000 when computing the claim for the lost sale.

(b) Where the plaintiff has incurred costs preparing for the contract or in partly carrying it out, these expenses cannot be included in the claim in addition to the basic loss, because they are part of the price which the plaintiff had to pay to secure his bargain.

113   Real life is not as simple as this, but it is useful to bear these basic rules in mind. Put shortly, a claimant cannot make a profit out of his contractual claim. This is in contrast to a claim founded in tort, which we discuss below.

114   In some claims for breach of contract it may have been impossible to complete the contract, or circumstances may have been such that the results of doing so would have been too uncertain to enable loss of profits to be calculated. In these cases the court or arbitrator will consider an alternative measure of damages, where recovery of out-of-pocket expenses may be substituted for loss of bargain.

115   In one case from our own experience, a client concluded heads of agreement on a potential acquisition and requested us to carry out investigative work in respect of the final contract. After the acquisition contract had been signed, it transpired that the other side were in breach of contract. However, working out the resulting loss of bargain or loss of profits was too difficult. It was therefore appropriate for the plaintiff to claim back the cost of the fees paid to lawyers and accountants for setting up the contract and carrying out the investigation.

Damages in tort

116   There are many kinds of tort or tortious acts, all with a common characteristic: that of a wrong inflicted by one person on another. Tort encompasses well-known civil wrongs: nuisance, trespass, slander, libel, conspiracy and negligence. The typical remedy is an action for damages against the person responsible for the injury. The damages are designed to compensate the injured party. The basic rule is that the injured party should be placed, so far as money can do it, in the same position as he would have been had the tort not been committed; in legal jargon this is referred to as the 'status quo ante'. Distinguish this from contractual damages, which are intended to put the plaintiff in the same prospective position he would have enjoyed had the contract been fulfilled. What is the difference, exactly? Let us consider an example. Mr X is let down under a contract by a supplier of carpeting and has to buy the same carpeting from another source at greater expense. He can claim the extra cost, since it stems from the contract, but he cannot go on to claim for damage to, for instance, his reputation. Mr Y, on the other hand, receives the carpet but it is then burnt in a fire caused by Mr Z's negligence. Y's claim against Mr Z will be tortious. It will be based primarily on the cost of replacing the carpet, but is likely to be much wider in scope than Mr X's claim and might well take account of, say, business interruption loss.

117   The diagram on p 15 demonstrates the requirements for a successful claim for damages in tort.

Damages arising from misrepresentation

118   Where the plaintiff has been induced to enter into a contract by a misrepresentation of fact on the defendant's part, he can sue for breach of contract if the representation constitutes a term of the contract, whether condition or warranty. The plaintiff is entitled to such damages as will put him into the position he would have been in had the misrepresentation been true.

119   If the representation does not constitute a term of the contract, then, although the plaintiff may be entitled to rescind (that is, turn the clock back and, for example, return the assets if they are still intact), there is no breach of contract and his only common law action is in tort – in deceit if the misrepresentation has been fraudulently made, or in negligence if it has been carelessly made.

120   Fraudulent misrepresentation is most often found in cases involving the purchase and sale of shares. In such cases the measure of damages is normally the purchase price paid for the shares less their actual value at the time of the purchase. In cases of negligent misrepresentation, the normal measure would be to restore the plaintiff to the position that he would have been in if the misrepresentation had never occurred.

SOME UNDERLYING CONCEPTS

Non-pecuniary losses

121   Damages are awarded to cover pecuniary and non-pecuniary losses. Pecuniary losses, which are usually based on loss of profit or loss of value, constitute the area most likely to require the accountant's skills. Non-pecuniary losses, which relate to circumstances such as 'pain and suffering', are generally fixed by the court. The accountant is unlikely to be concerned with non-pecuniary losses.

New for old

122   In certain claims – such as those related to construction – where a defective item of plant needs to be rebuilt or replaced, it is likely that the new one will be more modern than the previous one. It is often argued that, where as a result of tort an asset has to be replaced or rebuilt, some deduction should be made to reflect the resulting 'betterment'. The court will not make such a deduction from an award in circumstances of 'new for old' if, in the words of Widgery LJ: 'to do so would be

CAUSE OF ACTION IN TORT

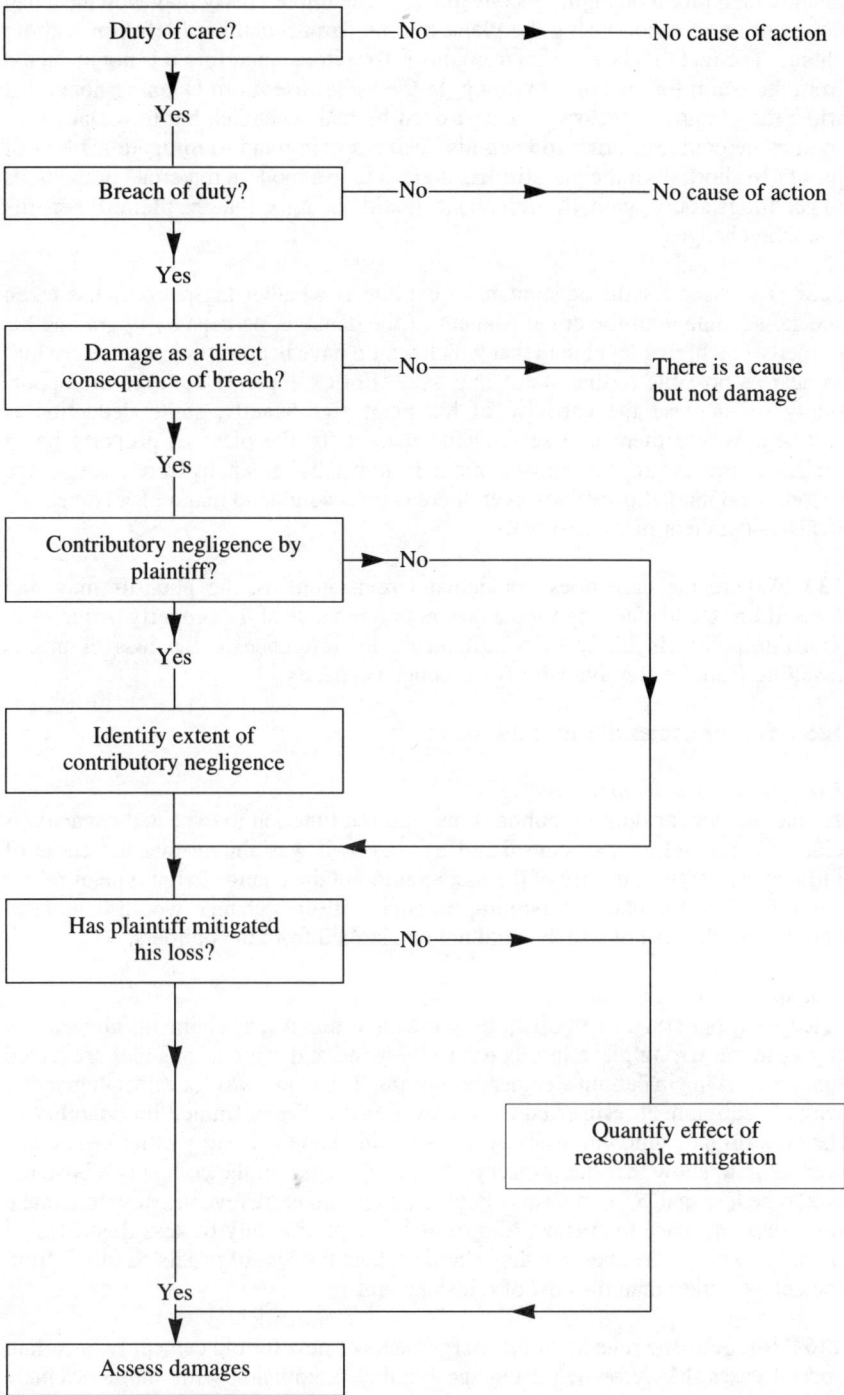

```
┌─────────────────────────┐
│     Duty of care?       │───No──────────▶──────No cause of action
└─────────────────────────┘
             │
            Yes
             ▼
┌─────────────────────────┐
│    Breach of duty?      │───No──────────▶──────No cause of action
└─────────────────────────┘
             │
            Yes
             ▼
┌─────────────────────────┐
│    Damage as a direct   │───No──────────▶──────There is a cause
│  consequence of breach? │                      but not damage
└─────────────────────────┘
             │
            Yes
             ▼
┌─────────────────────────┐
│ Contributory negligence by │──No──┐
│        plaintiff?       │        │
└─────────────────────────┘        │
             │                     │
            Yes                    │
             ▼                     │
┌─────────────────────────┐        │
│    Identify extent of   │        │
│  contributory negligence│        │
└─────────────────────────┘        │
             │◀────────────────────┘
             ▼
┌─────────────────────────┐
│   Has plaintiff mitigated │──No──▶──┐
│        his loss?        │          │
└─────────────────────────┘          │
             │                        │
             │            ┌───────────────────────────┐
             │            │    Quantify effect of     │
             │            │   reasonable mitigation   │
             │            └───────────────────────────┘
             │                        │
            Yes◀──────────────────────┘
             ▼
┌─────────────────────────┐
│     Assess damages      │
└─────────────────────────┘
```

15

the equivalent of forcing the plaintiffs to invest their money in modernising their plant, which might be highly inconvenient'.[2] The injured party may well have had no intention of modernising the plant, but the damage suffered left him with no choice. The fact that he benefits from this is fortuitous; therefore it is not deducted from the claim for cost of rebuilding. In the same case, Lord Denning noted that when the plaintiff's factory was destroyed he had no choice but to replace it as soon as he could, in order to keep his business going and to mitigate his loss of profit.[3] In short, if all the plaintiff has done is to use modern materials or methods to get things going again, the defendant should not argue that the plaintiff benefits from the change.

123   The issue for the accountant to explore is whether the plaintiff has taken special advantage of the circumstances of the damage, perhaps by upgrading his property to a higher level than that which would have been sufficient to return him as near as possible to the 'status quo ante'. For example, if he takes the opportunity to increase the capacity of his plant significantly, some deduction is justified. Where there is a secondhand market for the plant or property being replaced, the award for reinstatement is normally given by reference to the secondhand market price; however, there is no secondhand market for something that was deficient in the first place.

124   Where the case does not demand reinstatement, the plaintiff may find himself limited to claiming for the diminution in value of the property in question. The diminution is likely to be calculated by reference to the loss of profits resulting from its non-availability or reduced capacity.

125   Two examples illustrate this point:

Example 1 – The incinerator
An incinerator for burning public refuse did not function to expected capacity. A claim for rebuilding was considered. However, it was shown that the cause of failure was not the capacity of the incinerator, but the change in the type of refuse being fed into the plant. Rebuilding to cope with this change would have been betterment, the cost of which could not be claimed from the builders.

Example 2 – The oil jetty
A jetty was built on a small offshore island oil terminal. The claimants alleged that it was in the wrong place in relation to the wind and sea currents and prevented tankers docking in certain weather conditions. The claim was for reinstatement by way of realignment, estimated to cost over $20m. We examined the viability of the oil terminal, which in its six years of trading had made substantial losses, and were able to show that the impact of the realignment on the company's business would be less than $1m in terms of cost savings and extra revenue. It would make no economic sense to spend $20m to improve profitability by less than $1m. If damages were to be awarded, they should reflect the loss of profits resulting from the defect, rather than the cost of reinstatement.

126   But quite the reverse of these arguments of new for old can apply in certain special cases. Mr X owned a vintage Bentley; a collision with another vehicle caused damage to the Bentley costing £100,000 to repair. He was awarded the damages even though it would have cost only £75,000 to buy a brand new Bentley.

16

LIMITATION TO DAMAGES

127 The court has established a number of limitations to damages where to award full compensation would be too harsh on the defendant. The plaintiff cannot recover damages:

(a) for that part of the loss which is his fault ('contributory negligence');
(b) for loss for which the defendant's conduct is not the cause ('remoteness as to cause');
(c) for loss which is not within the extent of protection of the particular tort or contract ('remoteness as to extent of protection');
(d) for loss which should have been avoided by the plaintiff ('mitigation'); and
(e) for loss which is too uncertain ('certainty').

We discuss these limitations below, distinguishing between those concepts applicable to contract and those applicable to tort.

Contributory negligence

128 Contributory negligence is an important feature of tort. The implications of contributory negligence by the plaintiff for a damages award have been summarised as follows:

> 'Where any person suffers damage as a result partly of his own fault and partly of the fault of any other person(s), a claim in respect of that damage shall not be defeated by reason of the fault of the person suffering the damage, but the damages recoverable in respect thereof shall be reduced to such extent as the court thinks just and equitable having regard to the claimant's share in the responsibility for the damage.'[4]

In other words, the fact that the plaintiff's negligence has contributed to the damage he has suffered does not affect his right to claim compensation, but it may reduce the level of compensation he obtains. The apportionment of blame and consequently of damages is up to the court. The accountant should limit himself to the identification of contributory negligence and leave the rest to the court.

Remoteness as to cause

129 The plaintiff must show that the losses for which he is claiming were caused by the defendant.

130 The onus is on the plaintiff to show that a particular item of damage is not too remote, before he can recover for it. Difficulties may arise where the consequences of a tort are affected by a new intervening force. This, however, is a large subject in itself and touches on the question of liability, on which the advice of a lawyer should be sought.

Remoteness as to extent of protection

131 The implications of this limitation differ for tort and for breach of contract. In both tort and contract, damage for which recovery is sought must have been reasonably foreseeable by the defendant.

132   In tort, the question of reasonable foreseeability appears to have been interpreted widely. For example, the pecuniary state of the plaintiff is of no consequence to remoteness or reasonability. Scrutton LJ said: 'You negligently run down a shabby looking man in the street and he turns out to be a millionaire engaged in a very profitable business which the accident disables him from carrying on. You have to pay damages resulting from circumstances of which you have no notice.'[5] In other words, damages appropriate to a millionaire rather than to a tramp.

133   In contract, the scope of protection is established by what was 'in the contemplation of the parties' when the contract was entered into. This statement is based on case law and is known as 'the rule in *Hadley v Baxendale*'.[6] This rule means that damages from a breach of contract should be:

(a) those arising naturally – that is, according to the usual course of things – from such a breach of contract itself; or
(b) such as may reasonably be supposed to have been in the contemplation of the parties at the time they made the contract, as the probable result of the breach of it.

134   If there existed special circumstances under which the contract was made and if these circumstances were communicated by the plaintiff to the defendant and were thus known to both parties, the damages would be the amount of injury which would ordinarily follow from these special circumstances. For example, suppose when entering into a contract for the repair of a machine it was made clear that the repaired equipment was needed by a certain time because its absence would lead to loss of sales; if the defendant caused delay he would be held liable for the sales which were lost in consequence.

135   On the other hand, if these special circumstances were wholly unknown to the party breaking the contract, then the most he could be held responsible for would be the amount of injury that would arise generally from such a breach of contract. The law takes the view that had the special circumstances been known, the parties might have provided within the terms of the contract for damages arising from breach of contract due to the special circumstances.

136   The rule in *Hadley v Baxendale* was restated in the case of *Victoria Laundry (Windsor) Ltd v Newman Industries Ltd*,[7] where 'reasonably foreseeable' was said to depend on 'the knowledge actual or imputed of the party who broke the contract'.

Mitigation

137   Mitigation is a duty imposed on a party to proceedings to attempt to reduce the consequential effect of a breach of contract or tort. Three different, but interrelated rules concern the effect of mitigation on awards of damages:

(a) the plaintiff must take all reasonable steps to mitigate loss to himself consequent upon the defendant's wrong. The court will not award damages for any loss which the plaintiff could have avoided but failed, through unreasonable action or inaction, to avoid;

(b) where the plaintiff takes reasonable steps to mitigate the loss, he can recover for any expense or loss incurred in doing so. This rule holds, even if the resulting damage is, in the event, greater than it would have been had the mitigating steps not been taken; and

(c) where the plaintiff's mitigating steps are successful, the defendant is entitled to the benefit accruing from the plaintiff's action and is liable only for the reduced loss.

138   The case of *Beoco Ltd v Alfa Laval Co Ltd*[8] illustrates the importance of a plaintiff mitigating the effects of a breach of contract. The defendants were found in breach of contract in supplying a defective heat exchanger and failing properly to repair it when the defects became apparent. The heat exchanger subsequently exploded.

139   However, the plaintiff was found to have been reckless in using the heat exchanger without properly testing the repair and the court awarded it damages on the basis of the loss it would have suffered had it replaced the defective parts of the exchanger rather than have it repaired. The Court of Appeal overruled this judgment, restricting the plaintiff's claim to the cost of replacing the defective parts and such loss of profit, if any, as was incurred while the repairs were carried out. The plaintiff was unable to recover any loss of profit beyond the point when it allowed the repaired heat exchanger to be put back into service.

140   Where the plaintiff who has insured against loss receives insurance, the damages recoverable will not be diminished by the amount of the insurance. However, the insurer may have a right to recover the claim out of the damages awarded.

Certainty

141   Sometimes the court can accurately assess the actual damages suffered, for example, where because of injury a plaintiff was unable to work for a certain period, a loss of earnings results. Sometimes the court has to assess a lump sum to compensate a potential loss, for example, where because of injury a plaintiff will be at a disadvantage in the labour market if he loses his job, albeit that he has not lost his job yet. Sometimes the court has to assess the loss of a chance, for example, where a model is injured the night before competing in the Miss World finals. Sometimes the court will simply conclude that the damage is too remote to be properly quantifiable.

142   The extent to which certainty must be established to obtain damages claimed, is dealt with in case law. The following statements demonstrate the court's present attitude.

(a) 'The fact that damages cannot be assessed with certainty does not relieve the wrongdoer of the necessity of paying damages.'[9]

(b) 'Where the precise evidence is obtainable the court naturally expects to have it; where it is not, the court must do the best it can.'[10]

(c) 'As much certainty and particularity must be insisted on, both in pleading and proof of damages, as is reasonable, having regard to the circumstances and to the nature of the acts themselves by which the damage is done.'[11]

143   A commodity broking case provides an example. The loss of a general opportunity to trade was considered much too speculative to allow a money value to be placed on it.

144   However, damages can be received for future or projected loss – if reasonably anticipated – as the result of the defendant's wrong, whether such future damage is certain or contingent. Measuring loss of opportunity is expanded on later in Chapter 4.

An illustration

145   Several of the underlying concepts of damages may be illustrated by the following example.

146   We were engaged in a case involving defective natural gas storage tanks. It was alleged that design faults caused the whole plant, which was highly expensive and very profitable, to be shut down while remedial work was done. The plaintiff also took the opportunity to improve the storage tanks for reasons not connected with the defect. We appeared for the defendant and our accounting and economic report had to deal with the following issues.

- The remedial work: was it reasonably carried out at reasonable cost?

- The consequential 'loss of markets' damage: were the interruptions to the supply of overseas markets (especially Japan) caused by defective storage tanks?

- The consequential 'extra operating cost' claim: was it true that liquefied gas tanker ships operated very much less profitably because the pattern of voyage operations was distorted by the plant shutdown?

147   To investigate the claim we assembled a team of economists, accountants and shipping advisers, and also held discussions with academics versed in the economics of the natural gas industry. We concluded that the claims were largely unjustified and that mitigation had occurred through various economic events during the period of interruption, which had improved the position of the plaintiffs rather than the reverse.

148   In assessing the remedial work, we made a critical review of the programme – supervision, tendering and so on – which showed that much of the cost was due to mismanagement, or to delays unconnected with the defect complained of.

149   We also tackled the question of betterment or 'new for old'. The new tank storage was much more intricate than the discarded tankage. It seemed to us that at most the contribution in damages should be limited to the written-down value (historic) of the old tankage; indeed, as the new storage was so different, there were strong arguments for going below that figure on the grounds that the old tanks were obsolete and uneconomic and that their fortuitous replacement was a positive benefit.

150   As a result of our report for the defendant on these issues, the plaintiffs elected to settle the case before it was decided by the arbitrator, and for a figure very much lower than that originally claimed.

ISSUES AFFECTING QUANTUM

Taxation

151   The question may arise in quantum of how to take taxation into account in assessing damages. The impact of taxation on awards of damages is a complex subject on which we comment in more detail in Chapter 15.

152   The principal case which determined the court's attitude to the incidence of taxation in awards of damages was *British Transport Commission v Gourley*.[12] Here it was determined that the amount of damages awarded should take into account taxation where:

(a) the amount for which the damages are awarded as compensation would originally have been subject to tax in the hands of the plaintiff; and
(b) the damages awarded to the plaintiff would not themselves be subject to tax.

153   Where tax is leviable both on the damages and on the income for which the damages constituted compensation, but at different rates, the court does not adjust damages for the net difference arising. It awards damages on a gross basis and the plaintiff pays tax at the rate then applying.

154   It is generally thought that the assessment of the tax liability should be based on the present rates of tax, taking into account the present rates of reliefs and allowances available. The court should take into account any changes in taxation which have occurred between the date of action and the date of judgment, and any arising on budget proposals even though they are not yet law.

155   Where a claimant is an individual for the purpose of calculating the adjustment to damages, the income to which the damages relate is deemed to be taxable at the taxpayer's top rate of tax at the time. The court does not generally speculate on what will happen to the plaintiff's taxable circumstances in the future.

156   Capital gains tax (CGT) may also affect damages. Although not directly relevant in practice to the question of quantum awarded by a court, the decision in *Zim Properties Ltd v Procter (Inspector of Taxes)*[13] may be of consequence to a plaintiff. It was held that in certain circumstances a right to bring an action constituted an 'asset' for the purposes of CGT legislation. This issue is discussed in more detail in Chapter 15.

Interest

157   We invariably find that a claim for the awarding of interest is included in the closing paragraphs of a claim document. This complex topic is dealt with in Chapter 14. Briefly, when damages are awarded, interest if granted by the court is usually on a simple rather than compound basis. It usually accrues from the date of the breach of contract or tort and the rate of interest paid is that prescribed in the Supreme Court Rules for cases of death and personal injury; in other cases it is decided at the court's discretion. In our experience, lawyers find it helpful to have an indication of the amount of interest that may be awarded, particularly when they are considering settlement terms or payments into court.

Inflation

158   The high rates of inflation experienced in the late eighties focused attention on how far the court will take these circumstances into account when awarding damages. The court's approach appears to differ according to whether the claim is for breach of contract or in tort.

159   In a case of breach of contract, damages for losses relating to property are normally based on the market value of the property at the time when the breach occurred, because the party affected is required to mitigate his loss by going back into the market immediately to find another buyer or seller. So the effect of the change in the value of property over time is generally of no consequence. In tort, however, the plaintiff is not obliged to go immediately into the market to seek replacement and if reasonable attempts to mitigate have failed, the court may take account of changes in value between the date of the tort and the earliest time that the action could reasonably have been brought to judgment.[14]

160   The court's views on how inflation should be dealt with in damage awards were expressed in the judgment in *Mitchell v Mulholland (No 2)*.[15]

'No one doubts that an award of damages must reflect the value of the pound sterling at the date of the award and conventional sums attributed to, say, the loss of an eye have been adjusted upwards in recent years on that account. Inflation which has reduced the value of money at the date of the award must, thus, be taken into account.'

Insurance

161   Although insurance companies are seldom direct parties to a claim, they are often indirectly interested in the outcome of the case. For example, the insurers to the plaintiff may be seeking to recover the claim they have already paid out to him under his insurance policy. The insurer to the defendant may ultimately bear all or part of any damages awarded to the plaintiff. The expert accountant ought to remember the role of the insurers, even if they are only lurking in the background of a case.

162   An amount paid out by the plaintiff's insurer following the event which is the subject of the action, does not itself provide a basis for calculating the full quantum of loss. The insurance payment will have been determined under the terms of the policy, and will take account of the indemnity period and the extent of cover and may well fall short of the total loss suffered.

163   The court will not reduce the damages to reflect insurance monies received. The existence of insurance may nevertheless influence the computation of interest awarded on damages, since the court may award interest only on the part of damages not covered by the insurance proceeds.

164   The consequence to the plaintiff of having received insurance moneys should always be considered in the context of his financial position. In some cases of tort we have had strong reason to believe that the plaintiff would have ceased trading through insolvency but for the receipt of the cash proceeds of the insurance claim. Thus, rather than causing damage, the tort fortuitously injected new life into the plaintiff's business by giving rise to a claimable event under an insurance policy. To our knowledge, no legal precedent supports this contention but, if the circumstances of the case suggest that it is a possible argument, the instructing solicitor should be advised.

165 As observed, the existence and scale of the defendant's insurance cover has no bearing on the amount of damages that may be awarded against him. However, when reporting on a claim on behalf of a defendant, the accountant may be asked to distinguish between damages covered by the insurance policy and those excluded, so that the insurance company is in a position to assess this aspect. The possibility of this arising should be discussed at the outset with the instructing solicitor and if the latter wishes the expert to take account of such matters, the expert should obtain a copy of the relevant insurance policies.

Foreign currency

166 The award of damages for a claim based in a foreign currency was clarified in the *Miliangos* case in 1976,[16] when it was established that an English court may award damages in foreign currency. Damages payable in foreign currency are converted into sterling, for payment purposes, on the date when the court authorises the plaintiff to enforce judgment for a sum expressed in sterling. This topic is further developed in Chapter 14.

EXPROPRIATION

167 Political and religious unrest around the world has resulted in fairly frequent cases of expropriation of business and private assets – and not only in developing countries experiencing, say, a Marxist coup. Expropriation in the form of nationalisation has occurred in many developed countries, for example, in France where the banking system was nationalised. Expropriation, the compulsory transfer of the ownership of assets from private to public control, may be lawful or unlawful.

168 A number of conditions must be satisfied for an expropriation to be lawful. The first concerns the purpose of the expropriation. For many years the most important case in this area was expropriation of certain German interests in the *Polish Upper Silesia* case.[17] In this case, the Permanent Court of International Justice found that the only lawful expropriations of foreign assets were those for reasons of public utility, judicial liquidation and similar aims. Since that decision in 1926, international law has progressively recognised the rights of states to nationalise foreign property for a public purpose. These rights are now universally accepted.

169 The second main condition for a lawful expropriation is that there must be prompt payment of just compensation. The definition of what is considered prompt and what is just, is the subject of heated debate. It has to be determined individually for each case.

170 Claimants put forward a number of arguments in support of their view that the expropriation is not lawful and that they are therefore the victims of a wrongful action, for example, that:

(a) no compensation was paid or offered;
(b) the expropriation was discriminatory;
(c) the expropriation was in violation of the specific agreement; or
(d) the expropriation was not for the public purpose but was merely to avoid contractual obligations.

171 The distinction between lawful and unlawful expropriation is important, since it affects the compensation to be paid. The measure of compensation in the case of a lawful expropriation is less than for wrongful expropriation. In lawful expropriation, the compensation is limited to the enrichment realised by the nationalising state, with no compensation for lost profit. In unlawful expropriation, the question of international responsibility of states arises. Under this concept there is provision for 'restitutio in integrum', that is, putting the plaintiff into the same position as he would have been if rescission had been awarded, either through restitution in kind or its monetary equivalent if necessary. Damages for future profits will also be included. The leading case on this subject is the *Chorzow Factory* case.[18]

172 In instances of lawful expropriation, fair compensation will consist only of the just price of what was expropriated: that is, the value of the undertaking at the moment of dispossession. The choice of method for ascertaining that value depends on the nature of the asset involved. We deal with methods of valuation in compensation claims in Chapter 4.

173 The calculation of quantum in international legal disputes is complicated by the need to consider exchange rates. First, to establish the relevant date – particularly important where currency values have been fluctuating widely over a relatively short period. Second, to decide which exchange rate to use – some countries, particularly developing countries and those in the Eastern Bloc, use more than one exchange rate, for example, there may be an official rate and a black market rate. The effect of exchange controls and local regulations must also be considered in arriving at a just result.

COSTS OF PREPARING CLAIMS

174 A plaintiff may well incur significant costs in preparing his case, for example:

- legal costs;
- the accountant's costs for preparing quantum;
- expert advice on the basis of claims; and
- photographic costs, eg, as evidence of damaged machinery.

The trial judge will take these into account when costs are awarded. As they do not form part of the damages themselves, they should not be included in the claim. Costs incurred on experts' fees prior to the issue of a writ, will not usually be included in any award of costs by the judge.

POSTSCRIPT

175 Finally, a word of warning. The law on damages is not like a succinct set of rules that can be followed to answer the question: 'How much can I claim?' It is enshrined in case law which has been evolving over several hundred years, as judges interpret and apply the principles to changing commercial and social circumstances. The expert witness is strongly advised to seek advice from the solicitors and barristers handling the claim as to the precise heads of damage to be evaluated in each claim. He should also ask to see law reports of analogous cases – the judges' remarks are often enlightening especially as to what really influenced them in their decision.

NOTES

1 (1880) 5 App Cas 25, HL.
2 *Harbutt's Plasticine Ltd v Wayne Tank and Pump Co Ltd* [1970] 1 QB 447 at 473, CA.
3 Ibid at 468.
4 Law Reform (Contributory Negligence) Act 1945 s 1(1).
5 *The Arpad* [1934] P 189 at 202–203, CA.
6 (1854) 9 Exch 341.
7 [1949] 2 KB 528, CA.
8 [1994] 4 All ER 464.
9 *Chaplin v Hicks* [1911] 2 KB 786, CA.
10 *Biggin & Co Ltd v Permanite Ltd* [1951] 2 KB 314, CA.
11 *Ratcliffe v Evans* [1892] 2 QB 524, CA.
12 [1956] AC 185, HL.
13 [1985] STC 90.
14 *Sachs v Miklos* [1948] 2 KB 23, CA.
15 [1972] 1 QB 65, CA.
16 *Miliangos v George Frank (Textiles) Ltd* [1976] AC 443, HL.
17 (1926) PCIJ Rep, Ser A, No 7.
18 (1928) PCIJ Rep, Ser A, No 17.

Chapter 2

Loss of profits: how to calculate them

Collection and interpretation of data – Statutory accounts – Internal evidence – External evidence – Visiting the scene of the crime – Calculation of loss of profits – Lost sales – Gross profit – The cost of management time – VAT – Double counting – Summary – An aide-memoire to the assessment of damages

201   A common form of economic loss suffered by companies through breach of contract or tort is loss of profits. For many years insurance companies have provided protection for a variety of events or perils giving rise to loss of profits or 'consequential loss'. The insurance world now refers to such claims as 'business interruption claims'.

202   This chapter explains the concept of loss of profits, how to calculate them, and perhaps most important, the type of evidence needed to support the claim. Absence of contemporary evidence can be a big hindrance to a successful claim. We look at the subject largely from the perspective of claims under breach of contract or tort.

203   The expert accountant has many skills to bring into play in calculating loss of profits, but he will always need to establish the ground rules in advance. This will involve asking the instructing solicitor about the nature of the claim and obtaining from him a copy of the pleadings, which will contain the statement of claim. In Chapter 18 we outline the workings of the legal process and how claims are fought. Here we deal with the practical considerations involved in the computation or verification by the accountant of the quantum of the damage.

204   Whether an expert is asked to give help on behalf of the plaintiff or the defendant, he needs to consider all the strengths and weaknesses of his client's case and the claim for damages. He is, of course, looking for evidence to demonstrate the strengths of his client's case; at the same time, he should point out to instructing solicitors the weaknesses or the possible counter-arguments and alternative methods of calculating damage which might be put by the other side's expert. In the end, the expert's report should try, where appropriate, to dispose of possible counter-arguments by the other side. Success will depend on his ability both to think about the client's position with vision and to present the evidence in a clear and concise manner.

205   While the accountant may not be expected to be an expert in the industry concerned, he should, nevertheless, become sufficiently familiar with it to understand the basis of the claim and to put the claim into the practical context of the business concerned.

206 Each case must be treated on its own merits. Nevertheless, experience has shown that many cases have features in common.

COLLECTION AND INTERPRETATION OF DATA

207 Any assignment to calculate, or evaluate a calculation of, loss of profits, involves collecting and interpreting data from many different sources. A useful starting point is to obtain a copy of the relevant contract or the relevant parts of it.

208 As stated in Chapter 1: 'Where the precise evidence is obtainable, the court naturally expects to have it; where it is not, the court must do the best it can'. Therefore, gathering and examining documentary evidence to support a claim are important aspects of the work of the accountant and his role in assisting the court. If asked to comment on the quantum generally, rather than on a specific issue, he should try to inspect all the supporting documentary evidence: documents giving direct proof, for example, invoices in respect of costs incurred; or an analysis or best estimate derived from previous performance – for example, from historical gross profit margins shown by management accounts.

209 The process of 'discovery', which is described in Chapter 18, often results in a vast quantity of documents being made available by both sides. The expert should inspect such documents, to identify papers which support or contradict the claim, and should file and index them so that they can be found easily when needed. We say more about the control of paperwork in Chapter 21.

210 Attention to detail is a feature of this work. Errors in calculations, differences between amounts claimed and the supporting documents, and absence of support – however small – should be noted in the reports. The concept of immateriality, which may apply in an audit, has no place here. The court expects that expert accountants will be accurate in matters relating to figures and calculations. While the court may not be too concerned over small errors in the statement of claim, inaccuracy in small matters may be held against the expert when he is cross-examined on the important matters.

211 The expert accountant has several sources of information to which he can turn in calculating loss of profits. Some information is readily available; some will require a little detective work. He should not rely on the client, or even the solicitor involved (who might not possess the appropriate knowledge or expertise to ask for production of specific documentation), to provide all documentation to enable him to put forward the best case possible. It is important to request any documents or accounting records which ought to exist which could be helpful to the case.

Statutory accounts

212 Claims are often put together with no sense of reality or reference to the plaintiff's general financial position. The plaintiff's claim for damages must therefore be put into the context of his general financial position disclosed in the relevant statutory accounts. Where loss of profits is claimed, the expert accountant should prepare a schedule (using tables or graphs) comparing the profits disclosed by the statutory accounts with the profits as adjusted by the loss claimed. The trends disclosed should be examined and discrepancies interpreted.

213   This form of comparison may demonstrate the absurdity of a claim. In our experience, plaintiffs have a tendency to overstate loss of profits. In one case, for example, we reviewed a claim arising from the collapse of a factory roof. In addition to a claim for remedial work to the roof, the plaintiff made huge claims for disturbance of production – leading to greater unrecovered overheads – and for loss of market share for the main 'do it yourself' products. Our detailed examination of the claim showed up some serious weaknesses in the plaintiff's assumptions and calculations. It also failed the test of overall reasonableness. Taking the claims for loss of profits and for adverse variances at their face value, we added them to the reported profits for the two years in question. The result was totally unbelievable: it showed unit profit margins which were double those achieved in the years before and after the event, and unmatched by competition or by subsidiaries in other countries. It produced record annual profits for the company. In short, it was a colossal overstatement. By demonstrating this, we were able to help bring the plaintiff's expectations down to sensible levels and settlement followed without the need for court action.

214   It should be borne in mind that a judge or arbitrator is likely to lose patience with, and have less sympathy for, a claim which has been vastly overstated (either in the pleadings or in expert evidence) as opposed to one which has been realistically stated.

215   Statutory accounts may also provide revealing evidence about the plaintiff's business and general financial standing. The accountant should review the directors' report, the chairman's statement and notes to the accounts for relevant comments. For instance, it is revealing if:

(a) the claim represents a substantial loss of profits, but there is no reference to the problem in the accounts for the period when the incident occurred;
(b) poor results are attributed to factors unconnected with the claim, eg, economic recession;
(c) the claim seeks recovery for redundancy costs but the accounts indicate that provision for redundancy costs was made before events took place;
(d) the accounting policies described in the accounts are different from those the plaintiff is using to establish the quantum of the claim; or
(e) the financial strength of the company as shown by its accounts, appears inadequate to support the scale of business represented by the claim.

Internal evidence

216   In addition to the plaintiff's statutory accounts, the accountant may want to inspect a number of other documents when assessing claims. The list set out in the following table represents, in our experience, the type of data frequently used.

217   The plaintiff may have used only some of the information listed above to prepare his case and quantify damages. Consideration of all relevant information may support or contradict the assumptions on which the claim is based; considered use of this type of evidence in litigation will illuminate the strengths or weaknesses of the claim.

28

INTERNAL DOCUMENTS WHICH MAY BE RELEVANT TO LOSS OF PROFIT CLAIMS

Financial documents
Monthly financial and budgetary reports to management.
Board and management committee minutes.
General ledger.
Long and short range profit plans.
Consolidated company and divisional financial results of operations.
Cash flow information.
Departmental budgets illustrating actual versus budgeted results.
Capital expenditure programmes and investment appraisals.
Cost accounting data by product.
Break-even points.
Research and development expenditure versus planned expenditure.
Financial ratios, eg, inventory turnover rates;
                    return on investment;
                    working capital ratios;
                    ageing of debtors.
Sales and income analyses.
Product profitability studies.
Internal audit reports.
Tax returns.

Marketing documents
Long-term strategy and short-term objectives of marketing department.
Estimated market size and share of market by product.
Sales trends and forecasts.
Sales budget and delivery plans.
Advertising and promotion plans and costs.
Order intake and backlog.
Customer enquiries.
Customer order history.
Customer complaints, returns and lost order reports.
New product developments.
Competitive product analyses.

Production documents
Manufacturing capacity, programmes and production schedules.
Physical characteristics of existing plant.
Stock records.
Stock obsolescence reports.
Economic batch sizes.
Material usage and variance analyses.
Labour efficiency data.
Scrap and rework costs.
Maintenance problems and costs.
Quality control reports.
Purchasing budgets.
Make-or-buy study results.
Employee turnover.
Employee availability/shortage/absenteeism.
Time sheets.
Overtime costs.
Industrial relations reports.

218 Financial, marketing and manufacturing data should be analysed over the months or years before, during and after the claim period. Analyses might include graphical presentations, correlations and tabulations.

219 Budgets and forecasts, although by no means conclusive evidence of how things might have developed, do provide pointers. If different, the onus is on the plaintiff to show why the assumptions for the claim did not follow the forecasts. Alternatively, if original budgets form the basis of the claim, then the plaintiff's record of forecasting should be examined to see whether it has been reliable in the past.

220   Production data provide a means of establishing the company's capacity, its productivity, its level of stockholding and its costs of production. Careful study of this aspect of the plaintiff's business may indicate whether fluctuations in output all relate to the claimable event, or were caused by some other event. Similarly, consideration of the liquidity of a business which is claiming on the basis of growth in sales, will indicate whether it is reasonable to assume it could have afforded to fund that growth.

221   Where possible, supporting data should be reconciled to audited accounts. Any inconsistencies should be recorded and explanations sought.

External evidence

222   Claims for loss of profits should be viewed not only in the context of the plaintiff's own recent performance, current resources and existing plans, but also against the wider market. The accountant should consider the need to obtain and collate market data at an early stage; market data should be carefully analysed to establish whether the assumptions used in the claim for sales and sales prices, appear reasonable.

223   Press comment may be a useful source of corporate information. A number of databases now available provide a computerised wealth of press cuttings. The picture in press releases differs surprisingly often from that given in the claim documentation, thus providing contradictory evidence. Trade associations and journals may also be a useful source of industry information and market statistics.

Visiting the scene of the crime

224   Finally, the accountant may need to visit sites to get a clearer picture of the business under review and to put the claim in perspective. A visit will often help to distinguish between factors that flow from the event complained of and those that do not.

225   The advantage of visiting the 'scene of the crime' is well illustrated by a case where we were acting for an architect who was being sued for negligence over the design of a warehouse roof which had to be rectified. The plaintiffs argued that consequent delays to the project had disrupted their business, losing them sales and increasing their costs.

226   We looked at the costs of disruption from two angles. First, we deducted the alleged cost of disruption from the plaintiffs' total costs in their audited accounts. The resulting figure of costs was significantly below the normal level. Second, we looked critically at the individual items of cost claimed in the light of evidence we had gathered from our site visit. The plaintiffs had claimed additional costs arising because, it was alleged, fork lift trucks moving production items had to make long detours while the warehouse was being completed. Throughout our visit to the site, we saw no fork lift trucks moving goods but a number standing idle. It was clear that the plaintiffs' fork lift trucks were not operating at capacity and that any additional time in journeys would have been easily absorbed within the existing capacity of the trucks. Thus no additional costs were incurred.

CALCULATION OF LOSS OF PROFITS

227 Once the expert has collected and analysed the relevant information, the next stage is the calculation of the quantum of the lost profits. Lost profits are generally calculated by applying a rate of gross profit to the volume of lost sales. That sounds reasonably simple. But what rate of gross profit is appropriate, and what sales have been lost?

Lost sales

228 Lost sales may be determined by reference to cancelled orders. However, in most cases this information is not readily available and lost sales have to be estimated by projection. The court will accept the use of projections, provided they are reasonable and the best that can be achieved.

229 What constitutes a reasonable projection will vary in each case. Questions to ask include the following:

(a) Does it appear from stock records that the claimed lost sales could have been satisfied entirely or in part from existing stock?
(b) Is there evidence that enquiries or orders have been turned away by the plaintiff?
(c) Did the plaintiff have the capacity to produce the goods to make the claimed lost turnover?
(d) Do the projected sales trends look realistic in relation to the overall market trends?

230 The importance of the last two issues was brought home to us when we were asked by a major oil company to look at a claim for losses resulting from its disruption of supplies of petrol to a chain of petrol stations. The chain of petrol stations was unable to obtain bulk fuel deliveries from other suppliers and sued our client for the loss of profit on the sales of petrol lost because of the alleged short deliveries.

231 We carried out a detailed check on the daily sales and stock records kept by each garage during the period of disruption. In only one garage did we find that the stock in hand at the end of the day was below the level of sales to be expected for the following day. In all other cases there was sufficient fuel in the garages' storage tanks to supply an average day's sales. Sales were down, but this did not seem to be in any way related to lack of supply. A recent substantial increase in prices probably accounted for the drop in the public's demand for petrol.

232 We looked also at the employees' wage records. We found no evidence of any reduction in overtime levels worked or in the stations' operating hours, which suggested that customers had not been turned away.

31

233 In another case we were called in to review a claim for loss of profit in a sugar refinery. The plant comprised a series of interlinked tanks through which passed liquid and unrefined sugar. The claim related to the collapse of one of the last tanks in the process chain and it made a number of assumptions about the output of that tank.

234 We examined the production process and identified a bottleneck in the system that made it impossible to produce enough intermediate product to satisfy the throughput attributed to the collapsed tank. The plaintiff scaled down his claim for loss of profits accordingly. This illustrates the importance of establishing that the plaintiff has adequate production capacity to meet his sales projections.

Gross profit

235 The value attributed to lost sales should be the sales value (net of VAT) of those goods which cannot be sold, but which are already manufactured and where there is no alternative use for them. The value attributed to sales of goods not yet manufactured should be the gross profit on those lost sales. For this purpose, gross profit is generally the sales value less the variable costs of manufacture, distribution and sale. The plaintiff's assumptions for sales prices and underlying costs need to be examined carefully.

236 Experience has shown that the following issues should be considered.

(a) Can the claimed gross margin be reconciled to statutory or management accounts? (see para **212**).
(b) Has the plaintiff made proper adjustments for all variable and semi-variable costs? For example, has the loss of turnover resulted in savings in:
  (i) advertising?
  (ii) sales expenses?
  (iii) employer's national insurance contributions?
  (iv) despatch and delivery costs?
  (v) repairs and maintenance?
  (vi) insurance premiums?
  (vii) pension costs?
(c) What costs has the plaintiff incurred as a result of taking reasonable steps to reduce or mitigate the losses arising? Reasonable costs will generally be allowable, but unreasonable costs or costs which are fixed and must be incurred regardless of the claimable event, where they are identified, should be highlighted in accord with the concept of mitigation discussed in more detail in Chapter 1.

The cost of management time

237 We often see claims for damages which include expenditure of managerial time in putting right the problem that is the subject of the claim. Two points arise here. First, managerial time tends to be a fixed cost of a business. The plaintiff will not usually pay directors more money for doing this part of their job. On that basis, one can argue that extra management time is not a real cost to the plaintiff. However, the plaintiff may be able to show that management attention was diverted from more profitable activity and that loss was suffered thereby.

Following the decision in *Tate and Lyle Industries Ltd v Greater London Council*[1] it seems that, if the plaintiff fails to record details of the managerial time spent on remedying the situation, the court will not speculate on quantum by awarding some percentage of expenditure.

VAT

238 Where the plaintiff is registered for VAT, he can recover VAT charged on most of the costs he incurs from HM Customs & Excise. Consequently, it is inappropriate for the plaintiff to seek to recover VAT from the defendant as well, because by doing so he would be compensated twice for the same costs. Therefore, VAT included in quantum which has been recovered from HM Customs & Excise should be disallowed, unless special circumstances indicate otherwise.

Double counting

239 Many claims for loss of profits spring from damage to, or destruction of, plant. Such claims tend to include both repair or replacement of the plant and the profits lost because the business was deprived of the use of the plant. Where the plant has a limited life, an award of loss of gross profit may be seen as sufficient compensation for the loss of use of the machine, so that to award machine repair or replacement cost as well would be double counting. However, where the machine needs to be repaired or replaced to mitigate the consequential losses, the costs would normally be allowable, where reasonable.

240 In a boat-building case we worked on, the boatyard's wooden moulds were destroyed by fire, preventing the company from making glass fibre hulls. If the wooden moulds had had either a limited physical life or were likely to become obsolete, then it would have been appropriate to claim only for the loss of profit on the boats that could have been built in the remaining life of the moulds. However, it was demonstrated that, provided the moulds were kept in good repair, they could be used indefinitely; therefore, to mitigate the loss of profit it was appropriate to rebuild the moulds from scratch. The loss of profit related only to the number of hulls that could not be made or sold in the period of rebuilding.

241 Another area of potential double counting is where the plaintiff claims both wasted expenses and loss of profits. For example, a plaintiff may claim the costs of buying and installing a machine and training staff to use it. He may also endeavour to claim the loss of gross profit arising because the machine failed to produce the expected sales. But damages are intended to put the plaintiff back in the position he would have been in but for the wrong. If the plaintiff had made the sales for which he is claiming loss, he would have had to incur the costs of buying and installing the machine. He cannot be given compensation both for the lost sales and for the means of making those sales.

242 This point was recognised in the case *Cullinane v British 'Rema' Manufacturing Co Ltd*[2] where it was held, on appeal, that the plaintiff could not claim both his capital loss (expenditure incurred) and his loss of gross profits. The plaintiff was therefore required to choose between these two claims; he could either seek to be put back into the position he would have been in if the contract had not been made (ie recover his net outlay) or claim what he could have received if the contract had been made (ie the gross profit on the lost sales).

SUMMARY

243 The computation of loss of profit is a complex tapestry into which is woven law, evidence, expectations, business awareness, accounting and economics. The expert accountant must keep a wary eye on all of these aspects. A methodical approach is essential. The tabulation opposite helps to summarise the key points discussed in this chapter.

NOTES

1 [1981] 3 All ER 716.
2 [1954] 1 QB 292 at 308, CA.

AN AIDE-MEMOIRE TO THE ASSESSMENT OF DAMAGES

This aide-memoire is designed to provide the reader with a short checklist when considering the quantum of a claim for damages.

1 Is the action in tort or for breach of contract? Has a copy of the claim and defence been provided?

2 If the action is in contract has a copy of the contract been provided?

3 Has a company search been arranged?

4 Does the claim look sensible in relation to recent statutory accounts?

5 Do the statutory accounts disclose any other information which tends to support or contradict the claim?

6 Has a thorough review been made of all papers disclosed following discovery?

7 What further documents ought to be obtained?

8 Are papers filed to facilitate rapid retrieval?

9 Is there adequate support for specific items in the claim?

10 Are calculations associated with the claim accurate?

11 Can other specialists assist in the review?

12 Have the appropriate external sources of data been identified?

13 Has the plaintiff made appropriate allowance for savings in variable costs and overheads in the loss of profits calculations?

14 Are costs claimed in respect of mitigation of damages reasonable?

15 Did the plaintiff take reasonable steps to mitigate losses?

16 Has the plaintiff claimed as additional costs of working, fixed costs which would have been incurred in any event?

17 Does the claim include property replacement costs and loss of profits such that there may be double counting in the claim?

18 Are there any other aspects of the claim which may represent double counting?

19 Has VAT been properly excluded from the quantum of damages?

20 Does the claim include matters which might be considered too remote?

21 Is there evidence to indicate the possibility of contributory negligence?

22 Has the plaintiff included any costs of preparing the claim in quantum?

23 Was the plaintiff covered by insurance? If so, what implications might the receipt of insurance money have on the quantum?

24 Will the defendant's insurers require the quantum to be specifically analysed for claim purposes?

Chapter 3

Breach of warranty claims

The legal status of warranties – Examples of financial warranties – Proving breach of warranty – Materiality – De minimis clauses – Hindsight – Post-balance sheet events – Consistency – Stock provisions – Collecting old debts – Completion accounts – Damages arising – The general rule – The value as warranted – The value as was: opposing arguments – Double counting – Conclusion

301 The 1980s will be remembered by many in business as a decade of notorious corporate takeover battles. These represented only the tip of the iceberg. Many hundreds of acquisitions of one company by another were taking place outside the limelight.

302 Those involved with these mergers and acquisitions will be only too aware of the many hours devoted by the company directors, their lawyers, merchant bankers and accountants in drafting and arguing over the terms of the sale agreements. Common to many such agreements were extensive financial warranties.

303 The 1990s may well be remembered by commercial litigation lawyers in years to come as the era of warranty claims. Deals put together during the bull markets of the late 1980s are not proving to be as fruitful as was expected and disappointed acquirors are looking closely at the warranty clauses for some financial relief.

The legal status of warranties

304 Warranties are given by vendors to purchasers and form a part of the contract of sale. However, in law they are only collateral to the main purpose of the contract. Thus a breach of a warranty does not constitute a breach of the contract itself. It can give rise to a claim for damages, but unlike a breach of contract 'condition', it does not convey a right to treat the contract as repudiated.

Examples of financial warranties

305 Financial warranties can be conveniently divided into two broad categories: general warranties and specific warranties. General warranties we define as relating to the purchased business or its accounts as a whole. Examples of such warranties include those relating to the truth and fairness of its accounts, the consistency of its accounts with those of prior years, and the absence of adverse changes in its financial position since the balance sheet date. Specific warranties we define as those relating to a particular part of the purchased business or its accounts. Examples of specific warranties include those relating to the collectability of debts, the valuation of stock, the loss of major customers.

306　In many of the contractual disputes in which an expert accountant acts, he is concerned only with the quantum of the claim. In warranty claims, the accounting expert is usually concerned with both liability and quantum. In other words, his evidence will assist the court to decide whether or not there have been breaches of the financial warranties and if so, how the damages might be calculated.

307　Some examples of financial warranties typically found in company sale agreements are set out in the table below. We return to a number of these examples later in this chapter.

Proving breach of warranty

308　Of course, specific and general warranties are interrelated. However, our experience is that it is easier to prove breach of a specific warranty than a general warranty. For example, it may be fairly straightforward to show that specific debts were not collected by the purchased company within the warranted period. It is another matter to prove that this meant that the reserve for doubtful debts in the accounts was inadequate as a result of which the accounts did not show a true and fair view.

EXAMPLES OF FINANCIAL WARRANTIES

'The Accounts comply with the requirements of the Act applicable to the Accounts; and have been prepared in accordance with all applicable Financial Reporting Standards and Statements of Standard Accounting Practice and where none are applicable with generally accepted accounting practice; and show a true and fair view of the affairs of the Company as at the Accounting Date and of the results of the Company for the accounting period ending on that date.'

'The Accounts fully provide or reserve for, or fully disclose, all liabilities of the Company as at the Accounting Date.'

'The Accounts fully provide or reserve for all bad debts as at the Accounting Date and adequately provide for all doubtful debts as at the Accounting Date.'

'The Accounts are not affected (except as disclosed in the Accounts) by any extraordinary, exceptional, unusual or non-recurring events, circumstances or items.'

'Each of stock and work-in-progress was included in the Accounts at a figure not exceeding the amount at which it could in the circumstances existing at the Accounting Date reasonably be expected to be realised in the normal course of business of the Company except that any redundant or obsolete stock was written off.'

'The amounts due from debts as at the Accounting Date will be recoverable in full in the ordinary course of business and, in any event, not more than six months after the Accounting Date except in respect of amounts specifically provided for in the Accounts as being bad or doubtful debts.'

'There has been no material adverse change in the financial or trading position or prospects of the Company since the Accounting Date.'

Materiality

309   In order to prove that accounts do not show a true and fair view, it is necessary to show that the errors, misstatements or omissions relating to those accounts are material. Materiality is a concept to which accountants often refer and so it is perhaps helpful to set out what accountants mean by this concept. It has been codified within the Statement of Auditing Standards 'Auditors' Reports on Financial Statements'. The relevant paragraphs are reproduced below.

> 'A matter is material if its omission or mis-statement would reasonably influence the decisions of a user of the financial statements. Materiality may be considered in the context of the financial statements as a whole, any individual primary statement within the financial statements or individual items included in them.
>
> A qualified opinion is issued when the auditors disagree with the treatment or disclosure of a matter in the financial statements and in the auditors' judgement, the effect of the matter is or may be material to the financial statements and therefore those statements may not or do not give a true and fair view . . .'

310   This definition provides plenty of scope for argument and expression of opinion. It is a fruitful area for an expert accountant. But a plaintiff who can only sue by reference to an alleged breach of a 'true and fair view' warranty will be well advised to ensure that the breach is clearly material before embarking on such litigation.

De minimis clauses

311   Warranties are like guarantees. If the warrantor states that debts are fully collectable, then the purchaser is entitled to expect every pound to be collected. What happens if he is one pound short? A breach of warranty has occurred and there is a potential claim for damage. This would clearly be a ludicrous state of affairs. To overcome such potential difficulties, warranty schedules are usually drafted with 'de minimis' clauses. In effect, these provide that a purchaser can only bring a claim if the total of all breaches of a given warranty or group of warranties exceeds a certain sum of money.

312   As stated at the outset of this chapter, there are two facets to warranty claims. The first is to prove that there has indeed been a breach of warranty. The second is to calculate what the damage for the breach should be. In the next part of this chapter we address a number of the issues which commonly arise in proving breach of financial warranty.

Hindsight

313   Many breach of warranty claims are brought to court because the purchasers are generally disappointed with their investment. It has not worked out as they had hoped and they are looking for some compensation. They perhaps find they cannot sell all the stock that they bought as part of the acquired company. Perhaps a large customer unexpectedly goes into liquidation and the amount it owes can no longer be recovered. Such matters can be demonstrated by reference to hindsight. The issue of hindsight is rarely absent in a warranty claim. The relevance of hindsight and how it impinges on a breach of warranty depends largely on the terms of the warranty itself. The expert will have to treat each warranty on its individual merits.

Post-balance sheet events

314 Where the warranty at issue is the truth and fairness of a set of accounts, the issue of hindsight is addressed in Statement of Standard Accounting Practice 17 'Accounting for Post-Balance Sheet Events'. Post-balance sheet events are defined as 'those events, both favourable and unfavourable, which occur between the balance sheet date and the date on which the financial statements are approved by the directors'. Such events are further distinguished between 'adjusting' and 'non-adjusting' events. Adjusting events are post-balance sheet events which provide additional evidence of conditions existing at the balance sheet date. For example, if a customer owing a substantial sum of money at the company's balance sheet date went into receivership between that date and when the accounts were approved by the directors, it would be proper to adjust the balance sheet to reflect a reserve or provision against that particular debt. Non-adjusting events are post-balance sheet events which concern conditions which did not exist at the balance sheet date. For example, it would not normally be appropriate to adjust the book value of stock to reflect losses as a result of a catastrophe, such as fire or flood, which occurred after the balance sheet date.

315 So, when considering a breach of a 'true and fair view warranty', the expert will need to be satisfied that the alleged adjustments do not arise either as a result of any events occurring after the directors approved the accounts, or from non-adjusting events between balance sheet date and directors' approval.

316 Of course, where hindsight merely confirms a view which ought reasonably to have been taken at the time the accounts were approved by the directors, the expert is entitled to refer to such hindsight.

Consistency

317 The issue of consistent accounting is at the heart of many breach of warranty disputes. When a company is taken over by another company the new owners soon impose their own management style and way of doing things. This will include accounting procedures and practices. It may even lead to different accounting policies being applied in drawing up the acquired company's annual accounts. The accounting expert will be familiar with the concept of 'consistency' because it is one of four fundamental accounting concepts underlying periodic financial accounts of a business. However, some guidance may be helpful for those instructing the expert.

318 The consistency concept is that 'there is consistency of accounting treatment of like items within each accounting period and from one period to the next'. Two further definitions must also be stated.

(1) 'Accounting bases are the methods developed for applying fundamental accounting concepts to financial transactions and items for the purpose of financial accounts, and in particular:

(a)   for determining the accounting periods in which revenue and costs should be recognised in the profit and loss account; and

(b)   for determining the amounts at which material items should be stated in the balance sheet.'

(2) 'Accounting policies are the specific accounting bases selected and consistently applied by a business enterprise as being, in the opinion of the management, appropriate to its circumstances and best suited to present fairly its results and financial position.'

319   A reader of a set of accounts will usually find the accounting policies listed just before or just after the profit and loss account and balance sheet. But even reference to the same accounting policies listed in two consecutive years' accounts will not necessarily be sufficient to establish consistency of accounting treatment.

320   This can best be understood by reference to an example relating to accounting for stock and work in progress. Typically, the stated accounting policy for stock and work in progress will include the following words:

'Stock and work in progress is valued at the lower of cost and net realisable value.'

Cost is usually purchase price or the cost of manufacturing the stock. Accounting standards allow a company to include an allocation of certain manufacturing overhead costs. Some discretion exists for how this allocation should be done.

321   Net realisable value is the actual or estimated selling price less all further costs to completion and all costs to be incurred in marketing, selling and distributing.

322   This is clearly a matter where discretion exists and judgment has to be exercised. For example, management may look at each individual stock line and decide whether or not net realisable value is less than cost. Alternatively, companies with many lines of stock may adopt a formula to assess this which they consider is reasonable, based on, for example, past experience. There is no single correct answer. Rather the answer lies somewhere in a range of possibilities.

323   Difficulties arise in warranty claims because some companies apply the accounting policy in a way which gives a relatively low value for stock, whereas other companies apply the accounting policy in a way which gives a relatively high value for stock. One might refer to these alternatives as the pessimistic approach and the optimistic approach respectively.

324   When a company whose management have a pessimistic approach purchases a company whose management had an optimistic approach, consistency can break down even though the stated accounting policy remains the same. The expert accountant when asked to consider warranty claims where consistency is at issue, must have regard not only to consistency of stated policy, but the manner in which the policy is applied in practice.

325   Sometimes, however, the concept of consistency is taken too far. Some plaintiffs argue that it is appropriate to use accounting policies which are not generally accepted accounting practices, merely because to fail to do so would be inconsistent with the previous year's practice. Unless the sale agreement specifically provides for this exception, it is no part of the concept of consistency for accounts to be consistently wrong.

Stock provisions

326 A change of ownership often gives rise to a change of management. This in turn can have a significant effect on the way an acquired company trades, particularly so when a family business is taken over by a large conglomerate. It is surprising how often new management will identify substantial quantities of obsolescent stock which the former owners claim to have had no difficulty disposing of.

327 Two examples come to mind from our recent experience. The first concerned a company producing paint and ancillary products for the DIY sector. Their customers included chain stores for whom they produced 'own label' products. From time to time these chain stores would change their product requirements, leaving the manufacturers with surplus items unsold. The new owners regarded these goods as obsolete. The former owners had good links with street traders and after repacking were able to dispose of the stock to such traders at reduced prices. But even after price cutting, the former owners were still able to recover at least the cost of the product and so no provision was necessary.

328 The second example concerns a company operating in the toiletries and cosmetics markets. Here fashion can change frequently, particularly as regards packaging. The new owners regarded all stock in old packaging as obsolete. The former owners were able to group together old lines into 'gift packs' to be retailed at the lower end of the market during the Christmas season, and so recover most if not all of the cost of the stock. This argument did not extend, however, to unfinished goods where the company held an imbalance of parts, for example, more bottles than lids. In these circumstances it is generally not unreasonable for the new owners to regard the excess parts as obsolete and of little or no value.

Collecting old debts

329 Breaches of warranties relating to the collectability of debts are, in principle at least, easier than most to prove. For example, it is a matter of fact, not judgment, whether or not a debt has been collected by a certain date. Despite this, there is often suspicion in the minds of defendants in these circumstances, as to whether the new owners have used best endeavours to pursue and collect the debts. After all, they may suggest, it is easier to collect the damages for the breach of warranty than chase after a lot of individual debtors.

330 When faced with these circumstances, the expert should establish whether the actions of the owners have been reasonable in all the circumstances. For example, it might be that a decision by the new owners to stop sending monthly statements to their debtors would be regarded by the court as evidence of insufficient effort to collect the debts.

41

331 The issuing of credit notes is another common feature of warranty claims. It is often alleged by defendants that the new owners issued credit notes to cancel debts, rather than take the more difficult route of pressing for payment. Debtors of acquired companies do sometimes take advantage of the new owners' lack of knowledge of the day-to-day running of the company. They may dispute deliveries. They may try to send surplus stock back. The expert should be alert to such possibilities. Conversely, the new owners may find that the accounting records are so disorganised, and the control over accounts receivable so loose, that they are unable to prove debts when challenged. In such circumstances the court might be sympathetic to the plaintiff's willingness to issue credit notes against book debts.

Completion accounts

332 Sales of companies rarely coincide with their accounting year ends. As a result, sale agreements typically require completion accounts to be drawn up as at the date on which the sale is completed. It is a matter for agreement between the parties in each case who is to be responsible for preparing such accounts, be it vendor or purchaser. Usually the party which does not produce the completion accounts is given the opportunity to 'audit' the accounts once they are prepared. There is usually a time limit for this, during which the other side's auditors are given access to the working papers underlying the completion accounts. It is important to know and observe such limits since they are sometimes 'of the essence', ie it is no good complaining after the limit has expired. If, following this exercise, the completion accounts present a worse financial picture for the acquired company than shown by its previous audited (and warranted) accounts, this can lead to arguments about when the deterioration occurred. It may be necessary for the expert to consider whether the deterioration reflects a change in the way the accounts have been drawn up, a genuine deterioration since the previous audited accounts, or a deterioration which should have been reflected, at least in part, in the previous audited accounts. Such disputes can lead to much detailed accounting analysis. In some cases reference may be necessary to the auditors of the previous accounts, particularly if the company's own accounting papers are inadequate. In some cases the expert will have to resort to reconstructing the previous accounts to ascertain whether or not they fairly presented the company's financial position at that time.

Damages arising

333 So far in this chapter, we have discussed the expert's role in proving or otherwise a breach of financial warranty. His other role is assisting the court in determining the damage which flows from the breach.

334 When the acquisition is originally negotiated and settled, the parties rarely give thought to the subject of damages. It is most unusual to find that an agreement specifies how damages are to be calculated. Rather, the parties seem to be content, consciously or unconsciously, to leave the court to decide the amount of any damages arising.

335 The actual method to be employed in calculating the damages depends on the nature of the warranty which is in breach. Financial warranties often require financial calculation to prove the breach. It is sometimes – erroneously – thought that these same figures automatically provide the measure of damage. So, for example, if stocks are over-valued by £100,000 is the damage itself not also £100,000? The answer is: 'not necessarily'.

The general rule

336   Damages for breach of warranty under the general rule are arrived at by considering the difference between the position the person relying on the warranty would have been in had the representation been true and the position he is actually in as a result of it being untrue.[1] Applied to warranty claims involving the sale of a company, this becomes the difference between the market value of the shares had the warranties been true and their market value as they were in reality ('the value as was').

The value as warranted

337   The market value of the company or shares, had there been no breach of warranty, ie had the warranties been true, is normally taken to be the purchase price. There is a presumption that the original sale was negotiated between willing buyer and willing seller and that the price represented a 'market value'. It is possible, however, that the price paid does not represent the market value of the company or shares because the purchaser was willing to pay more than the market value for its own reasons. An example of such a reason is where the purchaser anticipated that it would be able to make substantial overhead savings by integrating the purchased company into its organisation. However, strong evidence of such reasons will be needed in order to persuade the court that the purchase price is not appropriate. In the absence of strong evidence to the contrary, the court is likely to accept that the purchase price represents the market value of the company or shares.

338   In some cases, payment of a part of the purchase consideration may be deferred to some future date from the date of the sale agreement. The damages should be quantified as at the date of the sale agreement. Consequently, an allowance should be made for the time value of the deferred consideration, because the purchaser would have had the benefit of using those funds in the period from the date of the sale agreement to the date of the payment.

The value as was: opposing arguments

339   The calculation of the value as was can require the court to decide between a calculation based on a change in net assets and one based on multiplying earnings.

340   Consider a case where a liability is omitted from the accounts which causes a breach of warranty on the company's net assets. What loss is suffered by the purchaser? At a minimum, the purchaser would argue that the loss is the amount needed to discharge the liability. If the company had been purchased by reference to a multiple of its stated profits, then the missing liability caused those profits to be overstated. Thus, the purchaser might argue that the loss suffered should be the omitted liability appropriately multiplied.

341 The vendor, on the other hand, may argue that the company was purchased for its future profit earning capacity, and furthermore that the omission of a liability does not have a direct effect on that earning capacity or on the value of its shares. The measure of damages in this example might be the effect on the price that a reasonable purchaser would have paid had he become aware of the liability during negotiations.

342 The expert will have to weigh up these arguments in the light of the factual evidence at his disposal. In particular, he will have to consider whether at the time of the sale agreement the liability would have been considered to be the result of a one-off event or was likely to be recurring. No simple rules of thumb can be given.

343 Where it is clear, from the way in which the original price was fixed between the parties, that the price was based on a multiple of warranted profit and the breach of warranty is such that it is likely to affect future profits, it would seem reasonable to argue for damages based on a multiple of the overstatement of net profit.

344 The vendors in these circumstances may seek to argue that some of the error relates back to earlier years, and that if this is taken into account, it is not the whole of the overstatement of profits to which the multiplier is applied. This argument may be theoretically sound, but difficulties may arise in proving the point. It is likely that the prior years' accounts have been audited. Unless the audit opinion on those accounts has been qualified, or unless there is reliable evidence to show that they were incorrectly drawn up, the vendors may find little practical comfort in this argument.

Double counting

345 Where claims are brought for breach of a number of warranties within one agreement and damages for each breach are sought, the possibility of double counting can arise. This is particularly so if claims are made both for deficiency in a company's net assets and for over-valuation of its shares. The expert should draw this to the attention of those instructing him. It is not for him simply to omit the part that represents double counting. Counsel may well prefer to present the damages claim under a series of alternatives. This can be particularly helpful to the court where the judge may see fit to find breach of some warranty clauses and not others.

Conclusion

346 Finally, a word of caution to those entering into agreements which include financial warranties. Before the deals are struck, guidance from an accounting expert who has seen what happens when breaches are made or alleged could be worth its weight in gold. The tendency so often is for relationships to deteriorate after the disposal of the business is over. A quick review of possible causes of dispute (for example, so-called 'exceptional' factors) before the signing of the agreement, will identify those topics which might later provide the purchaser with an excuse or reason to seek variation of the consideration stipulated, and enable the vendor to prevent such reasons or excuses becoming a cause of friction.

NOTES

1 *Firbank's Executors v Humphreys* (1886) 18 QBD 54, 60, CA.

Chapter 4

Valuations for court purposes

The role of valuations in disputes – Compensatory damages – Share valuations – Lost opportunity – Estate and trust cases – Divorces – Expropriation of companies – Duties of a director – The negligence of a valuer – Using valuation theory to test reasonableness of claims – Defining the entity to be valued – Methods of valuing a business entity – The price/earnings method – Discounted cash flow method – Dividend yield valuations – Special purpose valuations – Valuation of net tangible assets – Liquidation basis – Replacement cost – The choice of concepts for litigation purposes – Some oddities explained – Market capitalisation and asset values – High multiples and capitalisation rates – Information gathering – Loss of investment opportunity – Methods of measuring the value of lost investment opportunity – The importance of assumptions – The valuer's liability for negligence – Summary

401 A good understanding of valuation methods is an essential weapon in a forensic accountant's armoury. In the interests of brevity we have had to be selective in our discussion of valuation in this book. We are concerned in this chapter with valuations arising from disputes rather than with those relating to, say, a transfer between two parties where, for tax reasons, a value has to be struck. Readers should refer to Appendix D for more information on two principal techniques which can be applied in valuing businesses.

THE ROLE OF VALUATIONS IN DISPUTES

402 There are many types of court case where a valuation is required and where a report by an expert accountant may therefore be needed. Some examples that arise in practice are discussed below.

Compensatory damages

403 Typical of compensatory damages is the case where the plaintiff had been promised an interest in a business which for some reason is denied to him or has failed to measure up to the worth represented by the seller. Much conjecture may be involved in such valuations, for example, where the valuer has to decide what the business would have been worth if the action complained of had not occurred.

Share valuations

404 Disputes over the valuation of shares, which may also require expert evidence can arise in management buy out situations or where a capital reconstruction takes place. The valuation of shares may also be relevant in disputes arising where a company buys back its own shares or in circumstances where minority shareholders are being treated unfairly or unjustly.

Lost opportunity

405 Valuation of lost opportunity has become an expanding area for expert accountants. The financial markets in Britain are being ever more closely regulated and corporate behaviour (for example, in relation to 'concert parties' and other methods of manipulation of markets) is likely to come under the scrutiny of the courts. If the court finds that, through foul play, someone has deprived his rival of the opportunity of acquiring a business, for example in a takeover battle, damages based on the value of the loss of net benefits which would have accrued to the latter will need to be argued.

Estate and trust cases

406 Situations arise where a shareholder is in a position to purchase stock from the estate of a deceased person or from a trust. The trust representatives have a fiduciary responsibility to be fair to all beneficiaries and not to sell out cheaply. An independent appraisal is desirable. If a dispute occurs, the usual requirement is to re-examine the independent valuation critically.

Divorces

407 Sometimes one or both of the partners in a marriage are running a business which needs to be valued for the purposes of identifying the financial resources of the parties. The business may be either spouse's livelihood as well as the biggest single asset of the married couple. Valuations of businesses in these circumstances can be clouded by distrust and secrecy. Quite often, expert testimony on their value has to be presented in court. The presentation of financial evidence in divorce cases is dealt with in Chapter 7.

Expropriation of companies

408 When one comes to deal with the expropriation of companies it is very important to look at the terms laid down by whichever tribunal is charged with fixing the compensation. If the company which has been acquired has been a going concern for some time and has been producing profits, then the measure of loss is generally to determine the value of its future stream of earnings by reference to past achievements and future forecasts. If, on the other hand, the company is still in the start-up phase of its life, it will probably be essential to turn to some form of discounted cash flow, which takes account of the remaining investment that should be made before positive cash flow will result.

Duties of a director

409   In recent times there has been an increasing number of cases (both civil and criminal) involving allegations that directors of companies have breached their duty to the company. It may be alleged, for example, that directors have been negligent or have acted in bad faith by securing a personal gain in buying or selling shares in the company. Evidence provided by the expert accountant on the valuation of such shares is often relevant to such allegations.

The negligence of a valuer

410   A valuation may be the subject of an action in court where a valuer himself is facing a damages claim arising from his failure to exercise reasonable skill and care. In these circumstances the expert accountant may be called on to provide an opinion on the probity of the procedures followed and the methodology used in the valuation. At the end of this chapter we discuss a number of court cases dealing with the issue of the valuer's liability for negligence.

Using valuation theory to test reasonableness of claims

411   The expert accountant must always be aware of the alternative courses of action which the claimant of damages has open to him. Valuation theory is often important here. For instance, a claim is made that a piece of plant or a factory was unable to meet its design requirements; a figure of £x is put forward as the measure of damage (lost profit). The question should be asked of the claimant: 'If you receive your claim in full, will you invest it in the improvement of the plant?' If the explicit or implicit answer is: 'No, I will use it to reduce my bank overdraft' certain adverse conclusions might be drawn about the value of the business and the economic case for the basis of the claim.

412   Or consider a situation where, following destruction of the item in question, a more modern or larger unit is put in its place. Again, business valuation principles can be applied – perhaps to demonstrate that the book value of the old plant was unrealistic because the plant was uneconomic either in size or through out-of-date technology.

DEFINING THE ENTITY TO BE VALUED

413   Fundamental to the valuation process is the determination of whether the value of the total *assets* of a company, or the *equity* in the total assets, is required. The expert valuer must ensure that clear instructions are received to this effect.

414   Great care is needed to define exactly the entity or specific asset that is the subject of the expert's appraisal. The expert and the instructing lawyer should also agree precisely:

(a) the purpose of the task; and
(b) the date or dates of the valuation.

415   Case law or other legal principle will be of critical importance. Sometimes values can alter greatly within a short time as a result of certain events and it may be that those events will be deemed by the courts to have mitigated the damage. Substantial changes in the investing public's perception of the value of quoted shares in general are demonstrated by the stock market crisis of October 1987. Sudden changes in a company's performance can likewise have a big impact on values.

416   In cases of expropriation the expert valuer needs guidance on the extent to which he should remove the influence of the prospective expropriation (or other adverse influence) from his valuation methodology.

417   Sometimes the expert will need to produce valuations for different times in the life of the business, since the legal guidance may be unclear as to which date is likely to be decisive in the court hearing. Normally, business values depend on an assessment of future income; such assessments in turn depend partly on a review of the past to indicate the risk associated with the prediction of future income. In some situations, for example, an uncompleted project, no history will exist for the entity being valued. Claims in such circumstances stand or fall on the accuracy of estimates of cash flow for several years ahead; such appraisals can be highly speculative and the courts may well view them with reserve. There will be other situations where the expert may be asked to establish a fair value as a measure for compensation by considering what has been spent on the project to date, or what the replacement cost will be, or by establishing some similar method of comparison.

METHODS OF VALUING A BUSINESS ENTITY

418   Since value, like beauty, is in the eye of the beholder, no absolute rules can be laid down. Nonetheless, as we have already seen, the context of the dispute is important and the measurement of damages must be put into the legal framework which is laid down by practice in the courts, by terms of the agreement or indeed by statutory definition. Usually, fair market valuation – 'the price at which the interest would change hands between a willing buyer and a willing seller, both being informed of the relevant facts' is the measure required. The instructions will indicate whether this or some other standard of value is expected from the expert.

419   The courts have recognised that valuation is not an exact science, and that different experts can, with perfect legitimacy, hold widely differing opinions as to the value of the same item. This was seen in the recent case of *Axa Equity & Law Home Loans Ltd v Goldsack & Freeman*[1] where it was held that a valuer was not negligent in valuing an asset for more than it subsequently realised where the result was within a 'proper bracket of valuation'. In *Private Bank*[2], a margin of 15% was considered to be a reasonable 'margin of error' where the property was unusual and it was thus difficult to achieve a level of precision.

420   The two most commonly used methods of valuing a company or an operating business, are discounted cash flow (DCF) and the price/earnings (P/E) method, which we explain below. A third method, the dividend yield basis, is usually used to value minority shareholdings.

421 In certain specialised industries or activities, values may be established by reference to the assets belonging to a company, not its future profits or cash flows. An example where this approach is used, is property development companies which are worth the current value to a purchaser of the portfolio of properties.

The price/earnings method

422 In practice the DCF method is a little sophisticated. It therefore remains common in valuing an ongoing business entity to rely on the more simple price/earnings method. This takes an estimate of future maintainable profits as a surrogate for the future cash flows and multiplies this earnings figure by an appropriate price earnings ratio. We explain this method in detail in Appendix D. The choice of P/E ratio reflects inter alia expectations about growth, or lack of it. A high multiple is accorded to a business with relatively high growth expectations, and a low multiple to one with lower or negative growth prospects.

Discounted cash flow ('DCF') method

423 As a concept, DCF analysis is relatively simple. It is based on the generally accepted theory that the value of a business depends on the future cash flows of the business at present day values. Discounting is used to take account of the widely accepted preference for money now rather than money in the future. This is often referred to as the 'time value' of money. Thus, as an example, the receipt of £100 in one year's time is attributed a lower economic value than £100 received today. The difference between the two economic values is the discount.

424 The mathematical technique used in DCF analysis is the reverse of that used for calculating compound interest, a concept more familiar to laymen and perhaps the courts. Compound interest takes a capital sum today and, by the application of an interest rate, adds interest to the sum year on year, interest being calculated on principal and accrued interest in future periods. It is possible in this way to compute what a given sum, invested today at a given rate of interest, will be worth in a given number of years' time. By contrast, as we have seen, DCF will take the sum expected in the future and discount it back to the present day.

425 By expressing all cash flows on a present day basis, the costs of an investment can be compared with the returns from that investment, the difference being the net present value (NPV) of the investment.

426 In terms of this methodology, the cash flow (not the profit) that the company or business will generate each year is discounted back to a current value. A simple cash flow valuation illustrating this principle is shown opposite.

DCF analysis requires the following:

(a) a forecast of future cash flow estimates over a relevant period of time;
(b) the choice of an appropriate discount rate; and
(c) the estimation of the terminal residual value at the end of the time period.

DCF methodology is explained in detail in Appendix D. It is natural that when two or more parties are seeking to come to agreement, it can be difficult to reconcile views on such matters as:

Year	*Cash flow receivable*	*Present value at 10% pa*
1	100	91
2	120	99
3	140	106
Total cashflows	360	
Present value of cashflows		296
* assuming cash flow is received at the year end		

(a) economic conditions in the future;
(b) business expectations, including competition and level of demand; and
(c) the competence of management to grasp opportunities.

427 So, because long-term projections often lack credibility (or at least mutual acceptance), many business valuations end up being based on historical data.

Dividend yield valuations

428 The price/earnings and discounted cash flow methods of valuation are used to value a controlling interest in a company. Valuations of minority parcels of shares in private companies are often based on the capitalisation of dividends rather than maintainable earnings. This is in recognition of the fact that a minority shareholder is not in a position to direct, and often not even in a position to influence, the distribution of dividends or the investment of retained profits. As a result, the value of such a shareholding is generally restricted to its right to receive dividends.

429 Thus, for valuations of small minority interests in unlisted companies, the dividend yield method is often used. This involves computing a capital value for the shares such that when the dividends actually paid are expressed as a percentage of this capital value, it produces a reasonable yield when compared to the yield that could be derived from a comparable listed investment. Some discount would normally be applied to reflect any restriction on transferability of the shares and the absence of a ready market for the shares.

430 Dividend valuations of businesses do not otherwise differ fundamentally from other cash flow valuations, of which they represent a special case. We have deemed this method to be of little relevance to the sort of disputes we describe in this chapter.

Special purpose valuations

431 In some specialised industries and activities, values are established by methods which do not conform to the main routes described above, for example: news agencies, estate agents, insurance brokers, medical and dental practices, accountancy practices, petrol stations, hotels, public houses and off-licence shops. Each have traditional valuation formulae applied to them, often based on a simple multiple of turnover. These businesses tend to be cash oriented, and the true net profits in a given period may be difficult to determine. The methods used for evaluating such units provide a useful cross-check on conventional methods, ie methods based on the capitalisation of future earnings.

VALUATION OF NET TANGIBLE ASSETS

432 There will be occasions when the needs of the case require a valuation of a particular trading asset or group of trading assets, as distinct from the overall business valuation. The value of an asset or group of assets will normally be based on the open market value of the asset; however, the determination of such values is best determined by specialists who are fully aware of the prevailing market conditions. As it is beyond the scope of the forensic valuer to determine specific asset values where he has no particular expertise, we have not considered the asset basis of valuation in any detail.

433 Net assets may be measured in a number of different ways. There are fundamentally two alternative bases: namely, to measure by reference to their costs or to their current 'value'.

434 When the net assets are measured by reference to their cost, the source of information is the business balance sheet which records original prices paid for them by the company. This basis is known as 'historic cost'. As the assets are depreciated over the years, the remaining balance is called the 'book value' or the 'written-down historic cost'. It should be evident that book value is not necessarily the price that the asset would fetch if sold in the market, or what it would cost to replace.

435 When net assets are measured by reference to their current value, it is usual to adopt one of four approaches:

(a) the price that would have to be paid at today's date to purchase an asset equivalent to the existing asset (the 'current replacement cost'). If the replacement asset in question is partly worn out, it is termed 'written-down replacement cost';
(b) the current open market sales value of the asset;
(c) the 'forced sale' value of the asset, ie the amount likely to be obtained if it were put on the market in circumstances where the seller either has to take the best price obtainable in a fixed period or as soon as possible; or
(d) the net present value of all expected future earnings from the asset.

436 Each of these values may be supplemented by the premium which a purchaser is prepared to pay, reflecting such factors as potential economies of scale, reduction in competition, the securing of a source of supply or outlet for products. The premium is unique to the purchaser. The existence of this special value means that the purchaser is prepared to pay a consideration which is over and above the value which other purchasers are prepared to pay.

437 The phrase 'the going concern value' is often used; strictly, this is not a system of valuation: the phrase simply states that the valuation rests on the assumption that the company can continue to trade for the foreseeable future, for example, it has adequate funds for doing so.

438 The economic value of a company's assets tends to be the one which causes most discussion in legal disputes, ie the present value of expected earnings.

Liquidation basis

439 Typically, assets sold on a liquidation basis will realise significantly less than would be the case if the asset was sold in the normal course of trading on a going concern basis. For instance, the cost of stock and work in progress sold in these circumstances by auction will generally have to be discounted significantly in order to attract buyers.

440 This method is likely to be appropriate for valuing controlling interests of entities facing liquidation. Alternatively, the liquidation basis may be relevant for those entities operating at a loss and with little prospect of making future profits, or with a low profit rate compared with the asset base of the entity.

Replacement cost

441 The replacement cost basis of valuation is based on the concept of replicating or duplicating a business from scratch. The Sandilands Report 1975 was an attempt to prescribe suitable methods of valuing assets in periods of high inflation, such as the 1970s. According to this report, the replacement cost method is likely to be the most appropriate method of valuation in seeking to calculate the loss which a business would suffer if deprived of an asset. In certain circumstances the report recommends that assets may also be valued on the net present value or the net realisable value basis.

The choice of concepts for litigation purposes

442 No definite rules can be laid down, and clearly the requirement of the court should be the fundamental consideration in determining the valuation approach to be adopted. Sometimes more than one approach will be appropriate. Case law may indicate the preferred course to be followed. Time should always be taken to examine all the options available.

443 As a general guide, however, although value needs to be determined in the context of each assignment, most independent valuations of shares and businesses tend to use the term as meaning:

> 'the price that would be negotiated in an open and unrestricted market between a knowledgeable, willing but not anxious buyer and a knowledgeable, willing but not anxious seller, acting at arms length.'

444 As we have already made clear, valuation on the basis of earning power is the concept which most often has relevance in court cases. For instance, if a family business is being valued it is likely that it will be determined by this route.

445 It is perhaps helpful to consider what concepts are to be applied when the dispute is more extreme between the parties. Take for instance a claim for lawful or unlawful expropriation. If his business has operated profitably, the claimant may well argue for an economic valuation. But he will also look at replacement value on the grounds that the underlying asset should not be taken from him 'on the cheap' in what is really a forced sale.

446   If his business is still in the start-up phase, the claimant will use book value as a starting point, taking the line that as a minimum he should receive back what he has spent. He will also look for compensation for the lost opportunity to make profits in the future, attributing an element of economic value to the assets.

447   A claimant may in certain situations be justified in looking for a valuation which includes elements of all three approaches (net realisable value, replacement value, and economic value). Consider, for instance, a business which has not only a profitable operation, but also a redundant office building, a large unused bank balance, and mineral deposits (or a land bank) which will take care of many years' requirements. Here he should argue for economic value for the profitable operation, net realisable value for the surplus office building and the cash, and replacement value for the mineral deposits (or land bank).

448   We hope that the discussion of alternative valuation concepts set out above will demonstrate the subjectivity and choice which exists in this area. The merits of each type of valuation approach adopted by the claimant will need to be looked at critically by the defendant's experts. It is unlikely that one method alone will be sufficient for arguing the case in court.

SOME ODDITIES EXPLAINED

449   The following apparent oddities arise in valuations at times, puzzling lawyers and others concerned with values.

(a) How does market capitalisation relate to asset values?
(b) How do multiples relate to capitalisation rates?

Market capitalisation and asset values

450   Some people expect there to be a relationship between market capitalisation and asset values. Financial commentators talk about underlying asset values being X% more or Y% less than the quoted price, as though the relationship is direct. The reality is that shares are normally valued on earnings capability, not on underlying assets. A financial services company, for example, with virtually no tangible assets may have a capitalisation of millions of pounds. Alternatively, if a company can be broken up and sold off, asset values may be important.

High multiples and capitalisation rates

451   Some people, seeing a share quoted at 25 times reported earnings, think that this implies that the shareholders are content to buy shares that will give them only a 4% net return. However, investors are more interested in the future earnings capacity of a company. If this year's earnings double, the multiple will halve to 12½ times. If profits double again, the multiple will drop to 6¼ times. Conversely, if profits halve, the multiple will double to 50 times reported earnings.

INFORMATION GATHERING

452 As with many aspects of accounting work for litigation, a thorough approach to the way that information is gathered in preparation for valuation is essential. The court will want to be satisfied that the valuation presented to it is both reasonable and soundly based.

453 The following sources of information should be considered in a valuation:

(a) a site visit to the business;
(b) information about the business, its competitors and prospects, obtained by interviewing those responsible for running the business;
(c) share market statistics published by the stock exchange;
(d) the annual reports and audited accounts of the company or business being valued, taking into account, where appropriate, a period of time reflecting the economic cycle of the business;
(e) government papers, industry studies and statistics;
(f) a review of literature about the business and its market environment, including brokers' reports, financial journals, trade journals and newspaper reports;
(g) a review of papers about the business's financial position and future prospects, including detailed management accounts, board minutes, profit forecasts, market surveys;
(h) reviews of similar businesses;
(i) examples of recent valuations of part or all of the business, such as recent share transactions; and
(j) the company's Articles of Association, to check whether any restrictions exist on the transferability of shares.

454 The scope of the investigation will depend on the nature of the valuation and on whether the valuer has access to people and papers. Instructing solicitors will appreciate an early indication of the types of documents which ought to be seen, particularly if they need to apply for discovery of the papers from the other side.

LOSS OF INVESTMENT OPPORTUNITY

455 There is a growing area of litigation in connection with lost investment opportunity, for example, loss of opportunity to do something, caused by someone else's wrongdoing. The basic rules of calculation follow those described in Chapter 2 dealing with loss of profits, but, at the risk of some repetition, the subject of lost investment opportunity deserves separate study. It is important to say that the rules are not clear in law. A number of cases have argued that damages for the loss of an opportunity should be recoverable, but to date there has been no conclusive authority on the point. Certain cases of this type have been founded on the tort of unlawful interference or conspiracy to injure. The House of Lords' recent finding that it is not necessary to show that the intention to cause injury was the predominant purpose of the alleged unlawful action, is likely to increase the incidence of cases of this type.

456 First let us distinguish the concept of loss of profits from the concept of lost opportunity. Loss of profits is normally regarded by the courts as a form of pure economic loss (unless an element of physical damage to property or person also enters into the claim). Where such a loss is purely economic, the courts are normally reluctant to allow the recovery of damages in respect of that loss in a claim based on the tort of negligence (the notable exception to this 'reluctance' is in the case of professional negligence, where economic loss does feature in awards of damages). Accordingly, where property is damaged, any immediate economic loss which arises as a result will be recoverable as damages, but future economic loss is less likely to be recoverable, on grounds of uncertainty. In *Department of the Environment v Thomas Bates & Sons Ltd*[3] the House of Lords held that the diminution in value of a lease due to negligent and defective building was pure economic loss and so not recoverable. The building itself, while not fit for its intended purpose was not physically damaged, nor was it an imminent threat to health and safety. This case followed the decision in *Murphy v Brentwood District Council*,[4] where it was held that the Council was not liable for defects in a house in circumstances where there was no injury to persons, no risk to the health and safety of others and where there had been no damage to other property arising out of the defect.

457 The concept of loss of opportunity caused by a wrongful act, has to be viewed differently. Here the loss complained of is the loss of the chance to earn profits in the future, rather than the loss of profits themselves. If such damages are recoverable, the claimant in respect of such a loss has to satisfy the courts, on the balance of probabilities, that he stood a certain percentage chance of obtaining the benefits of the opportunity he claims to have lost.

458 The role of the expert accountant would be to calculate the total value of the lost opportunity. It is for the court to make such discount as is necessary to reflect the element of uncertainty present.

459 It is also for the court to select, perhaps from a range of models or methods, what is most appropriate for remedying the tort or contractual defect.

Methods of measuring the value of lost investment opportunity

460 As we have said, one or more methods can be employed to value loss of opportunity. The key formulations are set out below.

(a) The use of a replacement model. We have lost the bargain so what will it cost to find an equivalent? Such an approach might be appropriate to value, for example, a picture, some property, an oil field, or perhaps a company which has a unique character. Sometimes, the opportunity lost is so unique that an equivalent is very hard to find.
(b) The valuation of the future profit potential. Here the need is to calculate what extra profit would have been enjoyed by the intending purchaser which was not itself fully represented in the price at which the bargain was going to be struck. This is an 'incremental profit approach' and might well be appropriate in a claim connected with insider trading or where, through trickery, a bid for a company fails and the plaintiff has to sue for damages.
(c) The break-up value. Normally, this will not be appropriate for going concerns, but it should always be considered as a partial alternative. For instance, where there is a high element of cash or spare land and buildings, or some valuable

product brands which could be disposed of without injuring the rest of the business, the break-up value should be brought into the equation.

(d) The original investment value or written-down historic value. This may well be a valid approach where there has been an expropriation of a company.

(e) The inflation adjusted book value of the assets. This is really a variation of (d) and simply allows for the loss in monetary value which has occurred since the original investment was made. It is particularly relevant when the country in which the company operates has suffered from high monetary inflation.

461 Perhaps the most difficult approach is method (b), namely, valuing the future profit potential. There is a need to estimate what would have been the outcome had there been a complete success in terms of, say, an acquisition of a business or company. We have already discussed the two principal routes for putting a value on future earnings: the discounted cash flow technique and the price/earnings multiple.

462 There is a simpler approach to valuation of profits, and that is to add them all up between the date when the tort or contractual break occurred and the date of the judgment. If this is done, together with interest, it often produces a figure which a court will be prepared to accept as a reasonable and conservative estimate of lost opportunity. It is deficient in that it excludes any future losses arising after the court hearing. But it should not be overlooked that judges generally take the view that the damage will not be suffered for an infinite period; there will be other bargains about and it will be up to the plaintiff to mitigate his loss by seeking those other bargains.

THE IMPORTANCE OF ASSUMPTIONS

463 When an accountant prepares his valuations for court purposes, he should give special thought to the appropriateness of the assumptions underlying his work. It is surprising how often it bears fruit to ask the other side's valuer, in cross-examination, what his instructions were when asked to prepare a valuation and to see his letter of instruction. It is a truism that valuations are no better than the assumptions on which they are based; however, for forensic valuations, one should add a further limitation: valuations based on verifiable assumptions will be preferred to those based on theoretical or speculative ones.

464 The decision in the case of *Anangel Atlas Compania Naviera SA v Ishikawajima-Harima Heavy Industries Co Ltd (No 2)*[5] shows the importance of being able to justify the assumptions involved in financial models.

465 The case concerned damages arising from a breach of a 'most favoured customer' clause. The plaintiffs not only claimed the difference in price between the final cash price of ships sold to them and those sold to another party which was given better terms, they also claimed loss suffered due to differential credit terms on which finance was provided to buyers. In order to do this, Anangel's expert employed a concept of 'net finance benefit', which he defined as the net loan cash flow discounted at the opportunity cost of the funds. This represented the return that the purchasers of a vessel would be able to obtain by investing in their own business funds made available as a result of the credit terms.

466   The judge rejected the concept of 'net finance benefit', accepting the defendants' submissions that if such a claim was reasonable under the agreement, it ought to be capable of being calculated by competent accountants rather than a team of high powered accountants. Also, it should not be necessary to use data to which they, the defendants, could not reasonably have access, nor should it involve the use of assumptions. The judge also questioned the assumptions that the past rates of return were a guide to the future, and that rates of return on equity were a better measure than, for example, bank deposit rates.

467   The message from this case was that the court would subject both valuation techniques and assumptions to careful scrutiny. In particular, it was a warning to an expert whose methodology for calculating loss is too theoretical.

The valuer's liability for negligence

468   In undertaking a valuation, a valuer implicitly warrants to his instructing client that he has a reasonable degree of skill and knowledge, and that he will exercise reasonable skill and care in preparing the valuation report which is sought. A serious failure to exercise reasonable skill and care may leave the valuer liable to a claim for damages for losses occurring pursuant to a breach of contract. There may also be an extended duty of care to third parties in certain circumstances, by operation of the law arising in tort.

469   There is a view that a valuer who may be otherwise negligent for a valuation, should not be held liable for a drop in the value of an asset subsequent to the valuation which could not reasonably have been foreseen at the time of the valuation. This argument was accepted at first instance in the *Banque Bruxelles Lambert*[6] case, where a bank lent money to a company on the strength of a valuation of certain properties, but the properties realised significantly less than indicated by the valuation once the property market collapsed.

470   In any contemplated legal action against valuers, the activities of the plaintiff will need to be examined. In *Banque Bruxelles* referred to above, the measure of damages payable to the bank was reduced by 30% as a result of the bank's contributory negligence in failing to discharge its own obligation to investigate the implications of a price discrepancy. This case demonstrates that even though a valuer may have been negligent in his approach, users of valuations cannot simply place blind reliance on their professional advisers: they must act sensibly and in accordance with their own practices. The Court of Appeal has subsequently overturned this judgment[7] and it is expected that the point will be referred to the House of Lords for a final decision. It is clearly a very contentious area, with implications for causation in professional negligence actions generally, and has been subject to considerable debate.

SUMMARY

471   Out of necessity, this chapter has merely touched upon the areas of most common concern to expert accountants. There are several excellent books on valuation, some of which we list in our bibliography. Valuation is a forward looking exercise. No set of circumstances is precisely the same as the one which preceded it. Prices can be volatile and influenced by mood as well as reason, and so one cannot always achieve exactitude.

472 In all cases, the forensic accountant engaged to prepare a valuation should ensure that his opinion is:

(a) independent;
(b) based on the best available information in circumstances where there is admissible evidence to prove all of the necessary underlying factual assumptions in court;
(c) verifiable to the greatest possible extent;
(d) formulated on the basis of the relevant legal principles (as communicated to the valuer by the legal advisers);
(e) formulated using the most appropriate methodology; and
(f) presented to the court in a logical and coherent manner.

NOTES

1 *Axa Equity & Law v Goldsack & Freeman* [1994] 23 EG 130.
2 *Private Bank & Trust Co Ltd v S (UK) Ltd* [1993] 9 EG 112.
3 [1990] 2 All ER 943.
4 [1990] 2 All ER 908.
5 [1990] 2 Lloyd's Rep 526.
6 *Banque Bruxelles Lambert SA v Eagle Star Insurance Co Ltd* [1994] 31 EG 68, QBD.
7 (1995) Times, 21 February.

Chapter 5

Construction contract claims

Introduction – The nature of the construction industry – A typical
construction project – The construction litigation team – Types of
contract – Fixed price contracts – Cost-plus contracts – Bills of
quantities or unit price contracts – Time and materials contracts –
Turnkey contracts – Standard form contracts – Variations –
Provisional sums – Direct loss and/or expense – Overheads – Loss
of profit – Increased cost of working – Finance charges and interest
– Under-tendering – Inflation – Analysis of claims – Variations to
contract – Delay – Disputes concerning original specification –
Summary

Introduction

501 Disputes involving construction contracts figure strongly among the assignments offered to the forensic accountant, partly because of the complexity and size
of such contracts in which the amounts disputed often run into millions of pounds.
An accountant with knowledge of the construction industry can clarify the issues
at the heart of the claim and his work can sometimes bring the parties together.

502 What was contractually agreed will play an important role in determining
how a construction claim is formulated. While being ready to explore with the
lawyers all important contractual decisions relating to the analysis of the claim,
the expert should guard against making judgments on legal matters. The tendency
nowadays is for the accountant's report not only to deal with quantum, but also to
cover legal interpretation and such aspects as engineering theory. Where an
accountant gets involved in interpretation, he ought to add disclaimers such as:
'We are conscious that in certain areas of this report we may have trespassed into
the field of contractual terms and that this raises questions which are in essence
matters of law rather than accountancy. However, we have only done so where it
is necessary to respond to certain matters which had been put to us'. The solicitors
running the case will then have to ensure that the appropriate legal, engineering or
other expert is consulted if necessary.

THE NATURE OF THE CONSTRUCTION INDUSTRY

503 The construction industry covers a wide spectrum of entities, from the
small jobbing building firm to the sophisticated multinational contracting
corporation. It is a very competitive industry, where tendering for work is routine.
In recent years, supply has generally outstripped demand for construction

services. As a result, tenders have often included virtually no allowance for profit or contribution to overhead costs. The rationale for low tendering is threefold. First, even an unprofitable contract provides work for a work force during lean times, keeping it together until the better years come. Second, it opens the door to work on variations to the contract resulting from architects' or clients' alterations, or from delays or unforeseen circumstances. Variation work can be quite profitable, particularly if tender rates are not applicable. Third, it can often produce a positive cash flow for a substantial part of the contract, to the benefit of other parts of the contractor's business. In some quarters, the practice of obtaining work with a low tender and making a profit on claims seems to be increasingly relied on. We have even come across one contractor which boasted that all of its major contracts were loss making before claims, but profitable after successful prosecution of claims. Much of the information underlying the complex claim presented to us by this contractor stood up well to detailed verification. But we were able to show, by examination of the accounts of the subsidiaries and sites involved, that if the claim was valid, the contract as tendered would have been the sole highly profitable contract for some years. In other words, the amounts claimed were literally incredible and further investigation soon revealed the logical flaws underlying the claim.

A typical construction project

504 Nothing could be simpler, in theory, than a building contract in which one person formally agrees for valuable consideration (ie money) to carry out building or engineering work for another. However, in practice, problems abound. In the following example we introduce the players in a typical construction contract and point out some of the common problems that arise.

505 An employer proposes to construct a new factory on his land. He employs an architect, who in turn engages a quantity surveyor and possibly a consultant engineer on behalf of the employer. The architect discusses the employer's plans with him and prepares and obtains approval for the detailed plans which the quantity surveyor will then evaluate to ascertain the quantities of materials and work (detailed in the 'bills of quantities') necessary for the factory.

506 The employer then invites contractors to tender for the construction of the factory on the basis of the work of the architect and the quantity surveyor. The contractor normally estimates the cost of the works from the information supplied to him supplemented by his own enquiries. He also takes into account the timescale for doing the work. The contractor then submits his estimate or tender for the work. Normally, several tenders are invited to ensure that the work is competitively priced. The contractor will be aware of any time penalties that will apply for late completion of the work.

507 Next, the employer selects his contractor, normally with assistance from the architect. The lowest tender usually, but not always, wins the contract. A binding contract comes into existence between the contractor and employer when the contractor's tender is accepted without qualification.

508 The contractor may in turn engage sub-contractors to assist with the work. Sub-contractors can be engaged directly by the contractor and are often referred to as 'domestic' sub-contractors. Sub-contractors can also be nominated by the architect as agent for the employer, in which case there is usually a direct warranty between the sub-contractor and the employer, the consideration for which is the payment of 'sub-contractor direction' by the employer. Such sub-contractors are termed 'nominated'. It can be important to distinguish between the type of sub-contractor relationship, because claims in contract and tort can differ widely depending on the nature of the sub-contractor's relationship with other parties. However, general responsibility for performance and completion of the contract remains with the main contractor. The architect supervises the construction work and normally arranges for interim payments against the agreed contract value as stages of the work are completed. The measurement of work done may also involve the quantity surveyor. After evaluation, the employer usually retains amounts (normally 5% of the contract sum during the contract) for up to one year during the defects liability period after the contract is completed.

509 Retention moneys are normally released in two portions of 2½%; one, on the issue of the Certificate of Practical Completion when the building is substantially complete, and the other on the issue of the final certificate. Final certificates are normally conclusive evidence that the contractor has been paid all moneys due and the building is in compliance with the contract conditions. Arbitration notices are usually issued within the fixed period (laid down in the contract) after the issue of the final certificate, but can also be issued during the course of the contract.

510 On completion, the architect normally issues a 'completion certificate' for the factory building works and determines the final total value of the contract. In this valuation the architect may have to take into account:

(a) additional work required and authorised via variation orders;
(b) defects in the work of either the main contractor or the nominated sub-contractor;
(c) delays in the work caused by the employer, for example, those relating to delivery of free issue materials, lack of access, inadequate instructions or the absence of drawings and variation orders.

511 If the architect and contractor cannot agree on the value of the contract as amended, it may be referred to the employer. If they still cannot agree, the dispute over settlement normally proceeds to the courts or to arbitration, with the contractor suing for recovery.

512 If the factory is completed late, the employer may consider suing the main contractor for economic loss, if that was not already dealt with under the terms of the contract by way of liquidated damages. Liquidated damages are a fixed amount, stipulated in a contract to be paid by way of damages in the event of a breach of the contract. The amount of the liquidated damages sum is a genuine pre-estimate of the damage which would probably arise from breach of contract. Liquidated damages clauses do not deny the employer the right to claim general damages for breach of contract. However, it has been held that if an employer enters 'nil' in the relevant liquidated damages clause, he is denied the right to recover for any loss.

513 The contractual relationship must be carefully considered when dealing with legal disputes. In our example, the architect and the quantity surveyor act as agents of the employer and owe him a duty of professional care. The architect is usually responsible for:

(a) designing the factory within the employer's indicated price range;
(b) obtaining a competitive price for the construction work from a competent contractor and sub-contractor; and
(c) supervising the construction work in accordance with the designs, price and timetable.

514   The quantity surveyor is responsible for working from the drawings and information supplied by the architect to prepare a bill of quantities detailing the items and work required to construct the factory, including site clearance, foundations, bricklaying, cladding, painting and so on. Contracts normally include an amount for preliminaries, such as the erection of temporary site huts for the contractor's staff and architect's representatives, supervision, insurances, supply of site services and mobilisation of equipment. In some contracts these items are not detailed – instead, rates per hour by grade of worker or job are supplied. The quantity surveyor can be asked by the architect to provide data analysis for making claims for moneys for extensions of time.

515   The contractor and his sub-contractors have to carry out the work in accordance with the contract with the employer. The relationship between the main contractor and his sub-contractors must be studied with care, since one or more of the sub-contractors may have the same or similar duties as the main contractor.

516   If a dispute arises as a result of a construction contract, new players enter the game. We call these players the 'construction litigation team'.

517   New forms of contract, like construction management, give rise to different contractual arrangements and the use of nominated sub-contractors is now rare, although use is still made of 'approved' suppliers which can achieve similar results to nomination. Such contracts can include 'project managers' as well as architects and quality surveyors.

The construction litigation team

518   The members of a typical construction litigation team are illustrated in the diagram overleaf.

519   Because of the complexity of many construction related cases, more experts may be involved. This causes additional problems for the solicitors in co-ordinating the flow of information between the team members. The experts generally deal with different aspects of the case, but there may well be overlaps, for example, the work of the expert quantity surveyor may have implications for the accountant. Although the accountant cannot demand information from the other experts on his side of the case, he should seek liaison between the professions; there is nothing worse for him than to find himself being contradicted by another expert on his own side. In the end, the solicitor will have to determine whether it is necessary for the accountant to be briefed on the other experts' reports. Further complications arise when there are co-defendants each with their

CONSTRUCTION LITIGATION TEAM

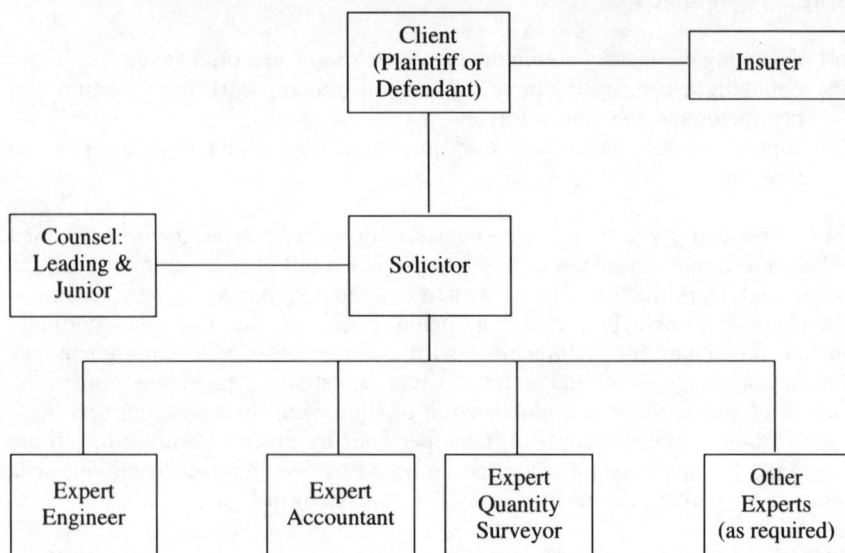

```
                    ┌─────────────────┐          ┌─────────────┐
                    │    Client       │          │             │
                    │ (Plaintiff or   │──────────│   Insurer   │
                    │  Defendant)     │          │             │
                    └─────────────────┘          └─────────────┘
                             │
┌─────────────┐      ┌─────────────────┐
│  Counsel:   │      │                 │
│ Leading &   │──────│    Solicitor    │
│   Junior    │      │                 │
└─────────────┘      └─────────────────┘
                             │
        ┌────────────┬───────┴───────┬────────────┐
  ┌──────────┐ ┌──────────┐  ┌──────────┐  ┌──────────┐
  │  Expert  │ │  Expert  │  │  Expert  │  │  Other   │
  │ Engineer │ │Accountant│  │ Quantity │  │ Experts  │
  │          │ │          │  │ Surveyor │  │(as required)│
  └──────────┘ └──────────┘  └──────────┘  └──────────┘
```

own team of professional advisers. Often it makes sense for the accounting expert to act for co-defendants, who will then share the cost of his work, rather than each support their own expert.

TYPES OF CONTRACT

520 In dealing with construction cases it is important to know the principal types of contract. While many factors, such as construction techniques and financing arrangements, may have influenced the terms of a contract, management is usually most concerned by the risk factors. In assessing the type of contract to negotiate, the contractor will have carefully estimated the cost of performing the work, the equipment requirements, the timing, the use of sub-contractors' opportunities for profit, and the risk element.

521 The more usual types of contract include:

(a) fixed price or lump sum contracts;
(b) cost-plus contracts;
(c) bills of quantity or unit price contracts;
(d) time and materials contracts; and
(e) turnkey contracts.

Fixed price contracts

522 Under the fixed price or lump sum contract, the entire work is performed for a single price. For instance, suppose that you arrange for a garage to be built for the price of £15,000. Provided it is completed as required in the contract, with no alterations, the contractor is entitled to £15,000, the agreed price for the work.

Fixed price contracts are not generally subject to claims as a result of subsequent fluctuation in costs or quantities to the contract, since the work has been estimated on a 'fixed' basis. However, if alterations in scope are imposed upon the contractor, or the quantity changes are substantial, for example, more than say 15% of the original specification, he is entitled to compensation. The larger contracts include a schedule of rates as the basis of valuation of any extra work.

Cost-plus contracts

523 In the past, cost-plus contracts have been favoured by contractors and governments where the work has been difficult to define in advance. Cost-plus contracts provide for reimbursement of defined costs incurred, plus a fee for the contractor's services. These contracts are open to abuse by the contractor; the work may take considerably longer than planned, justifiably or not, and since the costs tend to increase proportionally with time, the contractor receives a higher fee. On the other hand, they protect the contractor from abuse by the employer.

524 Normally, these contracts require the best efforts of the contractor to complete the work and only costs incurred honestly and properly are to be reimbursed. If the costs are increased because of the contractor's inefficiency, they are likely to be disputed by the employer. The related fee will then be at risk. The contract terms should carefully specify the reimbursable costs, the overhead recovery percentages and the contractor's fees. The costs should be fully defined, so that the employer is protected against waste by, or excesses of, the contractor.

Bills of quantities or unit price contracts

525 Bills of quantities or unit price contracts commit the employer and contractor to performing specific tasks at an agreed or fixed price per task. Normally, the work involved in the project is broken down into precise estimates of labour hours, quantities of work materials and so forth. The breakdown is based upon an analysis of all the drawings for each part of the task. As part of the tendering procedure, the contractor is required to price the bill of quantities and provide a total contract sum, subject to any variations later in the project. The rates or prices in the bill of quantities normally form the basis for the architect or engineer to value agreed variations during the contract's life. However, there is provision, even in standard form contracts, for variations to be valued at rates or prices other than those in the bill of quantities where the latter are inappropriate due to the nature or extent of variations. These additional items are often referred to as 'starred', appropriate 'star' rates being agreed between the parties. If the bill of quantities does not provide any relevant rate, the contractor is generally entitled to a fair and reasonable rate. Star rates are generally based on an extrapolation or interpolation of the bill of quantity rates.

526 Typically, the bills of quantities are divided into phases of work or trades, such as site clearance, excavation, concreting, brickworks, asphalting, electrical works, painting and finishing, and drainage. 'Preliminary items' of generalised expense relate to the project as a whole, such as insurance and mobilisation costs. Preliminary items may be fixed as a total sum or on a periodic basis, where the charge varies directly with the length of the contract period. Contractors do not always set out the preliminary items when they put forward their tender, on the assumption that they will be fixed with the owner when the final contract is written. Alternatively, they may not be explicitly defined, being dealt with within rates for the work.

527 The contract must specify how each job will be measured. The forensic accountant need not concern himself with the details, as measurement is the responsibility of the supervising engineer, but he should at least be aware of some of the problems which may arise. Take excavation, for example. The rates for excavation in rock will be different from excavation in soft soil. Furthermore, in both cases the rates may or may not include pumping costs in wet conditions. The rules of measurement can be extremely complicated and involve a considerable amount of professional skill on the part of the engineer and quantity surveyor. For this purpose standard methods of measurements are often used, for example:

(a) civil engineering standard method of measurement;
(b) standard method of measurement (for building contracts); and
(c) methods specified in the contract documents.

Time and materials contracts

528 Time and materials contracts are similar to cost-plus contracts. Generally they provide for payment to contractors on the basis of direct labour hours at agreed fixed rates. These rates are usually composite rates incorporating amounts for the actual labour cost, overheads and profit. The cost of materials and other items are specified in the contract. Sometimes bulk materials for specialised equipment, for instance specialised steel for offshore construction work, may be provided by the employer on a 'free issue' basis.

Turnkey contracts

529 The phrase 'turnkey contract' or 'turnkey project' came from the United States, probably originating from the oil industry. Under these contracts the project is handed over complete and ready for use: the 'key' can be turned and everything will be ready to operate. The contract may also involve the transfer of technology and the training of the team to run the project after physical completion.

530 Other expressions, such as 'design and build', 'build operate and transfer', 'design, construct, manage, fund' or 'package deal', have similar connotations. The chief implication is that the employer hands over complete responsibility to the contractor for designing a building or plant to meet the stipulated aims and requirements.

531 A turnkey contract does not necessarily mean the use of one contract throughout the entire project; the 'turnkey' part may apply only to, say, the camp site, with the rest of the project subject to bills of quantities. The primary advantage claimed for a turnkey contract is that the ultimate costs are lower and more easily controlled. A further advantage often claimed is that construction is rather quicker under this method. Whether this is really so is debatable. A turnkey contract can involve a higher tendering cost and can leave the owner with less control over the project.

532 Since the contractor is free to innovate within his turnkey contract, the completed structure might well be a matter for argument. This is a notorious source for disputes, especially if the performance of the plant does not measure up to the original intention. In this type of contract, where the employer requests the contractor to design a structure that will do x, y and z, and build it for an agreed price, the employer carries the major risk that the structure will not operate as specified.

533 Forensic accountants can help to resolve contentious issues in such cases. In the dispute following a turnkey contract to design and build a municipal incinerator, that was mentioned earlier in Chapter 1, the basic requirement was that the incinerator should consume all the rubbish collected in a particular area. During the delay between accepting the design and completing the project, the nature of the rubbish (or 'arisings' as they are quaintly called) altered considerably; much more plastic, from yogurt cartons, plastic bags, pvc toothpaste tubes and so on, was collected, which upset the calorific value and overturned other assumptions. In consequence, the incinerator dealt with some three tons per hour less than had been expected. The district council concerned claimed huge economic damage. Enquiry revealed that the engineer considered that no real defects had been observed during the hand-over tests, other than those associated with the change in the nature of the rubbish.

534 The incinerator had at no time failed to deal with all the rubbish collected in the area. We also established that the alternative to incinerating – dumping in gravel pits – would cost rather less than using the incinerator. The claim was settled for a fraction of the amount initially pursued.

STANDARD FORM CONTRACTS

535 Most construction contracts are drawn up under a standard form contract. In the UK, the body primarily responsible for drafting standard form contracts is the Joint Contracts Tribunal (JCT). The JCT represents principally public sector employers, architects, contractors and sub-contractors. Its members include various professional bodies, trade associations and the like. Before issue, JCT standard form contracts have to have the approval of all constituent members.

536 The principal JCT 'Standard Form of Building Contract' covers bills of quantity for major works for local authorities and for private work. There is a separate version for each type of employer. The standard is known as JCT80. JCT80 was designed to supersede the previous standard JCT63, although the latter is still used from time to time.

537 An accountant involved in building claims disputes should be aware of the existence of JCT80 and other standard form contracts such as PSA/1 with Quantities (General Conditions of Contract for Building and Civil Engineering Works), the ACA Form (a Form of Building Agreement published by the Association of Consultant Architects) and FIDIC (Fédération Internationale des Ingénieurs-Conseils), since the basis of the claim will often be contained within the terms of those standard forms. The terms of JCT80 have been extensively dealt with by Dr John Parris in his book *The Standard Form of Building Contract JCT80* (Collins) and also commented on very clearly in *Building Contract Claims* by Vincent

Powell-Smith and John Sims (Blackwells). A new standard form which can be used on all engineering contracts has been produced. It is the 'New Engineering Contracts' form, it is designed to stimulate more foresighted management of contracts. It is hoped that it will lead to a reduction in the incidence of claims.

538 The standard forms provide a methodology for dealing with and evaluating claims arising in the course of performance of construction contracts. These claims may be for additional costs arising from variations to the contract through, for example, changes in design or methods of construction. They may be for direct loss for expense arising, for example, from delays or rescheduling of work. We describe these two types of claims below. Provided the contractor follows the procedures for making a claim, he has a means within the contract for resolving disputes. The fact that certain claims may be quantified by reference to the contract does not prevent a contractor seeking damage under common law rights for breach of contract or under the law of tort. The contractor cannot, however, be compensated twice for the same item.

VARIATIONS

539 Variations are generally valued by the appointed quantity surveyor. Where the bill of quantities contains rates for the compensation of material, labour and so on involved in the variation, these are used for valuing the variation. Where work is of a similar nature, the bill of quantity rates are used, subject to an appropriate allowance for difference in conditions. If the bill of quantities provides no suitable yardstick, the items comprising the variation are valued at 'fair' rates and prices.

540 To determine 'fair' rates or prices, the quantity surveyor normally takes account of the prices contained in the original bill of quantities. If the contract was priced competitively or at a loss, then similar pricing will be applied to variations.

541 Where variations cannot be measured reasonably, valuation on a 'daywork' basis may be used. In essence, daywork rates means either a schedule of rates which may be based on a working rate agreement or actual cost plus a percentage – such percentage being established as an industry norm – to cover overheads and profit. The norm can change over time, reflecting the extent of competition in the industry.

542 'A *quantum meruit* valuation' – that is, one based not on the terms of a contract but on 'how much is deserved' for work done – is not normally used by the architect or quantity surveyor unless the contract authorises him to do so.

543 Because bill rates are the prime source for valuing variations, errors or inconsistencies in the rates appearing in the bill of quantities can give rise to difficulty if they come to be applied for variations. For this reason a bill is generally scrutinised for such errors before the contract is signed. Where such errors are discovered in lump sum tender contracts, it is often the case that the contractor is asked whether he wishes to stand by his rates. If not, the rate and pricing can be corrected. However, because the individual item will now not add up to the lump sum, a percentage adjustment is applied to all the items on the bill in order to compensate for the error, so that the amended bill still adds up to the original lump sum tender price.

544   When, later, the bill is used to price variations, the quantity surveyor must ensure that any percentage adjustment to the rates is taken into account.

Provisional sums

545   Sometimes an employer puts a contract out for tender before he or the architect has decided on the detailed specification of some part of the building. In these circumstances, a general description for the works is given and the architect or quantity surveyor puts in a 'provisional sum' for the work. Although these are estimates they are based on what is considered likely to be expended.

546   When the work has been completed and the work valued, the provisional sum is replaced by the actual value of work carried out. This may be valued at actual price or, under JCT80, as if it were a variation.

DIRECT LOSS AND/OR EXPENSE

547   Standard form contracts commonly allow for claims to be made if contractors suffer direct loss and/or expense because progress on the contract is materially affected by factors outside the contractor's control. Direct loss is considered to mean, in these circumstances, losses caused by the event complained of, not the result of an intervening event. This definition flows from case law and particularly the rule in *Hadley v Baxendale*[1] which we touched on in Chapter 1.

548   A common misconception is that loss and/or expense claims can only arise if the architect has awarded an extension of time. In *H Fairweather & Co Ltd v Wandsworth London Borough Council*,[2] it was decided that under the JCT standard form contracts an extension of time is not a condition for reimbursement of direct loss and/or expense. The significance of extensions of time is that they serve to limit claims by the employer, for liquidated damages for late completion of the works.

549   In practice, claims on construction contracts often involve a number of events whose effects interact. In such circumstances, the courts may not require the losses caused by each separate event to be separately identified and the claimant may adopt a global approach in quantifying his claim. The principle is, however, subject to a number of important qualifications:

(a)   the events must be complex and interact in such a way that it is difficult, if not impossible, to make an accurate apportionment of the total extra cost between the various causative events;

(b)   there must be no duplication within the amounts claimed; and

(c)   if profit is irrecoverable under any of the heads underlying the claim then the entire global claim must exclude profit.[3]

550   Typical heads of a construction contract claim for direct loss and/or expense are:

● on-site establishment costs;

● general or head office overheads;

- loss of profit;

- increased cost of working; and

- financing charges and interest.

551   It is established as a matter of principle that claims for appropriate head office costs are allowable as part of a claim for direct loss and/or expense. This is based on the decision in *FG Minter Ltd and Drake & Scull Ltd v Welsh Health Technical Services Organisation*[4] that recoverable 'direct loss and/or expense' are sums which would be recoverable as damages at common law. Whether wasted management time can be recovered may depend on the existence of adequate records of the wasted time.[5] The calculations of loss of profits described in Chapter 2 are therefore relevant to these claims. The claimant is entitled to recover the difference between what it would have cost him but for the delay and what it actually cost him. The rates used in the bills of quantities are generally irrelevant for this purpose. A number of features of these claims merit specific comment here.

Overheads

552   A claim for overheads is a difficult area, but one which must be tackled in any review of a contract dispute. Some contractors divide their overheads between preliminary items and bill of quantities items without giving precise indications of what they have done. As a result, when a major change goes to the heart of the contractual price arrangements, the contractor may claim that the unit rates in the bill of quantities are inadequate. For instance, if less work is done than was foreseen in the original bill of quantities, he might claim that he has failed to recover his off-site and on-site overheads in full. Alternatively, if he has done more work than was contemplated in the bill of quantities, he may claim additional overheads on the grounds that the levels of supervision and skill required in the off-site and on-site offices were so great, that the overheads went well over the sums he had expected when he submitted his tender. These are fertile areas for dispute and accountants are well placed to advise on the solution. Ideally the accountant should, if possible, examine the total overheads incurred, period by period and category by category. Remember, the purpose of the claim, or damages if it becomes a common law claim, is to put the claimant back in the position he would have been in but for the event being complained of.

553   On occasion, claims are evaluated by reference to tender rates including provisions for sub-contract costs. Care must be taken that the amounts claimed represent genuine costs. It is, therefore, necessary to determine how much has (or is likely to have) actually been paid to sub-contractors after taking into account any claims and counterclaims. It is also necessary to investigate any recoveries that have been made by way of insurance claims. A related area which needs careful handling, is the extent to which losses arising out of any event have already been reimbursed by way of a claim against the main contractor. Since there is a tendency for settlement to be made on a lump sum basis, this area can give rise to significant differences of opinion upon which the accountant can often shed useful light.

554   At an early stage in his work, the litigation accountant will have to consider what jurisdiction is relevant. Many large construction contracts are carried out abroad. A claim may have to be quantified on different bases, depending on which jurisdiction is relevant. For example, in a case in which we were involved, a claim for unjust termination would probably have failed in England since it was common ground that the contract was a 'loss leader' and that it would have made a significant loss if it had carried on to completion. This was no bar to the recovery of a substantial sum, however, since the relevant jurisdiction held that the doctrine of unjust enrichment served to prevent the employer receiving a benefit without incurring a cost. It is up to the accountant expert to be aware of the various possible routes towards quantification of a claim. Before he commences on his report, the proper basis should be agreed with the legal experts.

555   Since overheads tend to be fixed in the short to medium term, a variation to the contract or a delay does not necessarily affect the off-site costs. Nevertheless, in the contracting industry such overhead costs have to be paid for out of work done. The costs are generally a function of time, although method related overheads do also occur, for example, where due to delay a concrete batching plant has to be decommissioned then remobilised. If delay occurs, these costs continue without any contract income to cover them. In many cases it is appropriate for this loss to be included in the claim. A word of warning, however: the contractor may have a number of contracts or claims in progress which are all contributing to overheads. The accountant, therefore, needs to assess whether a further claim for overheads will represent an over recovery. Similarly, if other parts of the bill of quantities make allowance for local office overheads – for example, in the on-site costs – double counting may occur.

556   Contractors frequently price bills of quantities at rates which cover preliminary and off-site overhead costs. As a result, when there are substantial variations, which are priced at these rates, the contractor receives through variations, a contribution to his on- and off-site overheads. Substantial variations often cause delay in the general progress of the works. Therefore, claims for variations tend to go hand in hand with loss and expense claims for delay. If the expert accountant is retained to assess the loss and expense claim, he should take care that there is no duplication of this claim within the measured variations in the final account.

557   In our experience, the contractor sometimes objects to the disclosure of project costs to an investigating accountant. In a dispute, such objections should not be sustained if the contractor is alleging that there has been a fundamental change in his expectations on overhead costs. As a rule, if a major extension has been made to the contract, the contractor should be willing to reveal all project costs.

558   Scepticism arises if the contractor says that a major increase in the scope of the project will add to the unit cost of overheads, where there is no change in the nature of the overheads required to service the change of scope and the time period is the same. After all, common sense says that spreading the overheads over a greater amount of direct output produces some economy of scale. The contractor may have left out altogether the overhead contribution when pricing the job (perhaps because he was short of orders). A major extension in the scale of the work will then clearly hit him hard, particularly if the extra work prevents him from taking on other, more remunerative, work.

559   If, on the other hand, he has had to do much less work than that allowed for in the bill of quantities, the contractor may not be able to recover the overheads built into his costs. Whether his claim is realistic or not will depend on circumstances; if the time needed to do the job has decreased, he may be able to fill the remainder of the time with other work, thereby mitigating his loss completely.

560   Computing the amount of overheads to allow in a claim, is fraught with difficulty. The industry and the courts have endeavoured from time to time to establish formulae for deriving the amounts, for example, by computing contract overtime costs per day or per £1 of direct cost. Appendix E lists some of the formulae and their pros and cons. Inevitably, there is a trade off between simplicity and fairness. The important thing is to choose the most appropriate approach for the individual claim. But a word of warning: courts and arbitrators often have little sympathy with the application of standard formulae by experts. It is often better to look at each case on its merits.

Loss of profit

561   Although many contracts explicitly do not allow claims for profit, a contractor may be entitled to claim for loss of profit if he can demonstrate that he would have earned that profit but for the delays, disruption, changes or whatever he is complaining of. He has to show that, where there is disruption or delay, he has been prevented from earning a profit elsewhere in the normal course of business. That is to say, because his resources have been tied up on a delayed contract, he has not been able to take up other contracts.

562   Faced with this sort of claim, we find it helpful to analyse the contractor's general level of profitability, looking, for example, at his general business performance as disclosed by audited accounts or the profitability of a range of recent similar contracts.

563   We also consider whether the market at the time was active or slack. Sometimes a contractor computes his claim for loss of profit based on the profit percentage he builds in to tenders. This can be misleading. There can be a considerable difference between expected and actual profit, and careful attention should be given to this aspect of a claim.

Increased cost of working

564   Although, clearly, performance on the contract in dispute is of primary importance, faced with a claim for increased cost of working we find it helpful to analyse the contractor's general level of profitability and throughput. For example, we may look at his general business performance as disclosed by audited accounts or the profitability of a range of recent similar contracts and compare planned and actual production as shown on the management production schedules. Amounts claimed in respect of alleged idle time, should be restricted to loss of profits and overhead recoveries which could have been achieved on other profitable work that it is reasonable to believe would have been carried out in the absence of breach.

565 Plant hire rates are often an issue in cases of idle time, although in many instances plant is hired for a fixed period. Provided the delay does not result in the hire period being extended, there is no loss. Where the plant is owned, it may also be appropriate to relate the loss to a hire rate; some adjustment will be necessary to eliminate the profit and overhead contribution built into the hire rates. Alternatively, the loss may be reflected by a depreciation charge. In this case, we expect to see a lower than normal rate applied since idle plant tends to depreciate more slowly than active plant. Maintenance costs may also be relevant, but their impact will depend on whether idle plant needs more or less maintenance than the working plant.

566 It is important to identify the specific factors causing the delay and whether these were the fault of the employer or the contractor. Also, it must be ascertained whether these delays affected the critical path of the contract schedule. (The critical path is the longest sequence of steps in the construction programme.) It should be noted that the critical paths can change and that there can be more than one critical path.

567 Increased costs often arise in cases of delay and disruption because of inflation and the effort needed (for example, overtime working, inefficient working) to restore the project to its original timetable. Such claims should be accounted for in detail and relate cause to effect.

Finance charges and interest

568 In Chapter 14 of this book we discuss in some depth the subject of awards of interest in claims. Under the concept of direct loss and/or expense in the JCT Forms, finance charges, and in particular interest on money expended, are allowable as a head of claim, as is loss of interest on money diverted from interest-earning investments. However, simply applying a reasonable commercial rate of interest to the losses under other heads of damage is not enough. The claimant must produce supporting evidence to demonstrate his loss, for example, proof that he incurred overdraft interest.

569 Furthermore it has been established that the contractor has an obligation to update the employer continually with the accrual of finance charges. There is, of course, a general need for the contractor to keep contemporary records of extra expenses incurred and their causes if, at a later date, disputes have to be negotiated or settled.

UNDER-TENDERING

570 We have already stated that some construction industry contractors deliberately under-tender, either because they are desperate for work or because they hope, by careful claims creation later, to make good any price shortfall in the original quotation. We have also said (para **540**) that if an item was priced at a loss, that price should also apply to variations if the tender conditions existed at the time of the variation.

571 It may be useful, with the assistance of the employer's engineering advisers, to assess the extent to which the contractor has under-tendered when quoting for a contract. No precision can be claimed for such exercises, especially if the employer (the defendant in this instance) has not seen the details of the plaintiff's original tender. Even then, however, clear clues may demonstrate under-tendering.

572 If the contractor (or his sub-contractor) has under-tendered by a factor of, say, two or three, disaster will follow. He may be able to prove legally that he was misled as to the work required, the difficulty of the design, or the quality of the rock he had to excavate. But to support his assertions, he will have to show that there was good reason for his tender price to be, say, half of the next lowest price.

573 The accountant must get down to the basics behind the contractor's estimate. This will often involve taking a view of the number of labour hours required for a particular part of the contract, or perhaps of the weight of metal required, in addition to the question of overheads.

574 A clear indication of under-tendering by a sub-contractor may arise where the main contractor has priced some work which he is undertaking and which is the same, or very similar to, work sub-contracted to someone else. If the main contractor's assessment of the cost is, say, twice that of his sub-contractor, the latter is putting himself in peril and should not look to later claims for variations or disruption to recoup his initial error.

575 In short, the courts will not feel disposed to let a contractor off the hook if he has under-tendered or been careless, or has simply failed to appreciate the risks he is undertaking.

INFLATION

576 Increased costs can often be the subject of a claim where there has been significant inflation since the contract was signed. The investigating accountant should beware of a claim for generalised increased costs – particularly for unit prices – showing standard increases in all costs over a period. Costs fluctuate, and the relationship between the costs in a claim for different periods may not be linear. Price indices and statistics, widely available from libraries and government departments, should be reviewed to determine whether the trend claimed is in line with costs in the country as a whole. Care must be taken to ensure that the country index chosen is relevant, bearing in mind the source of the materials or plant concerned.

ANALYSIS OF CLAIMS

577 The variety of problems found in construction claims is considerable; in the tables on pp 75–76 we have broadly divided the causes between those arising from variation, those from delay, and those from disputes as to original specification. (Disputes as to original specification are distinct from variation disputes in that they go to the heart of what information the contractor was given originally when he was requested to tender.) We have then described the effect that these basic causes can have on direct loss and/or expenses and have suggested areas of enquiry for the accountant to follow through.

VARIATIONS TO CONTRACT	
Effect on claim	*Areas for enquiry by the accountant*
Increase in preliminaries	Was genuine additional expenditure incurred?
Changes to materials used – both volume and type	Are unit rates valid? Were materials necessary?
Change in labour mix	Were genuine additional costs necessarily incurred or did the work absorb idle labour?
Additional labour hours	Are the rates applied appropriate?
Change in plant and machinery usage	What was the real cost of the plant usage?
Allowance for overheads and profit	Were any additional overheads incurred? Was there loss of opportunity to carry out other profitable work?
Allowance for financing costs	Was the company a net borrower of funds and, if so, at what rate did it borrow?
Additional costs arising through acceleration of work	Were the additional costs directly attributable to acceleration of work or do they reflect inefficiency by the contractor?

DELAY	
Effect on claim	*Areas for enquiry by the accountant*
Increase in preliminaries	What additional charges were actually incurred?
Idle direct labour	Could labour have been redeployed or laid off?
Idle plant and machinery	Was there any alternative use for plant and machinery?
Additional overhead costs	Were there any genuine increases in indirect costs and overhead expenditure?
Demobilisation and remobilisation costs	Were these costs genuinely increased, for example, to mitigate loss?
Extra remedial costs and costs of making good after delay	Did the delay cause deterioration to the works which had to be made good before recommendation?
Escalation to unit rates on productive work	What increase in underlying costs rates impacted the project?
Loss of profit	Did the delay give rise to loss of profit opportunity elsewhere?
Additional financing charges	Was the company a net borrower of funds and, if so, at what rate did it borrow?

75

DISPUTES CONCERNING ORIGINAL SPECIFICATION

Effect on claim	Areas for enquiry by the accountant
Increase in preliminaries	Was proper cognisance taken of preliminaries in the original tender?
Additional materials	If genuine, were they acquired at best rates?
Change in labour usage and mix	Are rates for different labour grades appropriate?
Additional wear and tear on plant and machinery	What rates of depreciation are applied to plant – was any fully written off?
Additional overheads	Was the original overhead recovery rate appropriate? Has the change in specification affected indirect costs in any way?

SUMMARY

578 In looking at claims for construction costs, it is initially desirable to assess their overall reasonableness by some broad tests: the costs of the principal components of most contracts tend to conform to a similar pattern. For example, the costs of design and supervision and project management seem to bear a direct relationship to the value of the contracting work performed. Experience has shown that design and supervision costs usually represent some 10–15% of total construction costs; project management costs tend to represent 1–3% of the total. Contract overheads range as follows:

Site overhead	3–10%
Head office overhead	5–10%
Engineering and supervision	7–21%

These guidelines should not be considered definitive, as they do tend to change from time to time reflecting market and competitive conditions, but they may help the expert accountant to consider the overall reasonableness of a claim and to direct his work towards those areas where the claim appears unduly heavy.

579 Finally, thought should be given to the pros and cons of settlement versus continued dispute. Almost always there are commercial considerations to be taken into account. What is the potential prize? What is the cost of winning it and what are the chances of success? Construction claims, whether heard by the courts or in arbitration, tend to lead to lengthy trials. We know of a case which was expected to last nine months to a year. When the experts' reports on quantum were exchanged a few days before trial, it became clear that the quantum gap between the parties was so small that it made the litigation uneconomic. The case settled.

If the quantification of damage had been given a higher priority in preparation for litigation, much expense would have been saved.

NOTES

1 (1854) 9 Exch 341.
2 (1987) 39 BLR 106.
3 See *J Crosby & Sons Ltd v Portland UDC* (1967) 5 BLR 121, QB, Donaldson J; *McAlpine Humberoak Ltd v McDermott International Inc* (1992) 58 Build LR 1; *Imperial Chemical Industries plc v Bovis Construction* (1992) 8 Const LJ 268.
4 [1980] 13 BLR 1.
5 *Tate and Lyle Industries Ltd v Greater London Council* [1981] 3 All ER 716.

Chapter 6

Personal injuries

Information gathering – Calculation of loss to date of trial – Special damages – Income – Benefits – Taxation – Deductions – Calculation of future loss – Uncertainty – Multiplicand and multiplier – Time value of money – Actuarial evidence – Children generally – Calculation of other relevant factors – Loss of or reduction in pension – Future disadvantage in the labour market – Loss of job satisfaction – DIY activities – Expenses – Interest – Negotiations between parties – Contributory negligence – Structured settlements – Fatal accidents – Case examples – Summary

601 The increasingly complex claims arising from personal injury which can, unfortunately, affect anyone, may lead to the need for expert help from both lawyers and accountants. In this chapter we describe the background to the subject before explaining the role of the accountant and how his skills may be brought to bear most effectively. Our aim is to provide a guide and summary of the matters arising in personal injury claims without quoting in depth the references to legal cases which will be found in more detailed publications. The traditionally recommended book for personal injury practitioners is *The Quantum of Damages* by Kemp & Kemp.

602 Approximately one quarter of a million tort claims for personal injury are made each year, of which approximately 50% are at least partly successful. Personal injury may be inflicted by dangerous premises, animals out of control, breaches of statutory obligations (for example, as to work conditions), or straightforward negligence on the part of the defendant, for example, the driver of a motor car. Since only a quarter of victims of accidental damage consider claiming compensation, the percentage of those injured who recover compensation for accidents is low: about 12% for accidents at work and 25% for road accidents.

603 Under English law, a person injured in an accident has no automatic right to compensation. To obtain it he must show, if necessary in a court of law, that the accident was the fault of another person. It will be for the legal adviser to discover whether or not the person allegedly at fault (the defendant) is insured. Insurance may affect the defendant's ability to pay any damages awarded and will influence the lawyer in his advice to the plaintiff as to whether to proceed. Under English law, some forms of accident are compulsorily insured, principally those relating to motor insurance and employer's liability. Other types of risk which may involve injury to others are also commonly insured against, the principal ones being property owner's liability, product liability and professional negligence, for example, by a doctor or surgeon.

604 In the early stages of a claim for personal injury compensation, the lawyers will primarily be concerned with matters of liability. Only months, or perhaps years, later will they get down to detailing the quantum of the amount to be claimed by the injured person. Commonly, the main constituents of the claim will be damages for pain and suffering, loss of amenity, cost of care and pecuniary loss, for example, loss of earnings.

605 The assessment of damages for pain and suffering, loss of amenity and cost of care is a matter for solicitors or counsel who specialise in this branch of the law. Based on experience, they will be able to assess with some degree of accuracy the amount that a judge will award for pain and suffering and loss of amenity. However, they will be less able to make an accurate assessment in respect of pecuniary loss. Here the involvement of an accountant specialising in personal injury cases will often be helpful, and sometimes essential. Such a specialist accountant will be careful not to stray beyond his brief into matters that are for lawyers or other experts, such as the medical advisers, to deal with. As already mentioned, the legal adviser will wish to discover if the defendant is insured. It is often advantageous for a defendant not to disclose whether he is insured, or if so what the limits of his cover are. A plaintiff may be put off by the worry that there are insufficient funds to satisfy the claim.

606 Before the actual commencement of proceedings, the plaintiff is entitled to discovery of documents held by the defendant. For example, in a medical negligence case the defendant may hold case notes and records which will enable the plaintiff's medical adviser to come to an initial view as to liability. At some point the plaintiff will require a full medical report, but the lawyer will normally only ask for this to be completed when the question of liability has been investigated and when it is clear that his client has a good case. In a serious case of injury there is little point in obtaining the report in the early stages of the claim when the plaintiff's condition may not have stabilised.

607 Personal injury cases will usually involve expert evidence. There will be one or more medical reports setting out details of the plaintiff's injuries and there may need to be a separate report on the quantum of damage underlying the claim. The court rules on disclosure of reports to the other side only apply to those reports on which a party intends to rely; if a party does not wish to call the doctor or the engineer to give evidence, there is no need to disclose that report since he will not be relying upon it at the trial.

608 In most cases an experienced solicitor will prepare the calculations for a straightforward personal injury claim. For routine cases a checklist is used; this identifies all the typical items which enter into a damages claim, in particular the lost earnings up to the time when the claim is made. The claim should allow for any wage increases that the plaintiff would have received since the accident. The plaintiff's other losses and expenses, for example, expenses of attending medical examinations, prescriptions, telephone calls, should also be listed and evidenced. In more complicated cases specialist help is required, particularly in relation to claims for future pecuniary losses. If an accountant or an actuary is commissioned to prepare a report then his report has to be disclosed to the other side if it is to be relied upon at trial. The defendant's solicitors may challenge such extra cost on the grounds that the plaintiff's solicitor could do the calculations himself. However, this risk of challenge should not deter the plaintiff where the calculation of the true level of lost earnings and the likely level of future profits becomes a large part of the claim, for example, if the plaintiff is self-employed or the director of a small company. Sometimes, a plaintiff will have lost his pension rights through enforced early retirement following the injury, in which case an actuary's view will assist in the formulation of the claim.

609 As with other claims arising from tortious damage, the underlying objective is to place the injured person back into the position he would have been in had the accident not occurred. In the case of a wage earner away from work for a short period, the assessment of the loss can be reasonably precise, in other cases the assessment of 'what might have been' is necessarily speculative.

610 The work of assessing pecuniary loss can be conveniently broken down into five stages:

(a) information gathering;
(b) calculation of loss to date of trial (past loss);
(c) calculation of future loss;
(d) calculation of other relevant factors; and
(e) a recent development: providing advice on structured settlements.

INFORMATION GATHERING

611 At this early stage one needs to establish the following.

• The plaintiff's age.

• His relevant medical history before and after the accident. This information helps to identify periods when the plaintiff was away from work, and also the relationship between the plaintiff's disabilities and fluctuations in his income and expenditure.

• His career history. For a young injured person, a knowledge of his academic ability is important. For an older person, the career achievements to date ought to give some guide as to what his future prospects would have been. The job description, at the time of the accident, should be as detailed as possible. Consideration of the achievements of comparable employees may also provide useful indicators of earnings potential. Personnel files will be a good source.

• Details of his earnings. For an employed person, copy pay slips, P11Ds, P60s or letters from employers will normally suffice. For a Schedule D taxpayer – that is, a self-employed person working alone or in partnership – copies of the accounts for at least three full years before the accident, and for all periods since the accident, will be needed. These should be supported by corporation tax and/or income tax computations and assessments.
(The accountant may well need access to accounting records. When he is acting for the plaintiff, this will not normally present a problem. If he is acting for the defence, it may be more difficult and court permission may need to be sought.)

• General information on the plaintiff's trade, profession or employment sector. Government or industry statistics may suffice, but often there is the need for detailed research into the more general aspects of a plaintiff's potential earnings. For example, consider the situation where a self-employed butcher suffers relatively minor injuries in a road traffic accident and subsequently his earnings reduce significantly. The plaintiff may assert that the reduction is wholly attributable to his injuries. However, this may be coincidental; the key cause may have been the opening of a new superstore in the area, or changes in meat consumption, or significant adverse price movements.

612 In short, the accountant should obtain the fullest possible information so that he is in a position to understand fully the individual's pre-injury attainments, his further aspirations, and the factors which would have served to limit those aspirations, both injury-related and otherwise. Having assembled this information, he should prepare the first part of his draft report, which sets out background, career and earnings to the date of the accident. This introductory section of the accountant's report is of crucial importance in giving the judge background information, and in bringing together the salient factors, including the opinions of other experts. A balanced picture should be painted which sets the scene for the calculation of loss to the date of the trial.

CALCULATION OF LOSS TO DATE OF TRIAL

Special damages

613 What is termed 'past loss' is the diminution of income from the date of the accident to the date of the trial. Past loss is considered as special damage and is eligible for interest, as opposed to future loss which forms part of general damage and does not rank for interest. Interest on damage claims is considered further in Chapter 14.

614 At the time the accountant receives instructions, the trial date may or may not be known. Calculations may be prepared up to an assumed or notional trial date. The hearing may not take place until many years after the accident. Although lawyers and insurance companies are frequently blamed for delays in bringing injury cases to trial, often the medical effects of an accident can only be fully established after a long period. The calculations produced may therefore need to be updated more than once.

Income

615 In the case of an employed ('Schedule E') plaintiff, the calculation of past loss is relatively simple. A review of salary scales from the date of the accident to the assumed date of the trial is the starting point. If the plaintiff has been working for a large organisation, such scales will be available. If not, a review of the salary progression of similar employees should provide the information. Trends in the particular employment sector will also be relevant. Possible promotion increments also need to be considered; here the employer's views will be helpful, but not necessarily conclusive. Employers sometimes, out of loyalty, overstate promotion prospects, particularly in cases of severe injury. The views expressed by the employer should be examined critically and the pre-accident career pattern of the plaintiff should be compared with that of comparable employees.

616 For a self-employed ('Schedule D') plaintiff, the calculation of past loss may well be more complicated. If he is a partner in a firm, the earnings of the other partners will be a guide. One aspect to be considered will be the impact of the plaintiff's incapacity on the total partnership income. The smaller the firm, the more significant will have been the impact. Difficulties may be encountered in obtaining information concerning the partnership accounts if the plaintiff is no longer a member. Partnership accounts and related information are not publicly available and the assistance of a lawyer may be required in accessing such data.

617 The case of the self-employed plaintiff who is not in a partnership, for example a sole trader, typically gives most difficulty. His business may have ceased altogether or may have been continued under the control of a manager. Levels of turnover and profits for several years before the accident provide a starting point, although information will also be needed about special circumstances affecting those years; the aim should be to 'normalise' the results, ie to remove special non-recurring factors. Once normalised, the resulting trends, together with information provided by trade statistics, will provide a basis for estimating lost earnings in the years up to the date of trial. Any calculation based on trend analysis must be reviewed objectively, as trends can be easily manipulated.

618 All sources of income must be taken into account. For example, a plaintiff may have been receiving directors' or consultancy fees from other companies as well as his own. A spouse's salary should not be included where he or she gave up their job to care for the plaintiff following the accident. Such loss is dealt with separately by the court under cost of care.

Benefits

619 It may also be necessary to calculate the value of lost benefits when assessing the loss to date of trial. Such lost benefits may include reduced pension entitlement, the loss of use of a car, health insurance premiums, a subsidised mortgage, living accommodation, staff discounts or any other benefit the plaintiff derived from his business or employment. The value of the benefit of a car, for example, is a matter for evidence and is unlikely to be the same as the taxable value of the benefit.

Taxation

620 A notional deduction should be made for tax and national insurance contributions from earnings. The reason for this is that damages arising from personal injury, of which loss of earnings is only one element, are not taxable in the hands of the plaintiff. Since the aim is to place the plaintiff in the financial position that he would have been in but for the accident, a notional deduction must be made for the tax and national insurance he would have paid. This treatment follows from the decision of the House of Lords in *British Transport Commission v Gourley*.[1] (The Gourley Principle and the impact of taxation on damages claims are discussed in Chapter 15.) Taxable benefits included in the loss of earnings claim must also be taken into account in computing the plaintiff's notional tax liability. Claims may even be admissible in respect of income which the plaintiff has failed to disclose to the Revenue, but such income should be assessed net of taxation and national insurance. Because of the tax and national insurance deductions, it is convenient to assess earnings on a fiscal year basis; however, this may not be practicable, for example, for a Schedule D plaintiff whose financial year ends on some date other than 5 April. Whatever basis is used, annual gross earnings should be shown, with the accountant's best estimate of tax and national insurance deductions.

Deductions

Actual net income

621   In cases where the plaintiff has not been totally incapacitated by his injury, he may have been able to generate some income, although at a lower level than his pre-accident capacity. It is the plaintiff's duty to mitigate his loss, even if this involves retraining in order to exploit alternative earnings capacity. His claim must give credit for the actual income and benefits enjoyed, net of taxation and national insurance. Furthermore, tax must be calculated separately on actual and projected earnings. This treatment ensures that the claim, which is based on the difference between the respective net of tax amounts, correctly accounts for relevant personal allowances, standard or higher tax rates and national insurance thresholds.

State and other benefits

622   If the plaintiff receives state benefits and/or allowances as a result of the injury, these may have to be deducted from the damages calculation. The treatment of such receipts has been subject to recent changes in legislation. Whilst we recommend that the expert accountant be guided by his instructing solicitor in this area, a summary of the rules follows.

623   The Law Reform (Personal Injuries) Act 1948 s 2 governs the position in relation to accidents or injuries sustained up to the end of 1988. It provides that one half of the following benefits accruing to the plaintiff in the five years beginning with the date of the accident, are deducted against any claim for loss of earnings:

- sickness benefit;

- invalidity benefit;

- non-contributory invalidity pension;

- severe disablement allowance;

- injury benefit; and

- disablement benefit.

624   The following are examples of other benefits which are deductible in full and without time limit (provided they can be set against a similar item of damages under the rules, up to 1988):

- unemployment benefit;
- statutory sick pay;
- supplementary benefit;
- family income supplement; and
- industrial rehabilitation allowance.

625 Lord Bridge's judgment in *Hodgson v Trapp*[2] clarified the principle that, prima facie, receipts that a plaintiff would not have been entitled to but for the injury '. . . are to be set against the aggregate of the plaintiff's losses and expenses . . .'. It follows that receipts from attendance and mobility allowances have to be deducted from the 'cost of care' heads of damage and not included in the income section of the claim.

626 For injuries suffered after 1 January 1989, the Social Security Act 1989 s 22 and Sch 4 introduced new rules which provide that deduction is only to be made in respect of 'relevant benefits'. These rules do not apply in 'small' claims, ie where total damages do not exceed £2,500. The benefits are deductible in full (in contrast with 50% previously) for a period of up to five years from the date of the injury, but, unlike the previous rules, cannot be taken into account in respect of future periods beyond the date when compensation is settled. 'Relevant benefits' include:

- attendance allowance;
- disablement benefit (including disablement pensions) payable in accordance with ss 57 to 63 of the 1989 Act;
- family credit;
- income support;
- invalidity pension and allowance;
- mobility allowance;
- reduced earnings allowance;
- retirement allowance;
- severe disablement allowance;
- sickness benefit;
- statutory sick pay; and
- unemployment benefit.

627 The 1989 legislation has also revised the mechanics of dealing with such receipts. The insurer or defendant must compensate the Secretary of State for the amount of benefits paid to the plaintiff. The Secretary of State provides the insurer with a certificate of total benefit stating the sum which the insurer has then to deduct from the total amount of damages payable to the plaintiff.

Non-deductible items
628 Certain receipts which arise because of people's benevolence, or which stem from arrangements made by the plaintiff prior to the injury, are not to be deducted from the claim. Such receipts include charitable donations and other

gratuitous benefits, insurance receipts, state retirement pension and pensions generally. The principle that a pension is a reward for pre-injury service and, accordingly, should not be deducted is well established.[3] The House of Lords has recently held that this applies even to a disability pension to which the defendant has contributed in its capacity as employer of the plaintiff.[4]

CALCULATION OF FUTURE LOSS

Uncertainty

629 The third step in calculating pecuniary loss in a personal injury claim is the computation of future loss of earnings, which is no different in principle from the calculation for past pecuniary loss but is surrounded by greater uncertainty. Lord Scarman once said: 'There is really only one certainty; the future will prove the award to be either too high or too low'.[5]

630 Most of the factors relevant to assessing past loss will be known even, for example, the possibility of redundancy, since the position of the plaintiff's employers and the general economic climate from the date of the accident to the date of trial can be established. No guidance of comparable reliability is available in the assessment of future loss.

631 The different factors which may have some bearing on the future are numerous and will vary from case to case. The principal matters to be taken into account are:

● plaintiff's life and working life expectancy;

● likelihood of economic, industrial, and technological changes;

● possibility of sickness or unemployment;

● promotion and other career prospects; and

● the value of receiving a future income stream as a lump sum.

Multiplicand and multiplier

632 The courts have developed a convention for the assessment of future loss of earnings; this involves taking the product of two elements, known as the 'multiplicand' and the 'multiplier'. The 'multiplicand' is intended to represent the plaintiff's annual loss subsequent to trial. As already explained, this figure will be based largely on past statistics but, if appropriate, adjusted to reflect expected changes in career or employment prospects. The multiplier is the number of years' equivalent of the multiplicand that the plaintiff is considered to have lost. Because the award is generally of a lump sum payable immediately after the trial, the multiplier is designed to reflect many factors, in particular the plaintiff's life expectancy and the time value of money (ie the principle that £1 today is worth more than the same amount at some future date). That said, the multipliers used by the courts have in fact evolved through reported decisions, rather than by rigorous mathematical calculations. It follows that the choice of multiplier is very much a matter for the lawyers to advise upon.

633 Because there is often a diversity of views as to the plaintiff's future career prospects (as to the likelihood of both advancement and unemployment), expert accountants are often asked to furnish the lawyers with several alternative figures for lost earnings, based on varying projections of the plaintiff's career path. Often, these can be conveniently produced by varying the inputs to a single computer spreadsheet model. For example, the inputs can be changed so as to reflect varying assumptions, as to when an employed plaintiff might have received significant promotions. An alternative approach to using a range of assumptions is to select as the multiplicand an annual figure somewhat higher than would be indicated by the assessment of past loss; however, in order to gain acceptance of this approach, it is usually necessary to have available calculations supporting the higher earnings figure.

Time value of money

634 In making assessments of future income, the accountant must disregard inflation. The courts in injury cases have usually left out of account the risk of further inflation. They also disregard the possibility of high interest rates. Money should be treated as retaining its value at the date of judgment. It is implicit in this approach that projected earnings for the purposes of the calculations should exclude any element of inflation, as distinct from pay rises due to the career progression. Interest rates appropriate to times of stable currency, such as 4% or 5%, are generally adopted (see below) and hence discount rates of that order are to be applied in calculating the present value of a capital sum equivalent to the plaintiff's future income stream. Current tax and national insurance rates should be used in the projections; there should be no attempt to forecast them unless, perhaps, the Chancellor has already announced changes in a Budget speech.

635 The establishment of index-linked Government stocks has prompted calls for a reassessment of the validity of multipliers based upon interest rates such as 4% or 5%. This is because returns on such stocks fall into the range 2½% to 3½% before taking into account adjustments to include inflation. Indeed, the Law Commission recommended in 1994 that there should be legislation requiring the court, in any proceedings for damages for personal injuries, to take account of the net real return that a plaintiff would obtain if the award were to be invested in index-linked Government stocks.[6] If future earnings were discounted at the lower rates obtainable from such stocks, there would be significant increases in the multiplier and, hence, the level of damages awarded.

636 The proper approach to the choice of multiplier is thus an open question. Where many years of life expectancy remain, the courts have recently held that, on the basis of past experience, the plaintiff could with negligible risk, invest his award in equities in the expectation of earning a real return in the range 4% to 5%. On this basis, the traditional approach to assessing the multiplier has been upheld. It remains to be seen whether a lower rate, such as that favoured by the Law Commission, will be held appropriate in cases when life expectancy is lower, when it could be reasonable for the plaintiff to invest his award in risk-free Government securities in order to be protected against the short-term fluctuations in returns on equities which undoubtedly occur.

Actuarial evidence

637 Over the years, a number of efforts have been made to introduce actuarial evidence to the court in support of loss of earnings calculations. The court has tended to reject such evidence, preferring instead to use, as a rule of thumb, the multiplier/multiplicand approach described above. It is said that a judge must appraise the facts of an individual case and not the outcome of statistical averages on which actuarial calculations are based.

638 In 1982, in an effort to bridge the gap between the judicial viewpoint and the actuarial viewpoint, the government set up a working party of actuaries, barristers and solicitors who prepared a set of actuarial tables[7] intended to give the legal profession some guidance in the choice of an appropriate multiplier. The working party also supported the use of the index-linked Government stocks discussed above.

Notwithstanding the findings of the working party, the courts continue to determine multipliers primarily by reference to previously decided cases. They appear to regard actuarial evidence as, at best, an ancillary method of checking a computation already made by the multiplier method. There has been the empirical observation that the multipliers actually applied by the courts tend not to be altogether out of line with those indicated by the actuarial tables. The debate will no doubt continue. The Law Commission report of September 1994[8] recommended that the Ogden Tables should be admissible evidence, and that legislation should require courts to have regard for true rates of net return based on index-linked Government security.

Children generally

639 Inevitably, the younger a child is at the date of the injury, the more subjective is the process of assessing future earnings. Not only does the career the child would have pursued have to be conjectured, but there will be no indication of how he or she would have performed in that career, what their promotion prospects would have been and so forth. Whatever earnings estimates are made have to be discounted to take account of the fact that the child would not have received the earnings until he reached working age.

640 In assessing the potential earnings of children, the courts use a number of approaches. Most common appears to be the use of Government statistics on average wages. The concept of an average wage needs to be applied with care; it should take cognizance of the background of the child in question and the education he would have received. Also, if circumstances indicate that the child could have been expected to perform above the norm, it may be appropriate to uplift the average wage levels. An alternative approach is to look at the earnings and employment history of the child's father and use this as the basis of assessment of the child's prospects. This could be appropriate if, say, the father runs a family business which the child could have been expected to take over on the retirement of his father. This approach was deemed appropriate in *Cassel's* case,[9] where the child injured at birth was compensated at a level which took into account the fact that his uncle and grandfather had both been successful QCs.

CALCULATION OF OTHER RELEVANT FACTORS

641 We have so far been dealing with damages arising directly from loss of earned income, but other issues can also arise. The following are common subjects for research.

Loss of or reduction in pension

642 A diminution of earnings will frequently result in a reduced pension. Calculating the pension that the injured person would have received, had it not been for the accident, is subject to predictions not only of the value of any pension fund, but also of the estimation of possible earnings. Pension loss is often remote in time and therefore tends to be heavily discounted by the court, firstly because of the benefit of receiving a lump sum immediately, and secondly because of the various contingencies that might occur in the interim, not least the possibility that the claimant might still have died before pension age from causes unconnected with the claim.

643 Pensions are often linked to final salary. The assumed pension at retirement should be based on the assumptions that have been adopted to calculate loss of earnings; in theory, the present value of that pension can be determined by actuarial methods. Another approach is to obtain a commercial quote on the value of the pension. A 1985 case[10] (in which, incidentally, the courts gave their clearest indication of their antipathy towards actuarial evidence in personal injury claims), set out in some detail the judge's calculation of pension loss. The expert accountant may find that his instructing solicitor asks him to adopt a similar approach.

644 For the self-employed person, assessment of pension loss is all the more complicated. Here, the likely pension would depend on:

- level of contribution,

- performance of investment fund, and

- retirement age,

the first two of which are factors which are not capable of precise measurement. A practicable and convenient expedient in such circumstances is provided by incorporation within the total past loss, and also the future multiplicand, of an amount equivalent to the tax relief which would be enjoyed based on historic rates of premiums paid by the plaintiff – thereby compensating the plaintiff for the loss of tax benefit previously enjoyed on pension contributions. By this means, the fund of damages will be grossed up to a lump sum, out of which an amount may be invested to purchase a deferred annuity for the plaintiff which should approximate, when paid, to the shortfall of his likely pension caused by the injury.

Future disadvantage in the labour market

645 Awards are sometimes given under a separate head of damage for future disadvantage which the plaintiff will suffer in the labour market; these are often referred to as '*Smith v Manchester* damages'.[11] The amount is intended to protect the plaintiff in situations where his current earnings, which indicate the level of the multiplicand, may diminish or be at risk in the future by virtue of his injury. Such awards, being distinct from future loss of earnings and, by their nature, not scientifically quantifiable, should not be included by accountants in calculations of lost future income from employment.

Loss of job satisfaction

646 A similar head of damage, which again comes outside the accountant's remit, is for loss of job satisfaction. A fireman obtained such compensation when he was forced to change to another job as the result of an accident. He suffered loss of job satisfaction as a result.[12] This damage would usually come within the categories of pain and suffering and loss of amenities.

DIY activities

647 Often, lawyers for the plaintiff maintain that because the injured person performed various 'do it yourself' work in the home, such as decorating, general repairs and gardening, this work will have to be paid for in the future. The value of this free labour, once established by evidence, is commonly dealt with, as regards future loss, by taking the assumed value as an individual multiplicand and applying to it a multiplier. That multiplier will not necessarily be the same as that which will be adopted for the purpose of assessing loss of earnings; this is because the age at which an individual stops working for a living may well be different from that at which he would give up DIY activities.

Expenses

648 Severe injuries, such as those which render the victim paraplegic or tetraplegic, lead to significant nursing and medical costs for the remainder of life. Additionally, there can be heavy costs in adapting a house to make it suitable for a disabled person. Sometimes the plaintiff and his family have to move house, for example, to a bungalow. An accountant's help in quantifying the financial cost can be helpful here (but he must keep in mind the court's approach to decided cases). The evidence on such matters is normally assembled by the lawyer, sometimes with the aid of experts on that particular topic, but tabulating the figures in a manner which fits the rest of the submissions can sometimes be a task for the accountant.

Interest

649 The plaintiff is not automatically assumed to claim interest on his damages. The writ should also include a claim for interest. One must differentiate between special damages (ie financial loss up to the date of the trial) and general damages (for example, compensation for pain, suffering and loss of amenities). For special damages, interest generally runs at half the rate of the High Court Special Investment Account rate (formerly known as the Short-term Investment Account rate) whereas for general damages, interest is at 2% from the date of the service of the writ. (These low rates follow from the assumption that the plaintiff benefits through inflation by having the date of trial postponed and so does not need a high rate of interest; this is no longer necessarily so and the time may be ripe for it to be challenged.)

650 The claims for future loss, for example, future loss of earnings from the date of the trial, do not attract interest.

651 It must be appreciated that interest can be a sizeable element, especially if the case takes a long time to come to trial. It is a big component in the calculation of whether or not to accept an amount paid into court in settlement of the dispute.

Negotiations between parties

652 There is a tendency for all letters between people engaged in the conduct of the case to be headed 'without prejudice', despite the fact that these words are usually only necessary when suggesting values or inviting settlement of a claim.

653 There will first be an exchange of views on liability. Usually the defendant's insurers will play a major role. The insurers will wish to know the approximate amounts involved. Both sides will try to learn the strengths and weaknesses of the other side's case so that further instructions can be taken. At this stage, the claimant's representatives will not reveal the details of the client's case and may well not pass across the medical reports. Most insurance representatives are experienced and will know the precedents that exist. The insurers will prefer that the commencement of the proceedings is delayed, in case the claim can be settled and thus the expense and inconvenience of the proceedings avoided. If the case is strong on liability, the lawyers for the plaintiff may well ask for an interim payment, even before proceedings are commenced.

654 If the case seems reasonable from a liability point of view, the lawyers for the plaintiff may be tempted to postpone proceedings on the basis that if it is good on liability, it will settle. However, delay in issuing the writ has many attendant risks attaching to it, particularly since interest does not start running on general damages until service of the writ has occurred. In these preliminary negotiations, discussion will sometimes revolve around the percentage of contributory negligence on the part of the plaintiff.

655 It should be noted that when negotiations take place they are almost invariably 'subject to the payment of the plaintiff's costs'; that is, negotiations relate only to the basic compensation, not to the legal costs of the matter.

Contributory negligence

656 Frequently, a defendant in either a motor accident or a works accident will conclude his defence by stating that the plaintiff's accident was caused wholly or partly due to his own (the plaintiff's) negligence. It will not be the part of the accountant to deal with this issue, but it is worth remembering that contributory negligence is not concerned with whether the plaintiff is partly responsible for the cause of the damage but whether he is partly responsible for the damage itself. For instance, failure to wear a seat belt can be contributory negligence if it contributed to the damage, even though it did not in any way contribute to the cause of the damage.

STRUCTURED SETTLEMENTS

657   It was held in *Kelly v Dawes*,[13] that parties to a personal injury action may agree on a structured settlement, whereby the defendant's insurers invest a proportion of the total sum payable to the plaintiff in the purchase of an annuity which would provide an index-linked annual sum for the remainder of the plaintiff's life. The Inland Revenue and the Association of British Insurers have agreed a procedure whereby periodic payments to a plaintiff, funded by an annuity purchased by the insurer from a separate life office, may be treated as payments of capital, and so not subject to income tax.

658   The result is that, because of the tax advantages to the plaintiff, the total damages payable may be less than the sum which would have been payable as a single lump sum payment. The insurer can pay (at less cost than the lump sum that would otherwise be payable) an annuity which would yield higher benefits than the plaintiff could have expected from the lump sum. The financial gain to both parties arises largely from the tax saving.

659   Other advantages accrue to both parties. In particular, from the plaintiff's perspective, the worry of administering a large capital fund is removed, and annual income is protected against inflation and guaranteed for life. (Studies in Canada have revealed conventional awards are dissipated at an alarming rate. After five years some 90% of awards have been totally exhausted.)

660   In order that the plaintiff preserves some of the flexibility afforded by a lump sum settlement which is lost under an annuity arrangement, the settlement may provide for a lump sum to cover past loss, plus a reserve sum for contingencies in the future and an annuity settlement over the remainder of the plaintiff's life. It should be borne in mind that any changes in the tax law could alter the present position.

661   Once a structured settlement has been agreed between the parties, an application must be made for the court's approval. It has been recommended that solicitors present a report of accountants or other financial experts as to the fiscal and investment advantages to the plaintiff of the structured settlement proposed, with particular regard to life expectancy and likely future costs of care. Because, at present, the court can only approve, rather than order, a structured settlement, such arrangements require the agreement of the parties.

662   It is unlikely that awards of less than £100,000 would merit consideration, but advisers could well find themselves open to charges of professional negligence if they fail to consider the possibility of structured settlements in appropriate cases.

663   However, these potential savings can give rise to practical difficulties, particularly since the insured may seek to negotiate a part of the potential savings into the overall settlement figure. Structured settlements are more typically applied to larger claims and, as a consequence, the potential savings are significant and may amount to 10% or more of the damages, dependent upon annuity rates at the time.

664   Insurers may argue that they require reimbursement for the increased administrative burden which accompanies such arrangements, and, more importantly, the adverse cashflow consequences which result from the present arrangements.

665   However, the Law Commission has recently recommended changes to the present system which would remove those problems for the insurer, enabling him to close his files much sooner.[14]

666   In the meantime, discount will remain a feature of settlement negotiations.

FATAL ACCIDENTS

667   The Fatal Accidents Act 1976 provides that, if an injured person has a cause of action arising out of injury, such a cause of action shall not be lost if the injury results in death. An action for recovery of damages may be brought by or on behalf of a dependant of the deceased. Calculations of quantum in a fatal accident case must follow the steps outlined above. However, the death of the injured party restricts the quality of the information available, for example, the consideration of the future business plans of a Schedule D taxpayer. The fundamental difference from injury claims is that, here, the measure of damages is now generally the loss suffered by the dependants after the plaintiff's death; it is not the loss suffered by the plaintiff.

668   Section 4 of the Act, as amended by the Administration of Justice Act 1982, provides a departure from the general principle that the quantum of damages should be sufficient to place the wronged parties in the pecuniary position that they would have been in if the wrong had not occurred. It states that:

> 'In assessing damages in respect of a person's death in an action under this Act, benefits which have accrued or will or may accrue to any person from his estate or otherwise as a result of his death shall be disregarded.'

For example, damages would not fall to be reduced just because the deceased was prudent enough to take out a life assurance policy.

669   The consequences of s 4 could, however, be more dramatic. We were recently involved in a claim by the widow of a multi-millionaire living off unearned income in a tax-free environment. It was common ground that she had suffered no loss since the deceased's investments were inherited by her and the stream of unearned income was not affected by death. But it was argued that s 4 required this inheritance to be disregarded. The widow thus stood to double her wealth, which before death was very considerable but after death (after applying s 4) was nil. By the time the case came to court, it was clear that damages were either in excess of £1 million or nil, depending upon the correct construction of s 4. Not for the first time since 1982, the matter was settled on a compromise basis and the true intent and effect of s 4 in such circumstances, remains to be seen.

670 Once the loss of earnings figure is calculated, the value of the loss of dependency must be assessed. In the absence of better information, dependency for a widow with two or three children is usually assessed at 75% of net income, and for a widow without children at 66.66%. To challenge these commonly accepted percentages involves detailed enquiry into the deceased's lifestyle. Clearly, dependency would be lower in the case of a man who had very expensive hobbies, and thus less income available for his family, than for a man who had no such hobbies and was educating his children privately.

671 The apportionment of the award between the widow and the children is a matter for the lawyers. It is no longer significant in the assessment of the total amount of damages in respect of deaths after 1 January 1983, following the introduction of the Administration of Justice Act 1982. It can, however, still be relevant where a widow remarries because, although the widow's claim does not end, her remarriage may terminate the dependent children's claim.

672 Having determined the appropriate multiplier, taking into account the various uncertainties of the case, the approach now varies from that in an injury case. In non-fatal cases, the multiplier is assessed as at the date of trial. For fatal accident claims, it is determined as at the date of death, because uncertainty over the future arises at that date, rather than trial date. The actual period from death to the date of trial is deducted from the assessed multiplier, leaving the balance of the multiplier to be applied to the multiplicand in order to obtain the present value of loss of future earnings. Thus:

Assumed multiplier	15.0
Period to date of trial	3.5
Balance of multiplier	11.5

CASE EXAMPLES

673 A wide variety of personal injury cases arise in practice. We set out below five examples of personal injury cases in which the writers have had experience.

Boy aged 15 at the date of the accident

674 In this matter the plaintiff suffered severe head injuries with consequent brain damage. The plaintiff had enjoyed a happy and stable family background, and his academic attainment prior to the accident was in the superior to gifted range. The plaintiff had expressed an interest in a career in merchant banking. We also considered, on his behalf, alternative careers in both chartered accountancy and the law.

675 Our research relied upon published data on earnings at various levels within these alternative professions. We also had regard for the various benefits which attach to such positions, notably company car and pension.

676 Our assessment envisaged that the plaintiff would have the prospect of attaining earnings at the upper end within these professions, although our report was structured so that the court would be able to adopt a lesser level of attainment should that be considered more appropriate. We made extensive use of computer graphics in order to provide visual information on earnings streams during a professional career.

677 We also prepared a separate assessment of loss of earnings on behalf of the boy's mother, an experienced teacher, who was forced to retire from her profession due to the stress caused by her son's injuries.

678 In both cases, our reports assisted instructing solicitors to achieve satisfactory out of court settlements.

Professional Rugby League player

679 In this instance we were instructed, on behalf of insurers, to consider a substantial claim for loss of earnings suffered by a New Zealand national who had played Rugby League on a professional basis, both in New Zealand and the UK. The plaintiff had also supplemented his earnings from Rugby League with other out of season income from manual employment.

680 Our research was wide-ranging, including discussions with the Rugby Football League, and with executives of Rugby League clubs in the UK. We also engaged our associated office in New Zealand to carry out similar research in that country.

681 We identified that the assumptions which had been applied in assessing the plaintiff's loss of earnings were, in many instances, fundamentally flawed. Even if those assumptions were adopted, the quantum of the plaintiff's losses remained significantly overstated, due to the use of inappropriate and excessive estimates of income levels.

682 We also considered the average retirement age in order to determine the appropriate multipliers which ought to be applied. As a consequence of these various issues, we were able to effect a robust reassessment which enabled insurers to negotiate a substantial reduction of the plaintiff's claim.

Civil servant aged 39

683 In this matter, the plaintiff again sustained severe brain damage. As a consequence of her injuries, and due to cash constraints within the family, her husband was obliged to cease trading both in his own business and also in another related activity which he operated in partnership.

684 In this particular instance, insurers asked us to consider collectively all heads of claim and to bring together the results of our own enquiries with the findings of other qualified experts. As a consequence, our report comprised a comprehensive assessment of all losses suffered by the plaintiff under a host of headings which included matters such as transport, professional and gratuitous nursing care costs, accommodation, appliances, aids and equipment, loss of earnings and pension, state benefits, and Court of Protection costs. We made extensive use of financial modelling techniques in order to simplify the assessment of irregular future expenditure requirements, reducing these to simple discounted multiplicands.

685 We were able to assist the court by simplifying the complex financial assessments offered by other experts. By adopting a common approach to presentation of the various heads of claim, we were able to present a more easily understandable assessment, which assisted insurers in effecting a satisfactory out of court settlement.

686 This composite approach had the added advantage of identifying duplication of claims, particularly in the areas of gratuitous nursing care offered by the plaintiff's husband, coupled with professional care costs and claims in respect of loss of earnings suffered by the husband as a consequence of the need to provide such care to the plaintiff.

Self-employed hairdresser

687 In this particular matter we were instructed to act for the plaintiff. The plaintiff had initially trained as a hairdresser on leaving school and had subsequently carried on in business as a hairdresser in self-employment for some five years. However, following her marriage she had left that employment. Many years later, the marriage failed, and the plaintiff determined to start a new life and to return to hairdressing. Prior to that venture taking off, she suffered injuries in a road traffic accident which prohibited any such return. Assessment of losses was rendered all the more difficult due to the passage of time since she had last been involved in hairdressing, and also because there was little evidence as to the likely earnings which she might have achieved but for her injuries.

688 Our approach in this instance was, therefore, to provide an assessment of a range of earnings as a hairdresser in employment, and to suggest possible premia above those levels to recognise the likely additional rewards that would be attainable in self-employment.

689 Our assessment culminated in an out of court settlement, during the lunchtime recess on the first day of trial.

Partner in a professional firm

690 This case involved the death of a 37 year old partner in a professional firm with a number of branch offices in a small geographical area. We were acting for the defence. The assessment of his share of the profit was complicated: the profit sharing arrangements had varied over time, and branches had opened and closed according to profitability. Only after a detailed investigation of the part played by the deceased partner, particularly in relation to his involvement in the opening and closing of branch offices, were we able to make a projection of his earnings which was acceptable to both sides.

SUMMARY

691 An accountant acting in a personal injuries case must convert a complicated situation into easily understood figures. His aim should be to lay objective information before instructing lawyers so as to give the court a clear picture and, as far as possible, an uncomplicated series of options. Lawyers should be able to provide help as to what damages are obviously too remote to be included in the calculation.

692 The accountant should beware of becoming involved in matters which are properly the concern of lawyers and the court. As in all expert work, he should also avoid a partisan approach: it only reduces the value of his report as evidence, and can also militate against a reasonable out of court settlement.

NOTES

1 [1956] AC 185, HL.
2 [1989] AC 807, HL.
3 *Parry v Cleaver* [1970] AC 1, HL.
4 *Smoker v London Fire and Civil Defence Authority* and *Wood v British Coal Corpn* [1991] 2 WLR 1052, HL.
5 *Lim Poh Choo v Camden and Islington Area Health Authority* [1980] AC 174, HL.
6 *Structured Settlements and Interim and Provisional Damages* (Law Com no 224) at para 2.31.
7 *Actuarial Tables with Explanatory Notes for use in Personal Injury and Fatal Accident Cases* (May 1984) HMSO.
8 See footnote 6.
9 *Cassel v Hammersmith and Fulham Health Authority* [1992] PIQR Q168.
10 *Auty v National Coal Board* [1985] 1 All ER 930, CA.
11 *Smith v Manchester Corpn* [1974] 17 KIR 1, CA.
12 *Champion v London Fire and Civil Defence Authority* (1990) Times, 5 July.
13 (1990) Times, 27 September.
14 See footnote 6.

Chapter 7

Divorce

Establishing the financial resources – The best approach – Developing questionnaires – Valuing shares in a family company – Farming businesses – Lloyd's underwriters – Pension arrangements – Family trusts – Tax aspects – The financial settlement – Raising the cash – Quantifying the wife's 'reasonable requirements' – Computing the capital sum – Expert evidence – Conclusion

701 In modern society divorce is commonplace. No longer is the emphasis of litigation on the obtaining of a divorce itself, but on the custody of children and the financial settlement. The role of accountants has hence become more significant in divorce cases.

702 The Matrimonial Causes Act 1973 s 25 (as amended by the Matrimonial and Family Proceedings Act 1984) requires that in dealing with financial provision in connection with divorce, the court shall have regard to the following:

(a) the income, earning capacity, property and other financial resources which each of the parties to the marriage has or is likely to have in the foreseeable future, including, in the case of earning capacity, any increase in that capacity which it would in the opinion of the court be reasonable to expect a party to the marriage to take steps to acquire;
(b) the financial needs, obligations and responsibilities which each of the parties to the marriage has or is likely to have in the foreseeable future;
(c) the standard of living enjoyed by the family before the breakdown of the marriage;
(d) the age of each party to the marriage and the duration of the marriage;
(e) any physical or mental disability of either of the parties to the marriage;
(f) the contributions which each of the parties has made, or is likely in the foreseeable future to make, to the welfare of the family, including any contribution by looking after the home or caring for the family;
(g) the conduct of each of the parties, if that conduct is such that it would in the opinion of the court be inequitable to disregard it; and
(h) in the case of proceedings for divorce or nullity of marriage, the value to each of the parties to the marriage of any benefit (for example, a pension) which, by reason of the dissolution or annulment of the marriage, that party will lose the chance of acquiring.

703 Accordingly, the court has to form a reliable estimate of the financial resources of the parties and of their requirements. Those advising the parties are similarly concerned to obtain such information. Where the financial picture is complex, an accountant's report, setting out the position clearly and comprehensively, can be very helpful. It may be appropriate for separate reports to be prepared by accountants acting for the husband and for the wife, in which case they should be exchanged at an early date so that the accounting matters in issue can be clearly established. The courts are becoming increasingly concerned at the costs of calling conflicting expert evidence from accountants and valuers, and are tending to encourage experts to get together to produce a joint report setting out what is agreed and what remains in issue between them. The possibility has also been canvassed that there may come a time when the duplication of expert evidence will be replaced by the appointment of a single expert by the court, but so far as we are aware this practice has not yet been applied.

ESTABLISHING THE FINANCIAL RESOURCES

The best approach

704 The preparation of the accountant's report can have much in common with fitting together a jigsaw puzzle. Typically, most of the pieces are in the possession of the husband. For the purposes of what follows, it is assumed that the wife's financial position is relatively straightforward, although in practice this may not always be so.

705 The most economical approach to a dispute is for a detailed report to be prepared first by the husband's accountants, or by accountants with specialist knowledge of the matrimonial finance field. Assets may have to be revalued and the CGT consequences of such revaluations calculated; the data for this is nearly always more easily accessible to those advising the husband. Where accountants act for the wife, their task is simplified if they can start from a comprehensive report prepared on behalf of the husband. Attention can then be more readily focused on the real areas of difference. These are typically the valuation of unlisted shares and the raising of liquid capital to effect the settlement.

706 Regrettably, accountants' reports are seldom commissioned on behalf of husbands and all too frequently affidavits of means (that is, statements setting out the husband's sources of wealth and income and other benefits) are sworn by husbands in which the financial position is far from clear and is incomplete.

Developing questionnaires

707 Faced with an incomplete statement by the husband, it becomes necessary for those advising the wife to bring in accountants of suitable experience to help to identify what is missing. They will be well placed to contribute to the development of a questionnaire, under Rule 2.63 of the Family Proceedings Rules 1991, to be put to the husband. The production of this questionnaire is important so as, on the one hand, to ensure that the right questions are asked and, on the other, to avoid asking questions that are irrelevant. The questionnaire is normally a collaborative venture involving accountants, counsel and solicitors. Counsel will give preliminary advice on the general areas to be explored and may also be called upon to settle in detail the final terms of the questionnaire. The accountant must frame the questions so that they extract the financial information required and cannot easily be evaded.

708 An outline of the matters typically covered in such a questionnaire is set out in the box below.

DETAILS TO BE REQUESTED IN THE QUESTIONNAIRE

Freehold and leasehold property

Description and current value of each property.

The family company

Copies of accounts for three years, including detailed trading and profit and loss accounts for each company in the group.

Draft or management accounts, forecasts and budgets for periods since the last accounts, including those provided to lenders in support of company borrowing.

The Memorandum and Articles of Association.

The number of shares held by each of the parties and how the remainder of the share capital is held.

Transactions in shares of the company.

Transactions between the husband and the company (including detailed accounts showing balances due).

Information as to the use of the company to support the family's standard of living.

The interest of each of the parties in the company pension scheme.

Other investments

Current details of portfolio of listed investments – cost, date of acquisition, current value.

For unlisted investments, copies of accounts and sufficient other information to enable the reasonableness of the valuation to be assessed.

Sources from which any recent investments have been made.

Taxation

Copies of tax returns for three years together with all supporting schedules submitted to the Inland Revenue.

Information to enable the potential CGT liability arising on the disposal of each asset to be established.

Bank accounts

Copies of bank statements for all accounts in which the husband had a beneficial interest at any time in the past three years, annotated to explain substantial items above a defined amount.

Other accounts

Similar information in respect of any account with stockbrokers, solicitors or others.

Credit cards

Copies of all credit card account statements on which the husband has a signature, for a period of one year, identifying by whom the expenditure charged to the card is (a) paid and (b) borne.

Settlements

Particulars of all settlements made by the husband, with a copy of the trust deed and accounts for three years.

Particulars of any settlement under which the husband is a beneficiary or discretionary object.

---

709 Questionnaires must be tailored to the circumstances of each case. Care must also be taken to match the extent of the enquiry to the amounts at stake in each category. In this respect, Family Division judges have expressed concern about the heavy legal costs being incurred in family provision matters. In *Evans v Evans*[1] it was noted that:

> 'while it was necessary for legal advisers to have sufficient knowledge of the financial situation of both parties before advising a client . . . the necessity to make further enquiries had to be balanced by a consideration of what those enquiries might be likely to achieve and the increased costs which would be incurred.'

710 The aim is to obtain information which will satisfy those advising the wife that full and fair disclosure of the husband's resources has been made, and that the standard of living of the parties has been fairly depicted. This may call not only for questions about the existing assets, liabilities and income but for the identification of the source and application of significant cash flows.

711 Production of credit card statements for a recent period, normally one year, can provide a valuable impression of living standards – which hotels and restaurants are frequented, where holidays are taken and which major shops are used. It is important to establish who bears the expenditure charged to the credit card accounts.

712 Sometimes the husband's financial disclosure is deliberately obfuscatory. Considerable detective work may be necessary in order to identify the loose ends from which the existence of undisclosed bank accounts or other assets may be traced. This is more likely to occur where the husband has planned the divorce prior to the commencement of the proceedings and consequently had the opportunity to organise his finances accordingly. In such circumstances, it may be necessary for the questionnaire to request information over longer periods of time than would normally be required. The accountant may be required to provide further assistance to counsel and the solicitors, in justifying to the court why such an extension is appropriate.

713 The answers to a first questionnaire may give rise to further questions and it may be necessary to devise a second questionnaire that will, if possible, prove sufficiently comprehensive to avoid the process of question and answer being protracted excessively.

VALUING SHARES IN A FAMILY COMPANY

714 In many divorce cases, the most substantial asset of the parties will be shares in the family company. Expertise in share valuation is then necessary to identify information needed and to frame the appropriate questions to include in the questionnaire.

715 The subject of share valuation is dealt with in Chapter 4. In the context of matrimonial financial settlements, it should be noted that the Family Division tends to take a broad view of the background to family companies. If, for example, a family company is owned and run by three brothers with equal shareholdings and history shows that they always act in concert to the best mutual advantage, the court is then inclined to favour an approach that values the holding of one brother as one third of the value of the company as a whole, rather than looking at that holding in isolation as a one third minority interest without control.

716 If the husband's main livelihood is derived from the family business and it is also his main asset, its value will be of limited relevance to the settlement, unless it can be shown that capital can be raised without significantly reducing his shareholding. The court would be most unlikely to require a husband to part with control of his business. In a recent unreported case, the judge was disinclined to envisage even the reduction of a minority shareholding as a means of raising capital. However, there have been cases where the court has been prepared to countenance a disposal of part of a controlling interest to an extent that still leaves the husband with control. In such a case, it is of crucial importance to demonstrate how cash could be raised without loss of control of the business by the husband.

717 In circumstances where the value of the business is really no more than the capitalisation of the personal earning capacity of the husband, the decision in *B v B*[2] as regards the extent to which a wife's advisers should go in seeking to establish the value of the husband's business, should be observed: 'Fine-tuned assessments of the value of a spouse's business, achieved at great cost to the parties, were meaningless and irrelevant where . . . the business produced the family's income and was not to be sold'. However, different considerations apply once the business has been built up to the stage where it has a value that is no longer solely dependent on the husband's earning capacity. In a recent case involving a property owner who maintained that all the property formed part of the business and that its value should be disregarded, the learned judge did not consider the *B v B* argument to be applicable.

718 If there are substantial other assets, the value of the family company does have an important influence on the settlement. If the husband is to keep the whole of his interest in the business, it becomes more reasonable for the wife to take a larger share of the other assets.

719 Sometimes the wife herself holds a substantial proportion of the capital of the family company. Where it is really the husband's business, the settlement of her claims will usually involve transferring her holding to him. There may be room for argument as to whether she is entitled as of right to the full value of her holding or whether she is, to some extent, holding her shares as nominee for her husband – in which case some lesser sum may be appropriate.

720 In valuing shares in the family company, the possibility of a future Stock Exchange listing, or the establishment of some other market for the shares, should be considered. Where there is a real prospect of such a happening, the foreseeable financial resources may be substantially greater and the means of raising cash will also be more easily identifiable.

Farming businesses

721 Different considerations arise when the family business is a farm. Typically, the capital value of the business will be based on land values, but the income from the farm will be low in relation to such values. This may be because profits are being ploughed back in improving the farm or because living expenses of the family are charged against the profits of the farm. It may then be difficult for the wife to demonstrate that the husband has the resources to pay substantial maintenance or to pay interest on the borrowings required to make a capital payment.

722 If there is some land which is not an essential part of the farm, for example, physically separated from the main farm area, it may be possible to propose the sale of such land to raise a capital sum, particularly if it is owned by the husband personally rather than through a company. The existence of agricultural tenancies may have a depreciatory effect on the value of the land. However, if both the freeholder and the tenant are within the family, it may be appropriate to take into account the totality of the family's interest, rather than to consider the value of the tenanted land in isolation.

Lloyd's underwriters

723 It is necessary to find out if the husband or the wife is a Lloyd's underwriter or 'Name'. Lloyd's accounting is complex and the underwriting results for each insurance year are kept open for three years so that, for example, the results for the 1990 underwriting year were not published until May 1993. The benefits accruing from Lloyd's underwriting consist of not only the underwriting profit (if any), but of investment income on the Name's Lloyd's reserves and underwriting assets, and capital gains on the increase in value of investments.

724 The underwriters' agents normally produce, annually, a summary of the income from all three sources in respect of each syndicate in which the Name participates, together with an indication of how the insurance years that have not yet been closed are progressing. These reports provide an important source of information regarding the Name's income and expectation.

725 Income tax and CGT at the standard rate are normally deducted in arriving at the amount distributed each year, and the net amount therefore has to be grossed up to arrive at the total income from this source. Allowance may have to be made for higher rate tax in computing the total tax liabilities.

726 Lloyd's Names have to demonstrate that they can meet the wealth requirements of Lloyd's appropriate to the level of premium income that they underwrite. This may be done either by the deposit of securities or, more commonly, by the provision of a bank guarantee. Where the bank gives a guarantee, it will normally require a charge over the Names' property or other suitable assets by way of security. Enquiries should be made to establish the nature of the Lloyd's security and to ensure that the assets concerned, whether deposited directly or charged to the bank as security, are included in the assessment of financial resources.

727 Where the wife is a Name, the question arises whether she should continue her membership of Lloyd's after the divorce. This will depend largely on the extent of the assets available to support her Lloyd's membership. In a recent (unreported) case, the wife's future requirements were projected on the basis that she would discontinue her membership of Lloyd's, since the only asset available to secure that membership was her house and she would have felt insecure in pledging the roof over her head to support underwriting activities which had the potential to produce a substantial loss if things went badly. From the husband's side it was argued that, in resigning from Lloyd's, his wife had spontaneously cut herself off from a substantial source of income which he should not therefore be required to make good. While the judge made no specific finding on this point, it appeared that he did not regard the wife's resignation from Lloyd's as unreasonable in the circumstances. This case was heard before the recent heavy losses incurred by Names on some Lloyd's syndicates and the proposed withdrawal of the wife from Lloyd's would probably now be accepted more readily as reasonable. In some cases now the ascertainment of the parties' financial resources may be made more difficult by the existence of substantial Lloyd's losses, the amounts of which cannot easily be quantified.

Pension arrangements

728   Recent legislation has made the pensions area increasingly complex and the accountant has an important part to play in reviewing the terms of the pension arrangements and seeing how a settlement can be designed to take them properly into account. One of the effects of divorce can be that a wife will cease to be a prospective beneficiary of her former husband's pension arrangements. Whether this is so depends on the precise terms of the pension scheme and these therefore require careful examination. It is not uncommon for pension schemes to make provision for a pension for a wife or former wife, and the wife's advisers should seek to protect her interests in this respect. If the terms of the settlement are such that she will be deprived of participation in the pension, this may be a valuable right for which she will need to be adequately compensated.

729   It is possible to apply actuarial techniques to estimate the value of that lost right. Since, in many cases, precise calculations may be unnecessarily complex and expensive, a simplified actuarial approach has been developed by certain barristers specialising in the field of family law and by Coopers & Lybrand actuaries. Their article: 'What price a widow's mite? An Actuarial Assessment of Lost Pension Rights'[3] provides a guideline to the 'prima facie lump sum to be paid to the wife by way of compensation for the loss of the benefit' and discusses the assumptions on which their approach is based. Such techniques can be helpful, provided that the limiting assumptions on which they rely are borne in mind.

730   There are, however, other means of compensating a wife for her loss of pension entitlement of which her advisers should be aware. For example, in the case of *B v B* referred to above, Anthony Lincoln J noted that in 15 years' time Mrs B's children would probably be independent. Mrs B would not need a four bedroomed house and could make provision for herself as regarded a pension out of the proceeds.

Family trusts

731   It is not open to a husband to remove his assets from the scope of his wife's claims by settling them on trusts which exclude her as a beneficiary. In a recent case, the wife had no difficulty in obtaining an order setting aside a transfer of assets by her husband to a trust that excluded her in this way. However, settlements made before the breakdown of the marriage, designed, for example, for tax purposes, may quite legitimately exclude both the settlor and his wife in favour of their children or grandchildren. It will normally be appropriate to review carefully all settlements created by the parties to the divorce, to see whether the assets settled would be available to either of them as part of the settlement of the wife's financial claims.

732 Either party to the marriage may be a beneficiary or a discretionary object of a settlement created by someone else, and these expectations will need to be taken into account. In these cases, however, difficulty arises in establishing the likelihood that he or she will actually benefit from it. Although trustees may produce evidence that it is not their intention to apply the trust assets or income for the benefit of the party concerned, the point may be taken by the other side that there is a real prospect that the trustees may change their minds at a later date. The court tends to take a realistic view in these circumstances. In one case with which we were concerned, trustees had said that they would not make money available to the husband. The judge made a financial order for a capital payment that would have left the husband in great difficulties if he had not benefited from such a discretionary trust, but he subsequently appeared to have no great difficulty in meeting the order.

TAX ASPECTS

733 It is not within the scope of this book to deal in any comprehensive way with the tax implications of divorce settlements. Generally, it will be necessary to take account of taxation in three principal circumstances:

- ensuring the correct amount is deducted for outstanding liabilities in estimating a husband's financial resources;
- accounting for all the capital gains tax implications of a realisation of all the assets at the values ascribed to them; and
- considering the tax consequences of alternative means for financing the settlement.

Assessing the outstanding tax liabilities in respect of income tax and CGT will normally be straightforward. The accountant adviser can, however, ensure that such liabilities are not overstated where in more complex cases there may be significant relief available from, for example, Lloyd's losses, or capital losses as opposed to capital gains.

734 In considering the capital gains tax arising on a realisation of all of the husband's assets, a distinction needs to be made between that part of the total liability which will actually arise on the disposal of those assets which are expected to be transferred or sold, and the deferred part that would arise on a sale of those assets which are expected to be retained by their present owner. In computing the CGT liability, the availability of roll-over relief, gift relief and retirement relief should be considered.

735 In those cases where a settlement is arranged soon after the breakdown of the marriage, it may be possible to take advantage of the exemption from CGT of a transfer of assets between spouses made in the same tax year as the separation, but generally in substantial cases it is unlikely that a financial settlement can be achieved in the same tax year.

736 The tax consequences of the various courses of action open to the parties in achieving a financial settlement will need to be carefully considered by the accountants, with particular regard to the most tax-efficient way of raising a required capital sum or effecting a transfer of assets between the parties. Areas of particular complexity may be the tax implications of using funds settled in trust and the separation of the parties' interests in jointly held property. In all of these areas it is important that the court and the legal advisers to both parties should have the clearest possible view of the tax implications.

THE FINANCIAL SETTLEMENT

737 Having once established the financial resources, the accountant adviser can play an important role helping to develop proposals for a financial settlement. This work may include all or any of the following:

- identifying ways in which cash can be raised and the fiscal consequences of various courses of action;
- helping to compile a budget of the wife's 'reasonable requirements';
- computing the capital sum necessary in a 'clean break' case to enable those requirements to be met.

Raising the cash

738 In most cases where the parties have substantial financial resources, the wife's claims will be met, in whole or in part, by the payment of a capital sum. Husbands frequently assert that they have no ability to raise the necessary liquid funds, but these assertions are often shown to be exaggerated once the financial arrangements have been determined. In one case with which we were concerned, the husband gave evidence that his business was going through a difficult period and he expected it to be three years before it had recovered to a point where he could raise any money by disposing of a minority interest. The court awarded the wife a lump sum deferred for three years. Within a few days of the hearing the husband made an offer to settle for a smaller lump sum, payable immediately. Sometimes the court orders a lump sum of a certain amount then adjourns for, say, a few months, to give the husband time to make proposals as to how the money should be raised. Accountants on both sides may be able to help the court with this.

739 It can be of great importance to persuade the court that a capital sum being sought by the wife is not only reasonable, in relation to the total financial resources of the husband, but is also capable of being raised in practice without damaging the family business. An experienced accountant can play a crucial part in persuading the court of this.

Quantifying the wife's 'reasonable requirements'

740 In order to establish the wife's 'reasonable requirements', it will often be necessary to produce a budget based on a combination of her own actual past expenditure and the husband's past expenditure in supporting the matrimonial home and meeting expenditure which in the future the wife will have to bear herself. Allowance should also be made for expenditure which may not have been incurred in the past but which might be regarded as reasonable. For example, even if the family have not taken a holiday for some years it would still be necessary to allow in the budget for reasonable holidays.

741 In many cases, it is possible to take a broad view of the wife's reasonable requirements without the need for the preparation of detailed budgets, but in some cases the detailed budget approach is appropriate and the accountant may be the person best placed to carry out the analysis that then becomes necessary. This involves not only an analysis of past actual expenditure but also estimates relating to a prospectively different regime in the future. For example, the wife of the owner of a large landed estate was faced with the prospect of re-housing herself in a house that was suitable, but less magnificent, than the one occupied by the family during the marriage. The projections had to be made on the basis of her new style of house, rather than on the family's actual past expenditure.

Computing the capital sum

742 It has been established by the courts in 'clean break' cases, ie those involving the payment of a capital lump sum rather than periodic maintenance payments, that it should not be assumed that the wife will live only off the income from the lump sum, but that the capital sum itself will be used up over her remaining life. In short, she is expected to live on a mixture of income and capital. This gives rise to a need to compute how much capital is necessary to sustain a given standard of living. We have developed a computer model which has been used in court on a number of occasions including the case of *Duxbury v Duxbury*[4] after which it has come to be known. The model is designed to evaluate the capital sum necessary to provide the net after tax annual sum necessary to meet the wife's reasonable requirements, assuming that she will live for a period exactly equal to her average actuarial expectation of life. The following factors are fed into the model:

- a stated level of annual inflation;
- a stated level of income return on the portfolio in which it is assumed that the lump sum will be invested;
- a stated average level of annual capital growth of the investment portfolio; and
- a stated annual percentage increase in the income tax reliefs and tax rate bands.

743 The model calculates the capital sum necessary if all the assumptions proved to be true, or the annual level of expenditure that could be provided from a given lump sum under those conditions. By evaluating variations in the assumptions, it is possible to test the sensitivity of the wife's requirements to variations in circumstances, such as:

- the receipt of a pension from a given date in the future;

- the receipt of a capital sum at a future date (sometimes when the children have left home the wife can reasonably expect to move to a smaller house, thus releasing capital to produce income to maintain her); and

- a change in the tax regime, for example, because of a change of government in the United Kingdom, or because the wife might move to a different jurisdiction at some future date.

744 The impact of the factors listed in para **742** can have a significant effect. A high income return may be obtained on the portfolio if it is invested in fixed interest securities, but it would then be vulnerable to the impact of inflation. Conversely, protection against inflation may be achievable but only at the expense of a low income return. The assumption normally made is that the lump sum will be invested in a mixed portfolio designed to balance these factors, giving, under present conditions, an average income return of the order of 4½% on the portfolio and capital growth at the rate of inflation.

745 The assumption is commonly made that the tax regime in operation at the time of the case will continue throughout the period of the projection, with reliefs and rate bands rising at the same rate as inflation. However, following the reduction in the top rate of tax to 40% it may not be realistic to assume that this situation will continue for 20 years or more into the future, and in recent years the increase in the income bands and allowances have lagged behind inflation. From the wife's point of view, it seems desirable to achieve a financial settlement that makes some provision for a deterioration in the tax regime in the future and therefore to put forward alternative calculations showing the effect on the lump sum requirement of various levels of future taxation.

746 While it is recognised that future events will inevitably diverge from whatever assumptions are made, the Duxbury model does enable a range of different assumptions to be evaluated so that the sensitivity of the capital sum required can be assessed. The results produced by such computations cannot, of course, be prescriptive of the capital sum to be awarded, but they have been referred to in the High Court as a useful tool to assist the judge in the exercise of his discretion. It has to be remembered that Duxbury calculations should be treated as the servant rather than the master. (There is sometimes a tendency in 'big money' cases to treat them as almost conclusive of the sum to be paid; this temptation should be avoided.)

EXPERT EVIDENCE

747 In the minority of cases in which the wife's application for ancillary relief actually comes to trial, the accountant may be required to give evidence as an expert witness, or possibly, where he is the husband's accountant, as a professional witness as to fact (for example, in relation to the husband's tax position). Guidance for the accountant faced with either of these situations is given in Chapter 19.

CONCLUSION

748 The late Joseph Jackson QC in his leading work on matrimonial disputes wrote:

> 'In general, insufficient reference is made to accountants in regard to both pure accountancy matters and in regard to financial implications of the matters in hand. It is far from unknown for the advice of an accountant employed by one side to be of the utmost assistance to both parties in working out their financial differences and requirements. It not infrequently happens that once the accountants have done their work agreements become possible since the basic facts are ascertained and agreed.'[5]

We would echo these sentiments and prophesy that the use of accountants in complex matrimonial finance disputes will continue to increase.

NOTES

1 [1990] 1 FLR 319 at 322.
2 [1989] 1 FLR 119.
3 'What price a widow's mite? An Actuarial Assessment of Lost Pension Rights' by Nicholas Mostyn, Philip Moor and Peter Singer QC, barristers, and Paul Meins and Tim Sexton, Fellows of the Institute of Actuaries, of Coopers & Lybrand Deloitte [1991] 21 FL 8.
4 [1987] 1 FLR 7, CA.
5 *Jackson's Matrimonial Finance and Taxation* (4th edn, 1986) Butterworths, at p 107.

Chapter 8

Professional negligence: accountants

General background – The court's view of professions – The main causes of trouble for the accountancy profession – Essential constituents of a successful negligence claim – Existence of a duty of care – The *Caparo* case – Extending the Caparo principle to takeover situations – A breach of that duty of care – Inadequate planning, controlling and recording of audits – Inadequate ascertainment of the enterprise's accounting system and improper reliance on internal controls – Failure to obtain relevant and reliable audit evidence – Errors in reviewing financial statements – Errors in reporting – General standards of competence – Foreseeable damage resulting from that breach – Foreseeability – Causation – Quantification of damage – Lost investment – Over-payment – Moneys wrongly paid out – Defalcations by directors or employees of audited enterprises – Cost of fresh audit and investigation – The expert's approach from the plaintiff's perspective – The expert's approach from the defendant's perspective – Carrying out initial reviews on behalf of litigants – Summary

General background

801   An expert accountant may be appointed by either a plaintiff or a defendant in an accountant's negligence claim, to give expert evidence on whether the work carried out met the appropriate standard of care. He may also be asked to assist the court on the quantification of damage suffered from the alleged negligent act.

802   The incidence of claims against accountants and auditors is increasing. For forensic accountants, acting for the plaintiff or the defendant in audit negligence cases has now become the single most important branch of their work. This chapter begins by considering the court's approach to professional work. It goes on to look at the essential constituents of a successful negligence claim and applies these to the practicalities of acting for the plaintiff or the defendant. Recent case law, for example, the *Caparo* and *Galoo* decisions, has been quoted in some detail. However, this book is not a legal treatise and, necessarily, the quotes are selective rather than comprehensive. Furthermore, this is an area of law which is constantly being refined as new cases continue to be brought before the courts, and appropriate legal advice should be taken where necessary.

The court's view of professions

803   The nature of professional work is that it is skilled and specialised and the work is mental rather than physical. A period of training is usually required, prior to qualification, and there will be a professional association which regulates entry and issues codes of practice. Professional practitioners are expected to go beyond the general duty of honesty; they are expected to observe high standards of service and to be concerned about confidentiality. Traditionally, professions operate in spheres where success cannot be achieved in every case. This is clearly the case for the doctor or the barrister, but it is equally valid for an accountant: he cannot guarantee success. Matters of judgment enter into his operations and no one can expect him to get it right every time.

804   It is useful to recall these characteristics of a profession, since they illustrate the underlying problems which have faced the courts in devising an approach to negligence claims. Broadly speaking, the solution which has been found is to require a professional to possess a certain degree of competence and to exercise a reasonable degree of skill and care in carrying out his work. The court does not expect him to be right every time.

The main causes of trouble for the accountancy profession

805   The underwriters of professional negligence ('errors and omissions') policies reported in Issue 25 (Autumn 1993) of the Bowring reports on professional indemnity, that by far the greatest concentration of claims against accountants arise from audits and from tax work in its various forms. Indeed, tax claims account for 57%, and audit work for 25%, of the total number of claims. In terms of value, the audit claims vastly outweigh those for tax work. The audit claims can be broken down as follows:

	%
Failure to detect fraud	24
Other audit negligence	32
Third party reliance	16
Other	28
	100

It is noted that third party reliance is on the decrease, probably as a consequence of the *Caparo v Dickman*[1] decision which limited accountants' liability to third parties (see paras **813ff**).

806   The message is clear cut. Tax and audit work together amount to around 80% of all claims brought against accountants. So far as tax is concerned, it has already been noted that this is a category where claims frequently arise, usually because of administrative failures rather than negligent advice. There is a tendency for the Inland Revenue authorities to 'go by the book' when dealing with taxpayers' affairs and it is very difficult for the clients to persuade the Revenue to allow a missed election, for instance, to be made on a discretionary basis. For the remainder of this chapter, discussion is concentrated on the topics of audit and accountancy preparation which continue to be the chief subject (in terms of value) of professional negligence cases.

ESSENTIAL CONSTITUENTS OF A SUCCESSFUL NEGLIGENCE CLAIM

807 The essential constituents are:

(a) existence of a duty of care;
(b) a breach of that duty; and
(c) foreseeable damage resulting from that breach.

In the first place, all these matters are for assessment by the lawyer. The lawyer will look in turn to the expert accountant for advice on (b), whether breach can be proved (ie whether the accountant has failed to exercise reasonable skill and care), and therefore much of the rest of this chapter dwells on what might constitute 'negligence', which is synonymous with 'breach' in this context. First, however, let us think about the existence and direction of the duty itself.

(a) Existence of a duty of care

808 The starting point when seeking to define what duty is owed and to whom it is owed is to examine the statutory or contractual requirements. For auditors of limited companies, the main duties are contained in the Companies Act 1985 s 236 which can be briefly summarised as follows:

(a) to make a report to members on the accounts laid before meetings of members;
(b) to confirm whether, in their opinion, the accounts present a true and fair view, and have been properly prepared in accordance with the Act; and
(c) to report, by exception, if the accounting records are inadequate, or the accounts are not in accordance with the accounting records and returns.

809 For the discharge of their duties, the auditors are given certain rights of which the most important are the right of access to the company's records and the right to require from the officers of the company such explanations and information as the auditors deem necessary for completion of their task.

810 For other duties carried out by accountants, the extent and nature of the task will be defined by the terms of his engagement by his client. Whether a duty of care exists when a professional accountant provides an opinion or advice depends on the circumstances of the case and how it relates to principles established in case law.

811 The standards of care with which the duty ought to be carried through, are discussed at paras **823ff**; what we must now consider is to whom the duty is owed. The leading general case on duty of care is *Donoghue v Stevenson*.[2] The unfortunate Mrs Donoghue became severely ill after consuming a bottle of ginger beer which was alleged to have contained the decomposing remains of a snail. Mrs Donoghue successfully sued the bottlers for negligence because the judge, Lord Atkin, expounded 'the neighbour principle' in which it was held that the test of the existence of duty of care was 'reasonable foreseeability'.

812 The contours of accountants' liability to third parties have been delineated with greater precision by the courts over the years since *Donoghue v Stevenson*;

the courts have, in particular, applied a wide variety of sometimes conflicting interpretations as to the scope of obligations entered into by an auditor; but as noted above, in February 1990 a more precise interpretation of auditors' duties of care emerged from the *Caparo* decision .

The Caparo *case*

813   The background was as follows. Touche Ross were the auditors of a quoted company, Fidelity plc. After Fidelity's 1984 statutory accounts were published, Caparo began purchasing shares in the company and subsequently launched a takeover bid. A little over a year later, in July 1985, Caparo commenced an action against Touche Ross and two directors of Fidelity, alleging that the published pre-tax profit of £1.3m should have been a loss of £400,000. Had the true position been known, Caparo alleged, it would have not have made the bid. The question of whether the auditors owed a duty of care to Caparo was tried as a preliminary issue.

814   The judge at first instance held that Touche Ross owed no duty of care to investors or to individual shareholders. The Court of Appeal agreed that a duty of care at common law did not exist between the auditors and a potential investor, but held that such a duty did exist between the auditor and an individual shareholder. The auditors appealed to the House of Lords which supported the judge's findings.

815   The reasoning of the House of Lords was as follows. A duty of care can arise in various circumstances. For example, when making statements in the course of his work, a professional man owes a duty of care to the client who employs him, and will be liable (in contract and in tort) for losses which his client may suffer arising from a breach of that duty.

816   A duty of care may also be owed to a third party (in the absence of a contractual relationship) if the professional is aware of the transaction contemplated by the third party, that his advice will be made available to the third party, and that the third party will rely on that advice in deciding whether to complete the transaction.

817   The situation is entirely different when a statement is effectively put into general circulation and might be relied on by strangers for many different purposes. It is almost always foreseeable that someone, somewhere, and in some circumstances, may choose to rely on a report or statement, but to hold a professional man liable to such a person would open up a limitless vista of uninsurable risk. Their Lordships placed great store by Lord Denning's dissenting judgment in *Candler v Crane Christmas & Co*[3] and its subsequent approval in *Hedley Byrne*.[4] There must be a 'special relationship' between the professional and third party for a duty of care to be owed.

818   Caparo had argued that the auditors should have expected that a takeover bid might be made and that this was sufficient to create a special relationship with potential bidders. This argument failed because there is nothing in the statutory duties of an auditor to suggest that Parliament intended those duties to protect the interest of investors in the market. Statutory accounts are published with the principal purpose of providing shareholders, as a class, with information relevant to exercising their proprietary interest in a company. They are not published to assist individuals, whether shareholders or not, to speculate with a view to profit.

819   Lenders might also wish to rely on statutory accounts. However, whilst the duty owed by the auditors to bankers and creditors who refer to statutory accounts was not an issue in this case, their Lordships took the opportunity of approving the decision in *Al Saudi Banque v Clarke Pixley*[5] that no such duty was owed. (They did not consider in detail the position of a shareholder who relies on the audited accounts in deciding to sell shares.)

Extending the Caparo *principle to takeover situations*

820   The application of the *Caparo* principle was discussed by the Court of Appeal in a later case, *Morgan Crucible Co plc v Hill Samuel Bank Ltd.*[6] In late 1985 Morgan Crucible launched an ultimately successful hostile bid to take over First Castle Electronics plc ('First Castle'). Morgan Crucible subsequently contended that First Castle was worthless and that in making its bid and then, more particularly, in increasing its offer, it had relied upon misleading defence documents. These included a profit forecast issued by First Castle's directors which was supported by reports from Hill Samuel (merchant bank to First Castle) and Judkins (reporting accountants to First Castle). Morgan Crucible alleged that the directors and financial advisers were each negligent in making representations in the defence documents which had caused its loss. Morgan Crucible argued that its bid placed it in a position of 'proximity' to all the defendants and that therefore they each owed Morgan Crucible a duty to take reasonable care in making statements in defence documents.

821   Following the *Caparo* decision, the defendants applied to strike out the claim, and Morgan Crucible sought leave to amend its statement of claim, the principal purpose of the amendments being to restrict the claim to representations made by the respective defendants after Morgan Crucible's bid became known, ie during the course of the takeover battle. The judge at first instance rejected the application on the grounds that, following *Caparo*, the defendants had no case to answer. The Court of Appeal overturned this decision. It distinguished *Morgan Crucible* from *Caparo* on the basis of the assumed facts. In particular, it assumed that in making representations about First Castle's profit forecast in the defence documents, the accountants were aware that Morgan Crucible would rely on them for the purpose of deciding whether or not to make an increased bid and intended that they should do so. On this assumption, the Court of Appeal decided that the proposed amendments to the claim were not bound to fail at trial. In the event, the case settled before the full trial and so the court did not have to make a decision on the basis of full facts. The *Morgan Crucible* case was essentially about negligent misstatement, not a case where a duty of care may arise due to the relationship between the parties. As such, it is a sign post rather than a clear landmark in the developing law relating to accountants' negligence.

822   Another case relating to the duties of accountants in a takeover was decided by the Court of Appeal in *James McNaughton Paper Group Ltd v Hicks Anderson & Co.*[7] Here, in contrast with the *Morgan Crucible* case, a friendly merger was negotiated between the plaintiff company, McNaughton, and another company, the target. The chairman of the target company had asked his accountant to prepare draft accounts which were later found to have been negligently prepared. McNaughton claimed that they had relied on them and were owed a duty of care. However, the Court of Appeal ruled otherwise, the reasoning being:

(a) the fact that they were 'draft' accounts put the reader on notice that more work was needed on them;
(b) it was known to the purchasers that the accounts had been prepared with great speed to meet a tight timetable;
(c) the target company was plainly in a poor state and the acquirer could be expected to consult with his own advisers; and
(d) this was a transaction between experienced businessmen who should have been aware of the risks.

(b) A breach of that duty of care

823   If a duty of care does exist, what is the standard of duty of care that is owed? We have seen that it will differ from individual to individual according to his professional expertise and according to the circumstances of the case.

824   Whether an accounting or audit default amounts to negligence will depend on the circumstances and on the legal principles which have evolved. The guiding principles were established almost a century ago in the well-known case *Re Kingston Cotton Mill Co (No 2)*.[8] It was held there that a breach of duty of care takes place if there is a failure to take such reasonable care as a reasonably competent person, having the skill which the defendant held himself out as having, would have taken. The test that the court will apply is whether, without the benefit of hindsight, a responsible body of professional opinion would have supported the action taken by the professional at the time. The court is not concerned with best practice, but with reasonable common practice. In summary, was what was done reasonable, in the circumstances, at the time?

825   A professional person is not negligent if he follows reasonable practice that a body of professional opinion would have supported. It follows that a starting point in assessing 'reasonable practice' is to examine the standards laid down by his professional body. The Institute of Chartered Accountants in England and Wales and similar bodies in England, Scotland and Ireland have developed accounting standards, auditing guidelines, and practice statements which, prima facie, could be taken by the court as evidence of reasonable practice (see Appendix F). The degree of expertise assumed to be reasonable will vary with the skill claimed by the professional. If any accountant claims to have special expertise, for example as a tax adviser, the courts will judge his actions in terms of the reasonable common practice of tax specialists, and not of accountants in general.

826   In the case of *Lloyd Cheyham & Co Ltd v Littlejohn & Co*,[9] Woolf J said of Statements of Standard Accounting Practice (SSAPs):

'While they are not conclusive, so that a departure from their terms necessarily involves a breach of the duty of care, and they are not, as the explanatory foreword makes clear, rigid rules, they are very strong evidence as to what is the proper standard which should be adopted and unless there is some justification, a departure from this will be regarded as constituting a breach of duty'.

827 The Statements of Auditing Standards (SASs) should be briefly explained. SASs are divided into 6 groups as follows:

(i)   responsibility;
(ii) planning, controlling and recording;
(iii) accounting systems and internal control;
(iv) evidence;
(v)   using the work of others; and
(vi) reporting.

The first group of SASs covers the general objectives of auditing as well as issues such as fraud and error, law and regulations and the going concern basis. Groups (ii) to (v) deal with auditors' duties in the course of the actual audit, preparatory to writing the report.

SASs contain basic principles and essential procedures ('Auditing Standards') which are expected to be followed in the conduct of an audit. They also contain additional material giving guidance on:

(1)   procedures by which the auditing standards may be applied;
(2)   the application of the auditing standards to specific items appearing in the financial statements of the enterprises; and
(3)   the audit problems relating to particular commercial or legal circumstances, or to specific industries.

Reference is made below to some of these statements and the manner in which they should be viewed as evidence of reasonable practice when advising the court on negligence claims.

Inadequate planning, controlling and recording of audits

828   SAS 200, 210, 220, 230 and 240 make it very clear that the auditor should plan and control and record his work. It is vital that the audit should be properly planned and controlled and that the tests devised by the auditor are appropriate to enable him to express an opinion on the financial statements. In the case of *Pacific Acceptance Corpn Ltd v Forsyth*,[10] the judge recognised that it was usual practice in all but the simplest audits for an auditor to lay out a written programme of work, and that the programme served many purposes. He also concluded that the failure of an auditor to keep such a programme up to date would tend to indicate that there were shortcomings in his work and was evidence of negligence.

Inadequate ascertainment of the enterprise's accounting system and improper reliance on internal controls

829   SAS 300 para 2 provides that the auditor should obtain an understanding of the accounting and internal control systems sufficient to enable him to plan the audit and to develop an effective audit approach. Paragraph 27 of the same statement provides that: 'if auditors ... expect to be able to rely on their assessment of control risk ... [they] should plan and perform tests of control'. It has long been established that an auditor is entitled to rely on the internal control system (see *International Laboratories Ltd v Dewer*[11]). However, before placing any reliance on them there is a need to ascertain the systems and to assess their operation and effectiveness.

Failure to obtain relevant and reliable audit evidence

830   SAS 400 para 2 states that: 'auditors should obtain sufficient appropriate audit evidence to be able to draw reasonable conclusions on which to base the audit opinion'. The statement emphasises the requirements of sufficiency and appropriateness of audit evidence. The statement gives certain general presumptions regarding the reliability of audit evidence:

- evidence from external sources is more reliable than that obtained from the entity's records;
- evidence obtained from the entity's records is more reliable when the related accounting and internal control system operates effectively;
- evidence obtained directly by the auditors is more reliable than that obtained by or from the entity;
- evidence in the form of documents and written representations is more reliable than oral representations;
- original documents are more reliable than oral representations; and
- original documents are more reliable than photocopies, telexes or facsimiles.

The application of the techniques of inspection and enquiry has been the subject of a large number of reported professional negligence claims against auditors (an auditor's reliance on an oral answer to his enquiry of a particular person, rather than on the inspection of material documents, if available, can often be damning).

Errors in reviewing financial statements

831   SAS 470 states that auditors should carry out such a review of the financial statements as is sufficient in conjunction with the conclusions drawn from the other audit evidence obtained, to give them a reasonable basis for their opinion on the financial statements. Our experience of litigation suggests that the last stages of the overall review ought to receive greater attention than any other stages of the audit. Problems become particularly acute when a matter requiring further investigation arises or comes to light at a very late stage of the audit. If more time is needed, the auditor should ask the board to have, for instance, the annual general meeting adjourned; urgency or lack of time is no excuse and will not provide a defence to a negligence action (see *Pacific Acceptance Corpn v Forsyth*[12]).

Errors in reporting

832   The product of an auditor's work is his report upon the enterprise's financial statements. If there has been error or negligence in conducting the audit then this may have some reflection and unfortunate impact on one or other sentences in the standard audit report. For example, if there has been inadequate inspection of material documents then qualifications ought to have been voiced in the report, or there should have been a disclaimer of an opinion. The requirement is that a qualified audit report should leave the reader in no doubt as to its meaning (*London & General Bank*[13]).

General standards of competence

833   Published standards are not the only sources of reference on reasonable practice. Firms of accountants produce practice manuals for their staff and partners which may set higher levels of professional excellence than the published standards. Whether these documents mean that those firms owe a higher duty of care to their clients, in other words 'by their own standards will they be judged', is unclear, but failure to meet internal guidelines will certainly make adverse inferences easier to draw.

834 Regardless of standards, published internally or externally, there remains the very important factor of reasonable skill and care being applied to the task. The expert giving evidence in a negligence case concerning, say, an audit will typically want to establish the following.

(a) Did the auditor seek adequate reliable evidence?
(b) Did the auditor investigate properly any material unusual matter which came to his attention?
(c) Did the auditor exercise reasonable professional judgment in forming his opinion ?

835 Below we describe some of the most common causes of claims for audit negligence, based on the experience reflected in the reports of professional indemnity insurers.

836 Certain accounting assignments obviously fall within what we may call high risk areas, such as assessing profit forecasts, and these will generally be preceded by the complete armoury of fully documented caveats and disclaimers so as to avoid the risk of litigation. Such caveats and disclaimers may still not provide a complete defence to a legal claim. Yet in reality it is the more routine duties, particularly those relating to the audit, which give rise to claims. Recent years have witnessed concerted attempts by firms to 'rationalise' their audit efforts, by developing audit techniques and written audit programmes to address directly the risk factors implicit in the audit process.

837 However, reliance on programmes will not of itself suffice. Certain problems keep on cropping up in negligence cases, even though the auditor concerned has conformed to his firm's procedures. Most obvious are the following.

(a) The use of inexperienced audit staff, lacking the training and experience appropriate for the responsibilities allocated to them.
(b) Lack of continuity. There may be insufficient continuity of staff from one audit to another resulting in the unsatisfactory follow-up of critical phases of the current audit.
(c) Incomplete written evidence. This is a particularly damaging aspect of many auditors' working papers.
(d) Inadequate compliance testing. Too much reliance may have been placed on controls supposedly operated by client staff without first ensuring that these controls are operating in accordance with the procedures laid down by the finance department.
(e) Unjustified sample sizes. Inadequate sample sizes for audit tests may lead to incorrect conclusions being drawn.
(f) Defective partner reviews. Subsequent enquiry may reveal a failure on the part of the audit partner to ask the 'right questions' when reviewing financial statements. There may also have been a failure to focus on the most revealing relationships and ratios, or to make full use of comparisons with earlier

periods, or with forecasts, or with the results of other businesses in similar trading circumstances. An inadequate review of the post-balance sheet period may also lead to audit failure.

(g) A failure to relate the findings of the audit as a whole to the opinion expressed in the audit report. This defect will normally come directly from a failure on the part of the partner responsible for the audit to take into account (or even to seek) the views of others. If he fails to draw the right conclusions, the highly concentrated and costly audit effort is nullified.

(h) A failure to distinguish flexibility from compromise. No matter how much effort is made to avoid unpleasant confrontations with the client, deeply held and differing views may on occasion render them inevitable. All auditors are naturally prepared to demonstrate flexibility in an understandable and reasonable desire to accommodate the view of the board of directors on matters of accounting treatment, especially since no individual can claim possession of divine insight on complex judgmental issues. However, that fateful step onto what has elsewhere been referred to as 'the slippery slope' is taken when the auditor loses his sense of proportion and where acquiescent compromise begins or takes over.

(i) Rigid adherence to a set programme, resulting in a failure to spot problems which a bit of lateral thinking might have picked up (ie fraud).

838 It will be seen that many of the above points relate to the judgment made by the partner in charge of the audit. An experienced view is needed from him in order for him to judge whether the financial statements are plausible in all circumstances. He needs, therefore, to possess sufficient knowledge of the client's business to enable him to make both intelligent enquiries, and a reasonable assessment of the responses to them. Not only should he be aware of the general nature of the organisation, its assets and liabilities, but he should also have an understanding of the accounting matters peculiar to the business and to the industry of which it is a part.

(c) Foreseeable damage resulting from that breach

839 There are two tests to pass here.

(i) Was the damage foreseeable?
(ii) Was the damage caused by the breach of the duty of care?

(i) Foreseeability

840 The case which established the general principle of foreseeability was *The Wagon Mound*.[14] As a result of negligence, furnace oil was discharged on to water in a wharf where a ship, the Wagon Mound, was moored. The following day, while the plaintiffs were welding, molten metal fell into the water and ignited the oil which then destroyed the Wagon Mound. The oil was believed by the plaintiffs and defendants to be non-flammable. It was held that the fire and consequent damage were not foreseeable; although the defendants' negligence had caused the loss, compensation would not be awarded because the damage was not foreseeable.

841 If the 'foreseeability test' is passed, liability for damage extends to all loss caused by the negligence which could reasonably have been foreseen at the time of the negligent act.

(ii) Causation

842   The loss must derive directly from the negligent act and not have some other cause. For example, although it may be clear that there were material errors in a set of audited accounts, it is often far less clear that the plaintiff relied wholly or even in part on those accounts in taking the action that gave rise to his loss. It is reasonable to pose the question: 'If the audit had been of the highest standard would the plaintiff have taken different decisions?' It is surprising how often the answer is that it would have made no difference - the loss would have been incurred in any event.

843   An important judgment on the question of causation was given recently in the case of *Galoo Ltd v Bright Grahame Murray*.[15] This was an action for damages against the auditors of a company which had been allowed to continue to trade and had been supported by large loans from its holding company, Hillsdown Holdings. Galoo went into liquidation in 1991, following massive losses, and Hillsdown claimed that a series of negligent audit reports had meant that it had lent money to a company that should have been wound up years earlier.

844   The Court of Appeal held that the proper method for determining 'reasonable cause' in such actions is a two-part process. First it is necessary to ascertain that the allegedly negligent act allowed an 'occasion for damage' to occur. The second step is to apply common sense in deciding whether the act was in fact the 'effective or dominant cause' of such damage. An act that merely provides the occasion for loss cannot necessarily be said to have caused the damage.

845   Applying this principle to the *Galoo* case, the court found that the fact that the subsidiary had sustained trading losses after the issue of the audit report (which report was assumed to be negligent solely for the purpose of the argument) did not necessarily mean that the losses were caused by the assumed negligence. It was determined that although the unqualified audit report provided Galoo with the opportunity to continue to trade and incur losses, those losses flowed from the trading rather than the provision of the audit report. Moreover, it was found that the acceptance of a loan cannot of itself be described as a loss causing damage and, if anything, it is a benefit to the borrower.

846   The decision means that in future it will be the plaintiff's responsibility to show a causal link between any audit negligence and subsequent trading losses incurred by the company. It will not be sufficient simply to show that the negligent audit work enabled the losses to be sustained. Damages for trading losses suffered, loan obligations incurred and other losses forming part of the company's normal activities will, in future, be far more difficult to recover from auditors.

QUANTIFICATION OF DAMAGE

847   In addition to giving evidence as to liability, an expert accountant may also be asked to assist the court on quantum, that is, the amount of the loss suffered from the alleged negligent act. This work requires an analysis of factors causing the loss to be carried out and an evaluation of the financial consequences that would have followed if the alleged negligence had not occurred. The usual remedy for breach of duty by an auditor is an award of damages.

848 The chain of causation, ie between the breach and the actual loss, must be established if damages are to result. Only those damages caused by not having fulfilled the duty as, say, the auditor of the company, can be recovered. The chain of causation may be broken by the act or omission of the plaintiff or by some third person. An accountant's liability for loss may also be reduced to the extent that it may have been a result partly of his own fault, and partly that of the plaintiff. A question that frequently arises is whether an auditor sued by the company for a negligent audit of its accounts, may have his liability reduced on the grounds that the directors or the management of the company were themselves negligent in their control of its accounts or affairs. In the New Zealand case of *Nelson Guarantee Corpn Ltd v Hodgson*,[16] the judge said that he would have held the executive of the plaintiff company 50% contributory negligent had the plaintiff company not failed in its claim against its auditors for alleged negligence in not discovering earlier the defalcations of an employee. On the other hand, in the Australian case of *Simonius Vischer & Co v Holt and Thompson*[17] one judge held that the defence of contributory negligence was not available to an auditor as a matter of law in such circumstances.

849 Whether the claim is brought in contract or tort, or by way of a misfeasance summons, the fundamental principle governing the measure of damages is that the plaintiff must be put, so far as money can do it, in the position he would have occupied if the negligent act had not been committed. There are certain types of loss which are of common occurrence and are considered below. The discussion is not necessarily definitive and ultimately the appropriate measure of loss, and the types of loss, depend upon the facts of each case and upon the advice of the lawyer.

Lost investment

850 Where the profitability of an enterprise is over-stated in a prospectus or in an accountant's report, due to negligence on the part of the accountant, and in reliance thereon a person is induced to make an investment in the enterprise which he would otherwise not have made, then if the enterprise becomes insolvent and the investor loses his investment, the normal measure of damages will be the amount of the original investment.

Over-payment

851 In consequence of negligence by an accountant, the investor may pay more for acquiring shares in a company than he would have done if proper advice or information had been given. The measure of damages recoverable against the accountant is the amount of the over-payment. This amount is calculated by comparing what would have been paid for the shares if proper advice or information had been given, with what was actually paid.

Moneys wrongly paid out

852 Where, in consequence of the negligence of the auditors of a company, its shareholders are induced to vote for dividends which would not have been voted if the auditors had properly discharged their duty, the normal measure of damages recovered by the company is the amount that it had wrongly paid out.

Defalcations by directors or employees of audited enterprises

853 Where, in consequence of an auditor's negligence, the defalcations of a director or an employee are not discovered, the normal measure of damages recoverable in the claim against him by the defrauded enterprise is as much of the defalcations unrecovered from the director or employee as would have been prevented if the auditor had properly performed his duty. It is arguable that if the defalcations are so material as to lead to the collapse of the business, for example through insolvency, and these material defalcations would have been prevented if the auditor had properly performed his duties, then the measure of damages will be the loss in the value of the whole business; this may require an earnings valuation to be made.

Cost of fresh audit and investigation

854 When consequent upon an auditor's negligence a fresh audit or a fresh investigation is necessary, the cost thereof, together with incidental legal expenses, would be the measure of damages against the auditor.

The expert's approach from the plaintiff's perspective

855 In preparing a report and giving oral testimony later at trial, the forensic accountant will generally develop his material based upon the records available to the plaintiff in the first place. A major part of his role will be designed to see if a proper audit has been done and the extent to which statutory duties and auditing standards and practices have been adhered to.

856 The usual approach is to highlight the losses caused to the plaintiff from the production of erroneous financial statements (or from the defalcation or whatever is the cause of the action) and relate them to the magnitude of the operations involved, the nature of the records and so forth. The end result should be to show how the plaintiff's situation suffered from the defective auditing and to develop a comparison of the 'but for' position with the actual financial position of the plaintiff, the difference being the measure of damages (see the discussion of the *Galoo* judgment earlier in this chapter).

857 The expert must be careful in distinguishing between negligence and an error of judgment when judgment was properly exercised. An audit involves making a judgment on certain matters which, at the time the audit takes place, cannot be proved with certainty; for example, provisions for slow moving or obsolete stock. Where the defendant professional's judgment is disputed, the plaintiff must prove either that no judgment was exercised or that the accountant's judgment was exercised negligently. If the latter, the plaintiff must demonstrate that any reasonable accountant would, on the facts in front of him, have come to a different view. In assessing such matters, the expert should exclude hindsight from his consideration.

858 In many cases, negligence claims will rest heavily on assertions regarding the failure to follow published auditing standards. The expert should be on his guard against being led by counsel to take too extreme a view on the responsibilities of auditors or accountants; for instance, it is not reasonable to expect that the very best and latest practice adopted by a leading firm of accountants necessarily represents the 'norm' which is being followed by the general body of the profession.

859 As with much litigation, the number of documents to be inspected can be enormous. Not only will the expert wish to see all the auditor's working papers, but he will also wish to inspect all papers which might have any bearing on the extent of reliance placed on the audit work, and papers relating to the losses claimed and their cause.

860 The expert should take a balanced view and not go overboard on trifling slip-ups. For example, close scrutiny of an audit file will almost always identify one or two examples of work which could have been performed better. A few such weaknesses do not in themselves constitute negligence. The expert accountant will have to consider the nature and extent of the audit work done, the way the work was recorded on the audit files, and the extent to which the audit partner exercised judgment in dealing with the matters at the heart of the negligence claim. He will also have to consider whether any errors in the audited accounts are material. What is material may vary according to the context. Immaterial errors are unlikely to constitute negligence.

861 When auditors are alleged to have failed to detect or report financial irregularities, the details will appear in the statement of claim which, depending on the division of the court, may either be lodged with the court as part of the writ or be served separately and therefore not become a public document. The claim can comprise such matters as:

(a) the losses subsequent to the irregularity beginning;
(b) overpaid taxes, to the extent results were overstated;
(c) dividend wrongly paid out of bogus profit; and
(d) audit fees for poor work.

862 The lines of argument can be that, had the problems been brought to light, imprudent conduct of management would have ceased, new management would have been introduced and if necessary, new capital obtained. Clearly the *Galoo* judgment described above must be borne in mind if this approach is adopted.

The expert's approach from the defendant's perspective

863 When an expert is called to assist the defendant's lawyer in the preparation of the case, the expert will be operating in a hostile environment. The writ will have been issued, the accusations of negligence made and, maybe, the damages quantified. The major role for the expert will be examining the circumstances of the alleged defective audit and refuting, where possible and where justifiable, the suggestion of negligence; he will also be expected to examine critically the other side's assessment of damages (which in normal circumstances will have been exaggerated materially) and, if instructed by counsel, develop alternative and more realistic estimates of damage.

864 The preparation of accounting testimony in such circumstances can be a complicated matter requiring ingenuity. It may be that many of the critical records are no longer under the control of the defendant's original client. Discovery may yield the missing information but usually a defence is required well before the detail can be obtained, which can be amended subsequently. Generally, one of the side objectives will be to challenge the plaintiff to provide reasons and data to support whatever is being alleged to be the basis of his (the plaintiff's) claim. Such data, when forthcoming, may provide the basis for challenging the financial and accounting theories of the plaintiff.

865 The accountant who accepts a defending assignment must bring to the attention of the court the ambiguities which exist in the business environment; this applies also to accounting standards and published guidelines. Basically, such standards are developed to apply to as many conditions and events as possible; they become generalisations which apply to the majority of situations. But there will be exceptions and mitigating circumstances which will excuse or justify a departure from those generalised codes of conduct. There are numerous qualifications (for example, that the true and fair view should be paramount) which may mean that the laid-down standards fail to be appropriate for the complexities of real-life situations.

866 The same ambiguity exists in statutory and case law, and experts should not necessarily be put off because there seems to have been a parallel case where audit negligence has been judged to have occurred. In short, defendants' experts must be critical, creative and, if justified, unorthodox in their approach. Hard work and plenty of lateral thinking will be needed here.

867 Public perceptions can sometimes be wide of the mark. There is a perception held by the public in general, and perhaps by the investing public as well, that the accounting and auditing profession can in some way prevent loss or fraud. Indeed, in a period of economic decline and business failures, frustrated shareholders, creditors and bankers have a propensity to regard the auditors as responsible for failing to stop the inevitable or, at the very least, to provide an appropriate warning. However, auditors will not be found liable simply because financial statements are subsequently shown to be misleading. They will only be found liable by the court if their actual performance is shown to have fallen short of that of a reasonably competent auditor, and that this was the reason the fraud or the error in the financial statements remained undiscovered, and the cause of the plaintiff's loss.

868 It is not unusual for banks to take negligence actions against accountants, for example, where they have claimed to rely on, say, a valuation before making a loan to a customer. Expert accountants are frequently asked to advise on the strength of such claims. Banks are acutely aware of the relationship between profit generation and risk. From this it is clear that successful financial management of a bank rests principally on risk evaluation: if excessive caution is exercised then opportunities are lost by the bank to more astute competitors. If, on the other hand, genuine risks are underestimated or ignored, the penalties can prove to be crippling, as indeed was the case in the early 1970s and the early

1990s when there was an ill-conceived expectation that property values would continue indefinitely to rise. The shattering consequences of that particular example of blind optimism are now part of banking legend. The expert accountant's role in such cases is therefore twofold:

(i) to determine whether the accountant's work was negligent, without the benefit of hindsight; and
(ii) to assist the defendant's solicitors in determining whether the bank relied on the accountant's work.

Carrying out initial reviews on behalf of litigants

869 The expert may initially be approached by the plaintiff when he is considering litigation. The expert's brief will be to advise on whether or not there is sufficient merit, on the basis of the information available to the plaintiff (ie an accountant's report) to justify pursuing a claim in the court. In these circumstances the expert will normally wish to see all the relevant papers already in the plaintiff's possession and to interview those who might have some knowledge of the way the prospective defendant carried out his work. He will also wish to establish, as best he can, the nature of the loss suffered and to consider whether it appears from information he has gathered that the auditors should have identified the problems in question. He should also consider with the legal advisers whether the loss actually stemmed from the auditor's alleged errors.

870 During this initial review, the expert will be at a considerable disadvantage since he will not usually have seen the defendant's papers. These will normally only become available through the discovery process, and to obtain discovery it is necessary to lodge the claim and complete the pleading process. When the auditor's files are ultimately inspected, the expert might find that, in the event, the defendant's papers show they have the making of a good defence. When advising a prospective plaintiff who is intent on pursuing a claim, the expert accountant should ensure that his client is aware that discovery may dent what seemed, prima facie, to be a good case.

871 The purpose of a review by an expert in the first place is to consider with the legal advisers whether the company should start an action for negligence against the auditors. Initially it would be based on a desk review of the papers provided, since the expert would probably not be allowed access to the audit files or working papers of the auditor concerned. (Later, if access to the audit files is achieved through the discovery process, then much else will result.) The review should be planned to deal with all material items having a bearing on the financial statements, and it is useful to summarise, if necessary using estimates, those transactions which have been excluded, undiscovered, or in some way distorted, and to relate those exclusions, omissions or distortions to the total financial statements. In this initial review it is also necessary to measure the net cumulative cash outflow or inflow arising from such defects.

872 The initial report may well be followed by an expanded initial report which will form the basis of the statement of claim or the technical part of it. It should be as comprehensive and thorough as possible; it may well be the report on which an early out of court settlement is negotiated.

SUMMARY

873 The courts have recently redefined the duty of care owed by an accountant, and it is therefore essential to be up-to-date with case law in this area of professional negligence. Assistance should obviously be sought from the client's legal advisers. Following *Caparo* it would seem that:

- the purpose of the annual audit is to give existing shareholders information on the company's past trading. It is not for the protection of potential investors or for others who enter into business relationships with the company;

- accounting firms acting as auditors should be less exposed to claims arising from takeovers as a result of their audit work on past sets of accounts of the company acquired;

- the liability of reporting accountants for a public issue has not been affected; and

- large investors and bankers should commission their own reports before they invest or lend. The small investor, who might be relying solely on the basis of statutory accounts, does so in the knowledge that such accounts were not necessarily drawn up with that in mind.

874 Accountants will be asked to act as experts when the question of liability for negligence comes to be determined in the courts. It is clearly invidious to criticise or question the competence of a fellow professional. However, the public interest requires that it should be done, so long as the expert is satisfied from his review that there is a good case to be made by the plaintiff.

875 An expert accountant who is called to assist the court on the matter of liability should recognise the need for impartiality and consistency and should guard against arguing for different standards, according to whether he is acting for a plaintiff or for a defendant. Expert witnesses really do win or lose these cases: it is clearly crucial for counsel to get the right expert, ie one who really does have the authority and experience to speak about the subject in question.

876 It will be very important to the lawyer and the client that the individual expert, from the firm he has chosen, is the right expert for the case, that is, one whose own expertise is in the area of accounting or auditing complained of. It may be necessary to have several expert accountants, giving evidence on different technical aspects, or to have the report in the name of one expert, who is in turn assisted by specialists familiar with the litigation process and the particular requirements of writing an expert witness report.

877 A charge of negligent execution of an auditing assignment is one which requires careful consideration and a high degree of proof; no hard and fast standards of universal or timeless application exist in any specific (as opposed to general) form and each case must be judged on its own terms. The closest we can come to an absolute formulation are the words 'reasonable care and skill' used repeatedly by Lindly LJ in the 1895 case of *London and General Bank*.[18] However, the degree of care and skill which measures up to the word 'reasonable' at any time and in any particular circumstances, will depend upon several contributing factors, including:

(a) the extent to which the auditor's suspicions should already have been aroused by attending circumstances, by mutually irreconcilable explanations or by past experience of the client in question;

(b) the prevailing standards of the profession at large, to the extent that they have been formulated and have a direct bearing on the matter in question; and

(c) the view of the expert witnesses called to give evidence on the extent to which, in their opinion, the auditor's conclusions were justified by the evidence presented to him, and whether his conduct as a whole accorded with that demanded by contemporary professional standards, whether or not officially formulated in published documents.

NOTES

1 *Caparo Industries plc v Dickman* [1990] 2 WLR 358.
2 [1932] AC 562, HL.
3 [1951] 2 KB 164, 179 to 184.
4 *Hedley Byrne & Co Ltd v Heller & Partners Ltd* [1964] AC 465.
5 [1990] 2 WLR 344.
6 [1991] 2 WLR 655.
7 [1991] 2 WLR 641.
8 [1896] 1 Ch 331; 2 Ch 279, CA.
9 [1987] BCLC 303.
10 (1970) 92 WNNSW 29.
11 [1993] 3 DLR 665.
12 See footnote 10.
13 [1895] 2 Ch 166.
14 *Overseas Tankship (UK) Ltd v Morts Dock and Engineering Co Ltd, The Wagon Mound* [1961] AC 388, PC.
15 [1995] 1 All ER 16.
16 [1958] NZLR 609.
17 [1979] 2 NSWLR 322.
18 See footnote 13.

Chapter 9

Commercial fraud

Introduction – The cyclical nature of fraud – Fraud's infinite variety – Conditions conducive to fraud – Fraud enquiries – Criminal investigation and prosecution processes – Powers to obtain information – Police procedures – Safeguarding documents – Documentary control systems – Interlocutory reliefs – Tracing the funds – Disclosure of information to third parties – Reports – The inter-relationship between civil and criminal proceedings – Fraud and the auditor – An overview – The auditor's responsibility to uncover fraud – Auditors' responsibilities to report fraud to regulators – Fraud alert factors – The court's view of the auditor's responsibility to detect fraud – Issues of causation.

INTRODUCTION

901 The vast majority of business transactions are conducted honestly and efficiently. In only a minority does misconduct occur, but it is worth noting that when it does, the amounts stolen can exceed by several hundred million pounds the total annual figure for burglary for the whole of England and Wales. So when fraud occurs it usually leaves chaos in its wake. It can cause enormous suffering, often to very vulnerable people who can lose a lifetime's savings to a crook. In recent years Parliament has made considerable efforts to redress the balance. In 1986 the Financial Services Act reached the statute book. It introduced a new system of regulation to cope with a post 'big bang' structure of the City, and the principal purpose of this Act was to prevent fraud. The following year a new Criminal Justice Act was passed and as a result the Serious Fraud Office was set up, the purpose of which was to improve the investigation and prosecution of serious and complex fraud. There still appears to be widespread concern about whether enough is being done to investigate and prosecute effectively those responsible for fraud.

902 This chapter begins with a description of the conditions which often apply in companies subjected to fraud. It describes the nature of fraud and the practical issues which an expert will meet in investigating it. At the end of the chapter we deal with the responsibility of auditors for uncovering fraud, including a review of case law which explains the court's developing views on this subject; this part of the chapter must be read alongside the more general advice given in Chapter 8 dealing with audit negligence generally, of which failure to discover fraud might be a part.

The cyclical nature of fraud

903   There is some evidence to suggest that corporate fraud has a cyclical life pattern. In boom conditions, when share prices are high, people use their company's paper to buy assets, usually by taking over other companies. They try to enhance the price of their own shares, or depress the price of the target company's shares, so that fewer of the acquiring company's shares have to be found to provide the purchase consideration. It is at this stage of the cycle that market manipulation fraud takes place. Sometimes the offeror pays cash or offers a cash alternative. He sees the target company replete with valuable assets and a special feature of this phase of the cycle is the financial assistance or share support fraud. Dishonest entrepreneurs emerge who cannot resist the temptation of finding a way to use the company's assets as a means of financing or helping to finance the purchase of the company's own shares. A spate of this sort of fraud seems to occur in the City every ten years or so, and their characteristics can be traced back to the South Sea Bubble.

904   The mischief, of course, lies in the unauthorised reduction of capital that occurs when a company's assets are used to purchase its own shares surreptitiously. The loss is suffered by the creditors who may see the company become insolvent, and those shareholders who have acquired their shares without the company's financial assistance, see their own shares rendered worthless.

905   As the economic cycle moves on so does the cycle of fraud. Boom conditions give way to recession. Bull markets turn into bear markets and take-over activity declines. So we experience a rather simpler system of fraud. People run short of money. They become increasingly concerned about supporting their lifestyles and their business, usually in that order, and they start re-financing themselves by issuing new shares or by borrowing. Banks continue to support their customers for a while in the hope of better times, but in the end insolvency sets in. During this period we experience deception, particularly of lending institutions, and also a fair amount of false accounting and fraudulent trading.

906   Then, as the recession deepens and the liquidators get to work, a yet more simple sort of fraud is discovered. We find that people have resorted to straightforward theft. We may then be getting towards the end of that phase of the cycle and coming back to the more sophisticated forms of fraud which we have described at the beginning of this section and so on.

Fraud's infinite variety

907   As Lord MacNaughten said: 'Fraud is infinite in its variety.' Fraud is not a specific offence in English criminal law, but there are a wide range of criminal offences which are commonly associated with fraud. These include offences under the Theft Act 1968, which are commonly used as a basis of substantive charges. For example, s 1 defines theft, s 15 deals with obtaining property by deception and s 17 makes false accounting a criminal offence. There are also offences under other statutes, for example, there are about 50 criminal offences of which directors and other officials may be convicted under the Companies Act 1985. Many of these are summary offences which would be dealt with by way of fine. However, there are more serious charges which would be prosecuted by way of indictment, for example, where a company's business was being carried on with an intent to defraud creditors. There are also offences under the Financial Services Act 1986, the Insolvency Act 1986, the Drug Trafficking Offences Act 1994 and frauds against the Inland Revenue and Customs & Excise which are prosecuted under common law. This list is not exhaustive, it merely serves to illustrate the wide range of legislation which is used to prosecute fraud.

908 Most frauds include the common constituents of deception, dishonesty and financial loss. However, not all start from an intention to deceive. Rather, they become the easy option when something goes wrong – unexpected losses arise, a share bid is threatened, the market trend is reversed, punitive or unforeseen legislation is introduced. The hitherto honest person seeks to recover his losses or to combat the effect of the crisis. He reacts to a situation and starts along a road of deception. As time goes on the web of deception becomes ever more complex and starts to involve other people who find themselves compromised and in the same sinking boat. Some fraudsters become so wound up in their deception that they find it difficult to distinguish between reality and the deception which they have created.

909 In business, fraud can be broadly categorised as 'management fraud' and 'employee fraud'. Management fraud is inherently more difficult to identify at the early stages, as senior management have the greater opportunity of covering their tracks.

910 Understanding the stimulus, business environment and methodology for fraud helps the investigating accountant to focus his thinking. The fact that so many frauds are bound to be discovered in the fullness of time does not appear to be a major deterrent to would-be fraudsters.

Conditions conducive to fraud

911 The conditions in which management frauds may occur are obviously rather different from those conditions where employee fraud will occur. The existence of any of the following circumstances will enhance opportunities for management fraud:

(a) excessive authority vesting in one person, eg a dominant Chief Executive;
(b) secretive management style;
(c) poor quality middle management often combined with a dominant Chief Executive;
(d) weak accounting systems and internal controls;
(e) complex transaction sequences or complex corporate structures;
(f) accounting policies which rely heavily on judgments of future events, and where the contingent risks are difficult to measure, even if an honest approach is taken; and
(g) related party trading.

912 The existence of these circumstances will make management fraud easier to carry out. We have already considered what motives or incentives will be conducive to fraud; some of the more common incentives for manipulating trading results and/or net assets are:

(a) management remuneration related to profits – this can be true for departments, individuals, such as dealers, or whole enterprises;
(b) significant management shareholdings;
(c) a desire to conceal bad management, particularly because of pride or worry about future careers;
(d) a need in a fast growing company to achieve or maintain a high share price to enable acquisitions to be made by the issue of the shares, or to enable borrowings to be made on a personal basis against a value of those quoted shares;
(e) evasion of taxation; and
(f) obtaining additional finance for the business from the bankers.

913 If some of the transactions involve offshore financial centres this will add to the opportunities for confusion. Frequent changes of auditors and legal advisers will also be a hallmark of unsatisfactory corporate governance. (These points were addressed by the Cadbury Committee in their report on corporate governance in 1992. Among other things, the Committee emphasised the importance of non-executive directors who might bring some independent influence and judgment to bear, particularly in cases where a dominant Chief Executive has been operating without sufficient challenge from his colleagues.)

914 When one comes to consider conditions conducive to employee fraud the list is a shorter one. Poor management controls and over reliance on individuals without any cross-checking through shared responsibilities, provide a fertile ground for employee fraud. Some common examples of this sort of fraud, which really amount to straight theft, are:

(a) bribes from suppliers;
(b) computer frauds, eg involving the manipulation of computer programs in order to direct funds into the hand of the fraudster;
(c) cheque and credit card frauds;
(d) diverting money and using other money to fill the gap (often referred to as teeming and lading); and
(e) forging management signatures on documents of authorisation.

915 Lastly, one has to consider the methodology for fraud. The Roskill Committee (which reported in January 1986) identified the following main methods.

(a) *Advance fee frauds* – these normally involve paying some form of up-front fee to the fraudster for a service to be provided, commonly for purporting to arrange a loan. The deception will often be elaborate, involving forged documents and carried out on an international scale. Most of these frauds involve a target who is willing to pay a fee for a loan, or other service, which he could not obtain through normal commercial channels.
(b) *Banking frauds* – raising bank loans on false security or through deception about a company's property values or its business and general financial standing. The money raised may be used to support an insolvent company or it may be extracted by the fraudster through a web of nominee companies. Such frauds include raising finance, such as bills of exchange or letters of credit, in respect of overstated or fictitious business transactions. Banks, together perhaps with insurance companies, are the institutions most prone to

fraud; when banks become insolvent it is often as a result of some major fraud.

(c) *Commodity frauds* – large and rapid swings in commodity prices and the opportunity to buy and sell forward in an international market has provided considerable scope for fraud. Such frauds may be perpetrated by companies upon investors in the commodity market. Commodity dealing is also used as a mechanism to conceal other frauds, partly because of the complexity of accounting for such transactions.

(d) *Computer fraud* – some computer frauds involve the manipulation of computer programs in order to direct funds into the hands of the fraudster. Such frauds include unauthorised access to computer systems controlling the electronic transfer of funds. The increasing use of computers in all forms of communication and money transactions, including credit cards, has given computer fraud an international dimension. Unauthorised access to computer systems in the UK is a criminal offence under the Computer Misuse Act 1990, but this legislation is normally used to prosecute people who hack in to computer systems, which is usually for non-fraudulent purposes.

(e) *Investment frauds* – these are frequently characterised by the offer of generous returns on funds invested. The vehicles for such frauds may be investment trust funds or false prospectuses. A generous return is sometimes explained by giving the impression that there is some special tax advantage to be gained by the investor through offshore arrangements. The fraud is often prolonged by the payments of good returns to those people who invested early out of moneys received from later investors.

(f) *Contrived insolvencies* – it is not unusual for a fraudster to contrive a voluntary liquidation in order to defraud creditors. In such cases the fraudster, or a connected party, may claim to be owed a significant amount by the insolvent company in order to be able to control voting and the appointment of a suitable liquidator.

(g) *False insurance claims* – claims may be false or partly overstated, eg, fraudulent arson, claims for theft of stock, or loss of profits claims based on false accounts.

(h) *Customs and EC fraud* – infringing the rules governing the import and export of goods from the UK and EC which are complex and at times open to interpretation. There are also frauds against the EC. These normally involve a fraudulent claim for a subsidy or grant.

FRAUD ENQUIRIES

916 When an accountant is appointed to carry out a fraud investigation he must be quite clear as to his role and terms of reference. Where he has been appointed to assist a regulator (for example, concerning a financial services misdemeanour) it is common for him to be given certain statutory powers of investigation, for example, with work from the Department of Trade & Industry ('DTI'), the Serious Fraud Office ('SFO') and the Securities & Investments Board ('SIB'). The expert accountant may also be given powers under the Insolvency Act 1986. He should know what his powers of investigation are, which mainly relate to obtaining documentary and oral evidence. The use and scope of such powers are increasingly challenged in the courts and great care must be taken not to abuse the powers – to do otherwise could lead to the admissibility of the evidence obtained by the investigator being contested.

917 Special skills may be required, for example, in banking, insurance or investment. Quite apart from technical knowledge, the expert accountant should also familiarise himself with the criminal investigation and prosecution processes. He should know the various powers he has to obtain information and to question individuals, and should learn about the documentary control systems in order to protect the integrity of documents and to ensure their admissibility as evidence. He should also have an appreciation of how civil and criminal proceedings can conflict with each other, in terms of precedence of enquiry and investigation.

918 Most of these matters have legal implications and it is important that the expert seeks legal advice during the course of his work at each new stage.

Criminal investigation and prosecution processes

919 Under English law, a criminal offence is either indictable or may be tried summarily. If indictable it must be tried in the Crown Court, and if it may only be tried summarily it must be tried in the Magistrates Court. Most fraud cases are indictable and have to be tried in the Crown Court before a jury. There are, however, certain types of offences which may be tried in either court.

920 The venue for trial will be determined before a Magistrates Court. The procedures to transfer a case for trial before a jury in a Crown Court are governed by the provisions of the Criminal Justice and Public Order Act 1994. The prosecutor is obliged to serve on the Magistrates Court and the defendant a notice of his case, which specifies the charges and includes a set of the supporting evidential documents. The accused may make an application in writing to the Magistrates Court to dismiss the case, or specific charges, made against him. After due consideration of the representations made by both the prosecutor and the defendant, the Magistrates Court will decide whether to dismiss certain charges, if it appears that there is insufficient evidence against the accused to warrant a trial by jury for the offence charged. Subject to the dismissal process, the Magistrates Court will transfer the proceedings to the Crown Court.

921 After that, a pre-trial hearing may be held prior to the case reaching the Crown Court jury. The purpose of a pre-trial hearing is to define and resolve those issues which need to be clarified prior to commencement of the trial before a jury. Such hearings are normally on legal matters and do not usually involve the expert accountant.

922 It is when the trial before the jury arrives that the report of the expert accountant will be used. Unlike witnesses of fact, an expert witness is able to sit in court before and after giving his evidence, and as a consequence he can gain a good insight into the main issues which are arising during the course of the trial. He should use this insight to form a view on how best he can help the court in clarifying the matters upon which he is likely to be questioned when giving evidence. There is sometimes disagreement between the defence and prosecution counsel as to whether the accounting witness is an expert or merely a witness of fact. (If the latter, his attendance in court may be challenged other than when presenting evidence himself.) So it is useful for the status of the investigating accountant to be clarified between counsel before his attendance occurs.

923 The conduct and ethical behaviour of the expert accountant in criminal cases should follow the same rules as for civil cases, described in Chapters 18 and 19. What arguably becomes more marked in criminal trials, is the effect of the adversarial system of trials which has evolved from common law; the trial becomes more of an open contest between skilled counsel who will seek to use a complicated set of court rules for their own advantage. In cases where the evidence of the expert accountant is crucial to the outcome of the case, he can expect to be vigorously cross-examined. He should be at pains not to become biased, or upset, or, worse still, to express ill-founded opinions in the face of what may appear to be a personal attack. The expert accountant should try to present his evidence in as simple and as clear a manner as possible. He should remember he is there to assist the court in understanding what are sometimes complex financial situations.

Powers to obtain information

924 One of the features of fraud is that it is predominantly a document-based crime. If the authorities cannot obtain the relevant documents there is no hope of finding out what happened, let alone prosecuting anyone responsible. Often, the crucial documents are in the hands of banks or professional firms who have strong obligations of confidence to their customers and clients. Major fraud cases usually involve the analysis of thousands of documents and there has to be a means of obtaining these by law to enable the investigations to take place.

925 The powers under the Criminal Justice Act 1987 s 2 provide such means of investigation in cases which are controlled by the Serious Fraud Office.

926 There are other powers laid down by statute. For instance, the police are governed by the Police and Criminal Evidence Act 1984. Inspectors appointed by the DTI or the SIB are governed by the Companies Act 1985 and/or the Financial Services Act 1986. Liquidators' powers of investigation are governed by the Insolvency Act 1986 and the Inland Revenue's powers are set out in the Taxes Management Act 1970.

927 Obviously, when an expert accountant is appointed by any one of these authorities to assist them in their work, or indeed to assist defendants who are being investigated by these authorities, he should be familiar with the particular statutes which apply.

928 The powers to obtain evidence usually include the power to interview relevant persons. Where an interview is carried out under the Criminal Justice Act 1987 s 2 there is an obligation to answer questions, and if the person being interviewed fails to answer without reasonable excuse, or tells lies in the course of the interview, he commits a criminal offence which can be punished by a term of imprisonment. These powers are viewed by some defendants with considerable suspicion, as a serious curtailment of the right of silence, and there has been much debate in Parliament as to whether it is an infringement of personal liberty and privacy. However, there are certain safeguards. The transcript of an interview carried out under the authority of the Criminal Justice Act 1987 is not generally admissible in evidence before a court. Further, a legal professional privilege applies when someone is being questioned, and a person need not answer questions if they have reasonable excuse. Interviewers should bear these possible objections in mind, although it has to be said that it is likely that investigators in serious fraud cases will retain their existing powers to require answers to questions, and indeed a Royal Commission has recommended this.

Police procedures

929   Interview procedures adopted by the police are governed by the Police and Criminal Evidence Act ('PACE') 1984 and the accompanying codes of practice. These procedures are designed to ensure that evidence is obtained from witnesses without applying any oppression. If it can be shown that the police did not comply with PACE it is possible that the evidence so obtained would be inadmissible. While civilian investigators are not statutorily bound by PACE, the codes of practice act as a useful guide on some practical points which an expert accountant should bear in mind when interviewing potential witnesses, including:

● when a suspect should be cautioned;

● the conduct of interviews, including the procedures adopted when tape recording an interview; and

● the right to have legal representation.

Safeguarding documents

930   Fraud investigation work has many characteristics of a financial investigation. Documents are very important to provide evidence, but it is only through interviewing people that the true purpose of a transaction or event is likely to be established.

931   Fraudsters are unlikely to give accurate information freely. Usually they cover up a truth with false information or denials of involvement. It is important that interviews are planned properly in order to distinguish between truth and deceit.

Interviewing skills are vitally important, and many accountants do not have them. The police are trained at asking 'when', 'who', 'what' and 'how' questions, where inexperienced investigators tend to adopt a long winded approach which suits most fraudsters. It is necessary for the investigator to plan a strategy for interview and to brush up on his interviewing skills.

Documentary control systems

932   Having the right documentary evidence to hand is often the key to a successful interview. Such documents are not merely restricted to those supporting accounting transactions; they include circumstantial evidence. For example, even if a fraudster neither kept a diary nor made notes of meetings, the chances are that others did and that these records, for example, secretaries' diaries, shorthand pads or telephone log books, will be useful sources of reference as to who was where, when and with whom. One must range widely, and not focus solely on the principal documents, nor concentrate on any preconceived notions as to the nature of the fraud.

933 As remarked earlier, fraud is predominantly a document-based crime. It is important that the investigator has set up an efficient documentary control system, usually with the aid of a computer. Such a system must be designed to secure the integrity of any documents which are to be used in evidence. Common features of such a system include the following.

- The capability of establishing from whom, where and when the documents were obtained. In some cases it may be important to identify not just from which premises the documents were obtained, but from which room and from which desk.

- Physical control over original documents in order to establish that they have not been subsequently altered or tampered with.

- A facility to obtain continuity of documents.

- A search facility in order to identify specific documents to aid investigation work.

934 The above features of a documentary control system apply to original documentation which may be produced in evidence. If the expert wants to work on certain documents he should take photocopies or use a computer image, since original documentation may be the subject of forensic examination, for example, by the police. It is particularly important that original documentation is secured and protected as soon as possible, and with a minimum of handling. Forensic examination is normally required for criminal cases, but on occasions it is also required for civil cases. There are a number of private sector forensic laboratories who provide services similar to those of the police, for example, handwriting expertise and finger printing.

935 Frauds are difficult to detect and also difficult to prove with absolute certainty because a fraudster will have deliberately set out to cover his tracks. Documentary evidence will sometimes be forged so as to leave a false trail. For this reason the work of the forensic accountant must be very painstaking; the picture in the jigsaw puzzle must be restored even though from the outset it is likely that key pieces will be missing.

Interlocutory reliefs

936 Often the key to a successful fraud investigation is to gain early access to accounting records, documents and bank accounts. It assists if the regulators and enforcement agencies concerned have at their disposal certain search and seizure powers. Some of these powers require the consent of courts, others do not. For example, the police need to apply to the courts for a search warrant under PACE and the Inland Revenue need to apply under the Taxes Management Act 1970 s 20. Other regulators, such as Customs & Excise, the SFO and DTI Inspectors, have standing powers under the relevant legislation which avoids the need to apply to the courts.

937 The civil law equivalent to such search and seizure powers is found in certain interlocutory reliefs, commonly involving Mareva injunctions and Anton Piller orders. Mareva injunctions have the effect of preventing a person from dealing with his assets except in the particular respects identified in the court order. An injunction may be granted in respect of overseas as well as UK assets. Where assets are situated overseas, in order to make the injunction effective, it is necessary to apply to the appropriate overseas court in order to establish an equivalent order. To do so it is usually necessary to appoint local advisers, and the legal process can be lengthy and expensive.

938   It is necessary for a plaintiff seeking a Mareva injunction to show that there is a good arguable case, and that unless it is granted there is a risk that any eventual judgment in favour of the plaintiff will not be satisfied, ie because of the risk of dissipation of assets. In turn the defendant may suffer a loss because of the injunction, and it follows that if it can be shown that the Mareva application was not justified then he has a claim in damages. Therefore, before applying for Mareva relief, due consideration should be given as to whether such an action is likely to be cost effective. The expert may be required to produce an affidavit in support of the application, showing all relevant facts and assumptions that have been made.

939   Anton Piller relief is a court order directed at the defendant, requiring him to permit certain individuals to enter designated premises in order to search and remove particular documents. Such relief is given by the court where it can be shown that there is good reason to believe that the defendant is in possession of certain evidence which is material to the claim, and where there is a risk of destruction of such documents if the plaintiff sought to request the disclosure of such evidence.

940   It is argued by some people that Anton Piller relief represents a breach of civil liberties. The courts require good cause to be shown before granting an order and would take a serious view of any misrepresentations by the applicant. Should an expert accountant become involved in supporting such an application, he should consider the importance of the documents which are being sought and whether they could be obtained or preserved by some other means. It would not be normal for an expert to take part in the process of serving the order, but if he does become involved he should be familiar with the court order, the obligations of the defendant and what action is available should there be non-compliance.

Tracing the funds

941   'Tracing' is a quasi legal term which describes certain formal techniques used to identify ownership of funds or assets derived from such funds. Such techniques are particularly relevant where the ownership of funds becomes obscure through money from a variety of different sources being intermingled in one bank account.

942   The tracing of funds for the purposes of civil litigation must have due regard to the law, for example, whether tracing should be carried out under the common law or in equity. Where an expert is involved in tracing funds through a series of bank accounts he must ensure that the underlying principles and any assumptions which he uses are agreed with instructing solicitors if his work is to be used in evidence. There are some clearly defined rules for the tracing of funds which are more dependent upon legal precedent than on accounting practice, hence the need to take advice from instructing solicitors.

Disclosure of information to third parties

943 With all fraud investigation work the question of disclosure of information to third parties will arise. This applies to civil, as well as to criminal fraud investigations. Where the expert is acting for a regulator the disclosure of information is normally covered by statute, for example:

- disclosure of information about a taxpayer's affairs by the Inland Revenue is statute barred by the Taxes Management Act 1970, except in certain defined circumstances including for the purposes of a prosecution for an offence relating to inland revenue;

- the SFO is governed by the Criminal Justice Act 1987 s 3, which sets out those bodies to whom it may disclose information;

- investigations carried out under the Financial Services Act 1986 are also restricted on the matter of disclosure by s 179 of that Act; and

- information obtained and reports produced under the Companies Act 1985 ss 432 and 447 on behalf of the DTI are restricted by ss 449 and 451 of that Act. In essence, disclosure of such information is at the discretion of the Secretary of State and unauthorised disclosure may be punishable by two years imprisonment or an unlimited fine.

944 Great care must be taken with disclosure of information in all fraud cases. Such work is normally very sensitive and is likely to have potentially harmful effects both to individuals and to companies. There is, therefore, the inherent risk of litigation should there be unauthorised disclosure of information. As mentioned above, there are gateways which will allow disclosure of certain information between regulators and third parties. However, the associated law and practice is open to some interpretation and if there is abuse it may be argued that the defendant will not receive a fair trial. If an expert has any doubt as to what information can be disclosed to other parties, he should take advice from his instructing solicitor.

Reports

945 The reports produced by an expert accountant during the course of a fraud investigation may be prepared for different purposes. At the start of an investigation the expert accountant may prepare a report on the evidence to hand in order to brief instructing solicitors as to the possible nature of the fraud, what further information may be required and possibly an opinion as to the merits of the case. The expert accountant may also prepare a report, probably in the form of an affidavit, in support of an application to the court, for example, for a Mareva injunction. He may also prepare a report in the form of a witness statement for use at the trial. It is important that the expert accountant is quite clear as to the purpose of his report, in order that he may address all those issues which the court or other users of the report may consider to be relevant.

946 Fraud investigators often face complex situations, some of which are never entirely unravelled. Their knowledge will increase during the course of the investigation as more evidence is obtained and witnesses interviewed. It is important for an expert to form his views on available evidence and not on hearsay or circumstantial evidence. The expert needs to recognise that the earlier written reports that he may have produced, say for interlocutory hearings, may well be used to discredit his evidence if they can be shown to be ill-founded.

947 In criminal proceedings the prosecution must disclose its case to the defence, including all the evidence in its possession that is relevant to the case. This includes the evidence of experts. Where the prosecution uses an expert accountant, the defence has a right to call its own expert. The defence needs to give notice that it intends to call an expert, but it does have the advantage of knowing the prosecution case. It is possible that at the pre-trial hearing, or possibly during the course of the trial itself, the judge may suggest that the expert accountants for the prosecution and the defence should meet in order to agree common ground. However, it is not necessary for the defence to disclose any expert evidence which it does not intend to use, nor to disclose dissenting views.

948 These procedures are designed to put the onus of proving guilt upon the prosecution. An expert accountant must understand the principles which govern evidence in criminal proceedings and take great care to ensure that his report includes all relevant matters and that full disclosure has been made of all relevant evidence, including unused material. Exactly what constitutes unused material is a legal matter. In recent times the categories of documents which fall to be disclosed have widened. In the *Guinness* case[1] the judge ruled that certain draft witness statements should be disclosed to the defence.

949 In most civil litigation work a lot of the detailed investigation work and drafting of the expert accountant's report is undertaken by professional staff who report to the expert witness. The expert is able to rely upon this work, after appropriate review, in reaching his opinion which is incorporated in his evidence. This is not necessarily the case in a criminal trial where the people who actually carried out the investigation work may be called to give evidence. It is important, therefore, that the expert should plan his work in such a way as to ensure that the appropriate person gives evidence at trial.

The inter-relationship between civil and criminal proceedings

950 The differing roles of expert accountants in fraud investigations can give rise to different objectives; this is so in civil and criminal investigation work. The former is usually primarily concerned with maximising financial recoveries whereas the latter is primarily concerned with obtaining criminal judgment in the public interest (or in defending the accused against such judgment). These aims are different and sometimes mutually incompatible.

951 Where an expert has been appointed to assist in a civil action, he should consider with instructing solicitors whether the fraud should be reported to either the police or regulatory authorities. In some cases there will be a statutory obligation to report the fraud, for example, in the financial services sector or in compliance with the money laundering regulations. In other cases there may not be a statutory obligation to report the fraud and the expert accountant will need to take account of ethical or moral reasons. He will also need to take account of the likely effects on the civil case. It is probable that the involvement of the prosecuting authorities will provide competition for documentary evidence. It may make interviewing witnesses more difficult and may prolong the civil case significantly. On the other hand, there may be compelling reasons to inform the prosecuting authorities immediately, for example, overriding public interest, such as a fraud in the public sector, or the risk of defendants or assets leaving the jurisdiction. It is also possible that the involvement of the prosecuting authorities may assist the process of obtaining interlocutory reliefs in the civil proceedings.

952 It will be necessary for those involved in the civil action to continue with their investigations using civil remedies to obtain information, as the police and other prosecuting authorities are normally unable to disclose the information which they have obtained using their own powers, to civil litigants. Witnesses in the civil proceeding may be reluctant to give evidence should there be associated criminal proceedings. People who are possibly subject to charge in the criminal proceedings may claim a right of silence on the basis that they are entitled not to incriminate themselves. This argument has been used against the s 2 powers of the Serious Fraud Office. In the case of *Re Arrows Ltd (No 4)* (1993),[2] a director obtained a court order that, should the liquidators examine him under the Insolvency Act 1986 s 236, then the SFO would be obliged to apply to the Company's Court for directions should they wish to obtain the transcripts of the examination. The court at first instance ruled that the transcripts should be released by the liquidators to the SFO upon the SFO giving an undertaking to the court that they would not use the transcripts as evidence against the director, save in the circumstances prescribed by the Criminal Justice Act 1987 s 2(8). That decision was overruled in the Court of Appeal, where it was held that the SFO should be released from such an undertaking. The House of Lords ruled that the SFO had a right to obtain the transcripts, but that it was a decision for the judge at the criminal trial to rule whether to exclude such evidence.

953 In another celebrated case, Mr Ernest Saunders, who was prosecuted for his part in the *Guinness* case, maintained that he was obliged to give evidence to inspectors appointed by the DTI which was obtained subsequently by the SFO and used unfairly against him at his trial. Mr Saunders took his case to the European Commission, who held that the use at the trial of incriminating evidence obtained from him under compulsory powers was oppressive, and substantially impaired his ability to defend himself against the criminal charges. They found that he was, therefore, deprived of a fair hearing within the meaning of the European Convention on Human Rights.

FRAUD AND THE AUDITOR

An overview

954 In Chapter 8, we describe the approach which an expert should take to negligence claims on which he has been asked to give an opinion. When the alleged negligence relates to failure by the auditor to discover a fraud, the expert should concern himself with the conduct of the auditor by reference to the reasonable professional standards at the relevant time. But he also has to bear in mind that the audit profession's view of its responsibilities in respect of detection of fraud may not be precisely in line with the findings of the courts over the years. Whether the 'watchdog not bloodhound' metaphor of the *Kingston Cotton Mill* (see para **968**) case in the nineteenth century is still valid in determining liability in negligence suits, is something of an open question.

955   Whether negligence can be proved or not will depend on whether the defending auditor acted with the standard of care of an ordinary skilled and competent man carrying out the same engagements. The matters the expert will be most likely asked to assist on will be as follows.

(a)   Should the auditors have lighted upon the fraudulent transactions?
(b)   If they did so, did they ask the right question about the transactions?
(c)   If they did so, did they reasonably accept whatever answers were given?

956   There will often be a supplementary role, particularly when engaged on behalf of defendant auditors, namely to examine and report on what actually caused the losses claimed by the plaintiff and when such losses could in fact have been stemmed if the auditors had identified the fraud during their audit.

The auditor's responsibility to uncover fraud

957   The knowledge that a company's financial statements will be audited deters many people from perpetrating the more obvious types of fraud. But many frauds are not discovered by auditors, especially if they result from collusion between directors and/or top management. Whether an auditor should be expected to uncover fraud is a matter which has been keenly debated in recent years. There has been a common misconception in the mind of the public that the principal purpose of an audit is to identify fraud. The accounting professionals have rightly defended themselves against this view, but nevertheless the expectation gap has remained.

958   In order to bridge the expectation gap the accounting bodies have, over recent years, issued various statements and guidance to auditors on the extent of their duty to detect fraud.

959   In February 1990 the Institute of Chartered Accountants in England and Wales issued an audit guideline (3.418) on the responsibilities of auditors for the prevention and detection of fraud. This confirmed that primary responsibility for the detection of fraud rests with a company's management. The directors have a duty to safeguard the company's assets and through management should exercise their responsibility primarily by the institution and operation of an effective system of internal control. There will, however, always be the risk that internal controls will fail to operate as planned. In addition, such controls are usually ineffective against management fraud because of management's ability to override controls.

960   The auditor's responsibility is properly to plan, perform and evaluate his audit work so as to have a reasonable expectation of detecting material mis-statements in the financial statements, whether they are caused by fraud, other irregularities or errors.

961   The accounting bodies felt that simply setting out guidance to auditors was not enough to deal with the public's misconception of an audit, particularly among readers of financial statements. So, in 1993, they issued Statement of Auditing Standards 600. SAS 600 requires that the auditor should explain the basis of his opinion by including in his report a statement that he planned and performed the audit so as to obtain reasonable assurance that the financial statements are free from material mis-statements, whether caused by fraud or other irregularity or error.

962 To complete the sequence, in January 1995 a statement of auditing standards on fraud and error was published (SAS 110). The purpose of SAS 110 is to provide standards, together with detailed guidance, on the auditor's responsibility to consider fraud and error in an audit of financial statements. SAS 110 reiterates that it is the responsibility of directors to take such steps as are reasonably open to them to prevent and detect fraud. It also makes clear that it is not the auditor's function to prevent fraud or error, but that an audit may act as a deterrent and should be planned and conducted in such a way as to have a reasonable expectation of detecting mis-statements arising from fraud or error which are material to the financial statements. The distinction between the respective responsibilities of directors and auditors can be seen in the table overleaf.

Auditors' responsibilities to report fraud to regulators

963 In certain circumstances, auditors have a statutory responsibility to report fraud. For example, they have a duty to report to regulators in the financial sector. Statement of Auditing Standards 620 deals with the duty of the auditor of a regulated entity to inform the regulator on relevant matters of material significance to the regulator. Fraudulent activity would certainly fall within this definition. There will often be a natural reluctance to report possible corporate misconduct because of the existence of a duty of confidentiality to one's client. However, auditors who can demonstrate that they have acted reasonably and in good faith in informing the appropriate authority of an instance of fraud which they believe has been committed, would not be held by a court to be in breach of their duty to their client. This would be so even if it is subsequently determined that no offence has been committed. However, auditors may wish to take legal advice before making a decision on whether a suspected fraud should be reported to the police or other authority in the public interest.

Fraud alert factors

964 As we have said, management fraud will often involve collusion and systematic covering up of the fraudulent activity by false accounting and dishonest explanations. Whether the auditor could reasonably be expected to find fraud will depend on the nature and extent of the cover up. However, in planning his audit the auditor should recognise that conditions exist in certain types of businesses which may increase the inherent risk of fraud. These include:

● high risk activities, such as businesses operating in volatile markets, transactions carried out in certain unstable countries, association with certain products or services which have a political risk, assets held in a fiduciary capacity;

THE RESPONSIBILITIES OF DIRECTORS

- To ensure that the company's assets are safeguarded and its activities are conducted honestly.
- To instigate effective arrangements to prevent and detect any fraudulent conduct.
- To ensure that any financial information is reliable.
- To prepare financial statements that give a true and fair view of the state of affairs of the company and its profit or loss for the financial year.

THE RESPONSIBILITIES OF AUDITORS

- The audit should be planned so as to assess the risk that fraud or error may cause the financial statements to contain material misstatements.
- The auditor should design audit procedures so as to have a reasonable expectation of detecting misstatements arising from fraud or error which are material to the financial statements.
- When auditors become aware of information which indicates that fraud or error may exist, they should carry out further work in order to evaluate the possible effect on the financial statements.
- Auditors should document their findings in relation to instances of fraud and discuss them with appropriate levels of management.
- Auditors should consider the implication of suspected fraudulent conduct in relation to other aspects of the audit, particularly reliability of management representations.
- If the auditors are unable to determine whether fraud or error has occurred because of limitation in the scope of their work, they should issue a disclaimer or a qualified opinion.
- Where the auditors become aware of the suspected or actual incidence of fraud they should consider whether the matter may be one that ought to be reported to a proper authority in the public interest.
- Auditors should report the matter to a proper authority in the public interest without delay and without discussing the matter with the entity's management if they conclude that the fraud has caused them no longer to have confidence in the integrity of the directors.

- where the measurement of items in the financial statements is significantly influenced by the exercise of management judgment, eg, contentious accounting policies; and

- where certain products or assets are highly susceptible to misappropriation or can be used to provide security.

965 Experience has shown that if the auditor identifies one or more of the following tell-tale signs during the course of his work, it may well be indicative of fraud, particularly if some of the common factors which arise in management fraud (see **911**) are also present:

- a serious breakdown in the accounting or information systems;

- the appointment of weak management in positions of authority;

- a negative attitude to the audit or attempts to undermine the auditors' independence and objectivity;

- incomplete or unsatisfactory replies to audit enquiries;

- resistance to independent confirmation procedures;

- over-reliance on faxes or similar documents, which are simple to falsify, to support transactions; and

- evidence of unduly lavish lifestyle.

The court's view of the auditor's responsibility to detect fraud

966 SAS 110 is now a mandatory standard for UK auditors. It is arguable whether it sets a new level of responsibility for auditors for the detection of fraud or whether it simply codifies existing practice. Whichever is the case, what is certain is that from 1995 onwards it will be held up in court as the definitive standard against which auditors who have allegedly failed to find material fraud will be judged.

967 But what of cases arising from audits which predate this standard? A brief look at some of the landmark cases both here and overseas may give some helpful guidance on the court's developing attitude to fraud and the auditor.

968 Frequently the issue of the auditor's liability has been approached in the courts by posing the question: 'Should the auditors' suspicions have been aroused?' The classic case is *Re Kingston Cotton Mill Co* (1896)[3] which for many years defined the duties of an auditor. In this judgment it was said that an auditor: 'is a watchdog not a bloodhound . . . He is justified in believing tried servants of the company in whom confidence is placed by the company'. Thus it has been said that an auditor should not suspect people of dishonesty in the absence of suspicious circumstances. If, however, there are suspicions, he must probe it to the bottom (*London Oil Storage Co Ltd v Seear Hasluck & Co* (1904)[4]) and report it to the directors and the shareholders.

969 In some other reported cases a somewhat tougher line has been taken by the courts towards auditors. In the Australian case of *Franksten and Hartings Corp v Cohen* (1959)[5] it was stated that:

> 'an audit was a skilled examination of such books, accounts and records as will enable the auditors to verify the balance sheet. The main objects of any audit are: (a) to certify to the correctness of the financial position . . ., (b) the detection of errors and (c) the detection of fraud . . . The detection of fraud is generally regarded of primary importance.'

970 In another Australian case, *Pacific Acceptance Corpn Ltd v Forsyth* (1970),[6] the defendants were the company's auditors. A professional negligence claim was brought in contract relating to four separate years' audits. The auditors were found to have failed to exercise reasonable skill and care. The principal default was failure to discover fraudulent and irregular features in loans made to certain fictitious companies. The judge was critical, inter alia, of the auditor failing to plan his work so as to pay due regard to the possibility of error and fraud.

971 Ultimately, whether failure to uncover an irregularity amounts to negligence depends on the relevant circumstances and, in particular, its materiality. The standards of care appear to have become more exacting as the profession's own operational standards have been tightened. Even so, an auditor is not a guarantor of the accuracy of the accounts. The fact that fraud was not detected in the course of an audit does not of itself prove negligence (see *Fomento Sterling Area Ltd v Selsdon Fountain Pen Co Ltd* (1958)[7]). On the other hand, the greater the number of undiscovered peculiarities, the more difficult it is for the auditor to resist a finding of negligence in failing to discover them (see *International Laboratories v Dewar* (1988)[8]).

Issues of causation

972 In most large fraud cases there will be some evidence to support a negligence action against the auditors. The quality of such evidence and the strength of the case is likely to be both varied and contentious. However, setting aside the question of negligence, it will also be necessary to consider in such cases whether the loss deriving from the fraud can be directly attributed to the failure by the auditors. An important judgment on causation is the case of *Galoo Ltd v Bright Grahame Murray*[9] which is described in Chapter 8.

973 It was alleged that the defendant auditors failed to identify that the plaintiff company's management had falsely inflated the value of the company's stock in its accounts, thereby making it appear profitable when in truth it was loss making. The plaintiffs argued that had the fraud been discovered, the losses would have come to light and the company would have ceased trading, thereby preventing subsequent losses. The Court of Appeal held that the fraud was not the dominant cause of the loss; rather the loss was caused by poor trading.

974 While the expert accountant's primary role in a claim for audit negligence in a fraud-related case will be to comment on the adequacy or otherwise of the defendant's audit work by reference to contemporary professional standards, there will often be a supplementary and at times very important role in commenting, from a financial or business perspective, on the cause of the losses suffered.

975 It is surprising how often much of the loss had already been suffered at the time the fraud should have been discovered. It is particularly important, therefore, to consider the question: 'If a perfect audit had been done, when would the fraud itself have been identified and further losses thereby prevented?'.

NOTES

1 *Guinness plc v Saunders* [1990] 2 AC 663.
2 *Re Arrows Ltd (No 4)* [1993] 3 WLR 513.
3 *Re Kingston Cotton Mill Co (No 2)* [1896] 1 Ch 331; 2 Ch 279, CA.
4 *London Oil Storage Co Ltd v Seear Hasluck & Co* [1904] 31 Acct LR 1.
5 *Franksten and Hartings Corp v Cohen* (1959) 102 CLR 607.
6 *Pacific Acceptance Corpn Ltd v Forsyth* (1970) 92 WNNSW 29.
7 *Fomento (Sterling Area) Ltd v Selsdon Fountain Pen Co Ltd* [1958] 1 WLR 45.
8 *International Laboratories v Dewar* [1933] 3 DLR 665.
9 *Galoo Ltd v Bright Grahame Murray* [1995] 1 All ER 16.

Chapter 10

Intellectual property disputes

Introduction – Damages for infringement – Preparation of the
financial report on damages – Remedy sought – Choice of royalty
rate – Identification of relevant sales – Special considerations for
the expert – Current developments – Employee inventions –
Computer software disputes – Patents Court – Compulsory
licensing – European intervention – Conclusion

INTRODUCTION

1001 Intellectual property is one of those jargon phrases, beloved of lawyers,
which gives the accountant on the Clapham omnibus little clue to its meaning.
The phrase covers the property rights conferred by the state on inventors, as a
reward for their inventiveness. It applies to such matters as copyright, patents,
trademarks and registered designs. It therefore covers books, designs, pictures
and other inventions of the mind such as films, computers, computer programs
and even microbiology. Legislation in this area seeks to prevent others from
copying an original idea and profiting from the intellectual efforts of the
originators.

1002 There is obviously a conflict between intellectual property rights on the
one hand – with exclusivity of use protected by law – and anti-monopoly and
consumer protection laws on the other. The first aims to maximise the returns to
the originator of an idea, to reward his past efforts and to encourage the making of
future inventions; and the second aims to minimise costs to the consumer and to
widen his choice of supply.

1003 Intellectual property disputes typically involve accountants if damages
have to be quantified where infringement of rights has been proven. This chapter
discusses infringement disputes.

Damages for infringement

1004 In an intellectual property dispute in England, the liability for
infringement is dealt with first, followed, in a separate hearing, by the question of
quantum. This is in contrast to most other commercial disputes where liability and
quantum questions are quite often considered in parallel. Expert accountants
become involved in the second phase of the action, ie when liability has been
decided in favour of the plaintiff and damages have to be assessed.

1005 Frequently, the purpose of intellectual property litigation is to drive a defendant or a prospective defendant out of the marketplace. The plaintiff here wants to obtain an injunction, thereby removing the threat of competition for the duration of the life of the intellectual property rights involved. The plaintiff is less concerned with obtaining financial reward for the loss he has suffered. The combination of a Mareva order (effectively freezing a person's assets) and an Anton Piller order (requiring the authorities to assist in the confiscation of his stocks, manufacturing equipment and records) is not likely to be laughed off by a pirate, especially if the next stage is the physical destruction of his stock and manufacturing equipment.

1006 If the purpose of the litigation is to obtain damages for infringement (after the pirate has been made to stop his infringing activities) the plaintiff must prove its loss. In general terms, the defendant will have to pay damages representing a percentage of the value of its sales of the protected goods. The percentage payable aims to transfer the profits from the defendant's illegal acts to their rightful owner; the profits are meant to be the profits which the plaintiff would have made if it had made the sales. Persuasive financial evidence is vital here.

1007 The court may also award damages for loss of reputation, especially where the defendant's infringing goods (for example, a copy of a designer shirt) are of inferior quality so that the plaintiff's standing in the marketplace has suffered. This type of damages applies only to a limited category of intellectual property rights.

1008 As an alternative to damages based on the profits which the plaintiff would have earned, the successful plaintiff is entitled to require the unsuccessful defendant to account for the profits made by the defendant on its infringing activities, ie the profits must be handed over to the plaintiff.

1009 When an accounting expert prepares his report he ought to be familiar with past legal precedents and of course the relevant statutes, so that his evidence in damages is consistent with them. However, most enquiries as to damages in this field of law are settled before, or during trial. Only two such cases have yielded a judgment dealing with the quantum issues in England in the last thirty years. Although the general principles to be followed are well-established, there is little legal guidance on how to apply the principles in practice.

PREPARATION OF THE FINANCIAL REPORT ON DAMAGES

1010 The general principles are as follows. The plaintiff:

- is entitled to the profits it would have earned on the sales lost to the defendant;
- is also entitled to a royalty on any additional sales made by the defendant;
- is entitled to recover any losses it has suffered because the defendant has pushed the plaintiff's selling prices for its product down;
- may also be entitled to its profits on lost sales of any ancillary products, if it can show that these other products would inevitably have been sold with the product which is the subject of the dispute; and

146

- may also be entitled to the defendant's profits on any additional sales of non-infringing products which the defendant has been able to make because of its infringement (eg, if the defendant immediately begins to sell a non-infringing replacement product, thereby taking advantage of the market share established during infringement).

1011 Before the financial investigation gets under way, the objectives of the work should be clarified from both a legal and a financial point of view. The accounting expert's team should meet the instructing solicitors, and usually counsel as well. The objectives will typically be to:

(a) deal with the definition of those products whose sales infringe;
(b) decide which products are to be excluded from the calculations. If, at this early stage, there is insufficient knowledge to answer this question, it must be established well before the evidence is finalised;
(c) agree the precise definition of the intellectual property rights in question. In a patent dispute, for example, this may mean identifying the scope of the patent which is the basis of the litigation. Intellectual property rights tend to be complex packages and it may be essential to consider whether any additional patents or other rights are relevant to the proceedings and, if so, what impact they will have; and
(d) gain an understanding of the relevant normal practices of the business. The proper definition of 'sales' is often vital here. For example, should it be the value of sales by the manufacturer to his wholesaler or the corresponding value of the sales by the wholesaler to his retailer? What about sales by distributors?

Remedy sought

1012 Assuming it has been established that the plaintiff's intellectual property rights have been infringed, the next step is to ascertain whether the remedy to be sought is damages or 'an account of profit' as described above. The most common remedy is damages. These are assessed as a percentage of sales of the infringing goods, following the usual commercial practice of voluntarily licensing intellectual property rights in exchange for a royalty on sales. Nevertheless, an 'account of profits' may be a useful back-up, showing, for example, that the royalty demanded by the plaintiff on the infringing sales is not excessive.

1013 As we have stated, damages are mostly exacted on the basis of a percentage of sales which an infringer should have paid to the plaintiff by way of royalty if he had wanted to operate within the law. At first sight this may seem straightforward, but in practice the choice of the appropriate royalty rate and the identification of the relevant sales present real problems.

Choice of royalty rate

1014 The first problem to be considered is the royalty rate which the infringer is liable to pay. The services of an independent licensing expert may be needed to identify:

- the strength of the intellectual property rights in question;

- the market considerations;

- the going rate in the industry for comparable licences;

- the expected profits which the licensee may make; and

- the extent to which the licensor should share in these profits.

1015   There may well be an argument about how the likely profits are to be split between a licensor and his licensee. (The courts may even take refuge in a 50:50 split when faced with a question which is difficult to solve, for example, who contributes most by way of an invention.) If, however, the owner has a valuable intellectual property right, he would, as a willing licensor, allow the licensee to share in his monopoly but only if he could take the lion's share of the profit. The damages should reflect this.

Identification of relevant sales

1016   The next problem is to identify which sales the royalty rate should be applied to. For instance:

- Should a royalty be levied on the whole value of the infringing product or only on the value of the patented element? If the latter, how can this value be estimated? If the former, how much should the royalty rate be reduced, if at all, to take account of the increased value of the whole product as compared to that of the patented element alone?

- How are the sales of ancillary parts to be treated?

- How are the sales of replacement parts to be treated?

- Should export sales be treated differently?

- Are intergroup sales to be ignored until they reach a third party buyer?

1017   The defendant may say that its efforts have increased the total market for the product beyond the level which the plaintiff could have achieved on its own. In other words, the defendant may claim that none of its sales has been made at the expense of the plaintiff's continuing sales. If this is held to be true, the defendant need only pay a royalty on its sales. Establishing the truth is likely to be difficult, because the plaintiff, as monopolist, will be unwilling to concede that its marketing strategy was not intended to maximise sales. The defendant may even argue that if it sold at prices below the plaintiff's, it increased demand for both its own and the plaintiff's products. As an argument about these issues will tend to involve speculation and allegations about marketing practices, impartial, objective analysis of the facts by an independent expert accountant should be helpful.

1018   In compiling information on relevant sales, the accountant must be clear about the periods to be covered by the enquiry. These periods will be determined by legal considerations and will not necessarily coincide with the infringer's accounting periods. Special arrangements will have to be made to ensure that sales, which relate to the opening and the closing periods, are identified correctly. The closing stocks also merit special attention, since the articles held will themselves infringe the continuing intellectual property rights.

SPECIAL CONSIDERATIONS FOR THE EXPERT

1019 Inventors, especially individual inventors, can be emotionally involved and litigious. Their passions can inflame the lawyers whom they instruct; people get carried away, thinking they can win an unwinnable case. It is incumbent on the expert, if his experience tells him his inventor client is fighting a hopeless case – for example, because he can see that the financial evidence needed to support the arguments will not be available or will be unhelpful – to recommend that the case be modified and unwinnable issues be abandoned.

1020 Intellectual property disputes often revolve around the question of adequate remuneration for the intellectual property rights in question. Answering this question may involve consideration of what is a normal or reasonable level of trading profit. Evidence about the profits usually made in the relevant industry can provide useful guidance. Whether a plaintiff or a defendant has been adequately rewarded for the risks which he has been bold enough to take, may also be in question. None of these issues can be answered easily or quickly. They are all subjective and no clear guidance on any of them is readily available, but an experienced accountant should be able to contribute to their solution.

1021 Maintaining confidentiality of certain trade information can be an important consideration in intellectual property disputes. Monopolists may be reluctant to reveal information, especially when faced with unscrupulous opponents, so 'discovery' may be resisted. It is up to the accountant to devise ways so that confidential information can be presented in such a way that its disclosure is not damaging, while at the same time serving the needs of the court.

1022 In our experience, it is fatal if clients keep back confidential information when their expert advisers need it. We believe that to provide the best assistance the accountant must be a full member of the team, with early access to all the relevant documents.

CURRENT DEVELOPMENTS

Employee inventions

1023 One of the consequences of the Patents Act 1977 is that employees are now entitled to compensation for their own inventions (s 40) from the employing concern, over and above their salaries. Such cases raise many difficult questions. Will the inventor's entitlement depend upon the profits earned by his employer, rather than on sales values? If so, does this mean that the employee will be free to review his employer's profit margins critically? Where will the inventor find the money to fight the case in order to prove his entitlement? How easy will it be for him to prove the nature of his contribution to the invention, especially if he was a member of a team? It is likely that an accounting expert would be needed to assist in sorting out such questions.

Computer software disputes

1024 Intellectual property law changes rapidly, reflecting the need to keep this important branch of the law abreast of technological developments.

1025 A notable development recently is in the area of computer disputes, especially software program infringement and negligence cases. For example, a buyer of software alleges that it does not do what he thought it would do, because the programmer did his work negligently or because the vendor misrepresented the abilities of the program. The buyer therefore sues for damages including consequential losses. These losses may be large if they include business disruption claims. To be of assistance, an expert must be able to call on the help of information technology specialists who have the expertise to provide independent advice about whether a given software program infringes copyright and to help with damages.

Patents Court

1026 Intellectual property disputes are notoriously protracted, vicious and expensive. It is sometimes said that only those with deep pockets and thick skins are able to seek the help of the courts to uphold their rights. In response, a new court, the Patents Court, was set up in 1990 to hear intellectual property disputes in a less formal, less costly and speedier manner.

Compulsory licensing

1027 Compulsory licensing of intellectual property rights is a mounting fashion, reflecting the inherent conflict between a monopoly and the public interest. Compulsory licensing becomes more complex if there is a large prospective class of compulsory licensees, some of whom have different interests and operate in a different fashion from others. Although recent experience in the pharmaceutical industry (in which we were heavily involved, assisting the inventors) suggests that the courts recognise the need to protect the interests of inventors, this will not necessarily always be the case. The Copyright Tribunal has shown a greater desire to advance the interests of all the parties involved, including the consumer. It will be interesting to see how multi-media licensing issues are resolved. The ready access to the Internet system, and its databases, may make it difficult for copyright owners to demand large fees for their works when parts of these are re-used in multi-media products.

European intervention

1028 Finally, intellectual property rights are increasingly the focus of European attention because of the inevitable conflicts between these rights and the basic European principle of the free movement of goods. Both the Commission and the European Court of Justice are increasingly becoming involved in addressing complaints about alleged abuse of monopoly rights.

CONCLUSION

1029 Intellectual property disputes have to be distinguished from other disputes considered in this book because they involve a very specialised area of law. With a good grasp of the issues and some experience of legal precedents, the accountant can make a valuable contribution by applying basic business and analytical skills.

Chapter 11

Reinsurance contract disputes

Introduction – The language of reinsurance – The cause of disputes
– The insurance cycle – Long tail liability – Net accounting – Choice
of currency for settlement – The role of the accountant –
Understanding and interpreting the reinsurance contract –
Reviewing the placing files – Checking compliance with the
contract – Confirming the accuracy, completeness and validity of
accounting information – Examples of matters affecting
reinsurance disputes – Confusion over classes of business – The
period of cover – Reallocation of risks – Allocation of claims – The
scheduling process – Collection and interpretation of data –
Central accounting systems – Sampling – Breach of warranty –
Misrepresentation – Conclusion

INTRODUCTION

1101 Accounting for insurance is founded on the principle of uberrimae fidei,
that is to say, utmost good faith. The insurer expects the insured (or his agent) to
be open and honest in giving information about the risk. The insured expects the
insurer or reinsurer to pay claims falling within the policy terms.

1102 The unquestioning reliance by parties to an insurance contract on 'utmost
good faith' has been put under great strain in recent years. The unprofitability of
many lines of reinsurance has resulted in numerous disputes between parties to
reinsurance contracts. The magnitude of losses that can arise on a contract
injudiciously entered into by a reinsurer, can have a significant effect on his
financial position and even threaten his solvency. Some reinsurers have resorted
to the courts in an attempt to relieve themselves from the burden of those
contracts.

1103 In this chapter we discuss the nature of disputes that commonly arise on
reinsurance contracts and explain the role that the expert accountant can play in
helping the judge or arbitrator to understand the way in which the contract was
operated in practice. It is often in the context of an arbitration that an accountant's
expertise will be brought to bear, because most reinsurance contracts provide for
arbitration in the event of disputes.

THE LANGUAGE OF REINSURANCE

1104 It is not the intention of this book to provide the reader with any more than
an overview of reinsurance and its problems. It is a highly technical subject and,

like so many, has a language all of its own. A brief introduction to principal terms will assist those who are unfamiliar with this branch of insurance to understand the subject matter of this chapter.

1105 Reinsurance arises when an insurance company itself insures against certain claims arising on its own direct insurance policies issued to the public, or on reinsurance accepted from other insurers. The company which purchases reinsurance protection is often referred to as 'the ceding company'.

1106 Reinsurance policies can be broadly divided into two main types, facultative reinsurance and treaty reinsurance. Put very simply, facultative reinsurance is where an insurer chooses to reinsure specific individual risks on a one-off basis (the reinsurer is free to accept or reject them); treaty reinsurance is where a reinsurer agrees to reinsure, not an individual risk, but portfolios of a particular type or line of business. The reinsurer is bound to accept each individual risk falling within the terms of the treaty. The two main types of treaty reinsurance are proportional and non-proportional. Proportional treaties include quota share treaties and surplus treaties. Non-proportional treaties include excess of loss treaties and stop loss treaties. Excess of loss treaties may be on a risk basis (where the reinsurer pays in excess of a stated amount or an individual risk) or on an occurrence basis (where the reinsurer pays when the aggregate loss from a specific occurrence, eg, flood, exceeds a stated amount). It is not within the scope of this book to explain the characteristics of each of these forms of treaty. Readers wishing to learn more should refer to textbooks on the subject, such as Carter, RL, *Reinsurance* (1979) Kluwer.

1107 For the most part, it is excess of loss and proportional treaty reinsurance contracts which are the subject of most disputes, and for that reason this chapter focuses on such contracts. One further type of reinsurance which can be a cause of disputes is known as 'run-off' reinsurance. Run-off reinsurance is where a reinsurer agrees, for a fixed premium, to meet all valid outstanding claims, or all claims in excess of a stated cumulative retention, in respect of specified underwriting years, which become due for payment after a stated date.

THE CAUSE OF DISPUTES

1108 The first sign of a dispute is often the refusal by a reinsurer to pay a claim. The ceding company or intermediary (broker or agent) may then sue under the contract for the claim to be paid. The reinsurer becomes the defendant or respondent. Alternatively, the reinsurer may be so surprised by the losses arising on the treaty, suspecting that he was not properly advised about the risk or that the terms of the contract had not been adhered to, that he himself brings an action for breach of contract against the ceding company. Whichever way round the action is, it is often the expert accountant who provides the financial ammunition used in the litigation that follows.

The insurance cycle

1109 A word about the profitability of insurance business. An unprofitable contract does not automatically signal foul play. There is a cycle in insurance in which the underwriting results swing from being generally profitable to being unprofitable every few years. In the profitable years the cycle is characterised by an increase in the numbers of insurers and reinsurers willing to sign policies or treaties. This increases the supply of insurance, or 'capacity' as it is known. The demand for insurance tends to be inelastic, that is, it does not change greatly from year to year. To compete for a limited quantity of business when capacity is high, insurers and reinsurers tend to cut their premium rates to get the business and sustain a cash flow for investment. The reduction in premiums causes the market to become unprofitable, certain insurers stop underwriting certain types of risk, and the underwriting capacity shrinks, allowing the premium rates to rise and the cycle to repeat itself once profitability has been restored. Some new underwriting capacity that enters the market at the top of the cycles may be inexperienced in international reinsurance – the so-called 'innocent capacity'.

1110   When faced by unexpectedly large treaty losses, it is not surprising that some may believe that they were misled when they entered into the reinsurance agreement or that mistakes have been made in the operation of the treaty. Since the reinsurers are frequently part of a chain of ceding companies and reinsurance intermediaries, it can take a long time for information to flow from the original direct insurer through to the ultimate reinsurer. The full extent of losses on a particular line of business or treaty takes some time to become evident. In the meantime the reinsurer, ignorant of the true position, may have renewed the contract for another year or more.

Long tail liability

1111   Much of the difficulty between the reinsurer, the insured and the brokers acting as intermediaries, has related to the so-called long tail liability classes of business involving product liability and professional indemnity claims. Many years may pass between the underwriting of the original risk, a loss coming to light and the settlement of the claim, although under 'claims made' policy forms (as opposed to 'losses occurring' forms) there should be no delay in the notification of a claim. Furthermore, there has been a tendency for the cost of such claims to escalate, especially as a result of legal action in the USA.

Net accounting

1112   Net accounting is another practice in the insurance world which can itself give rise to disputes or, if not the direct cause, can complicate other disputes. Net accounting is the process adopted by intermediaries (brokers or agents) whereby premiums received from one insurer or reinsurance under a reinsurance treaty, are used to settle claims under that treaty or a closely related one. This can cause major complications if, as is often the case, the premiums are in respect of one accounting year and the claims have arisen on a previous year's underwriting. Although they may fall under the same treaty, it may happen that the individual reinsurers to the treaty are different from one year to another. In these circumstances, where disputes arise, the accountant will have a valuable role to play in tracing through the various parties' accounting systems the cash transactions, to establish whether or not the net accounting has been prejudicial to any of the parties' individual interests.

Choice of currency for settlement

1113 Reinsurance is an international business, generally accounted for in certain key currencies: the US dollar, sterling and to a lesser extent the Canadian dollar. Ultimately, the insured's claim will be settled in his relevant domestic currency. With the extent of movement in exchange rates between currencies in recent years, substantial exchange rate differences have arisen in the settlement of insurance and more particularly reinsurance claims. This problem can be exacerbated by the delays which occur in the processing and settlement of claims on reinsurance treaties. Typically, exchange losses arising because of delays in settlement of claims are passed on to all the reinsurers participating in a treaty. But we have been involved with cases where a reinsurer who has settled a claim on the due date, is charged with a share of exchange loss arising on a subsequent late settlement by the intermediary. This was disputed on the grounds that such losses should be apportioned only to those who delayed payment.

THE ROLE OF THE ACCOUNTANT

1114 The accountant's role in reinsurance contract disputes usually includes the following main tasks:

- understanding or interpreting the contract terms;
- reviewing information provided to the reinsurer when the treaty was signed;
- checking compliance with terms and warranties of the contract; and
- confirming the accuracy, completeness and validity of accounting information produced by the ceding company to the reinsurer.

Understanding and interpreting the reinsurance contract

1115 In the London market, a reinsurer's participation in a reinsurance treaty contract is usually evidenced by the underwriter initialling a document called a placing slip, which has been prepared by an insurance intermediary or broker acting on behalf of a ceding company. This slip gives brief information about the type of reinsurance arrangement, the business being ceded to it and the terms of the contract. Much of the information on the slip is in the form of abbreviations and initials.

1116 It is very important that the expert accountant has a thorough working knowledge of the reinsurance market to interpret and understand this contractual shorthand. Often its meaning is at the heart of the dispute, and the abbreviations and initials used can have more than one meaning in common usage in the insurance market.

1117 Some doubts and inconsistencies can be clarified by reference to the full treaty wording in the signed contract of reinsurance, and the expert should ask to see this. It is not uncommon for the treaty terms to conflict with the conditions specified on the slip. If so, an examination of the placing files may provide clarification.

Reviewing the placing files

1118   The expert accountant will usually need to call for the placing files of the parties involved with the contracts, that is, the ceding company, the reinsurer and the placing broker or intermediary. In the event of litigation or arbitration, these files will be obtained by the process of 'discovery'. Placing files contain background information presented by the intermediary to the underwriter at the time the treaty is entered into or renewed, including data on premiums written and claims incurred on the business in recent periods. Any statistical information supplied does not form part of the contract unless it has been specifically warranted, but it may help to clarify the intention of the parties at the time the risk was placed.

Checking compliance with the contract

1119   The central role the expert accountant plays is to establish whether the terms of the reinsurance contract have been complied with, a task which is simple in theory but one which in practice may be fraught with difficulty. For example:

● contracts are typically very complex, with both express and implied terms;

● reinsurance is a grand paper chase;

● reinsurers' accounting and document controls can be very poor;

● delay of documents and information characterises reinsurance;

● substantial time can elapse between receipt of premiums and settlement of related claims; and

● the reinsurance market can straddle national boundaries and involve different currencies.

1120   It is essential that the expert accountant has a thorough and up to date knowledge of the reinsurance market, its practices and its structure. Much of the expert's work will be in ascertaining whether the ceding company has allocated to the treaty only that type of business specified on the slip or contract, that all such business has been so allocated, and that all excluded business has, in fact, been excluded. He will also want to satisfy himself that any pre-existing reinsurance arrangements and all commission terms have been accounted for correctly.

Confirming the accuracy, completeness and validity of accounting information

1121   Whether it is a dispute over the accuracy of treaty statements, net accounting or foreign exchange losses, the accountant has a crucial role to play in verifying the relevant accounting data and in analysing it in a way that can be comprehended by the judge or arbitrator. The transactions can at first sight seem an impenetrable maze and, in order to establish the facts, it is essential to work painstakingly through the undergrowth of treaty statements, premium and claims settlement advices.

EXAMPLES OF MATTERS AFFECTING REINSURANCE DISPUTES

1122 By way of illustration of the kind of problems on which the expert accountant may be engaged, we describe below some of the work which we have carried out.

Confusion over classes of business

1123 We had to check the scheduling of business to a treaty where the slip referred to cover for 'all risks written in the Fire Department'. We found that the Fire Department in this case was writing an unusually high volume of non-fire business. We had to review placing files to establish whether the true intention of the treaty was to cover almost exclusively fire business. Similar difficulties can arise with non-marine business written in the Marine Department.

1124 In another case, the treaty excluded certain types of business but permitted such excluded business where it was written incidental to a risk of a permitted kind. Judgment and experience were necessary to determine what proportion of the total business might reasonably be regarded as 'incidental'. Other exclusions may relate to risks originating in certain specified countries. The originating country may not be obvious at first sight and some tracing back through the chain of insurance may be necessary.

The period of cover

1125 Confusion can arise over whether the risk reinsured falls within the period covered by the treaty. Some risks are placed in the year preceding that in which they are due to come into effect. Conversely, because of delays in the passing of information through the various stages of reinsurance, some risks are only placed after the period of cover has come into effect. The expert accountant will be able to check that risks have been properly allocated to the correct treaty period, in accordance with established and accepted practice in the market.

Reallocation of risks

1126 Some treaties are structured in a way which permits some flexibility in the placing of risks on particular treaties. The underwriter may decide not to cede to a treaty business which he believes will produce a low loss ratio and therefore be profitable. In these circumstances we have found that some ceding companies have been tempted to reallocate a risk to a reinsured treaty if the risk subsequently becomes unprofitable. The expert accountant will be alert for unusual adjustments to treaty allocations.

Allocation of claims

1127 Of particular concern to a reinsurer is that claims allocated to the treaty are in respect of risks covered by the treaty. In this and the other circumstances we have described above, the expert will have an important role to play in scheduling the business passing through the treaty, inspecting the underlying records and generally verifying that the parties to the treaty have abided by the terms and conditions of the contract.

THE SCHEDULING PROCESS

1128 The sheer volume of transactions involved in a disputed treaty of any significance, particularly where the reinsurer has been involved with the treaty for several years, presents the expert accountant with a formidable task. But it is one which must be done in a thorough and methodical way, to ensure that the relevant data is identified and clearly presented to the court or arbitration in a form which facilitates an understanding of the facts and their decision.

Collection and interpretation of data

1129 It is important at an early stage in the assignment to decide how the data is to be collected, reviewed and presented. As with other areas of an expert accountant's work, the reinsurance expert can make a major contribution to the discovery process. An early meeting with instructing solicitors and counsel is essential. Because the expert's work will involve detailed inspection of many records, he must be quite clear at the outset about the purpose of the work and the end product for which counsel is looking. To have to go back to the documents later, for a second look for further analysis, will be very costly and a very inefficient use of resources.

1130 The scale and extent of analysis required in reinsurance disputes lends itself to the use of computers and spreadsheets. Computers can be used to list transactions in date order, to assist in sampling techniques, to allocate insurance business by type, and to present data in tabular or graphical form. The insurance world is used to using computers to process vast quantities of data, both for underwriting and accounting and also to provide data analysed in the statistical form required by government regulatory bodies. Opportunities arise to transfer such information in computerised form directly into the expert's analysis system.

Central accounting systems

1131 Knowledge, by the expert accountant, of the central accounting systems operating in the insurance market, is fundamental in cases involving detailed analysis of reinsurance transactions. In the UK these are currently the Lloyd's central accounting system, the Institute of London Underwriters' system (ILU) and that of the London Insurance and Reinsurance Market Association (LIRMA).

Sampling

1132 Reinsurance treaty transactions often comprise a very large number of relatively small value items. Individually, very few such transactions are material, but a small error rate applied across all the transactions can amount to a sizeable sum. The parties must agree at the outset of the investigation whether a statistical sampling approach to the transactions is the appropriate one to adopt. In an arbitration, a sampling approach may be specifically ordered by an arbitrator when he gives directions for specific accounting analysis to be prepared.

Breach of warranty

1133 Reinsurance disputes are not only about whether particular types of business, risk or claim are properly allocated to a treaty; they may also go to the heart of the treaty contract itself. Sometimes, treaties are entered into with warranties attaching to them in respect of information supplied to the underwriter about the risk. The expert accountant can play an important role in reviewing the documents of the ceding company or intermediary placing the business, to see whether warranties have been observed and proper disclosure was made to the underwriter.

Misrepresentation

1134 It is sometimes alleged that the underwriter was induced to enter into a reinsurance contract by the presentation to him of false or incomplete information about the risk and, in particular, past claims experience. We have found that advantage is sometimes taken of delays in the processing of documents to paint an unfair picture of the profitability of business. For example, the ceding company may have information about increasing levels of claims at the time it renews a treaty but, because those claims have not yet filtered through the accounting system on to the treaty statements, the business still appears to be profitable.

1135 The expert accountant who has a good working knowledge of the insurance market can review the steps taken by parties to a disputed contract and express an independent opinion on whether proper care was observed by those placing the business when the contract was entered into.

1136 This expertise can also be applied in cases involving allegations of error or negligence by intermediaries or brokers who are defending claims of malpractice or making claims themselves against their own insurers under their Errors and Omissions (E & O) cover.

CONCLUSION

1137 Disputes over reinsurance contracts are generally complicated, involving large volumes of paper, numerous transactions going back many years and, perhaps most importantly, substantial sums of money. The expert accountant with a good working knowledge of the reinsurance market and its systems can provide a valuable service in helping to resolve these disputes:

● by explaining the background to the business;

● by assisting with the interpretation of the contract;

● by scheduling or analysing the transactions under the contract;

● by reviewing the fairness of representation given at the time the reinsurance was placed; and

● by assisting the lawyer in deciding the most efficient way to develop the case.

1138 Resolving reinsurance disputes is never easy, but the expert accountant can certainly make it less daunting.

Chapter 12

Lloyd's disputes

Introduction – Limitation of claims: potential extension – Economic matters – Reinsurance to close – The LMX spiral – The role of the expert accountant – The *Gooda Walker* judgment – Issues of liability – Claims against underwriters – Failure to do competent underwriting – Claims against auditors – Failure to report/account properly – Causation of loss – Issues concerning damages – Categories of defendants – Conclusions

INTRODUCTION

1201 A great deal of litigation has been generated recently within the Lloyd's community and this book would not be complete without reference to it. It is not the purpose of this book to attempt a comprehensive description of the underwriting profession within Lloyd's, nor to describe the rather arcane accounting practices applied when reporting to Names on the results of the syndicates (Names are the members of Lloyd's that subscribe the capital base on which Lloyd's trades). It is assumed that the readers of this chapter have a reasonable understanding of the concept of Lloyd's and how it works. For those who wish to remind themselves of the organisation and usages of Lloyd's, a helpful guide is Macve, Professor, *A survey of Lloyd's syndicate accounts* (2nd edn, 1993) ICAEW.

1202 The involvement of accountants as experts or as witnesses of fact, will be considerable in these actions. Proper accounting has additional significance for Lloyd's syndicates, because syndicates are one-year joint ventures that are intended to distribute the whole of their profit to or collect the whole of their losses from Names each year. This is to be contrasted with a normal business enterprise which distributes only part of its earnings, and where the value of the investment of the member is determined partly by reference to dividend return, but also by reference to other factors, for example, dividend cover, earnings trends and perceived prospects.

1203 The current litigation is being pursued in the context of the Lloyd's Settlement Offer of 1993 which included a legal report endorsed by a High Court judge rating the chances of success of the various actions as 'high, medium, low or nil'. Although the offer was not accepted, there can be few situations where litigants and potential litigants have been given such a full public analysis of the strength of their case by an independent and respected source; added to this there have been a number of internal reviews, organised by Lloyd's, which have spelt out in some detail the unfortunate history of some of the syndicates which are now the subject of litigation.

Limitation of claims: potential extension

1204 Many of the allegations of negligence go back a considerable number of years. As a result, there are limitation difficulties with certain claims otherwise available to Names, ie claims could be time-barred (see Chapter 18).

1205 A case decided in the Court of Appeal in January 1995 (*William Hallam-Eames v Merrett Syndicates Ltd*[1]) extended the potential time limit for actions by a considerable degree, in cases where plaintiffs allege negligent underwriting or wrongful closure (ie where underwriters did not have the information necessary to make a rational assessment of potential liabilities for the RITC exercise). Under the Limitation Act 1980, claims are time-barred by the six-year limitation period. However, plaintiffs can stop the clock running where they can show 'deliberate concealment' (s 32) or 'special time limit for negligence actions where facts relevant to cause of action are not known at date of accrual' (s 14A). In this particular case (which related to Syndicates 417 and 418 of Merrett Syndicates Ltd) the Appeal Court held, inter alia, that:

(a) it was not sufficient (to bar the action) that a plaintiff should have known about the most directly causative act or omission on the part of the defendant; there must also be applied 'the principle of common sense';
(b) common sense would suggest that the act or omission of which the plaintiff must have knowledge must be that which is 'causally relevant' for the purpose of alleging negligence; and
(c) what is 'causally relevant' here is that the severity and scope of the risks were apparent and quantifiable.

1206 This decision seems an important one in the wider field of commercial litigation, not only because of the reference to 'common sense', but also because it is possible to envisage other circumstances, for example, in the construction industry, where risks are known, yet not apparent in terms of scope and severity, until after the six-year limit has passed.

1207 Accounting witnesses experienced in Lloyd's matters, will be called upon to give evidence for and against defendants in these trials. There will be a substantial task of analysis and of discovery, as part of the process of developing pleadings and collating the evidence. It is likely that accountants and actuaries will be brought into teams created for this purpose.

1208 While the cases are being presented by action groups representing all Names, the fact is that each Name has an individual case, although based on common causes of action. Part of the forensic accountant's exercise will be at an early or later stage to isolate the position of each Name or each group of Names, for example, new versus old Names.

Economic matters

1209 The insurance market, of which syndicates at Lloyd's are a part, is cyclical. It is also subject to particular uncertainties because of the length of time that can elapse between writing an insurance risk and settling all related claims. These business and economic features are of particular importance in establishing the profitability of the underwriting and, indeed, lie behind the concept of three-year accounting that is used by Lloyd's syndicates. (Lloyd's syndicates draw up accounts for a given year only after two further years have passed, during which trends in claims manifest themselves more clearly.) In any event, the result for any year is heavily influenced by the provision made for liabilities incurred but not reported, in respect of claims under policies entered into during past periods of trading. This provisioning exercise itself depends for its accuracy on an intimate knowledge of the nature of the business written by the insurance syndicate. It is fundamental in determining the reinsurance to close, which we discuss more fully below.

1210   It is important to appreciate the difference between a Name at Lloyd's and a shareholder in an insurance company. In the normal way, a shareholder of a typical limited company has no direct redress against management which acts recklessly and incurs large trading losses as a result. (In certain cases a creditor can have redress if he can prove recklessness.) Generally, the safeguard is to rely on market forces, ie if management behaves incompetently and incurs large losses, the shareholder will learn of this in the annual accounts and vote with his feet, selling all his shares. The most the typical shareholder can lose is the whole of his investment capital but no more. In the case of an unincorporated Lloyd's Name, although he has an annual opportunity to resign from a syndicate and avoid losses from future underwriting activity, he is still exposed to past losses for 'open years' (see below), and potentially for closed years if all subsequent Names become bankrupt and the Lloyd's central fund is exhausted (although the latter situation is only a remote possibility). Furthermore, he can lose more than the immediate capital he has put up to support his underwriting; he has unlimited liability like any other unincorporated trader. In itself it seems unlikely that he will get sympathy in the courts for this additional element of risk which is not present in a typical quoted company. He will, however, have a powerful cause for complaint if that risk was undertaken in ignorance of the true position, for example, through wrong accounting or inadequate reporting by those running the syndicate, or if the underwriting carried out on his behalf can be shown to have fallen below the standard of reasonable skill and care.

1211   The treatment of Names' losses for taxation purposes is also of relevance: wrong calculation of losses can have damaging consequences for that Name, in terms of losing the opportunity to get relief for his Lloyd's losses against his other taxable income. The procedure, very simply, is that managing agents agree annually the results of syndicates with the Inland Revenue without any intervention from Names. This is the case whether the syndicates are still underwriting or are in run-off. It is likely that this aspect will be given emphasis when some of the cases (for example, those alleging wrongful closure) come to be argued.

Reinsurance to close

1212   In order to close the account for a given underwriting period and to establish a trading result for that period, it is necessary to make an estimate of the outstanding liabilities. Once this is done the syndicate will enter into a reinsurance contract (normally with the Names constituting the syndicate for the following year, but it can be with another syndicate) for the new syndicate to take over the liabilities in respect of the year closing, and all years reinsured into it, in exchange for a reinsurance premium. This is known as the reinsurance to close ('RITC').

1213 If a syndicate is unable to establish its outstanding liabilities in respect of a year of account with sufficient certainty for the reinsurance premium to be equitable between the two sets of Names, then the year of account will be left open until such time as there is sufficient certainty for an equitable premium to be established. This is then known as a run-off year of account.

1214 It follows that the RITC is the most significant item in the preparation of the syndicate accounts and in the allocation of profit or losses in an equitable manner between Names on different years of account of a syndicate. The traditional wisdom has been that the Lloyd's three-year accounting period is long enough to see if reserves for outstanding claims are sufficient to ensure that the results can be determined without impact on later years' results. In many areas of insurance activity this does not hold good. The longer the 'tail' of business (ie the time taken to discover the incidence and extent of liability for loss) the greater the degree of uncertainty in estimating the claims in respect of a year's underwriting at the end of the third year. Thus, for example, third party liability insurance will generally have a much longer 'tail' than insurance for damage to property; and reinsurance of third party liability insurance will have an even longer 'tail', because the information about the ceding insurer's exposure to claims will tend to be incomplete for extended periods. The length of the 'tail' is at its most extreme when insurance reserves have to be made for latent diseases, in particular asbestosis, or for environmental pollution. Many such liabilities have arisen under 'losses occurring policies' where liability may come to light long after the expiry of the policy period.

The LMX spiral

1215 The LMX spiral has been the subject of considerable discussion and comment. It also lies at the heart of a number of the current cases involving Lloyd's syndicates. Therefore, some background information about the nature of the LMX spiral is appropriate in this chapter. 'LMX' is the abbreviation given to London Market excess of loss reinsurance. LMX business arises when the reinsurer and retrocessionaire of an excess of loss contract on another excess of loss or whole account contract, are both based in the London Market. The parties for this purpose can be either Lloyd's syndicates or companies. The LMX spiral arose from the interrelationship between many reinsurers in the London Market who had both inwards and outwards reinsurance excess of loss contracts with one another. These types of reinsurance arrangements developed within Lloyd's over many years, but they were brought into sharp focus during the 1980s by two principal factors.

1216 First was the substantial increase in underwriting capacity in Lloyd's syndicates, as the number of Names and syndicates grew rapidly. The result was a reduction in premium rates, making it increasingly difficult for reinsurers to find retrocessionaires willing to cover ever increasing layers of excess of loss. There were also financial advantages, because of solvency regulations, for syndicates to reinsure with other Lloyd's syndicates, and this amplified Lloyd's involvement in LMX business.

1217 Second was the increased incidence of major catastrophes, in particular the Piper Alpha oil platform disaster, where the loss on the London Market has been estimated at US$1.4 billion.

1218 To understand how the LMX spiral operates, a simple example may help. (Of course such examples are inevitably oversimplified and so care should be exercised in interpreting the example.) We assume in our example that there are only two excess of loss underwriters in the market, underwriter X and underwriter Y. Underwriter X purchases an excess of loss reinsurance contract for £10 million excess of £1 million, for each and every loss from underwriter Y. Underwriter Y purchases a similar contract from underwriter X.

1219 Suppose now underwriter X suffers a loss of £5 million. He retains the first £1 million and claims £4 million from underwriter Y under his excess of loss reinsurance cover. Underwriter Y receives the claim for £4 million. He retains £1 million for his account and claims the excess £3 million from underwriter X under his own excess of loss reinsurance contract. When underwriter X receives the claim for £3 million his £1 million retention has already been used up by the same loss, so he is able to claim the whole £3 million from underwriter Y under his excess of loss contract. This ping-pong process continues until underwriter X has used up the whole of the £10 million excess of loss cover. At this point X no longer has reinsurance protection and has to bear Y's claim for £3 million. In net terms, X ends up paying £4 million and Y pays £1 million. In arriving at this ultimate net position X will have received four inward claims, including the original direct claim, totalling £14 million, and made three outward claims on Y totalling £10 million. Thus the notion of the 'spiral'.

1220 In reality, there were likely to be a number of separate syndicates involved in the spiral and some non-Lloyd's insurers. Nevertheless the example does illustrate how, despite what may on the face of it appear to be adequate excess of loss cover, the spiral effect can render such cover ineffective. The problem has been further exacerbated by the pricing of excess of loss contracts, where successive layers of reinsurance were written at decreasing rates.

1221 The key issues arising for those involved in the LMX spiral cases are:

(a) the recognition of the 'aggregate' or total amount of claims that one 'event' could give rise to under excess of loss policies written;

(b) the amount of the probable maximum loss that the given syndicate would suffer if that event arose; and

(c) the nature and extent of reinsurance protection obtained by the underwriter by reference to the potential risks arising under excess of loss contracts.

The role of the expert accountant

1222 The purpose of the remainder of this chapter is to examine the various roles that the expert, or indeed the forensic accountant, can play in claims by Names. The roles can be divided into two groups:

(a) those pertaining to issues of liability; and

(b) those pertaining to issues of damage;

although there is some overlap between the two.

The *Gooda Walker* judgment

1223 One of the first of the major cases, brought by Names in the current round of Lloyd's litigation, to proceed to judgment is that involving the Gooda Walker syndicates. The judgment contains some very important rulings on matters which are likely to be key issues in succeeding Lloyd's cases, so we make no apology for quoting from this judgment at some length. We therefore include, throughout the remainder of the chapter, some of the key points made by Mr Justice Phillips in his judgment on *Deeny v Gooda Walker Ltd.*[2]

ISSUES OF LIABILITY

1224 In Chapter 8 there is an explanation of the essential constituents of a successful negligence claim, including reference to foreseeable damage and the standards of care normally owed by a professional in his particular profession. It would be for the lawyers to advise as to the duty of care which must be established, and to advise on what would constitute a breach of that duty in the case of an underwriter or an agent, whether that agent is the managing agent or the member's agent. Although the main focus will be on the principles and practice at Lloyd's, a wide experience of insurance practices, rating and reserving generally will be required for those experts who are brought in to assist on this aspect of the case, whether for the plaintiffs or the defendants.

Claims against underwriters

1225 As we have said, claims against underwriters fall into two broad categories.

(a) First, there are alleged losses caused by negligent activity and decision making on the part of underwriters in entering into various underwriting contracts. These cases include those involving the negligent writing of 'run-off' cover contracts for other insurers' losses. They also encompass those concerning unjustified involvement in the LMX spiral without adequate reinsurance protection or appropriate monitoring of aggregate limits of exposure.

(b) Second, there are alleged losses caused by a failure properly to report and account for the underlying losses or the failure to make sufficient provision for long tail business claims. These cases include those concerned with the failure of syndicates to set an equitable RITC and those where it is alleged that the level of claims incurred, but not reported, was so uncertain that it was impossible to set an equitable RITC and that therefore the years of accounts should have been left open.

1226 The role of the expert accountant in relation to the first group of cases on liability issues can include substantial work, including the collation and scheduling of relevant financial data so that other experts, such as underwriting experts, can consider the quality of underwriting decisions made.

1227 The role of the expert accountant on the second group of cases is somewhat different in nature. Ultimately, it could involve the giving of expert evidence on the procedures and practices adopted by the underwriting agent in deriving RITC. Prior to this, there will typically be considerable work to be done in drawing together or examining the relevant data available at the time the RITC calculations were originally performed. Many of the claims allege negligence on this issue going back to the late 1970s or early 1980s, and so the collation of such data is an extensive exercise given the age of many of the relevant documents.

1228 Next, consideration needs to be given to the sufficiency of the available documentation for the purposes of an RITC exercise.

1229 Finally, the expert will wish to consider whether or not, in his opinion, the actual calculation of the RITC figure was reasonably calculated in the light of the available data.

Failure to do competent underwriting

1230 In the *Gooda Walker* judgment, Mr Justice Phillips had the following to say about the reasonable expectations of Names:

'The fact that a Name who joins Lloyd's deliberately agrees to expose himself to unlimited liability does not mean that he anticipates or accepts that when he joins a syndicate the active underwriter will deliberately expose him to the risk of such liability. On the contrary the Name will reasonably expect the underwriter to exercise due skill and care to prevent him from suffering losses.'

'A Name at Lloyd's, with the assistance of his Members Agent, will want to structure his underwriting in a manner that accords with his means and with his attitude to risk . . . A Name needs to know the nature of the exposure that he is likely to run by joining a particular syndicate if he is to be able to structure his underwriting business in an appropriate manner.'

1231 The judge had this to say about planning:

'Absence of written underwriting plans cannot be treated as evidence of lack of competence. What was, in my judgement, important was not that a plan should be written down, but that a plan should exist and be followed.'

'In my judgement it was a fundamental principle of excess of loss underwriting that the underwriter should formulate and follow a plan as to the amount of exposure that his syndicate would run.'

1232 He addressed the question of exposure to substantial risk as follows.

● Aggregates and probable maximum losses

'In order to monitor the exposure that results from the business he writes, the excess of loss underwriter must be aware of his aggregates . . . To calculate his exposure to a single event he needs to know how many of the covers that he has written are exposed to the risk of a claim should that event occur. He thus has to divide into different categories the covers that can aggregate. In practice this is normally done by a system of coding the different categories. The more carefully the business is recorded under appropriately chosen codes the more confident the underwriter will be able to be as to the limit of his exposure to a single event.'

● Horizontal exposure (exposure to a sequence of catastrophes)

'The competent excess of loss underwriter had to give careful consideration not merely to his vertical exposure but also to his horizontal exposure. This was true whether he was writing high level catastrophe business in the spiral or low level reinsurance of direct business and it is axiomatic that the underwriter had to plan his pattern of reinsurance protection. In relation to true catastrophe reinsurance, to grant more reinstatements than those purchased would produce an area of obvious exposure.'

1233 The way in which the judge addressed the question of the required standard of skill and care is of particular note. The defendants advanced the following principles which they contended applied to the present case.

(a) 'The standard of skill and care to be exercised by a member of a professional calling is the degree of skill and care ordinarily exercised by reasonably competent members of that profession or calling.'

(b) 'The existence of a common practice over an extended period of time by persons habitually engaged in particular business is strong evidence of what constitutes the exercise of reasonable skill and care.'

(c) 'In situations which call for the exercise of judgement, the fact that, in retrospect, the choice actually made can be shown to have turned out badly is not of itself proof of a failure to meet the necessary standard of care.'

(d) 'The Plaintiffs cannot show a failure to meet the required standard of skill and care unless the error on the part of the underwriter was such that a reasonably well informed and competent member of the profession or calling could [not] have made it.'

1234 Mr Justice Phillips accepted these propositions but made additional comments about three of them as follows.

(a) 'The first proposition does not remove from the Judge the determination of the standard of skill and care that ought properly to be demonstrated.'

(b) The action was concerned with underwriting spiral excess of loss reinsurance, a very specialised type of business in which the London market is no longer involved to any great extent.
'In these circumstances I do not consider that one can automatically regard the practices of those who wrote spiral business as constituting strong evidence of what constituted the exercise of reasonable skill and care. It is necessary to approach this case with the possibility in mind that, for many involved, a significant involvement in spiral business may not have been compatible with competent underwriting.'

(c) 'The fourth proposition is based on a passage of the speech of Lord Diplock in *Saif Ali v Sidney Mitchell* [1980] AC 198 at 220:
"No matter what profession it may be, the common law does not impose on those who practise it any liability for damage resulting from what in the result turn out to be errors of judgment, unless the error was such as no reasonably well informed and competent member of that profession could have made. So too the common law makes allowance for the difficulties in the circumstances in which professional judgments have to be made and acted upon."
This passage was dealing essentially with the question of judgment. The Plaintiffs' case is not that errors of judgment were made, but that judgment was not exercised at all in that the underwriters never acquired the data on which that judgment might have been based.'

Claims against auditors

1235 Ever since 1908 each syndicate has been required to undergo a form of audit; the prime purpose of this audit was, however, concerned with the solvency test for individual Names and for Lloyd's generally, and was directed to establishing that each member of Lloyd's was able to meet his share of present and likely future claims from his syndicate.

1236 The role and responsibility of the auditor to Lloyd's syndicates has, however, changed over the period to which the Names' claims relate. In particular, it has become necessary for auditors to give a 'true and fair' opinion on the results of the closed years, but this has only been a requirement since the 1985 accounts were filed in 1986 (although some firms were giving such opinions on 1984 syndicate accounts and earlier).

1237 Auditors are now also required to review the reports of underwriters and managing agents in order to check that there is consistency between these reports and the relevant accounts. It is important to remember that, as with a company and its directors, the primary duty for drawing up the accounts lies with the underwriting agency. It is not for the auditor to adjust the accounts, but simply to report on them in the required form.

1238 The role of the expert accountant in respect of claims against auditors of Lloyd's syndicates, is to form and express his opinion on whether or not the auditor has acted reasonably in forming his opinion on the syndicate's accounts.

1239 The matters which are typically relevant in claims against auditors are dealt with in Chapter 8. The additional factors to be borne in mind when reviewing audits of Lloyd's syndicates will include, inter alia:

(a) the particular scope of the audit by reference to the type of report the auditor was required to give in the relevant year (see para **1236** above);
(b) the relevant Lloyd's bye-laws and other pronouncements made to Lloyd's panel auditors by the Committee of Lloyd's (which includes the implicit comfort Lloyd's requires on the adequacy of the syndicates' accounting records);
(c) the nature and extent of work performed by the auditor to ensure that Lloyd's solvency tests had been observed by the syndicate; and
(d) the extent to which auditors reported, or ought to have reported, on the activities of underwriters and underwriting agencies prior to the mid-1980s, when various alleged improprieties came to the public eye.

Failure to report/account properly

1240 The severity of long tail problems, and the inherent uncertainty they give rise to in the calculation of syndicate results, have been topics of increasing concern for insurers since the late 1970s. Many of the cases brought by Names relate to long tail insurance and are directed to proving one or more of the following:

(a) that under-reserving took place so that equity was not achieved as between one year of account and the next;
(b) that the uncertainty of outcome was so severe as to invalidate whatever reserving process was adopted, ie it was inherently wrong to close off the

accounts after the three year period, and instead the accounts should have been kept open for a longer time;

(c) that insufficient care was taken by the underwriters and the agents to ascertain the true position, or that past trends were deliberately ignored so as to show an improved position;

(d) that a degree of recklessness or lack of reasonable care entered into some of the underwriting decisions; and

(e) that disclosure of the problems being faced by syndicates was insufficient for the Names to be able to order their own affairs in an informed manner, ie to decide whether to stay with the syndicate or leave.

1241 There is global evidence for saying that the deterioration of past years' liabilities has been consistently understated. The table below shows Lloyd's global result for the underwriting years 1985 to 1991, together with the split between pure-year results and the increase in reserves for prior years.

Lloyd's Global Profit/(Loss)

	Total result £million	Pure result £million	Adjustment in respect of prior years' reserves £million
1985	196	not available	not available
1986	649	not available	not available
1987	509	1,306	(425)
1988	(510)	432	(578)
1989	(2,063)	(1,376)	(395)
1990	(1,862)	(937)	(925)
1991	(1,576)	(615)	(961)

Note: The trend of 'deterioration' in 1992 and beyond has continued at about the level of 1991; the full effect will not be clear until the Equitas operation is completed at the end of 1995.

1242 It is clear that a large proportion of the losses from 1988 onwards relate to deterioration of accounts which have been closed in prior periods (column 3); that is, they are not 'pure year' losses but are the results of inaccuracies in reporting the result of earlier years. The real issue is whether this was reasonably foreseeable in the earlier years, given the information then available.

1243 In the *Gooda Walker* judgment, the duties owed by members' agents to an individual Name were said to include the following:

'(a) to advise the Name which syndicates to join and in what amounts,

(b) to keep him informed at all times of material factors which may affect his underwriting,

(c) to provide him with a balanced portfolio and appropriate spread of risk, a balanced spread of business on syndicates throughout the main markets at Lloyd's,

(d) to monitor the syndicates on which it places the Name, and to make recommendations as to whether the Name should increase his share on a syndicate, join a new syndicate, reduce his share or withdraw,

(e) to keep regularly in touch with the syndicates to which the Name belongs, and

(f) to advise and discuss with the Name the prospects and past results of syndicates on which he could be placed.'

Causation of loss

1244 While many Lloyd's cases focus on failure to establish adequate claims reserves, other major cases concern allegations of negligent underwriting. Insurance is by definition the spreading of risk. The process of underwriting can encompass the exercise of considerable judgment and experience, and complexities enter into many of the transactions. The underwriter does not warrant that his net underwriting result will be profitable. The mere occurrence of loss, however large, does not actually mean that a case can be sustained by the Names against the underwriters or their advisers. The issue is whether the underwriter acted negligently in judging or rating the risk.

1245 In the conduct of these types of cases there will be considerable time spent in proving or disproving that the behaviour of the underwriters, agents or auditors concerned was incompetent or reckless.

ISSUES CONCERNING DAMAGES

1246 The general principles for the assessment of damages are discussed in Chapter 1. It is necessary to show that the loss suffered flows from the alleged negligence. The loss suffered by any individual Name will depend on when the negligence took place in relation to the years in which the Name was a member of the syndicate.

1247 This issue can be well illustrated by considering the position of members of a syndicate where it is found that a certain year of account has been closed in circumstances where no reasonable RITC could have been calculated. Had there been no negligence, the year would have remained open until such time as a reasonable RITC amount could have been calculated (or, alternatively, put into a 'run-off' mode where all active underwriting would cease – an increasing phenomenon nowadays).

1248 A further potential issue arises in relation to losses suffered by new Names on the pure year accounts for the years in which they have been Names. It might be argued that, but for the earlier years being negligently closed, they would never have joined the syndicate, and thus that all losses that flow from joining are claimable. This is essentially a legal matter. However, the recent judgment in *Galoo v Bright Grahame Murray*[3] suggests that the court is unwilling to extend damages to include losses not directly caused by the negligent act. In the case of new Names, the direct cause of pure year losses is clearly the unsatisfactory underwriting in the relevant pure years. It would be for the Names to show that misrepresentation of earlier years' results was the direct cause of their joining the syndicate.

1249 In summary, for claims involving allegations of improper closure of years of account, it is necessary to prepare a detailed analysis of plaintiff Names showing years of entry to and exit from the syndicate. It will also be necessary to analyse the syndicate's results as between pure years' results and prior years' adjustments. It will also be necessary to attribute the proportion of the syndicate expenses and investment income which relates to the actual provisions set up. The schedules can then be used in conjunction with data on the individual Names' percentages to identify which Names have suffered loss flowing from the negligence, and the quantum of their net losses to date.

1250 The question remains: how to calculate future losses? Should the court award a cap on future losses? (This has not been done in *Gooda Walker*.) Quantification of future losses will require some judgmental answers since no one can be sure as to the ultimate result of latent liabilities which have still to be met. There are three possible sources of information as to the ultimate loss caused by deterioration of past accounts:

(a) there is the prospect that the Lloyd's central run-off company, Equitas, will, in early 1996, take on past liabilities up to 1985 from relevant syndicates, and this will provide a figure based on current information; or

(b) one could refer to the figures published by Chatset or other market commentators, although these are based largely on published data and are by no means universally accepted as an adequate guide; or

(c) a current actuarial review of the claims experience could be carried out, together with an actuarial evaluation of an appropriate provision for future losses.

Sources (b) and (c) are, of course, potentially subject to the same type of uncertainties as existed when the original claims reserve estimates were made.

1251 Names on the syndicate for the year that should have been left open, who continued as Names into the future periods, would of course suffer losses to the extent that the relevant underwriting year gave rise to a net loss, such losses perhaps increasing from year to year as the claims experience deteriorated. Such Names will not, however, have suffered these losses through the erroneous closure of the year in question. Had it been properly left open, they would have lost in any event. Their loss stemmed from the original poor underwriting, not the erroneous closure of the year of account.

1252 By contrast, new Names entering a syndicate in a year following that which should have been left open, will suffer loss to the extent that claims for earlier years exceed the provisions incorporated in the RITC, subject to any adjustment that needs to be credited in respect of investment income earned on the reserves set aside to cover the provisions made.

1253 Some evidence of the court's willingness to adopt a hypothetical approach to calculation of loss in Lloyd's cases has been provided by Philip J's decision in the case involving the Gooda Walker syndicates. Here it was held that the underwriter was negligent in the way it accepted risks in the LMX spiral without calculating the overall exposure of the Names to loss. The judge has assumed that had a proper consideration of the risks been made, the underwriter would have purchased reinsurance to limit his Names' exposure. He has directed that for the purpose of considering damage, evidence is put before him on what reinsurance could have been obtained and its cost:

- '. . . the Plaintiffs are entitled to that award of damages which will place them in the same position as if the underwriting carried out on their behalf by each syndicate had been competently performed. That basic test is easy to state but difficult to apply.'

- 'To attempt to reconstruct the position that the Names would have been in had the Gooda Walker underwriters adopted a competent approach to vertical exposure to catastrophes would be an impossible task.'

- 'In my judgment the Plaintiffs should recover by way of damages such sums as will put them in the same position as if this exposure had been protected by reinsurance.'

- 'Interest ought to be recovered by Names on their primary losses from the dates that those losses were sustained.'

1254 While none of these approaches may produce the right result, it is accepted by the court that certainty is not a prerequisite for calculating losses (see Chapter 1).

Categories of defendants

1255 Many syndicate Names have formed Names action groups for the purpose of bringing claims against those they consider responsible for causing their losses. The defendants are typically the respective syndicates' underwriting agents, members agents, auditors and, in some cases, actuaries and brokers.

1256 The damages that are being sought by the Names in the various actions against underwriters and their advisers and auditors are far beyond the means of the underwriters, or indeed of their advisers. It follows that the insurers (ie the errors and omissions insurers, or the professional indemnity insurers) will in practice be standing in the shoes of those who are being directly sued. It is probable that the insurance limits will be much below the value of the total claims put forward, and this will be a matter for consideration by the legal advisers in each case.

1257 A typical writ issued in cases relating to under-reserving for long tail claims on behalf of Names against underwriters, members agents or managing agents is on the following lines:

(a) the defendant was under a duty to achieve equity between Names when assessing the reinsurance to close premium;

(b) at the material time (ie whatever accounting date is chosen for the pleadings) it was impossible to quantify the syndicate's liabilities arising from, for example, asbestosis and pollution claims with any reasonable degree of accuracy;

(c) because the degree of uncertainty was too great, it was impossible to achieve equity between Names no matter what analysis was carried out, and the methods used by the defendant were inappropriate in any event; and

(d) the defendant was therefore negligent in closing the year of account chosen for the pleadings.

1258 Sometimes the points of claim are very broad brush in this respect. Rather than concentrating on the detail of individual RITC decisions, the tendency is to assert as a matter of logic that the liabilities incurred by the syndicate were at all times so uncertain that it could not in any circumstance have been possible to assess an equitable reinsurance to close premium. There will, of course, be many other allegations other than the central ones referred to above.

CONCLUSIONS

1259 The Lloyd's settlement offer published by Lloyd's of London on 6 December 1993, provides good background reading to the foregoing subject matter. Few cases have yet been heard in the High Court and it will be important to keep abreast of developing case law and any subsequent settlement offers which might be published by Lloyd's in 1995 or later. We have dealt with two major causes of action, namely negligent underwriting and negligent fixing of RITC premiums, in this chapter; there will be other causes which arise from special facts which do not call for general comment here.

1260 For cases involving allegations of negligent underwriting, the accountant's skills in assembling and analysing data concerning, in particular, excess of loss exposure, will be of great assistance.

1261 The reinsurance to close calculation is the most significant item in the preparation of syndicate accounts. For the Names' claims in relation to the RITC to succeed, they must establish that no reasonable underwriter would have closed the year (or assessed the RITC premium at the level eventually fixed) in the light of professional standards and the reasonable market practices applying at the time of the decision. While with hindsight it is clear that many RITC decisions were wrong, the question which will have to be answered is whether without hindsight it can be proved that reasonable standards were departed from and that negligence resulted. It is here that forensic accountants will be most employed.

1262 The accountant will have to look at the reserving methods adopted and see whether, given the level of information available, a reasonable decision had been made in spite of the degree of uncertainty inherent in the exercise. There will be questions as to whether equity between Names was maintained when this policy was adopted to achieve closure. As far as claims against syndicate auditors are concerned, the forensic accountant will be asked to consider whether they obtained sufficient appropriate and reliable evidence to enable them to form unqualified opinions on syndicate accounts. Again, there will be particular focus on the way in which syndicates arrived at their claims provisions including the RITC.

1263 Finally, the accountant will be called upon to assist in the presentation of evidence as to damages, working hand in hand with expert underwriters and actuaries. Here the skills of the forensic accountant in presenting financial data in a form easily digested by the court will be of considerable advantage in an environment where financial complexity is paramount.

NOTES

1 [1995] 1 WLR 243.
2 *Deeny v Gooda Walker Ltd* [1994] 3 All ER 508.
3 *Galoo Ltd v Bright Grahame Murray* [1995] 1 All ER 16.

Chapter 13

Security for costs

Introduction – The purpose of an application for security for costs – Financial evidence – The report to the court – Conclusion

INTRODUCTION

1301   Suing someone in the courts for half a million pounds is fruitless if his total assets are a secondhand car and a heavily mortgaged apartment in Neasden. However generous the judge may be in his award, the result will be a waste of money and a waste of time.

1302   There is no way in law of safeguarding a litigant from pursuing a man who turns out to be of straw, although everyone who makes a claim must have this risk in mind. So far as legal costs are concerned, the matter is more hopeful. In general the successful litigant recovers some, but rarely all, of his costs from the unsuccessful litigant. But this rule is of little consolation if the latter is unable, and cannot be forced, to pay up.

1303   The question of costs is important in commercial life. All sorts of litigious attempts are made, often as a ploy rather than with a view to an ultimate hearing in court. To defend oneself against such ploys, perhaps with expensive interlocutory hearings, puts much money at risk. Seeking 'security for costs' can be the remedy. The defendant's legal advisers will consider whether to seek an award of security for costs from the courts early in the proceedings. There usually need to be good grounds to persuade the court that an award is necessary and justified. Financial evidence, in the form of a sworn statement which can be exhibited to the judge, can help. The purpose of the statement is to show that if the plaintiff does not give some form of collateral, he might well turn out to be a bad debt when the bill for costs is posted to him.

THE PURPOSE OF AN APPLICATION FOR SECURITY FOR COSTS

1304   An application for security for costs is designed to safeguard a successful defendant from failing to recover his costs from the plaintiff. The principal circumstances for such an application, set out in Ord 23, r 1 of the Rules of the Supreme Court, are:

(a) where the plaintiff is a foreigner and, therefore, outside the UK jurisdiction; or

(b) where the plaintiff is a nominal plaintiff suing for the benefit of some other person; or

(c) in the case of a plaintiff company where the terms of the Companies Act 1985, s 726(1) apply, namely:

> 'Where in England and Wales a limited company is plaintiff in an action or other legal proceeding, the court having jurisdiction in the matter may, if it appears by credible testimony that there is reason to believe that the company will be unable to pay the defendant's costs if successful in his defence, require sufficient security to be given for those costs, and may stay all proceedings until the security is given.'

1305 Where a plaintiff company is in liquidation, that is generally prima facie sufficient ground for ordering security for costs. The fact that a plaintiff is a nominal plaintiff is also a ground for security. The fact that the plaintiff's impecuniosity is brought about by the subject matter of the action will usually be fatal to the application for security.

1306 Security for costs cannot be awarded against a defendant unless he himself is making a counterclaim, in which case he can be ordered to give security for the costs of the counterclaim. When fixing the amount of security in respect of costs of the counterclaim, the court will disregard that 'portion of the costs which could in any event have been incurred by reason of the defence' (Goode, RM *Commercial Law* (1982) Pelican); in many circumstances, therefore, a counterclaim will not trouble the defendant, particularly where the chief reason for his entering the action is to fight off a spurious claim.

1307 Once told by the court to do so, the plaintiff must give security for costs by one of the following:

- a payment into court;

- provision of a bank guarantee; or

- an insurance company bond.

1308 The granting of an application for security for costs is discretionary and the judge will consider the justness of the circumstances in each case. It is particularly difficult to get an order for security for costs in a professional negligence case. A simple claim alleging the plaintiff's actual or suspected lack of funds is not grounds for ordering that security be given. In our experience, judges (reinforced by the plaintiff's lawyers) regard applications for security for costs as serious matters, and need to be persuaded that they are essential; hence the need for sworn financial evidence.

1309 To illustrate that such applications are not easy to win, it is perhaps interesting to look at the case of *Porzelack KG v Porzelack (UK) Ltd*.[1] Here the plaintiff, Porzelack KG, was resident in West Germany and traded in car care products. Its proprietor had set up a number of companies in the UK and elsewhere and each had failed. In 1986 the plaintiff re-entered the UK market, importing car care products under the name 'Porzelack'.

1310 At about the same time a separate and unconnected company began trading under the name Porzelack (UK) Ltd, selling similar products to those sold by the West German group. The West German concern applied in the UK courts for an interim injunction to restrain the other group from 'passing off the car care products it is selling as being the products of the plaintiff organisation'. The defendant applied for security for costs against the plaintiff.

1311 In spite of the foreign status and weak financial history of the plaintiff, the court did not grant the application, on the grounds that:

(a) it was unnecessary to grant security in the UK, because the defendant company would be able to get an order for costs in West Germany under West German law, which would be enforceable under the 1968 EEC Convention on Jurisdiction and the Enforcement of Judgments in Civil and Commercial Matters; and
(b) the plaintiff would not be able to afford to bring proceedings if it had also to find the security for costs on the scale demanded by the defendant.

The defendant's use of the same name to sell similar products to those of the plaintiff might have made the court unsympathetic to the defendant's position.

1312 An application for security for costs is often hard to win; the court assesses the merits of each side's case before granting an application. The successful case must be both reasonable and realistic.

FINANCIAL EVIDENCE

1313 The financial investigation and evidence required for an application for security for costs will vary with the circumstances of the plaintiff's financial standing. Drawing evidence and conclusions from recent accounts may be enough.

1314 The main problem we have faced with this type of work is obtaining an accurate picture of the financial circumstances of the plaintiff. First, the available financial information may be out of date: information based on statutory filing may be many months and sometimes years old. Second, the published accounts may not provide sufficient information for fair conclusions to be drawn, for example, there may be no information on the lines of finance available to the company, especially if its parent is foreign. Third, even where a company provides up to date management accounts, their reliability can be questionable as they are not audited. Finally, some companies file accounts taking advantage of the limitations on disclosure allowed to small companies. In these circumstances no profit and loss accounts are published.

1315 In work of this nature our enquiries have ranged widely and have covered the following.

(a) Publicly available information – namely, company credit status reports, press cuttings and the statutory information on file at Companies House. This information is freely available but may be seriously out of date.
(b) Information obtained from the other side in connection with the application, for example, unaudited management accounts showing the company's current trading position and balance sheet. Such information may be inaccurate.

1316 The information obtained from the other side tends to carry extra weight in litigation, if deemed to be reliable, because:

(a) it is usually more up to date than that which is publicly available;
(b) it may be concerned with the future, which is relevant to the question of security for costs; and
(c) it may address some topics, such as contingent liabilities, with more thoroughness than the publicly available information.

1317 The accountant's review of the financial position, whether revealed by published or internal sources, must cover trends in profits or losses and an assessment of the likely cash position in the future, after taking account of any liabilities. A review of the accounts to identify unusual or incorrect accounting policies, for example, expenditure carried forward as an asset in the balance sheet rather than written off, may produce valuable evidence for the accountant's report.

1318 Once he has reviewed the information, the accountant must then consider the following questions.

● How much are the legal costs likely to be? (The lawyers will advise on this.)

● Does the plaintiff have the financial resources to meet such costs?

● Are there any contingent liabilities which might affect the plaintiff's ability to pay costs?

● What lines of finance and credit are open to the plaintiff?

● How much does the other side depend on support from related or group companies?

● Are those group companies likely to be able to meet the costs in an application of this type?

● Does the group holding company have rights to siphon off the plaintiff's bank balance through bank set-off or similar arrangements?

THE REPORT TO THE COURT

1319 If the financial information indicates that the plaintiff may be unable to pay the costs, it is usual for that to be reported by way of affidavit. An example of an affidavit in the appropriate form is given in Appendix G to this book. Where we are unable to testify in this way, we often provide a report analysing the plaintiff's position without saying whether he is likely to be good for costs. This can be a helpful compromise and often provides useful background to counsel if he decides to go forward with an application.

CONCLUSION

1320 To state that a company will not be good for its liabilities is a serious charge and should not be made lightly. An application for security for costs will be considered very critically by the judge.

1321 Sometimes, after a thorough review, it is not possible to testify in favour of the application. The work has not been wasted, however. The report or review may show that the other side is in a financially stronger, or weaker, position than was previously thought. This information may be useful in negotiations, for example, in inducing the other side to produce more funds, guarantees or information. Alternatively, it may help to persuade the court to give greater urgency to the dispute, perhaps by bringing forward the date of the trial.

NOTE

1 [1987] 1 All ER 1074.

Chapter 14

Interest and foreign currency: their effect on damages

Introduction – Interest – Interest as damages at common law – Interest on damages – The interest rates to apply – The interest period – Interest on interest – Effect of foreign exchange on damages – Foreign currency liquidated damages – Conclusion

INTRODUCTION

1401 This chapter deals with two factors affecting the calculation of damages: interest and awards in foreign currency. On the whole, we have chosen in this book to avoid regular reference to underlying statutes and case precedents on which the question of liability is determined. However, in this chapter we think it is helpful for the authorities to be stated.

INTEREST

1402 In this section we give a brief overview of the present legal position on interest and, in particular, seek to remove the confusion between interest awarded as a part of damages and interest awarded on damages. The expert accountant will frequently run across reference to interest in claims documentation when he is involved in the review or preparation of a claim. Because some cases take years to come to trial, the effect of interest can add significantly to the sum being claimed. But because it can involve detailed mathematical calculations, some lawyers, in our experience, are reluctant to grasp the interest nettle.

1403 The terms and conditions of many contracts specify the provision of interest in respect of overdue sums. Where interest has been provided for, the court does not also award interest as damages for the lost time value of money, since compensation is deemed to have been provided within the contract. Where interest has not been specifically provided for, the court awards interest as damages for the lost time value of money in a very limited range of contractual claims. Statute now requires the court to award interest on damages in claims arising out of personal injury and wrongful death unless there are special reasons for not doing so. But in all other cases the court has discretionary power to award interest.

Interest as damages at common law

1404 Historically, in contract law, if interest was not expressly or by implication contracted for, where it was open at the time for the parties so to do, the law did

178

not give interest by way of damages. Successful litigants still do not obtain an award of interest as a matter of course. However, awards of interest on contractual disputes have been held appropriate in certain circumstances: where, for example, it was foreseeable at the outset that late payment would cause the plaintiff loss. In these circumstances, interest can be awarded as damages 'on the simple commercial basis that if the money had been paid at the appropriate commercial time, the other side would have had the use of it'.[1] As Lord Denning put it:

> 'In a commercial transaction, if the plaintiff has been out of his money for a period, the usual order is that the defendant should pay interest for the time for which the sum has been outstanding. No exception should be made except for good reason.'[2]

1405 As a result of these developments, the successful plaintiff may now recover interest where he can show that he has paid overdraft interest or has lost interest income as a direct result of being deprived of the use of funds. While the plaintiff does not always succeed in such a claim, a number of authorities support him. A good example is the case of *Bushwall Properties Ltd v Vortex Properties Ltd*.[3] In that case, the defendant, having sold properties to the plaintiff on instalment terms, then insisted on full payment immediately. To meet the payment, the plaintiff had to borrow money and to use funds which would otherwise have earned interest income. The judge decided that the plaintiff was entitled to recover the interest expense incurred and the interest income lost.

1406 An exception to this principle exists in the case of breach of contract to render services. In such a case there is apparently no common law authority for awarding interest, and no good basis for making an award under statute either.

Interest on damages

1407 Under statute, interest may be awarded on damages or on a debt. For High Court actions, the relevant provision is the Supreme Court Act 1981 s 35A, which states in sub-s (1) that:

> 'Subject to the rules of court, in proceedings (whenever instituted) before the High Court for the recovery of a debt or damages there may be included in any sum for which judgment is given simple interest, at such rate as the court thinks fit or as rules of court may provide, on all or any part of the debt or damages in respect of which judgment is given, or payment is made before judgment . . .'

1408 In addition, sub-s (4) states that:

> 'Interest in respect of a debt shall not be awarded under this section for a period during which, for whatever reason, interest on the debt already runs'.

1409 A similar section is included in the County Courts Act 1984 for county court actions. In addition, a statutory provision, in the Arbitration Act 1950 s 19A, as inserted into the Administration of Justice Act 1982 Sch 1, enables an arbitrator to award simple interest (never compound interest) if he thinks fit, at such a rate as he thinks fit.

1410 In cases other than personal injury and wrongful death, these statutory provisions give the court the following four-fold discretion:

(a)   whether to award interest at all;
(b)   what rate of interest to apply;
(c)   on what part of the damages in respect of which judgment is given, or payment is made before judgment, interest is to be paid; and
(d)   for what period between the date when the cause of action arose and the earlier of the date of payment and the date of judgment to award interest.

Although the statute gives considerable power to the court to decide on the merits of a particular case, it expressly disallows the giving of interest on interest, ie compound interest is disallowed (but see also para **1420**). The governing principle for all claims for interest on damage is held to be that interest should be awarded to the plaintiff, not as compensation for the damage done, but for being kept out of money which ought to have been paid to him (per Lord Herschell LC in *London, Chatham and Dover Rly Co v South Eastern Rly Co*[4]).

1411   In cases of personal injury and wrongful death, the court is obliged to award interest on damages exceeding £200 unless it is satisfied that there are special reasons to the contrary. However, if no claim for interest is pleaded the plaintiff will not be awarded interest.[5]

1412   The flowchart opposite may help the reader negotiate his way through the interest maze. It ends up with a number of questions to be addressed. The succeeding paragraphs give guidance on the answers.

The interest rates to apply

1413   In cases other than personal injury and wrongful death, the rate at which interest is awarded is at the discretion of the court. Certain rates are commonly applied. In commercial cases, the rate applied is theoretically the plaintiff's cost of borrowing, if he had to borrow money. It has been said that base rate plus 1% is appropriate in most commercial cases. Where damages in foreign currency are concerned, the court takes into account the rate at which a person could reasonably have borrowed the foreign currency in the relevant foreign country.[6] In other cases, interest is commonly awarded at rates fixed from time to time pursuant to the Judgments Act 1838.

1414   In personal injury claims, the court will split the damages into three categories, each of which is treated differently for interest purposes. The rate of interest to be awarded on the category deemed to be special damages, should, according to the Supreme Court Fund Rules, be 'a realistic rate'. The rules give as an example the average rate of interest allowed on money paid into court and placed on the Special Account (formerly Short Term Investment Account). For special damages awarded for the period until the date of trial, ie past loss, the rate of interest applied to the award depends upon whether or not the special damages are continuing, for example, loss of earnings. Where special damages are continuing, the court awards half the special account rate from the date of injury to the date of trial. In cases where special damages have ceased, there are conflicting Court of Appeal decisions as to whether the award should be half the special account rate from the date of injury to trial[7] or the full special account rate for the finite period during which the special damages were suffered.[8] For the category of damages awarded for loss of future earnings, there is a nil rate of

THE AWARD OF INTEREST UNDER SUPREME COURT ACT 1981 S 35(A)

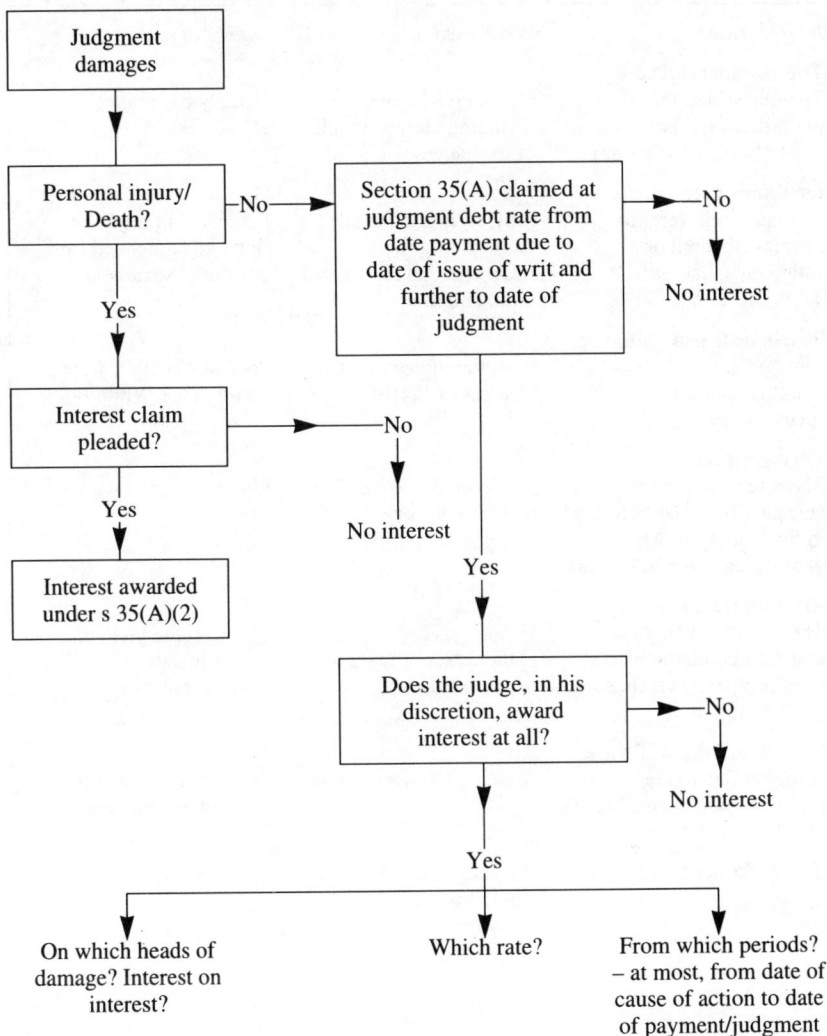

```
┌─────────────┐
│  Judgment   │
│  damages    │
└─────────────┘
       │
       ▼
┌─────────────┐         ┌──────────────────────┐
│ Personal    │  ─No─▶  │ Section 35(A) claimed │  ─No─▶   No interest
│ injury/     │         │ at judgment debt rate │
│ Death?      │         │ from date payment due │
└─────────────┘         │ to date of issue of   │
       │                │ writ and further to   │
      Yes               │ date of judgment      │
       ▼                └──────────────────────┘
┌─────────────┐                   │
│ Interest    │  ─No─▶  No interest
│ claim       │
│ pleaded?    │                  Yes
└─────────────┘                   ▼
       │                ┌──────────────────────┐
      Yes               │ Does the judge, in    │  ─No─▶   No interest
       ▼                │ his discretion, award │
┌─────────────┐         │ interest at all?      │
│ Interest    │         └──────────────────────┘
│ awarded     │                   │
│ under        │                  Yes
│ s 35(A)(2)  │                   ▼
└─────────────┘
```

On which heads of damage? Interest on interest?   Which rate?   From which periods? – at most, from date of cause of action to date of payment/judgment

interest. For the category of general damages awarded for pain, suffering and loss of amenities, the interest is 2% per annum.

1415 The table overleaf sets out the various rates available, when they apply and their source. Rates will vary from time to time, so regular reference to the sources will be necessary.

The interest period

1416 The maximum period for which interest can be awarded under the Supreme Court Act 1981 is from the date when the cause of action arose to the

RATES OF INTEREST

Interest rate	When used	Source of rate
The commercial rate The rate which the plaintiff would have had to pay to borrow the money	Commercial cases including claims on bills of exchange	Usually base rate plus 1%
Ordinary rate The court will refer to Special Account or Judgments Act rate	May be applied to all damage awards. Judgment Act rate is more common	Published in the White Book and amended by statutory instrument
The investment rate The rate at which the plaintiff could have invested the money	Personal injury cases [see para **1414**]	Special Accounts Rate – found in the White Book
Foreign interest rates The rate at which that currency could be borrowed in the country in which the debt should have been paid	If judgment is given in a foreign currency	Rate must be proved in evidence
True interest rate The rate that disregards that element in the market rates of interest attributable of 'inflation'	If damages are assessed at the date of trial in a depreciated currency	Based on the yield on index-linked government stock
'The wilful default' rate A higher rate to ensure no profit is made from a breach of fiduciary duty	Breach of fiduciary duty	Court's discretion under its equitable jurisdiction
The Judgments Act rate	(1) Judgments Act s 17 (2) Industrial tribunal awards (3) At the court's discretion (see above)	White Book

earlier of either the date of payment or the date of judgment. The actual period adopted is at the court's discretion, but tends to be related to the period during which the plaintiff is 'kept out of money' which ought to have been paid to him.

1417 Where the plaintiff has received insurance money under an insurance policy, interest will be allowed only on the balance of damages not covered by the insurance money. Also, following the decision in *Tate & Lyle Industries Ltd v GLC*,[9] the interest award may be adjusted downwards where it can be shown that the gross cost which is claimed was an allowable expense for tax purposes thereby reducing a later tax payment. Interest may be applied to the sum net of tax for the period following the date of the payment of tax.

1418 There may be some delay between the date on which judgment is given and the date on which the defendant meets the judgment debt. To compensate the plaintiff for that delay, interest is given under statute. Interest arising on judgments is covered by the Judgments Act 1838 s 17. For this purpose, a judgment will also include an arbitration award and debts due to or from the Crown by statutory instrument. Interest is payable on judgment debts at a specified rate fixed from time to time, and runs on the debt from the date of entering judgment until the satisfaction of the judgment.

1419 The provision for interest under the Supreme Court Act 1981 s 35A runs until 'the date of judgment', whilst under the Judgments Act 1838 s 17 interest is awarded from 'the time of entering up judgment'. Interest therefore should not accrue on the same moneys for the same period under the two Acts. This has raised uncertainties in cases where a final judgment follows an interlocutory judgment. Where there is a split trial in personal injury cases, the House of Lords determined in *Thomas v Bunn*[10] that interest runs under the Judgments Act 1838 s 17 from the date of the judgment which quantified or recorded the damages payable to the plaintiff, rather than from the date of judgment determining the liability. It is immaterial whether or not the judgment as to liability also directed payment of damages 'to be assessed'.

Interest on interest

1420 As stated in para **1410**, compound interest is effectively disallowed by statute. We might reasonably expect that the plaintiff is not therefore entitled to interest on an award of interest as damages. Recent cases indicate that this simple conclusion is not necessarily valid.

1421 In the case of *Bushwall Properties Ltd v Vortex Properties Ltd*,[11] Oliver J held that the plaintiffs were entitled to an award of statutory interest on the interest awarded as damages. He decided that the claim for interest as damages was simply a claim for the replacement of a sum of money, the quantum of which was calculated by reference to interest. Accordingly he saw no reason why statutory interest could not be awarded on this element of the claim.

1422 It is the practice of banks to compound interest by capitalising interest at, for example, quarterly or annual intervals. In *National Bank of Greece SA v Pinios Shipping Co No 1*,[12] the House of Lords upheld a bank's right to compound interest and Lord Goff concluded that: 'There appears to be no basis in justice or logic for terminating that right simply because the bank has demanded payment of the amount outstanding in a customer's account'. Consequently a bank's right to charge compound interest on the contractual debt until repayment, continues after the demand for payment has been made until all sums are paid or until judgment is given on the bank's claim.

1423 Our advice to the expert accountant is to discuss the implications fully with the legal advisers in any case where interest is involved in the calculation of quantum. The amount could have a bearing on pre-trial negotiations and in decisions on how much to pay into court to protect against costs if negotiations fail. Although some broad brush rules can be applied to calculate the figure of interest this may be of little use if the wrong principles are applied.

1424 Litigants who are awarded costs are entitled to interest on those costs. Interest runs from the date of judgment, not the date taxation of costs is completed, and is at the Judgments Act rate.[13]

EFFECT OF FOREIGN EXCHANGE ON DAMAGES

1425 In this section we consider how damages are calculated and settled. when some or all of the underlying transactions were contracted or were carried out in a foreign currency. The wide extent nowadays of international transactions in business inevitably results in many disputes which involve currencies other than sterling.

1426 The decision in 1976 in the case of *Miliangos v George Frank (Textiles) Ltd*[14] is an important one here. This case was complex. The plaintiff, a Swiss national, sold goods to an English company at a price expressed to be payable in Swiss francs. The goods and invoice were delivered but the price was not paid and two bills of exchange drawn in Switzerland were dishonoured on presentation. The plaintiff originally brought a claim for the price or, alternatively, the amount due on the bills of exchange expressed initially in the sterling equivalent of the sum due in Swiss francs as at the dates when payments should have been made. The plaintiff later amended his claim so as to claim the sums due to him in Swiss francs.

1427 For many years the general rule for the treatment of such claims had been:

(a) that all claims and all judgments had to be made in sterling;
(b) the damages were calculated in accordance with generally accepted principles;
(c) this calculation was sometimes in a foreign currency, which was then translated into sterling to arrive at a figure for the loss suffered; and
(d) the conversion to sterling was made at the same date as that at which the damages were calculated.

1428 However, in the 1970s frequent exchange rate fluctuations occurred and the fixed exchange rate regime of the commercial world tended to be abandoned in favour of a system of floating exchange rates. It thus became increasingly difficult to calculate the amount required as restitution to a plaintiff; the currency of the loss and the currency of the award no longer had a stable relationship.

1429 The decision in *Miliangos* in 1976 was to depart from the established practice described above and to 'award delivery in specie rather than by giving damages'. The effect of this decision was that while the breach date was still to be used for the calculation in foreign currency of the loss, the need to convert this loss into a sterling sum disappeared if the original claim had been for the foreign currency. However, a conversion date was still required, either in the court's judgment or in the claim, so that the claim could be enforced in this country. The date of judgment (rather than the date of breach as previously) is now the appropriate date for effecting this conversion.

Foreign currency liquidated damages

1430 The decision in *Miliangos* was extended to cover liquidated damages in the case of *Federal Commerce & Navigation Co Ltd v Tradax Export SA, The Maratha Envoy*.[15] In this case it was held that the *Miliangos* decision applied equally to claims for debt and claims for liquidated damages. The award in

Federal Commerce was denominated in US dollars, despite the fact that the designated law of the contract was English. Lord Denning said:

'Once it is recognised that judgment can be given in a foreign currency, justice requires that it should be given in every case where the currency of the contract is a foreign currency otherwise one side or the other will suffer unfairly by the fluctuations of the exchange'.

In taking this line, the courts were following the practice of commercial arbitrators in London, who had for some time been reaching settlements denominated in foreign currency, following the unsettled era of exchange rates.

1431   The determination of the appropriate foreign currency to use in awards for unliquidated damages for breaches of contract, where foreign currency is involved, requires separate consideration. Unlike disputes involving debts or liquidated damages, there will be no specific currency applicable to unliquidated damages. Some claims for unliquidated damages can result from businesses from two different countries agreeing to pay for goods in another country's currency and suffering damages in yet another currency. Lord Wilberforce has said: 'The first step must be to see whether expressly or by implication the contract provides an answer to the currency question. This may lead to selection of the currency of contract'.[16]

1432   There are also problems in selecting the right currency for damages in respect of indirect losses. A business may have to use its own domestic currency to purchase a foreign currency to pay for expenses such as repair work arising from a breach of contract. It was held in the House of Lords that damages for breach of contract in respect of sums expended in a foreign currency should be calculated, in the words of Lord Wilberforce in the *SEAS* case: 'In the currency in which the loss was felt by the plaintiff or which most truly expresses his loss'. This rule is in accordance with the principle that the court should compensate the plaintiff following the principle of restitution.

1433   Damages arising in cases of tort can also be awarded in foreign currencies. Once again, Lord Wilberforce expressed an opinion on this subject in *SEAS*. He said:

'It appears to me that a plaintiff who normally conducts his business through a particular currency and who when other currencies are immediately involved uses his own currency to obtain that currency can reasonably say that the loss he sustains is to be measured not by the immediate currencies in which loss first emerges but by the amount of his own currency which in the normal course of operation he uses to obtain these currencies. This is the currency in which his loss is felt, that is, the currency which is reasonably foreseeable he will have to spend'.

The key question appears to be, with what currency is the plaintiff's loss most closely linked? For example, if a foreign plaintiff bringing an action for tort suffered in the UK is able to show that his own domestic currency would be used to meet expenses in connection with the suffering which is the cause of the claim, then that would be the currency of the award.

1434   The position is not clear as to whether a loss suffered in a foreign currency has to be claimed in that foreign currency. However, supporting a sterling claim for a foreign currency denominated debt would be difficult if to do so would take advantage of exchange rate movements since the due date of payment.

1435   In calculating a foreign currency claim, it may be appropriate to indicate associated foreign exchange losses. For example, a plaintiff may have been due to receive payment in a foreign currency and he may have entered into forward currency deals to hedge his currency exposure. The failure to receive the foreign currency due will cause losses in the matching foreign exchange deal entered into as a hedge. Any such losses would need to be claimed under a separate head of loss. It would be necessary to prove that it was reasonable for the plaintiff to act in this manner and that the defendant could have foreseen such a loss.

1436   Lastly we have to consider what is the correct treatment of interest on damages awarded in a foreign currency. The rules are not clear but it seems possible that the courts would choose to apply the rate of interest applicable to the currency of the award rather than apply the UK interest rates applicable to sterling borrowings. In *Miliangos*, the interest rate awarded was that at which a person could reasonably have borrowed the foreign currency in the foreign country. The interest rate to be applied here is the general rate applicable to people in general, rather than the specific interest rate applied to an individual plaintiff's situation (unless interest is claimed as a separate head of damage, in which case we would expect the courts to look at the actual interest suffered or foregone).

1437   In some of the decided cases which relate to foreign currency damages, the principal sum has been awarded in one currency and then interest calculated at rates which relate to another currency. As a matter of economic common sense this seems to be wrong. A country's inflation rates, foreign exchange depreciation and interest rates are all inter-linked; the higher the inflation rate, the higher the interest rate and the softer the currency.

CONCLUSION

1438   The foregoing chapter demonstrates that the topics of interest and foreign currency are something of a minefield in the matter of damages.

1439   If an international dispute is under investigation, the expert accountant in preparing his report should take care to establish which foreign currency conversions are appropriate when damages are being calculated for purposes of a claim. This may require a careful examination of the circumstances in which trading transactions have arisen and the conclusions will need to be reviewed with the help of legal advice. The conclusions should be presented as part of the expert's report.

NOTES

1 *Kemp v Tolland* [1956] 2 Lloyd's Rep 681.
2 *Panchaud Frères SA v Pagnam and Fratelli* [1974] Lloyd's Rep 394, CA.
3 [1975] 2 All ER 214.
4 [1893] AC 429.

5 *Ward v Chief Constable for Avon and Somerset* (1985) 129 Sol Jo 606.
6 *Miliangos v George Frank (Textiles) Ltd (No 2)* [1977] QB 489.
7 *Dexter v Courtaulds* [1984] 1 All ER 70.
8 *Prokop v DHSS* [1985] CLY 1037.
9 [1981] 3 All ER 716.
10 [1991] 2 WLR 27.
11 [1975] 2 All ER 214.
12 [1989] 3 WLR 1330.
13 *Hunt v R M Douglas (Roofing) Ltd* [1988] 3 All ER 823.
14 [1976] AC 443, HL.
15 [1978] AC 1, HL.
16 *Services Europe Atlantique Sud (SEAS) v Stockholms Rederiaktiebolag SVEA, The Folias* [1979] AC 685.

Chapter 15

Taxation of damages

Introduction – Income tax and corporation tax on income – Income
or capital? – Wrongful dismissal – Treatment of interest – Tax on
capital gains – Revision of consideration following settlement of a
dispute over a sale and purchase agreement – Inheritance tax –
VAT – Damages subject to reduction for tax effects (the Gourley
Principle) – The tax period – Deductibility of damages for tax
purposes – The period of deduction for the defendant – Tax on
interest – Tax on awards made in foreign currency – Conclusion

INTRODUCTION

1501 In this chapter we give an overview of the issues requiring consideration
when advising on the taxation of damages and in determining whether damages
are subject to income tax, corporation tax, CGT, inheritance tax, VAT, or a
combination of these taxes. We describe circumstances where damages may be
awarded net of tax. We discuss how awards of interest may be treated for tax
purposes, how foreign currency awards are dealt with and also in which period
damages regarded as income may fall to be taxed. Finally we consider how the
defendant's tax position is affected by a payment of damages.

1502 Damages are awarded to compensate the injured party. The amount of
compensation is intended to put him back in the position he would have been in,
in so far as money can do so, had the injury or breach of contract not occurred.
The loss suffered and the settlement afterwards of the resulting litigation will
almost certainly affect the taxation payable by the plaintiff. The court, therefore,
has this in mind when considering whether taxation should be taken into account
in arriving at an award.

1503 The taxation consequences of any injury and of receiving the associated
compensation cannot, therefore, be ignored when considering damages in court or
in out of court settlements. Tax considerations will be material, not only to the
plaintiff, but also to the defendant, and can be an important aspect of any
negotiations for a settlement. In general, damages awarded by the court and sums
paid as compensation following an out of court settlement are treated similarly for
tax purposes.

1504 When considering the extent to which taxation may be of significance to
the assessment of damages, the expert accountant should have regard to:

(a) the circumstances of the injured party at the time the injury occurred;
(b) what happened and what gave rise to the injury;

(c) the jurisdiction in which the injured party is regarded as resident and carrying on his business activities for taxation purposes (these may differ, depending on the tax under consideration);

(d) if the injury occurred in some other country, the activities which the injured party was undertaking in that jurisdiction, the presence they had in that country and the tax consequences;

(e) the extent to which:

    (i) charges to taxation may have arisen, or should have arisen, as a result of the injury, or

    (ii) the injured party may have been granted, or entitled to, relief for losses and expenses associated with the injury compared with what would otherwise have been taxable income or gains;

(f) the tax consequences for the party receiving an award, including the date on which the award may be regarded as having been paid for taxation purposes (this date may be earlier than the actual date of payment);

(g) the circumstances in which the defendant or others may be able to claim some deduction from taxable profits, income or gains in his hands (which may be significant in determining his ability to pay the compensation); and

(h) whether, depending on to whom and how the award is paid, there may be opportunities to recover tax already paid, or to reduce potential tax payable, by the injured party or some other party.

1505 When considering these matters, the expert accountant should also have in mind:

(a) the extent to which an injured party may be under an obligation to account to others on an award being settled and, hence, their potential significance to those others for tax purposes and therefore to the obligations of the injured party; and

(b) the extent to which tax may have to be paid in more than one jurisdiction and the consequent need to minimise the risk of double taxation.

What may be exempt from tax in the hands of one taxpayer, or in one jurisdiction, may not be so in the hands of another, or in another state.

1506 What appear at first to be the obvious tax consequences of a claim and the settlement of the damages often turn out to be more complex on closer examination of the injured party's tax affairs. Many taxpayers negotiate, or grant themselves, concessions for tax purposes which are unique to their needs. Avoidance or evasion may be an issue. Conversely, offers structured to reduce the taxation payable thereon by the other side, or to maximise the taxation relief available, can often improve the chances of an out of court settlement. For this reason, it makes sense to obtain information about both the plaintiff's and the defendant's tax affairs so that advantage can be taken of these opportunities. It pays not to be surprised by unforeseen taxation consequences. It is also important to deal with potential tax issues during the pleadings stage, for example, when making requests for further and better particulars. The court is unlikely to allow representations about tax issues to be introduced only at the hearing.

1507 Having analysed what occurred and the nature of the compensation, the tax adviser should review the results in the light of the circumstances in which tax is payable and so we now highlight some of the issues that can arise when considering income tax, corporation tax, CGT, inheritance tax and VAT.

INCOME TAX AND CORPORATION TAX ON INCOME

Income or capital?

1508 Typically, damages received by way of compensation for loss of income or profits are taxable in the hands of the recipient in broadly the same way as the original income, for which the damages are the compensation, would have been. The same is true for reimbursed expenses. However, there are significant exceptions, and examples of these are given in the following paragraphs.

1509 Damages awarded in respect of the profit of a trade or profession may be subject to tax under Schedule D Case I or II, depending respectively on whether the receipt is a receipt of a trade or a profession. Furthermore:

(a) damages as compensation for the loss of trading income are treated as income receipts, even where the damages relate to the loss of, or damage to, an asset used in the trade;

(b) damages as compensation for destruction of the whole profit-making apparatus may be treated as receipts of a capital nature; and

(c) damages paid for the loss of the benefit of a trading contract will be a capital receipt if the failed contract constitutes the whole of the plaintiff's business – otherwise they are treated as income receipts for tax purposes.

1510 The mere fact that damages are quantified by reference to income does not necessarily mean that those damages are taxable income in the hands of the plaintiff. Compensation for loss of a complete business sector could be treated as a capital item and subject to tax on capital gains. In some cases where liability is disputed, a payment out of court may be in the nature of a gift and not subject to income tax or CGT. In such cases, the defendant may not be able to claim a deduction for tax purposes.

Wrongful dismissal

1511 Damages for wrongful dismissal from an office or employment are normally taxed under Schedule E to the extent that they and other termination benefits exceed £30,000 (£25,000 for terminations before 6 April 1988). If the payment arises under a contract, it may be taxable in full. Payment agreed to and made to plaintiffs after they have left their employment, in compensation for taxable earnings, should be paid after deduction of tax at the basic rate with the prior approval of the Inland Revenue. The tax deducted from such compensation may be limited to that due on the amount of compensation over and above the first £30,000. The defendants are responsible for accounting to the Inland Revenue for the sum so deducted. Such taxable damages can include the reimbursement of the costs incurred by the plaintiff in pursuing his claim unless, by concession, limited to legal advice. Therefore, other advisers in such cases should be instructed directly by the plaintiff's solicitors, who should also assume the responsibility for the payment of their fees and treat these as disbursements on his bill.

1512 Where the defendant company makes a payment into court in a wrongful dismissal case, consideration must be given to how to deal with income tax. The payment into court does not itself give rise to a liability on the defendant to account for income tax to the Inland Revenue because at that point the money remains the property of the defendant. However, a liability to account for tax at the basic rate could arise if and when the payment is taken out of court by the plaintiff.

1513 Unless some arrangement is made to withhold the relevant basic rate tax from the payment into court, the defendant will find itself paying both the gross claim and having to account separately to the Inland Revenue for the tax. In these circumstances it may be appropriate to pay the relevant sum net of basic rate tax into court, and at the same time to issue a form of Calderbank letter undertaking:

(a) to account to the Inland Revenue for the income tax withheld; and
(b) to provide the appropriate certificate of deduction should the payment into court be accepted by the plaintiff.

Treatment of interest

1514 Arrears of interest included as a separate part of the damages claim are subject to tax as interest. For example, consider a situation where an order is made directing the defendant to pay the plaintiff a net amount plus interest running at a prescribed rate from a prescribed date until the net amount is paid to the plaintiff. In this case, the interest will be liable to income tax in the hands of the plaintiff when it is paid.

1515 On the other hand, a lump sum awarded for loss of interest may be capital, even where the amount is arrived at by reference to the interest that has accrued over a period. For example, consider a situation where an order is made that the defendant should deposit a lump sum in the joint names of the solicitors acting for both parties. The order provides for a specified share of the balance on the account (comprising the original deposit plus the accrued interest to date) to be paid to the plaintiff on the occurrence of a particular event. In such a case the payment will not be taxable in the hands of the plaintiff, even though it includes accrued interest. Damages for loss of future interest or annual payments may be taxed as income or capital, depending on the circumstances. This is a complex area where the arrangements must be considered carefully with the tax legislation.

1516 Some forms of damages represent loss of income which, if received in the normal course of events, would have been taxable, but when received as lump sum damages on a settlement are not taxable. The most common of these is compensation for loss of income in personal injury cases which is discussed further at para **1529**ff.

TAX ON CAPITAL GAINS

1517 Compensation for the loss of an asset is generally taxable under the CGT legislation, but charges to income tax or corporation tax may also arise where capital allowances have previously been granted. Compensation for a wrong or injury suffered by an individual in his personal or business capacity is usually exempt, but this does not extend to losses in his finances, such as compensation for loss of goodwill, or the loss of a chargeable asset.

1518 Where a person suffers actual loss or damage, he is treated for CGT purposes (in the light of the decision in *Zim Properties Ltd*[1]) as having acquired, at that time, a separate chargeable asset for CGT (or, in the case of companies, corporation tax) purposes. This asset takes the form of a right to take legal proceedings ('the right').

1519 If the right arose on or before 9 March 1981, the injured party is deemed to have acquired this right for its open market value on the date that the right first arose. If the right arose after that date, and the party enjoying the right gave no consideration for its acquisition (which will usually be the case), he is treated as having acquired it for no consideration. If the right first arose before 31 March 1982 and was realised on or after 6 April 1988, or was acquired on the death after the former date of the claimant, the right is treated as acquired on 31 March 1982, or on death, for its open market value at the relevant time.

1520 In practice, the Inland Revenue is prepared to accept a valuation on the acquisition of such a right which gives rise to neither a chargeable gain nor an allowable loss in the hands of the plaintiff. In such circumstances, to the extent that the event giving rise to the right could be regarded as a partial or complete disposal of the damaged asset in the hands of the plaintiff, the right is regarded as having been acquired by him on the date the loss first arose for an amount equal to the cost or, if later, at the market value as at 31 March 1982, of the underlying asset which is attributable to the loss arising on that asset, plus indexation thereon to that date. The plaintiff should therefore not need to report or to pay CGT as a result of the partial or total destruction of the underlying asset.

1521 When the compensation or damages are received by the injured party, the right is in turn then treated as having been disposed of by the plaintiff for CGT purposes. Such a disposal may have to be reported by the plaintiff to the Inland Revenue and a computation of the gain arising included in his return. If the claim is unsuccessful, the professional costs in pursuing the claim may, nevertheless, be an allowable loss for CGT purposes. On the other hand, reliefs which might have been available if the underlying asset had been disposed of, namely, roll-over relief for the replacement of business assets, retirement relief and principal private residence relief, will not be available on the plaintiff recovering the damages, because the damages are not equated with the acquisition or disposal of the appropriate assets for such reliefs.

1522 In ascertaining what CGT may be payable on the settlement of the claim, it may be necessary to establish whether the damage to the underlying property has enabled the plaintiff or others:

(a) to realise an allowable loss on its subsequent sale; or
(b) to claim an allowable loss on the grounds that the property is of negligible value;

and, as a result, reduce the plaintiff's current or potential liabilities.

1523   As a concession, the Inland Revenue will allow plaintiffs to treat damages and compensation as arising from the underlying chargeable asset which gave rise to the loss. Thus, any chargeable gains and allowable losses can be computed as if there had been a partial or complete disposal of that asset. In computing the gain, the claimant may use the original cost of the asset, claim time apportionment, or revalue the asset as at 6 April 1965, or 31 March 1982 without regard to any disposal which occurred when the loss first arose. In addition, the Inland Revenue will:

(a) allow the compensation to be regarded as derived from the underlying assets and hence available for the reliefs mentioned in para **1521** above if applied appropriately; and

(b) extend time limits for claiming such reliefs.

1524   Under the same concession, where a right arises from an underlying form of property which is not a chargeable asset for CGT purposes (such as a private or domestic issue, or negligent professional advice), the damages or compensation for such assets may be treated as exempt from this tax in the hands of the plaintiff.

1525   When negotiating a settlement for a claim, plaintiffs should take care to ensure that where there is risk that the settlement may be liable to CGT, some grossing up of the settlement is sought to cover any tax payable. Defendants may wish to look for mitigation for any benefits obtained by the plaintiffs for losses claimed for tax purposes pending the settlement of the claim (see para **1522** above) and for arrangements for awarding or agreeing to compensation which limit the plaintiff's liabilities to CGT.

Revision of consideration following settlement of a dispute over a sale and purchase agreement

1526   Frequently, the expert accountant will be concerned with disputes over the amount of consideration which has passed between purchaser and vendor under a sale and purchase agreement. The settlement might be through a court action or through informal arbitration or conciliation. Typically, the dispute will relate to maintainable profits or to minimum assets warranted in the agreement. The Inland Revenue does not regard payments under a warranty or indemnity included in a purchase or sale agreement as coming within the principles in the *Zim Properties* case, and payments will normally affect the consideration given for the assets concerned. Due to the complex tax considerations and uncertainties involved, specialist advice should be sought.

INHERITANCE TAX

1527   Where an injury first occurred to an individual and that individual has subsequently gifted his rights, or died, the open market value of the claim at the time of the gift, or on his death, may be liable to inheritance tax in the hands of his personal representatives.

VAT

1528   Damages payable under a court order which are compensatory and do not relate directly to the supply of goods and services, are not subject to VAT.

Damages are, however, subject to tax to the extent that they are the consideration for specific taxable supplies by the plaintiff – where the dispute concerns payment for an earlier supply and VAT would arise only at the time of payment. Until November 1987, Customs & Excise treated out of court settlements in a different manner from damages awarded by court order. (In general, out of court settlements attracted VAT unless the original transaction had not been subject to VAT, for example, because the customer was outside the UK or, because the supply was not to be treated as made in the UK, the plaintiff was not, or not required to be, registered for VAT.) However, since November 1987, Customs & Excise have unified their policy and out of court settlements and damages awarded in court are treated identically for VAT purposes.

DAMAGES SUBJECT TO REDUCTION FOR TAX EFFECTS (THE GOURLEY PRINCIPLE)

1529 Where damages are awarded for the loss of income which, if it had been received in the normal course, would have been subject to tax, but the damages themselves are not liable to tax, then those damages must be reduced to take account of the tax for which the plaintiff would ordinarily have been liable. This is known as the 'Gourley Principle' after the case in which it was first applied.

1530 Whether the Gourley Principle also applies for damages awarded to a person for the loss of sums which would have been taxable as capital gains, is unclear. Because there is uncertainty, a plaintiff might argue for compensation to be grossed up for the capital gains contingency, even though in practice the contingency may not eventuate. The defendant might, on the other hand, argue the reverse on the assumption that the contingency can be ignored. Negotiations may have to strike a compromise on such matters in the absence of clarity in the legal arena.

1531 The difficulty that may arise in practice is well illustrated by the case of *Pennine Raceway Ltd v Kirklees Metropolitan Council (No 2).*[2] Pennine Raceway was granted a licence by the landlord to conduct drag racing on a disused airfield. Permission to use the land for this purpose was later revoked by the Council and the company successfully claimed damages in compensation computed by reference to loss of profits. In awarding damages, the Lands Tribunal made a deduction to reflect corporation tax which the company would have paid if the profits had been earned in the relevant years. On the basis that the damages would not be liable to tax, no grossing up for CGT was made. Subsequently, the Inland Revenue asserted that the damages would be taxable, either as trading income or as income from land or, more likely, as a capital gain. The Court of Appeal considered the possible liabilities to tax and decided that, in view of the uncertainty, there should be no reduction in the damages for tax.

1532 The calculation of the tax effect under the Gourley Principle is intended to reflect the tax which would actually have been paid. It is therefore necessary to consider in which period such sums would have become taxable. If the lost income for which damages are awarded would have been liable to tax before the award, the calculation of the relevant tax is simple because the rates of tax are known. Even if the past period is uncertain in length – say, there are tax losses available for set-off which lead to some difficulty in calculating tax precisely – there are, even so, some fairly clear parameters providing scope for negotiations between plaintiff and defendant.

1533 If, however, compensation relates to loss of future earnings, the unknown factors abound and the court has to take a fairly rough and ready approach to the subject of tax effect on damages. Based on past experience, the following guidelines can be offered as to the court's likely view of the case:

(a) it is inappropriate to speculate on future changes in rates of tax unless there is a reasonable expectation of change, for instance, a Budget proposal;

(b) where the plaintiff would have reduced his tax liability by, for instance, a deed of covenant for charitable purposes, or other legitimate means of tax planning, this is of relevance;

(c) where the plaintiff's rate of tax would be affected by a continuing private income – for instance, income under a trust – this is of relevance; and

(d) conversely, if an existing source of income is likely to cease, this is also of relevance and the plaintiff should argue for a lower effective rate of tax to be adopted.

THE TAX PERIOD

1534 The question of into which financial year the damages or settlement falls can be important, particularly in negotiations for and timing of settlements. In the case of damages subject to tax as income, the following principles apply.

(a) The case law in this area is complex and one of the factors to be taken into account is the proper accounting principles. However, as a broad rule, it would be unlikely that damages which are chargeable under Schedule D Cases I or II could be properly included for tax before there is some certainty that the award will be made, eg until the defendant admitted liability. This will vary depending on whether the claim is contested and on what is in dispute and is often a question of degree. Questions of reopening earlier accounts might arise. If there are future costs which are associated with the award, some provision or deferral may be allowed, but this is a matter for negotiation taking account of all the facts of a particular case.

(b) Damages for wrongful dismissal from an office or employment (which are taxed under the Taxes Act 1988 s 148) are treated as income arising at the date of termination.

(c) Damages in respect of interest and other types of loss may be taxable only when they are received, but it is necessary to have regard to all the facts and circumstances.

1535 The date of disposal for CGT purposes of a right of action may be the date the action is settled, but this will depend upon the facts. The time of disposal for damages falling within Taxation of Chargeable Gains Tax Act 1992 s 22 is the date the capital sum is received.

DEDUCTIBILITY OF DAMAGES FOR TAX PURPOSES

1536   There are a number of factors which need to be considered in deciding whether the cost of meeting damages is tax-deductible, and in what period that deduction should be made.

1537   Damages are deductible only where they are incurred wholly and exclusively for the purposes of the trade or profession and provided that the specific deduction is not expressly disallowed by statute. The tax treatment of the damages in the hands of the plaintiff is not relevant to the tax position of the defendant. Deductions cannot be made for:

(a)   expenses not wholly and exclusively laid out for the purposes of the business;
(b)   losses unconnected with, and not arising out of, a business; or
(c)   capital payments (for example, where damages are as a result of breach of contract connected with a fixed asset owned by the defendant).

1538   A trader cannot simply claim that the expense would not have been incurred if he had not been trading; he must justify it.

The period of deduction for the defendant

1539   The Inland Revenue will not allow deductions for potential damages; such deductions are not allowed until the plaintiff makes a claim and the defendant admits liability. Even then, a deduction will be allowed only if and when the amount payable by the defendant can be determined with a reasonable degree of certainty. A trader is therefore unlikely to be able to deduct an amount for damages payable by him before it is reasonably certain that an amount will be awarded and a figure can be put in on a reasonably accurate basis. Provisions charged in the accounts before that time are likely to be disallowed.

1540   However, the 1950 Court of Session decision known as *James Spencer & Co v IRC*,[3] on which the Inland Revenue rely for their approach to potential damages, was decided:

(a)   without reference to the facts of a particular situation (and, hence, the court was reluctant to decide on the issue); and
(b)   before the professional accountancy bodies issued guidance on contingent liabilities in SSAP 18 in August 1980 indicating that provisions should be made in accounts for such liabilities before arriving at net profits where it is probable that a future event will confirm a loss which can be estimated with reasonable accuracy at the date on which the financial statements are approved by the board of directors.

1541   Therefore, in light of:

(a)   the large amounts that are now being claimed;
(b)   the time plaintiffs often have to take to investigate and issue writs for claims in view of their complexity;
(c)   the fact that often some amount has to be conceded by defendants just to settle such claims; and

(d) the subsequent guidance from the professional accountancy bodies on providing for contingent liabilities where losses are probable;

it may be possible for potential defendants to argue successfully that the accounting principles now established for determining accounting profits, should prevail for determining taxable profits, where a payment for damages is almost certainly going to have to be made which can be quantified with a reasonable degree of certainty.

TAX ON INTEREST

1542 Arrears of interest obtained by court action are taxed in the same way as interest.

1543 The plaintiff will be liable to tax where he receives interest in respect of damages awarded in the following circumstances:

(a) where he has sued under a contract providing for interest, and has proved he is entitled to interest under the contract;
(b) under the Bills of Exchange Act 1882, where he has succeeded in an action for the dishonour of a cheque or bill of exchange;
(c) where the court awards interest in commercial and injury cases under the provisions of the Supreme Court Act 1981;
(d) under the Judgments Act 1838, on judgment debts between the date of judgment and the date of payment; and
(e) by the court under its equitable jurisdiction in cases such as breach of trust, breaches of fiduciary duty, or constructive trust.

1544 Interest under the categories described above is taxable as and when the interest is actually received. In some cases, such as for a bank, it may be appropriate in the circumstances to treat the interest as trading income. Interest awarded on damages in respect of personal injury or death is exempt where Taxes Act 1988 s 329 applies.

1545 In many cases, interest paid on damages will be annual interest. A trader who is not a company could deduct such interest which is laid out wholly and exclusively for the purposes of the trade. For companies, a deduction would normally be given for annual interest as a charge on income. If the interest is not annual interest, a deduction is available in computing trading profits only if it is laid out wholly and exclusively for the purposes of the trade. If there is a foreign element, the question of a deduction is likely to be more complex.

1546 Annual interest may be required to be paid under deduction of basic rate tax where Taxes Act 1988 s 349(2) applies, for instance where paid by a company, a local authority, or a partnership which includes a company as a partner, or where the payee is abroad. Interest is paid gross if it is:

(a) payable in the United Kingdom on an advance from a bank carrying on a bona fide banking business in the United Kingdom; or
(b) it is short interest; or

(c) it is paid by an individual or a partnership or a person living in the United Kingdom.

1547 Where an action is settled out of court, there may be some doubt as to whether an amount added to the agreed damages for interest would be treated as such for tax purposes. Moreover, in many cases, the question of whether or not there is an identifiable interest element will depend upon the precise facts and the details of the agreement reached. This can be a most complex area and expert advice should be sought.

1548 Interest that accrues on payments into court is usually taxable in the hands of the party who is regarded as the beneficial owner of the relevant amount pending the decision of the court. This remains the case even where the court subsequently directs that a party other than the beneficial owner should receive a lump sum out of such a payment. On the other hand, if the court subsequently directs that the other party should receive the payment, or a proportion thereof, plus the interest that has accrued on the amount awarded (ie in effect, the payment to the party is regarded as having been made on the date that the original deposit was made) such interest is almost certainly taxable in the hands of the recipient.

TAX ON AWARDS MADE IN FOREIGN CURRENCY

1549 Taxable damages awarded in a foreign currency must be translated into the sterling equivalent for tax purposes. Conversion of the currency into sterling may give rise to an exchange gain or loss which will be taxed as capital or revenue according to the nature of the damages. Where damages are trading receipts, the Inland Revenue accepts an average rate of exchange for the accounting period, or the rate at the date of the closing balance sheet where the plaintiff regularly maintains books in a foreign currency. In other cases the appropriate rate is that prevailing at the date of the transaction. The Inland Revenue usually accepts a reasonable method of calculating the exchange rate, provided it is consistent with methods used for dealing with other revenue and capital foreign currency items.

CONCLUSION

1550 The foregoing chapter demonstrates that the impact of taxation in the assessment of damages is something of a minefield. When settlements out of court are negotiated, a prior consideration of tax implications is especially worthwhile.

NOTES

1 *Zim Properties v Procter (Inspector of Taxes)* [1985] STC 90.
2 [1989] STC 122.
3 *James Spencer & Co v IRC* (1950) 32 TC 111.

Chapter 16

Regulatory work

Introduction – Company investigations – Statutory powers for
appointing inspectors – Practical aspects – The purpose and scope
of investigation – Rules for good interviewing – The stages of the
investigation – Disciplinary enquiries – The stages of enquiry – The
nature and powers of the committees – The stages of investigation –
Conclusion

INTRODUCTION

1601 This chapter consists of advice and explanations on the subject of carrying
out formal company inspections and professional disciplinary enquiries. There
are various published documents, notably the Investigation Handbook printed by
the Department of Trade and Industry, and the Joint Disciplinary Scheme &
Regulations, which set out the rules and procedures to be followed. Reference
should be made to these documents for a complete understanding of these topics.

1602 The subject matter of this chapter will also be of interest to those who are
invited to participate in a public enquiry either as a member of the appointed
committee or to appear before it so as to give evidence.

COMPANY INVESTIGATIONS

Statutory powers for appointing inspectors

1603 The powers of the Secretary of State for Trade and Industry to appoint
inspectors to investigate the affairs of a company and to report back to him, date
back to the middle of the nineteenth century. The purpose of most investigations
is to ascertain exactly what has happened where it appears that some form of
irregularity or misconduct has occurred, but where the circumstances and facts are
unclear and can best be determined by independent persons with the necessary
powers of investigation.

1604 Investigations of companies may be conducted by external inspectors
appointed by the Secretary of State, or they may be conducted on a more discreet
basis by officials of the DTI. Inspectors have statutory powers and duties which
are set out in the relevant legislation. They have complete responsibility for the
conduct of investigations and have discretion in the way in which they carry them
out. The appointment of external inspectors should be distinguished from those
instances where the DTI or other regulatory bodies delegate some of their powers

to 'competent persons' for investigation purposes. In this latter case, the responsibility for the investigation remains with the regulator, although the 'competent persons' are often expert accountants.

1605   Under current law, the powers of the Secretary of State to appoint external inspectors derive from the following statutes:

(1)   *Companies Act 1985 (as amended by the Companies Act 1989)*

    (a)   Appointments to investigate the affairs of a company.
- Section 431 – on the application of a company or of a prescribed proportion of its members.
- Section 432(1) – where so required by the order of a court.
- Section 432(2) – where there are circumstances suggesting—
  - that the company's affairs have been conducted with intent to defraud creditors or for some other unlawful purpose prejudicial to the members;
  - that the company was formed for a fraudulent or unlawful purpose;
  - fraud, misfeasance or other misconduct in connection with a company's management;
  - inadequate information having been provided to the members.

    (b)   Appointments to investigate the membership of the company.
- Section 442(1) – to determine the true persons who have a financial interest in the success or failure of a company or who are able to control or materially to influence its policy.

    (c)   Appointments to investigate share dealings.
- Section 446(1) – where there are circumstances suggesting that contraventions may have occurred in relation to statutory prohibitions on share dealings by directors and their families.

(2)   *Financial Services Act 1986*
- Section 94 – to investigate the affairs of an authorised unit trust scheme or of its manager or trustee.
- Section 177 – where there are circumstances suggesting that there may have been a contravention of prohibitions contained within the Companies Securities (Insider Dealing) Act 1985.

(3)   *Insolvency Act 1986*
- Section 218 – where it appears that a past or present officer or member of a company which is in liquidation appears to be guilty of a criminal offence in relation to the company.

1606   Accountants may also be appointed to assist the DTI and other regulators with the investigation into a company's affairs by delegation of investigatory powers. The types of investigation and governing statutes include:

(1)   *Companies Act 1985*
Appointments to inspect documents of a company.
- Section 447(3) – where there is good reason to produce specified documents, normally the books and records of a company, for inspection and to provide explanations in respect of them.

(2) *Companies Act 1989*
Appointments to assist overseas regulatory authorities.
- Section 84 – where a request has been received from an overseas regulatory authority to investigate a matter concerning investment business as defined by s 82 of the Act.

(3) *Financial Services Act 1986*
Appointments to investigate investment business.
- Section 106 – where there is good reason to investigate, under s 105, the investment business of any person authorised under the Act.

(4) *Criminal Justice Act 1987*
Appointments to investigate serious fraud.
- Section 2(11) – to investigate the affairs of a person suspected of an offence which appears to involve serious or complex fraud.

1607 The role of the accountant appointed to investigate under the above statutes will vary according to circumstances. Appointments under s 447(3) by the DTI are similar in some respects to appointments under s 432. The investigating accountant is expected to use his technical knowledge and skills to ascertain whether irregularities have taken place. However, the powers under s 447 are much narrower than under s 432. In essence, investigations under s 447 are limited to inspecting the books and records of a company and obtaining explanations in relation to them. The investigating accountant will normally produce a factual report, detailing the findings of his work, upon which the DTI will base a decision as to what future action, if any, should be taken. Reports under s 447 are never published and the DTI would resist disclosing their contents to third parties, other than to certain competent authorities for certain purposes, such as criminal proceedings or proceedings under the Company Directors Disqualification Act 1986.

1608 Appointments under the Financial Services Act 1986 may also be made by the Securities & Investment Board. An investigating accountant appointed under the Financial Services Act 1986 s 106 has wide ranging powers as defined by s 105. Reports of investigations under the Financial Services Act 1986 ss 105 and 177 cannot be published. Disclosure of information is restricted in a similar way as applies to investigations under the Companies Act 1985 s 447. The same basic principles apply where an accountant had been appointed to investigate allegations of serious fraud under the Criminal Justice Act 1987. Again, the investigatory powers are delegated to the investigating accountant, but there are severe restrictions placed upon disclosure of any information obtained. The accountant in these circumstances is effectively wearing the mantle of the regulatory body and should comply with their standards of operation and procedure.

1609 In the following paragraphs we give some practical hints in relation to investigations carried out by external inspectors, primarily those appointed under the Companies Act 1985 s 432.

Practical aspects

1610 External inspectors appointed under the Companies Act 1985 ss 431, 432 and 442, usually comprise a lawyer and an accountant. The former will be either a Queen's Counsel or a senior solicitor and the latter will usually be selected from among the senior partners of one of the larger firms of accountants. The investigatory work tends to be carried out by the staff of the accountant's firm. Inspectors will usually appoint a secretary to assist in the administration of the investigation; he will either be a senior member of the accountant's staff or a solicitor.

1611   The inspectors have statutory powers and duties which are set out in the relevant legislation. They have complete responsibility for the conduct of the investigation and discretion in the way in which they carry it out; guidance is offered by the DTI in the form of an official handbook, copies of which are publicly available through HMSO.

The purpose and scope of investigation

1612   The immediate purpose of most statutory investigations is to find out what has happened or what is happening when there are grounds to suggest some irregularity has occurred in the conduct of a business or of an individual. The longer-term purpose is to provide the Secretary of State with the facts on which to take remedial action if such steps seem to be warranted.

1613   The policy on announcements about the setting up of enquiries varies according to which section of the Companies Act 1985 or the Financial Services Act 1986 is being applied. Investigations under the Companies Act which are delegated to external inspectors are announced when they are set up, and the ultimate report tends to be published (although sometimes after a long interval). In contrast, investigations by internal inspectors, ie from within the DTI, are rarely announced since to do so would undermine the enquiry itself and might unduly damage the business of the companies concerned; in practice of course the existence of an investigation often leaks out.

1614   The powers of external inspectors are considerable. They can require explanations to be given and documents to be made available to them; failure to comply is an offence punishable by a fine. The enquiry is not a court of law; it is an investigation in the public interest in which all are expected to assist to the best of their ability. Lord Denning, in his judgment in *Re Pergamon Press Ltd*[1] said:

> '. . . I will try to state the considerations which are to be borne in mind in respect of an inquiry under the Companies Act. First and foremost when a matter is referred to an inspector for investigation and report it is a very special kind of inquiry. It must not be confused with other inquiries. Remember what it is not. It is not a trial of anyone nor anything like it. There is no accused person. There is no prosecutor. There is no charge. It is not like a disciplinary proceeding before a professional body. Nor is it like an application to expel a man from a trade union or a club, or anything of that kind. It is not even like a committee which considers whether there is a prima facie case against a person. It is simply an investigation without anyone being accused.'

Lord Denning went on to draw other distinctions between this form of investigation and a trial: 'There is no counsel for the prosecution, the investigation is in private; the inspectors must make their report holding nothing back'. Thus, in essence, he said that the rules of natural justice were not suspended but that much of the paraphernalia of court hearings were.

1615 These quotations from Lord Denning's judgment provide an excellent overview of how external inspectors should view their task.

1616 As a general rule, witnesses are interviewed on oath. Occasionally, inspectors will find it convenient to arrange for informal interviews so as to clarify certain issues ahead of the formal session. It is normal for both inspectors to attend the formal interviews; for the informal meetings this is not always the case.

1617 Inspectors have to act in a fair and reasonable manner in all other respects. Witnesses should be given reasonable notice of when an interview is sought; if possible they should also be told in general terms about the matters to be raised. A witness should also be supplied with a copy of his own examination unless there are compelling reasons for withholding it. The inspectors should give witnesses notice of the substance of matters which they intend to criticise. Their principal objective is to ascertain facts but it may be necessary for the inspectors to make criticisms of individuals or organisations in order to explain how and why events occurred. In doing so inspectors must provide those being criticised with an opportunity to correct or otherwise comment upon the evidence relevant to the criticisms which are proposed.

Rules for good interviewing

1618 It might be useful to dwell here on the basic rules and techniques for good interviewing. The lawyer in the team, who will do the lion's share of the questioning, will have learnt these rules from his court experience. The accountant may not have done so before he is faced with the inquisitional task.

(a) Be as polite as you can at all times. Nothing helps more to get to the truth than a courteous and enquiring approach. The tough approach is called for in some situations, but it is important to use this approach selectively for best effect.
(b) When asking technical questions, for example, accounting questions of a non-accountant, talk in a language that they will understand and feel at ease with. This can be done without the need for over-simplification or patronising metaphors; it is called 'courteous translation'.
(c) Trust is important. The worst pitfall is to misquote a document or a situation and then to pose questions on those hypotheses; there is always a need for accuracy. Likewise, do not seek to confuse or make unfair points.
(d) When making a point, look at the person being questioned.
(e) Keep notes, especially where your intention is to follow up a particular line of questioning with supplementaries. Clearly it is not the task of the inspector to keep full minutes, the official shorthand writer does that; but nevertheless a series of notes is vital for jogging the memory and referring back to an earlier part of the discussion which has taken place in the session.
(f) Decide the objectives to be achieved before commencing the interview. A clear plan of direction is vital. Often a detailed script of questions to be put should be made. It makes for succinctness and an efficient use of time.

The stages of the investigation

1619 The DTI will, at the outset of the investigation, brief the inspectors about the background to the investigation, and provide whatever documents it has which bear on the issues under enquiry. A timetable will also be discussed. Although inspectors are not full-time, they are expected to give the investigation top priority, and to complete their report as quickly as possible.

1620 We tabulate below the initial matters that the inspectors must consider and then the later steps as the investigation progresses.

AN ENQUIRY – THE INITIAL ARRANGEMENTS

(a) **Avoidance of conflict** The prospective inspector must make enquiries to ensure that he is independent of the case and that neither he nor his firm has a conflict of interest. For this purpose the DTI will usually supply a list of relevant parties with whom connections should be checked. The question of potential conflict must be kept under review even after the appointment. Cases have arisen where an inspector who thought he had no conflict had to resign due to the subsequent emergence of one.

(b) **Availability** There will be some periods during the enquiries when 100% dedication is needed and other times when a very substantial commitment is required, for example when writing the report. Given such commitment, the practising accountant will need to make sure that alternative arrangements can properly be made for covering existing commitments to his clients.

(c) **Indemnity** It is standard practice for the Secretary of State to indemnify inspectors against any personal liability which may be incurred as a result of the appointment. This includes the costs and expenses of any legal proceedings which may arise.

(d) **Fees** It is usual for time incurred by the inspectors and each member of the team to be charged at agreed hourly rates. Fee rates are a matter for negotiation with the DTI.

AN ENQUIRY – THE KEY STAGES

(a) **Obtaining access to relevant records** It is necessary to obtain access to records from a variety of sources, not simply those of the company which is the subject of the enquiry. Other sources of records may include those of individual directors, auditors, bankers, brokers and so forth. It is preferable for the originals of all such records to be taken to the inspectors' premises to ensure adequate control and continuing access. However, satisfactory alternative arrangements may be acceptable, such as segregation into a secure area on the company's premises, or the copying of files under the inspectors' control.

(b) **Reviewing the records** The records should be examined with a view to ascertaining relevant facts, identifying questions to be put to witnesses and detecting any potential malpractice or offences.

(c) **Interviewing witnesses** While witnesses may be seen informally to assist in conducting the enquiry, the substantive interviewing process is normally formal, with a shorthand writer in attendance. Some witnesses attend accompanied by their legal advisers. There can, however, be no question of a barrister or solicitor answering the inspectors' questions. A legal adviser can question his client and make representations on his client's behalf. The costs of that legal advice are never defrayed by the DTI.

(d) **Progressing the investigation and preparing a draft report** Based upon the information provided by witnesses, the inspectors may need to re-examine the records and seek fresh evidence on certain matters after which they will be in a position to prepare a draft report for the DTI. Reference to previously published inspectors' reports and to style notes published by the DTI will assist in this exercise. In preparing the draft report it may emerge that the inspectors wish to criticise individuals or organisations. Should this be the case, the substance of the evidence should be put to these parties and a response invited (see para **1617**). Such a response may be in writing or oral, in practice it is more convenient to conduct this process through correspondence.

(e) **Finalising the report** Having considered the responses to any provisional criticisms and any fresh evidence which may have emerged, the inspectors are then in a position to prepare their final report. This report will usually include an executive summary setting out an abridged version of the events and the more important facts and opinions emerging from the investigation. This summary ought to be written so that it can constitute a stand-alone abridged report.

(f) **Publishing the report** This is not the inspectors' province but that of a government department. The normal practice is for reports in respect of public companies to be published, but such publication will be delayed if there is the possibility of criminal proceedings occurring. Reports in respect of private companies are usually not published. Reports in respect of insider dealing enquiries are never published.

1621   The DTI liaises with other regulatory bodies in the UK who have responsibilities concerning the conduct of companies. Each of these regulatory authorities, for example, the SFO, the Securities & Investment Board, Bank of England and the Stock Exchange have specific powers of investigation. The extent to which the various regulators are able to disclose to each other information which they obtain under their powers is restricted.

1622   There are times when the activities of a particular company may interest more than one regulatory body and it is in the public interest to determine which regulator should take prime responsibility for a particular investigation. At one stage, external inspectors appointed under the Companies Act 1985 were obliged to complete their investigations irrespective of the interests of other regulators. However, where serious offences come to light it is desirable that all enquiries by either the SFO or the police should proceed as quickly as possible. Under the Companies Act 1985 s 437(1b), the Secretary of State may direct the external inspectors to take no further steps in their investigation if it appears that criminal offences have been committed. In such circumstances the investigation would be passed over to the SFO or to the police who would have access to the external inspector's report and supporting evidence.

DISCIPLINARY ENQUIRIES

The stages of enquiry

1623   Disciplinary enquiries under the Chartered Accountants' and Certified Accountants' Joint Disciplinary Scheme are very different from company inspections. They deserve mention here for three reasons. First, a limited number of accountants will find themselves instructed to give expert evidence so as to assist the enquiry body in coming to its decision. Second, an even more limited number of experienced professionals, and indeed some who are not qualified accountants, will be asked to serve on the tribunal itself. Third, there will be those who are accused of professional error and who will need to know how to conduct themselves to best effect in defending their position.

1624   The objectives of the scheme are to promote proper professional standards of behaviour by members and member firms and to secure adherence to published professional criteria (such as auditing standards) and to proper business practices.

1625   The scheme and its regulation are set out in public documents which describe the procedures for investigating and regulating the professional and business conduct, efficiency and competence of members and member firms. The scheme is administered by an executive committee which can appoint a committee of inquiry when it has received a 'complaint' on a matter which is of public concern and involves one or more members or member firms. (One example of such a matter could be a complaint by a member body in relation to a report by DTI inspectors containing criticisms of members or member firms.) A committee of enquiry usually comprises three persons, of whom two are members and the other a non-accountant, often a lawyer. Any adverse finding relating to a member or a member firm is subject to an appeal to an appeal committee.

1626   The 'complaint' will have originated from an investigation committee of one of the participating professional bodies in the scheme (for example, from the Institute of Chartered Accountants in England and Wales, the Scottish Institute or the Chartered Association of Certified Accountants), which will have reached the preliminary view that the efficiency, competence or honesty of a member or his firm 'gives rise to or includes questions of public concern'. Once the executive committee gets this missive it must act on it; it has no discretion in the matter although it can divide up the complaint into more than one topic and then allocate each topic to be examined by separate committees of enquiry.

1627   The committee of enquiry will reach a finding either that the complaint fails or that the complaint is justified, ie becomes an 'adverse finding'. If it reaches the latter finding, the committee has to give the member concerned the opportunity to make further representations, orally and/or in writing. After that is over, and assuming it is not satisfied, the committee is required to make recommendations which can range in severity from mild admonishment to exclusion from membership of the professional body.

1628   If a committee of enquiry reaches an adverse finding, the member concerned must then be given the opportunity of appealing to an appeal committee. The appeal committee may decide any relevant issue of fact or law; it even has the discretion to rehear witnesses or receive fresh evidence. Until the appeal committee has opined, no reports of the various enquiries referred to above can be published to the world at large.

The nature and powers of the committees

1629   It will be seen from the summary of the scheme at para **1623**, that the first level of enquiry (ie the investigation committee) consists of laymen – 'lay' in the sense that they are not legally qualified to sit as judges. Their qualification for appointment will be that they have significant experience in accounting matters.

1630   The second level of enquiry (the committee of enquiry) will consist of a majority of laymen (in the same sense used above) with at least one non-accountant, often a lawyer.

1631   The third level (the appeal committee) will consist of a majority of laymen (ie members of the accounting bodies) but chaired by either a judge or a Queen's Counsel.

1632   These distinctions (ie in the make-up of the committees) are important and should be taken into account when an expert is asked to assist, in some manner in their deliberations and investigations. The approach will inevitably be different, so a good rule to remember is 'know your audience and adjust your approach accordingly'. With the appeal committee the tendency will be for emphasis to be given to the legalities of the case, the burden of proof, the rules of natural justice and so forth. The expert accountant will find that there is much that is common with the tasks described elsewhere in this book relating to, for example, contract disputes, where he has to work closely with a lawyer who has charge of the overall conduct of the case. With the earlier levels of enquiry however the need will be to communicate with a different kind of audience where knowledge of the facts and of the standards of work to be expected of a professional will dominate their thinking. There will also be greater latitude as to the formalities observed during the earlier stages of enquiry. Each level needs to be treated with great respect and it is as well to be thoroughly prepared before making written or oral presentation to the committee concerned.

1633   Committees of inquiry may call upon members or member firms to provide relevant information and/or evidence but they have no statutory or other power to require such co-operation. A committee can also appoint an investigating accountant to make detailed enquiries on its behalf.

The stages of investigation

1634   When an accountant is asked to join a committee of enquiry he should take similar preliminary steps to those we have outlined at para **1620** in relation to DTI inspections.

1635   Unlike a DTI inspection, members of a committee of enquiry are unlikely to be involved in any detailed investigatory work; this is normally delegated to a separate firm of accountants; even so, some time normally devoted to practice will have to be set aside.

1636   After the initial formalities are concluded, the procedures noted in the table opposite should be followed (for detailed guidance reference should be made to the published regulations issued by the three professional bodies).

1637   In addition to the three members of the committee, there will be a secretary, who is usually associated with the firm which acts as investigating accountants, and a legal adviser to the committee. The legal adviser has an important role in advising the committee on procedure and on the drafting of the reports, especially the wording of the findings. If the matter goes to the appeal committee, the administration from then on is taken over by a separate group of people.

CONCLUSION

1638   It will be seen from the above that the atmosphere and procedures differ a great deal between one body of enquiry and another. Some tribunals act and feel more like well-run committees than a court of law; non-lawyers appear as advocates and there is a degree of informality about the whole business. Other tribunals are quasi-courts with great emphasis on formality. Anyone who is involved, as a member or as a witness or as someone who is defending his actions, would be well advised beforehand to establish where in this spectrum his particular committee lies. Discussion with someone else who has gone through a similar experience will be invaluable.

1639   There are the usual requirements for ensuring that the task is properly run and properly remunerated. It behoves an expert or investigator to check early on

COMMITTEES OF ENQUIRY – THE KEY STEPS

(a) **Establishing extent of investigations** Establishing the extent to which the matter under review requires detailed investigation is important. Where the complaint arises from the DTI report it is usual to proceed on the basis of the facts ascertained by the inspectors. Access may be sought to some of the records which were available to the inspectors and to transcripts of the evidence of witnesses. Where the complaint arises from other sources the committee may need to appoint investigating accountants. The investigating accountant's work should result in a report which sets out the relevant facts impartially; it should not contain opinion on the merits of complaint in terms of standards of professional behaviour.

(b) **Identifying the issues** After the facts have been established, the committee has to identify the issues which need to be put to the persons and firms under enquiry. Witnesses, including expert witnesses, may be asked to submit their evidence in writing in advance of the oral hearings, so as to reduce the length of the proceedings.

(c) **The hearing** If a member firm is under enquiry, rather than an individual, then it must appoint a designated partner to represent it at hearings. The member, or member firm's designated partner, can be accompanied by another member, a solicitor or counsel. (Unlike DTI hearings the evidence cannot be obtained under oath, since this would be contrary to the Statutory Declarations Act 1835.) A shorthand writer should be present so that transcripts can be provided to the committee and to each witness. Any member under enquiry is also entitled to ask for full transcripts of the hearings.

(d) **Formulating and submitting provisional criticisms** After completion of the hearings, the committee should be in a position to determine which criticisms have been sustained. The substance of such criticisms then has to be put to the parties under enquiry and their representations invited. The criticisms have to be accompanied by a clear reference as to the evidence which the committee has relied upon, identifying the relevant witnesses. (If the committee considers that no criticisms have been sustained then this is the end of the matter.)

(e) **Drafting reports** After considering the representations received in response to the provisional criticisms, the committee then prepares its report setting out its findings.

that the fees will be satisfactory, the terms of reference are clear, the timetable is reasonable, and that no conflict of interest arises. It is also important to obtain an indemnity bearing in mind the risk of subsequent proceedings, for example, for defamation.

1640 While the accountant's involvement is primarily designed to provide an input in his own discipline, an ability to explain accounting issues succinctly and to communicate well with lawyers will be a considerable asset. Finally, it is important that whoever takes on membership of an enquiry body or who seeks to advise that body, should have relevant experience for the task. Accountants who are invited to act as inspectors are not expected to have an extensive legal knowledge, nevertheless it is obviously advantageous for them to have had some prior experience of litigation, for example acting as an expert witness or as an arbitrator.

NOTE

1 [1970] 3 WLR 792.

Chapter 17

Balance sheet: capital reorganisations

Introduction – Companies Act 1985 – Group of companies –
Seeking the agreement of creditors – The steps to be taken on the
accounting side – Timetable – Other matters

INTRODUCTION

1701 Capital reorganisations of limited companies often require court consent,
so it is a subject which may properly be included in a book on forensic accounting
matters. Furthermore, the subject is not dealt with fully in most accounting text
books. This chapter deals with the most common points which arise and we have
also prepared, at Appendix O, an affidavit which touches upon some practical
matters.

1702 As a result of balance sheet valuation write downs or prolonged operating
losses, following Britain's recession of the early 1990s, many quoted companies
currently show a substantial deficit on their profit and loss accounts. The result of
this is that they are prevented from paying dividends. No company may make a
distribution except out of profits available for the purpose; the definition of
distributable profit is more restrictive for a public company than for a private one
(Companies Act 1985 ss 263(1) and 264).

1703 Unless the directors can remove the profit and loss account deficit they
may be prevented from raising fresh equity capital (because they cannot pay
dividends), or from taking many other steps, for example, the acquisition of
another business or a merger with another business, which might be in the general
interests of the shareholders. Directors can in certain circumstances go to court
and obtain consent to a reduction of the share premium account (which itself has
been created at a time when higher values were obtained in the marketplace) and
can thereby eliminate the deficit.

1704 The planning and execution of a share reduction scheme is very much in
the lawyers' province and circumstances vary as to the precise methods. It is an
exercise which requires the preparation of affidavits and petitions which have to
be submitted to the court in support of the application for reduction, and it is here
that the accountant can give assistance.

COMPANIES ACT 1985

1705 The Companies Act 1985 s 135 provides that, subject to confirmation by
the court, a limited company with a share capital may, if authorised by its articles,

reduce its share capital by special resolution. A company will normally have the necessary power in its articles. Reduction of the share premium account goes hand in hand with a reduction of share capital.

1706 Subsection 2 of s 135 specifies several situations which would qualify as grounds for a reduction:

'. . . the company may:
(a) extinguish or reduce the liability on any of its shares in respect of share capital not paid up; or
(b) either with or without extinguishing or reducing liability on any of its shares, cancel any paid-up share capital which is lost or unrepresented by available assets; or
(c) either with or without extinguishing or reducing liability on any of its shares, pay off any paid-up share capital which is in excess of the company's wants'.

1707 The categories listed are not intended to be exhaustive and it appears that the court is willing to confirm a reduction provided that a real or commercial purpose for doing so can be shown (*Re Ratner's Group plc* (1988)[1]). A reduction of capital for the purpose of restoring distributable reserves to what they would have been but for provisions for loss of value (which will have been written off against reserves in prior years) will be one such purpose.

1708 Reduction of capital is analogous to the cancellation of share capital which is lost or unrepresented by available assets within the meaning of s 135(2)(b), and therefore will be a reason with which the court ought properly to be satisfied.

1709 It is relatively simple to consider whether a single company should undertake a capital reduction scheme; it is less so for a group of companies.

Group of companies

1710 The rule in company legislation is that distributable reserves are decided by reference to the reserves of an individual company and not by reference to the consolidated group accounts. Hence the existence of deficits in some subsidiaries does not automatically have an effect on the distributable profits of the holding company; that is so long as the holding company does not feel it has to make a provision in its own balance sheet against its investment in the subsidiary companies by virtue of the past losses of those companies. This is very important; we are looking at the top parent company as an individual company. It follows that the consolidated accounts of the group may show a minus figure for distributable revenue reserves, yet the parent may be in surplus because it has not provided for underlying losses at subsidiary level, or indeed because the minus figure on the group reserves has been caused by a goodwill write off which results from accounting convention rather than value loss.

1711 So, it is important to consider when, in practice, a provision has to be made by the holding company against its investment in the subsidiaries. The answer is that a provision has to be made when 'a permanent diminution in value' arises. The test here is: 'Has the subsidiary the ability to trade out of its deficit and thereby restore the value of the investment from the parent's view point?' It is important to note that this test is not so tough as answering the question: 'Has the subsidiary got a value equal to the investment shown in the parent company's balance?'

1712 The value of the investment in subsidiaries, as shown in a parent company's accounts, is a matter which the directors should discuss with the auditors at the year end. (It has been known for a board of directors to seek an independent valuation, for example, from a merchant bank, of its subsidiary investments as a way of 'making good' the apparent deficit in tangible net assets. While such an exercise will meet possible audit objections on value, it will not solve the problem of distribution of reserves at subsidiary level if that subsidiary has a deficit of revenue reserves.) Realistically, one must expect auditors to require further provisions to be made in the parent company's balance sheet if the prospect is that those companies are not going to trade out of their deficit positions. Once it becomes clear that the diminution in value of the investment is such that it ought to be recognised in the parent company's balance sheet, and if the result of making the provision will be to create a deficit of distributable reserves at parent company level, then a capital reduction scheme should be considered.

1713 The confirmation by the court under the Companies Act 1985 s 135 has to have regard to the interest of the creditors (see below) and also ensure that the interests of the various classes of members are protected. In practice, writing down the share premium account in the holding company's accounts, by reason of a fall in value of its investment in subsidiaries, ought not to prejudice the rights of the creditors of the holding company. What is being done is to cancel share capital which has already been lost and which is no longer represented by available assets, due to the fact that the company has sustained heavy losses, evidenced by the decision to make a provision against the investment in its subsidiary or subsidiaries.

Seeking the agreement of creditors

1714 One of the main concerns which the court will have before sanctioning a reduction in capital will be to ensure that creditors at the effective date of the reduction of capital are fully protected. There is no difficulty in respect of those creditors who consent to the reduction of capital, but as to the other creditors the court has the discretion to require that a list of creditors be settled pursuant to the Companies Act 1985 s 136. In an ordinary case of reorganisation of capital, it is our experience that the court wants clear evidence that creditors are not being prejudiced. This will need to be covered in an affidavit which should make it clear (if this is so) that there is no intention to repay shareholders any money, or in any way to reduce shareholders' obligations in regard to subscription of unpaid calls or capital. Normally it is not so much a question of seeking individual creditors' permission for the reduction scheme, as seeing whether anyone has valid objections after being informed of the scheme, for example, through advertisements. If creditors then come back with objections, the court will become more protective and insist that a list of creditors be settled and that some form of guarantee be entered into.

1715 Should the court, in the event, require specific protection of creditors under a reduction scheme, then it may be expedient to obtain a bank guarantee covering all the non-consenting creditors and all the contingent liabilities of the company. If this guarantee has to be obtained it will have to be of a duration which is satisfactory to the court, for example, ten years in respect of any contingent liabilities. There may of course be circumstances where there are contingent creditors (for example, arising on a legal claim against the company) which cannot be valued precisely, nor indeed be consulted as to their wishes at the point when the scheme is put to the court. Legal advice will be needed here, but in practice contingent creditors will normally be ignored for the purposes of guarantee requirement. The amount of the guarantee which the court will require is the lesser of the amount released for distribution by way of dividends during the period of the guarantee and the amount due to all non-consenting creditors as at the effective date of the reduction of capital. We must emphasise that these are legal matters requiring the attention of a lawyer.

1716   There are other conditions which may be laid down by the court before sanctioning the scheme. In particular, the court will be concerned with ensuring that past provisions are not abused; the company is likely to be required to give an undertaking to the court that it will credit to a separate undistributable reserve the amount of any over provision, in relation to provisions which have been written off as a part of the reorganisation scheme giving rise to the application. The undertaking will be on the lines that a sum equal to the amount by which the value of any asset, at the effective date, shall upon realisation appear to have been understated, will be put back into capital reserves until such time as any debts or claims at the effective date of the reduction have been paid or satisfied.

THE STEPS TO BE TAKEN ON THE ACCOUNTING SIDE

1717   Once there is a clear need for action the programme would normally be as follows.

(a) A summary of all reserves, divided between distributable, non-distributable and deficits for each company in the group should be prepared. The origins of all reserves should be noted.

(b) A careful review of book values of assets and liabilities in each company of the group should be made to see if these book values are realistic. The reason for this is that it is pointless to go through a capital reorganisation programme only to be faced in the following year with a need for further major provisions, which were overlooked previously, and which put the group back into deficit on the profit and loss account.

(c) The parent company's balance sheet and profit and loss account should be prepared on a pro forma basis, after making full provision for the current year's trading losses and any losses relating to the investments in subsidiaries which stem from 'permanent diminution in value' (see earlier). If, on this pro forma basis, there results a net deficit in distributable reserves, then the feasibility of writing this deficit off against the share premium account should be assessed.

(d) If any subsidiary within the group has sustained a loss which leads to a deficit of distributable reserves, then it should itself prepare a programme of reduction of its own share capital. This is important, since unless a provision is made at subsidiary level for this factor, future profits earned by those subsidiaries will not be distributable to the parent company, and it will follow that the parent company will itself be destitute, ie have no income from dividend flows. Theoretically, a reorganisation of the parent company's capital could set off a chain of subsidiary capital reduction schemes.

(e) As part of the scheme, which will require consent of the court, an affidavit for each company needs to be signed, normally by the financial director of the group, setting out the history of recent trading in each company concerned, and the origins of the problem which is to be solved with the court's help. Occasionally, it will be desirable for this affidavit to be signed by one of the other directors, or an outside adviser, if very specialist matters need to be addressed. An example of such an affidavit is shown at Appendix O. In practice, the preparation of this affidavit frequently falls to be done by the advising accountant.

1718   These documents lead to the submission of a petition to the court, prepared under guidance from counsel. It sets out the purpose of the proposed reduction which will normally be to eliminate all of the deficits in reserves against a reduction of the share premium account, and explains how it is proposed that the creditors will be protected.

1719   Various other affidavits will be required from the chairman as well as from the person who is responsible for the financial direction of the company. These deal, inter alia, with the various statutory meetings which require to be held as part of the reduction programme. We have not shown an example here.

Timetable

1720   In the normal case, the timetable is arranged around the issuing of the annual accounts so that the special resolution to authorise the reduction of share capital can be proposed at an extraordinary general meeting held at the same time as the annual general meeting. It will normally be appropriate in such circumstances to include, in the circular accompanying the annual accounts, a pro forma statement showing the revised balance sheet once court permission has been obtained. Also, an explanation will be given to the shareholders in the circular of the reasons for the reduction of share capital. It will be necessary to agree with the court a timetable for the reduction of capital, such that the annual general meeting can be convened for an appropriate date.

1721   Typically, a reorganisation of the sort described above, which will include a reduction of the share premium account, will take about six months and the timetable might be as follows.

● **Month 1**   Instruct counsel to advise on the proposed reduction of the share premium account and settle the petition and affidavit evidence in outline.

● **Month 2**   Finalise the details of that scheme, see earlier.

● **Month 3**   Prepare a notice of the meeting to approve the reduction of share premium account. Twenty-one clear days' notice is required to be given to all members of the intention to propose the special resolution. Notice will be accompanied by an explanatory circular explaining the proposals to shareholders and recommending them to vote in favour. The circular and notice is sent to the shareholders together with the annual report and accounts.

- **Month 4** The AGM is held, immediately followed by an EGM at which the special resolution is proposed and passed. A copy of the special resolution has to be delivered to the Registrar of Companies within fifteen days.

- **Month 5** Assuming the special resolution is passed, a petition should be filed with the courts.

- **Month 6** A summons for directions is issued to consider the petition and evidence. The necessary advertisements are organised.

- **Month 7** The court hearing is held and an order for reduction should be drawn and made by the court and delivered to the Registrar of Companies. Reduction only becomes effective on registration of that order.

Other matters

1722 There have been cases where the court has refused to confirm a reduction whose sole purpose has been to avoid taxation or where the relevant company would have been able to eliminate the deficit without any assistance from the court. Tax advice is in any case essential before the details of a capital reduction scheme are finalised.

1723 It can sometimes be convenient to go for a reduction scheme in conjunction with a rights issue or some other form of capital raising exercise. If an excess of distributable reserves is needed in order to enable a rights issue, or other capital raising exercise, to be arranged, it is possible for the excess arising on a reduction of the share premium account (ie over and above what is needed to make good any permanent losses) to be transferred to a non-distributable special reserve which, after the rights issue and with the consent of court, can be transferred into a distributable reserve. For instance, the board would propose here the cancellation of the entire amount standing to the credit of the share premium account, a sum which would be in excess of the deficit on their profit and loss account, and which would normally have to be transferred to a special capital reserve.

1724 For example, consider a company with share premium reserves of £100,000 and with a revenue reserve deficit of £50,000. By means of a rights issue it raises a sum of £200,000 from its shareholders and at the same time proposes:

Step (i) The cancellation of the entire amount of share premium reserve (£100,000), with the elimination of the deficit (£50,000) and the creation of a (temporary) capital reserve of £50,000.

Step (ii) Following the raising of the £200,000 fresh capital, the temporary capital reserve of £50,000 would be transferred into a revenue reserve.

Note: Steps (i) and (ii) require sanction by the court and would comprise a series of steps which would be described in the petition. In this example it would be made clear to the court that the outside creditors of the company would be better secured after the two steps were completed, and that therefore no special protection (for example, a bank guarantee) would be needed for them as part of the petition.

1725 This is necessarily a simplified explanation in order to illustrate the practical side of a typical scheme where a company has to be recapitalised and where a precondition of raising capital is the creation of some distributable reserves. It will be observed here and earlier in this chapter, that reorganising capital contemporaneously with a rights issue means that the whole process is simplified since the benefit to creditors is almost axiomatic.

1726 Finally, one important practical matter: it is pointless to free up a company's reserves by a capital reduction scheme, and then go immediately back into deficit with another operating loss. The reduction of capital should only be contemplated after losses have been stemmed. Hence the need for thorough review on the lines of para **1717** above.

NOTE

1 *Re Ratner's Group plc* [1988] BCLC 685.

Part II

Legal procedure and practice administration

Chapter 18

High Court procedures

Introduction – The courts – The players in the judicial system – The judge – Solicitors and barristers – The barrister's clerk – Juries – High Court procedures – The writ – Pleadings – Joining third parties – Discovery – Summons for directions – Judgments – Appeals – Settling the case – Costs – Security for costs – The cost of it all – Steps in litigation

INTRODUCTION

1801 In commercial litigation the roles of the people involved, the wigs and the general formality, can be confusing to the first time expert witness. In this chapter we give a general description of the legal system and of the actors in it, and in particular of the role of the barrister. While proper respect is due to members of another profession, their presence should not overawe witnesses, expert or otherwise. Reading this chapter and the next one on cross-examination will perhaps help to dispel some of the mysteries.

1802 At the start of a case the accountant may feel comfortable because he can recall some snippets of his early law studies. However, he may soon find himself out of his depth on points of law, but disinclined to ask the lawyer to explain. It is vital to seek clarification at an early stage of any legal points which the expert does not grasp fully and, in particular, any which relate to the pleading of the claim, so as to avoid subsequent confusion and wastage of costs. We therefore set out in this chapter the processes which have to be followed when a claim is pursued through the courts.

1803 Lastly in this chapter we draw attention to the alarming rate at which legal costs mount up. Legislation is constantly expanding, notably in the field of consumer protection (for example, the Financial Services Act 1986) and no-one in business should be ignorant of the consequences of all this in terms of potential problems and expense.

THE COURTS

1804 The hierarchy of courts in England and Wales is set out in diagrammatic form overleaf.

THE HIERARCHY OF THE CIVIL COURTS IN ENGLAND AND WALES

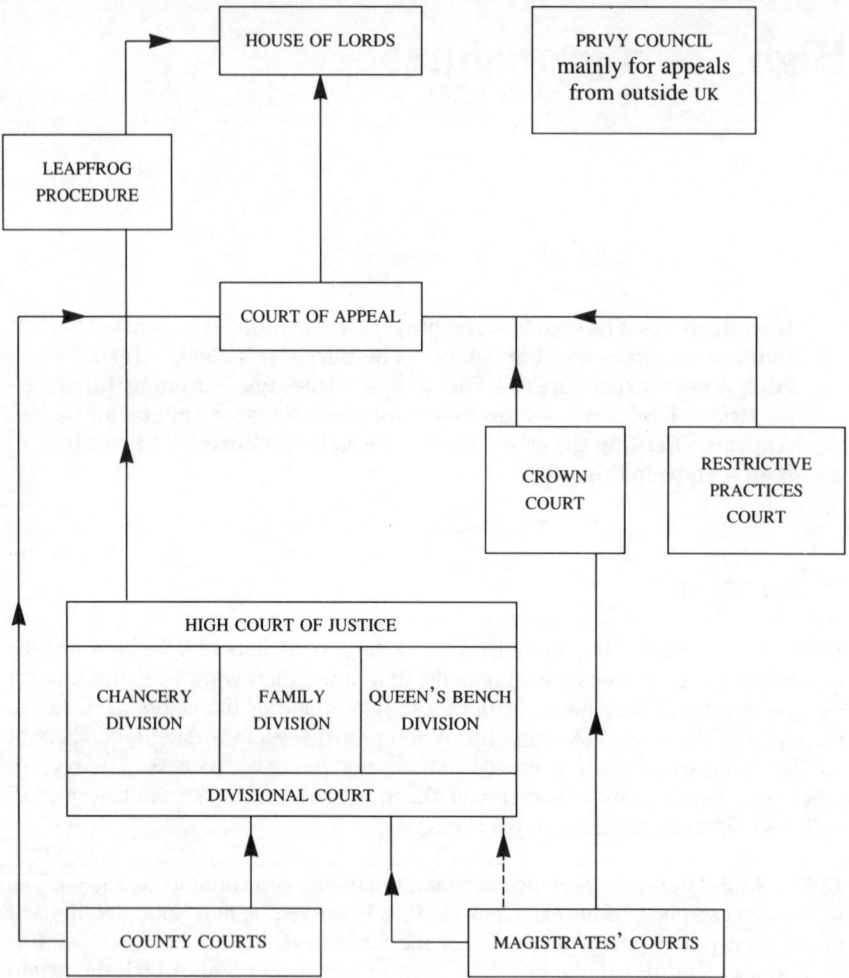

```
        ┌──────────────────┐         ┌────────────────────┐
        │  HOUSE OF LORDS  │         │   PRIVY COUNCIL    │
        │                  │         │ mainly for appeals │
        └──────────────────┘         │  from outside UK   │
                                     └────────────────────┘

┌──────────────┐
│  LEAPFROG    │
│  PROCEDURE   │
└──────────────┘

                    ┌──────────────────┐
                    │ COURT OF APPEAL  │
                    └──────────────────┘

                              ┌──────────┐    ┌──────────────┐
                              │  CROWN   │    │ RESTRICTIVE  │
                              │  COURT   │    │  PRACTICES   │
                              │          │    │    COURT     │
                              └──────────┘    └──────────────┘

   ┌────────────────────────────────────────────┐
   │          HIGH COURT OF JUSTICE               │
   ├──────────────┬──────────────┬───────────────┤
   │  CHANCERY    │   FAMILY     │ QUEEN'S BENCH  │
   │  DIVISION    │   DIVISION   │   DIVISION     │
   ├──────────────┴──────────────┴───────────────┤
   │            DIVISIONAL COURT                  │
   └──────────────────────────────────────────────┘

   ┌────────────────┐              ┌──────────────────────┐
   │ COUNTY COURTS  │              │ MAGISTRATES' COURTS  │
   └────────────────┘              └──────────────────────┘
```

Key

———————————— APPEALS

------------------- APPEALS BY WAY OF 'CASE STATED'

1805 Major commercial disputes will be heard in the High Court. Within the Queen's Bench Division is the Commercial Court, a specialist court whose judges are particularly experienced in complex commercial cases. Cases involving significant and complex engineering and financial issues are often referred to the Official Referees Department, which is a sub-division of the High Court. We summarise here the types of case heard in each court.

(a) Magistrates' courts are mainly concerned with domestic proceedings, eg, affiliation orders, separation and matrimonial relief orders; also with authorising recovery of small debts.

(b) County courts tend to hear the more minor cases, while the High Court tends to hear the weightier cases.

(c) The High Court has three divisions:

    (i) The Queen's Bench Division, which has jurisdiction over every type of common law civil action. The Admiralty Court and the Commercial Court are specialist courts within this division.

    (ii) The Chancery Division, which deals principally with matters formerly assigned to courts of equity, for example, partnerships, mortgages, trusts, companies, contentious probate, and with bankruptcy and revenue matters.

    (iii) The Family Division, which deals with all High Court business concerning marriage, family property and children, including adoption and wardship.

(d) The Court of Appeal deals with appeals on law or fact from any division of the High Court, from the County Court and from interlocutory orders made in chambers. Leave may be required for such appeals.

(e) The House of Lords hears appeals from the Court of Appeal provided the Lords or a lower court gives leave. The appeal can be heard direct from the High Court on a leapfrog procedure if it raises questions of law of general public importance.

THE PLAYERS IN THE JUDICIAL SYSTEM

The judge

1806 Judges are appointed by the Crown on the advice of the Lord Chancellor from among lawyers of not less than ten years' standing. In practice they are usually appointed from among senior barristers who have been appointed Queen's Counsel. The standard and expertise of High Court judges is world renowned, perhaps mainly because they are not career judges or political appointees, but have been appointed from the ranks of the most distinguished barristers.

1807 The judge is the umpire between the two opposing counsel. His intellectual skill and decisiveness should at least match those of the rival advocates. Judges should be impartial both in public and in private. They are expected to be apolitical and to avoid any financial transactions which would reflect adversely on their integrity.

1808 The essential skills of a judge are:

'the ability to identify the relevant points and assess the reliability of the evidence; the ability without discourtesy or impatience to retain control of proceedings; the ability to avoid premature conclusions; and the ability to come to a firm and fair conclusion without . . . fudging the facts or ducking contentious points of law.' (Lord Hailsham)

1809 But judges are human. Some place all the emphasis on a strict interpretation of the matter before them, say, a contract; others take a more sympathetic and equitable approach. A barrister in his advocacy takes note of personality; he notes carefully the impression he is giving to the judge. He tries to get the points across in a manner which appeals to the judge, and he has to assess how to deal with any difficulties the judge may have in accepting or understanding a line of argument.

1810 The expert witness should remember that judges are there to see fair play. In some tribunals and indeed in some UK courts, judges question the witnesses in some detail themselves. However, their role is that of an adjudicator, not an inquisitor. It may be easier for an expert to answer the judge who will genuinely be trying to get to the bottom of whatever point is troubling him, than cope with an advocate who may be bent on discrediting the line the expert is taking. But the expert should beware the seemingly innocent question from the judge. It is not unknown for an expert manfully to beat off questions hour after hour from the opposing advocate only to concede to the judge an unnecessary point when presumably off guard.

Solicitors and barristers

1811 A notable and peculiar characteristic of the UK legal system is the split profession. Practising lawyers are either solicitors or barristers, but not both. Very broadly, in major litigation solicitors deal with the preparatory stages of litigation, and barristers act as advocates in court and draft the formal pleadings.

1812 Most readers will be familiar with the solicitor's task. Solicitors, like barristers, are officers of the court. Since they only have limited rights of audience in the higher courts, they are rarely employed for the advocate's role in the United Kingdom. In overseas tribunals and in certain specialised arbitrations a solicitor is sometimes briefed to appear as the advocate.

1813 Barristers come in two tiers: Queen's Counsel (QCs) and 'juniors'. A 'junior' can be anywhere between 25 and 70 years of age; the term simply denotes his or her ranking at the Bar. Being promoted to QC is called 'taking silk', since the QC wears a silk gown in court. QCs represent about 10% of the profession. In most substantial cases (involving major points of law or large sums of money) at least one QC is normally retained, together with one or more juniors. The latter do much of the earlier preparatory work in conjunction with the solicitors appointed to handle the case, for example, the settling of the pleadings (see para **1827**).

1814 Barristers practise as self-employed individuals; so far they have not been permitted to form partnerships. They have recently been entitled to pool their fees with other people in their chambers, but few have so far availed themselves of this rule. They do, however, share expenses.

1815 The expert may well spend many hours in the barrister's chambers. The expression 'chambers' dates from the seventeenth century, when it meant a set of rooms let out as living (or occasionally work) accommodation. In London, most chambers are found in or around the Inns of Court (Inner Temple, Middle Temple, Lincoln's Inn and Gray's Inn); about three quarters of the profession reside in these inns, which have a collegiate atmosphere. There are also sets of chambers in other big cities in England and Wales.

1816 Because of the antiquity of many of the buildings, the conditions of working may sometimes strike outsiders as spartan. Carpets on the staircases are something of a rarity. The interior of a barrister's chambers gives the impression of a private study, perhaps a housemaster's study, rather than a modern office. Certain chambers, on the civil law side, specialise in particular aspects of the law and it is not uncommon for two barristers in the same set of chambers to find themselves on opposite sides of a case.

1817 In theory, if an expert is asked to discuss a matter with a barrister, a solicitor, being the barrister's client, should be present. The Bars' Code of Conduct provides for this practice 'save in exceptional circumstances', which have not been defined. However, in practice this rule is given a broad interpretation, with the tacit agreement of all sides, and counsel may discuss certain matters with the expert without a solicitor present. There is also increasing evidence of greater flexibility over some of the other traditional customs of the Bar. More frequently, barristers are holding meetings outside their chambers, visiting solicitors, lay client and experts' offices where it may be more convenient for the others involved in the case to attend.

1818 The question of the respective roles of solicitors and barristers has been an issue of debate among observers of the legal profession for many years. The efficiency of involving two legal professions, for example, to obtain counsel's opinion in certain technical matters, is questionable. Since 1989, chartered and certified accountants and chartered surveyors have been granted the right of direct access to barristers. Accountants may now directly seek counsel's opinion on a range of accounting, auditing, tax, insolvency and other advisory matters, particularly in connection with interpreting the Companies Act 1985, the Financial Services Act 1986 and related tax and financial legislation. However, any advice relating to litigation still requires the involvement of instructing solicitors.

1819 Other developments in the respective rights of barristers and solicitors have been introduced by the Courts and Legal Services Act 1990, although they reflect a deal of compromise compared with the more radical proposals which were contained in the earlier Green Paper. The most publicised provision allows the Law Society to grant solicitors rights of audience in the High Court. However, this has not been universally welcomed by the judiciary, albeit solicitors' rights of audience in the County and Crown Courts are now significantly wider.

1820 Despite these changes, there is still a debate over the more fundamental question of whether solicitors and barristers should fuse their respective professions or maintain the present independence. The solicitors are advocating change. The Bar are concerned that the skills of advocacy would be eroded and that independent specialist knowledge of the law would be less easily located and tapped. It remains to be seen whether the recent changes on direct access and the rights of audience are the start of a major change in the legal profession in this country. Change is inevitable but, given the conservative traditions of legal practitioners, it is sure to be gradual.

The barrister's clerk

1821 When a visitor enters a barrister's chambers he reports to the clerk's room. The barrister's clerk combines a number of functions – administrator, accountant, agent and, most important, business manager – for the chambers he represents. It is his task to ensure that a reasonable case-load comes into the chambers and it is he who is first contacted by the solicitors. There have on occasion been complaints voiced about the influence and authority exercised by clerks; but under the present arrangement the barrister cannot manage without one.

Juries

1822   Expert accountants rarely meet a jury. In civil cases, juries are used in the UK only in libel cases. Outside the UK, for example in the US, they are employed more widely; in communicating his message the expert has then to consider their needs as well as those of the judge.

HIGH COURT PROCEDURES

1823   Procedure in the High Court is governed by the Rules of the Supreme Court. The standard work on procedure is The Supreme Court Practice, known as the 'White Book'. The Rules of the Supreme Court lay down numerous time limits for particular matters. The parties may agree, or the court be requested to order a variation of these limits at the request of the parties, but the limitation period within which actions for breach of contracts in writing and for actions in negligence must be commenced is normally limited to six years from the date on which the cause of an action occurs.

1824   In this chapter we deal with High Court procedures in the English legal system. Those requiring knowledge of the equivalent procedures in Scotland should refer to appropriate reference books, for example, The Parliament House Book (Greens).

The writ

1825   The action starts when one party, the 'plaintiff', accuses another person, the 'defendant', of some wrong which is alleged to have resulted in injury to the plaintiff. This accusation is formalised when the plaintiff issues a writ, which on payment of a fee, is stamped by and filed with the court. Once issued, the writ is served on the defendant(s) together with an acknowledgement of service form. The ensuing steps are illustrated in the accompanying diagram on p 232 and described in more detail below.

1826   A defendant who intends to defend himself against the accusation contained in the writ must serve an 'acknowledgement of service'. The form of acknowledgement of service requires the defendant to state whether or not he intends to contest the proceedings. He must normally serve it within 14 days of the writ being served.

Pleadings

1827   Written statements setting out each party's case are delivered alternately to each side of the dispute and are called pleadings. The main object of pleadings is to define the issues between the parties. In addition to the writ, the pleadings include the statement of claim, the defence, the reply, occasionally the rejoinder, and even more rarely, subsequent pleadings. A defendant who feels that he has a claim or is entitled to a remedy against the plaintiff may, instead of bringing a separate action, make a counterclaim, which will be added at the end of the defence ('the defence and counterclaim'). The plaintiff will be entitled to serve a defence to the counterclaim, which may be followed by a reply to the defence to the counterclaim. In actions to be heard in the Official Referees Department (which are often of a complex financial or technical nature) Official Referees tend to use new technology and usually require careful pre-trial preparation to present the case in a digestible way. The pleadings usually incorporate a Scott Schedule which sets out in columnar form the cases of the plaintiff and defendant in a single document. An expert who is asked to advise on quantum issues will normally be sent copies of the pleadings as soon as he is instructed. Pleadings tend to be legalistic and may appear to be disjointed and highly repetitive. A précis is therefore useful.

1828   The pleading normally bears the name of the barrister who prepared it. It must be limited to a summary of the material facts (not a detailed chronology of all relevant facts) on which the party relies for his claim or for his defence. It does not contain the evidence by which those facts are to be proved; it should be as brief as the nature of the case permits. Certain matters must be pleaded if they are to be relied upon in arguing the case; this is to avoid later taking the opponent by surprise. Pleadings may be amended at any time up to and including trial. The time and nature of the amendment determines whether the leave of court is required.

1829   It is not possible to allege fraud unless strong evidence to support the allegation is available; any charge of fraud or misrepresentation must be pleaded with great care. This is of special relevance when, say, a business has been bought and one side feels that it has been cheated by the other, for example, by representations concerning the balance sheet position. Under the code of conduct for the Bar, a barrister cannot allege fraud unless he has clear instruction to do so and there is reasonably credible material to establish a prima facie case.

Joining third parties

1830   In addition to his right to defend the action and make a counterclaim, the defendant may join a third party in the action where he can reasonably claim a contribution, relief, or indemnity from that third party relating to the subject matter of the action brought by the plaintiff. A third party may also be joined where the defendant requires that any question relating to or connected with the original subject matter of the action should be determined, not only as between the original parties, but also as against a person not already a party to the action. Bringing third parties into the case adds to the complexities of administration; subsequent third parties can be numbered sequentially – we have heard of a case where there was an '18th third party'. Each party will have his own legal representatives, will call his own factual witnesses and may also seek to appoint his own experts. Sometimes the dissension between defendants, or between defendants and third parties, seems as bad as that between plaintiff and defendant.

Discovery

1831 After the close of pleadings in an action, the parties are required to exchange a 'list of documents' which are or have been in that party's possession, custody or power and relate to matters in question in the action. They include documents which, for instance: 'contain information which may enable the party applying for discovery either to advance his own case or damage that of his adversary, or which may fairly lead him to a train of inquiry which may have either of these two consequences.' The court will usually set time limits for the exchange of lists and arrangements for the inspection of the other side's documents. The process of giving and inspecting discovery is very time-consuming, but a detailed understanding of the relevant papers is critical for the expert. Such inspections are important for ensuring, for example, that there are no manuscript notes or matters of relevance which appear on, say, the carbon copy that do not appear on the original or vice versa.

1832 Both in theory and in practice, the obligations with regard to discovery are onerous and important. The test is one of relevance, not materiality, importance or interest. Confidentiality, or the fact that documents are internal, are not grounds for withholding relevant documents. A high professional duty is imposed on a lawyer and his client to ensure that the client retains and discloses all relevant documents. Some documents are however regarded as being subject to 'legal professional privilege' (ie relevant, but protected from discovery). These include:

(a) documents protected by solicitor/client privilege, ie communications between solicitor and client written for the purpose of getting legal advice or assistance for a client; and
(b) documents which are privileged only if litigation is contemplated, or pending, ie communications between a solicitor and a non-professional agent or third party which come into existence after litigation is contemplated or commenced, with a view to that litigation, for the purposes of giving advice or obtaining or collecting evidence.

1833 A party who obtains documents on discovery may use them only for the purpose of conducting his own case in that litigation. He cannot use them, for example, as a basis for working up a case against someone else in a separate set of proceedings. In our experience, the expert accountant is often asked to take part in the discovery process. He can assist in identifying the type of documents that the other side should have and which would be relevant to the financial issues involving quantum, as well as reviewing discovery provided by the other parties. He should get a clear briefing on the conduct expected of him and follow it meticulously.

Summons for directions

1834 It is a feature of every Queen's Bench or Chancery Division action that the lawyers of one or other, or both sides seek 'summonses for direction' ('applications for direction' in the Official Referees Department). One or more hearings will be arranged, attended by all parties to the action, usually in chambers before a Master, or in substantial cases, the prospective trial judge. The Master/Judge will be asked to decide how the case should be conducted up to trial and will lay down a procedural timetable. The involvement of the trial judge in such proceedings enables him to control the way in which the case will be tried and to keep things moving. Summons for directions are also used where, because of the complication of the case, the parties wish the judge to consider dealing with items in a defined order. For example, the judge may direct a timetable for discovery, and exchange of witness statements and, of particular relevance to the expert witness, that the experts should be limited to two on each side, or that experts complete their reports for exchange by a certain date. In complex cases, the judge may be asked to direct that the trial be split: issues of liability will be decided first of all, and only if liability is established, will quantum be considered at a later date. Similarly, a defendant may seek adjudication of a 'preliminary issue' (normally at a separate hearing, before the main trial), which, if successful, will dispose of the action.

Judgments

1835 In England, judgments are often delivered orally immediately after the conclusion of the oral arguments at the end of the case. In more complex matters judgment is reserved and delivered subsequently, and although delivered orally, may be handed down in written form at the same time. An oral judgment will usually be recorded by the tape recorder or the official shorthand writer and then transcribed. The House of Lords and now, commonly, the Court of Appeal hand down written judgments.

Appeals

1836 The normal period for giving notice for an appeal is four weeks from the date on which the formal written order is sealed by the court office, in the case of both a final judgment of the High Court and interlocutory cases.

Settling the case

1837 In general, 'settling the case' means agreeing to some sort of compromise between the parties before the end of the trial. This can happen at any time before the judge issues his judgment, either before the case comes to court or at some time during the hearing. An early settlement may arise because one party sees his prospects for a favourable outcome deteriorate and decides to cut his losses.

1838 Judicial statistics reveal that the proportion of actions settled before they come to trial is rapidly growing. Settlement is sometimes brought about by genuine agreement. In some cases, the fear of the enormous costs of the trial obliges the financially weaker party to give up. This is of course an unsatisfactory and sometimes unjust solution and has led to a discussion of alternatives such as 'contingency fees' which are dependent on the lawyer being successful in the action (see also para **2125**).

COSTS

1839 The court has full power to determine by whom and to what extent costs are to be paid. Such costs include fees, charges, disbursements, expenses and remuneration. The general rule is that 'costs follow the event', that is, the unsuccessful party must pay a substantial proportion of the successful party's costs, as well as his own. In matrimonial cases the courts tend to be less rigid in ruling that the loser pays costs. The court is more ready to look at who caused any avoidable expenses incurred, and to award costs accordingly.

1840 In order to protect himself against bearing these costs, a defendant may pay into court a sum of money which he considers will cover the judge's award of damages including interest in the event that the judge finds against the defendant ('a payment into court'). In those circumstances, if the award is less than or equal to the payment into court then costs arising after the payment into court will be awarded against the plaintiff even though he has won his case. This is because as a matter of public policy it is considered that the plaintiff should have accepted the payment into court and not continued with the action. In certain circumstances the same effect can be achieved by issuing a 'Calderbank letter'. This is a written offer made by one party to the other on a 'without prejudice' basis, but reserving the offeror's rights to ask the court to take note of the letter when awarding costs. In both circumstances the judge is not made aware of the payment into court or the written offer until after making his award.

1841 Except as explained above, a successful party is rarely deprived of his right to costs. But it is a matter for the judge's discretion. It is not unusual for the judge to order X to pay Y's costs, with 'such costs to be taxed if not agreed' – that is, analysed in detail by a court official known as the Taxing Master, whose job it is to decide whether they are reasonable. This can be a time-consuming and costly business, not least because of the immense detail required in preparing the analysis of costs. The drafting of bills of costs is a profession in its own right. Solicitors seek to agree costs wherever possible. The successful party does not normally get back the whole of his costs but only those which were reasonably and necessarily incurred (approximately 60%). Normally, the party reimbursing the cost is given the benefit of any doubt, except where costs are awarded on an indemnity basis, in which case the party being reimbursed gets the benefit of any doubt. The position requires care where costs are awarded against a party who was receiving legal aid. Although the Legal Aid Fund will meet his costs, it will not bear his opponent's costs awarded against him. In such circumstances, the award of costs to an ostensibly successful opponent may be a Pyrrhic victory. Often the unsuccessful party will insist that his opponent's costs are 'taxed'.

1842 Because of this system, lawyers have to keep detailed records of the time they spend on cases, including the timing of telephone calls, how long they are kept waiting in counsel's waiting rooms and so on. Increasingly, it seems, experts are expected to be able to produce similar details for taxing purposes. We recommend that such records are maintained since it can be difficult, if not impossible, to produce details after the event for taxing, which may take place years after the work is actually done.

Security for costs

1843 In appropriate circumstances, a defendant may be able to obtain security for costs, which amounts to a financial guarantee that the plaintiff can pay costs if required. The costs of a successful defendant may be irrecoverable if, for instance, the plaintiff is out of the jurisdiction, or is a company in liquidation, or for some other reason is unable to pay. The accountant may be asked to provide evidence to assist counsel in arguing for security for costs to be provided. We have dealt with this topic in more detail in Chapter 13.

THE COST OF IT ALL

1844 Under English law, someone who suffers a wrong is entitled to compensation for his losses if they were due to someone else's (the defendant's) fault. This is decided by legal battle. The plaintiff consults his solicitor. The solicitor sends a summary to counsel. If counsel thinks there is a reasonable chance of winning, the steps described in this chapter are taken to bring the matter to trial. The parties' solicitors serve on each other requests for 'further and better particulars', which are drafted by counsel. Somewhere along the line will be mini trials as the lawyers argue procedural points; the settlement of 'pleadings'; the processes of 'discovery'. The parties' solicitors then instruct their respective counsel to 'advise on evidence'. Finally, when all documents have been exchanged, the case is 'set down for trial' – that is, put in the queue of cases awaiting trial. From start to finish can take four years or more.

1845 Time is a great consumer of money. Over the years people have sought to simplify the system or resort to alternative systems such as arbitration. But as we show in Chapter 20, some arbitrations can be just as costly as the court system.

1846 As a former president of the Law Society said: 'There is no point in having the world's greatest system if it is so expensive as to be unavailable for a significant percentage of the population . . . It operates superbly for the few who can afford it' (Law Society Conference 1982).

1847 For the bigger and more complex cases, the present system is probably justified. For the lesser commercial disputes, and indeed for personal injury cases, a simplified system is required. We have had first hand experience on the continent of some effective methods of short circuiting the system, for example, by fixing severe time limits before and during the trial, by restricting the prolixity of the advocates, by curbing abuse of the discovery process, and by avoiding unnecessary paperwork. Perhaps the same should be tried in the United Kingdom.

STEPS IN LITIGATION

The time limits given are those set by rules of court. In practice, they are invariably extended by agreement between the parties or by order of the court.

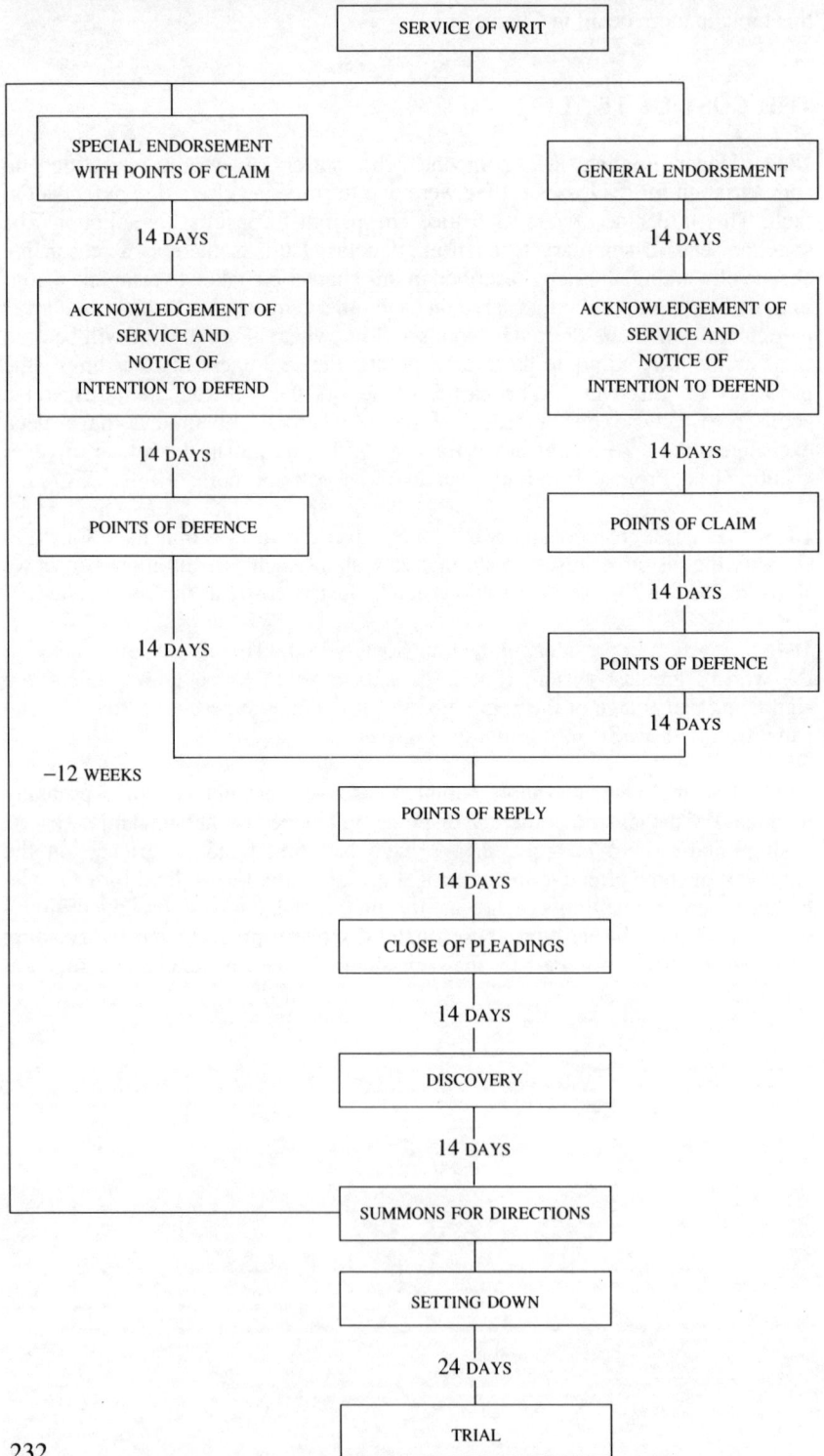

```
                        ┌─────────────────────────┐
                        │     SERVICE OF WRIT      │
                        └─────────────────────────┘

  ┌──────────────────────────┐          ┌──────────────────────────┐
  │   SPECIAL ENDORSEMENT     │          │    GENERAL ENDORSEMENT    │
  │   WITH POINTS OF CLAIM    │          └──────────────────────────┘
  └──────────────────────────┘
            14 DAYS                                14 DAYS

  ┌──────────────────────────┐          ┌──────────────────────────┐
  │  ACKNOWLEDGEMENT OF       │          │  ACKNOWLEDGEMENT OF       │
  │  SERVICE AND              │          │  SERVICE AND              │
  │  NOTICE OF                │          │  NOTICE OF                │
  │  INTENTION TO DEFEND      │          │  INTENTION TO DEFEND      │
  └──────────────────────────┘          └──────────────────────────┘
            14 DAYS                                14 DAYS

  ┌──────────────────────────┐          ┌──────────────────────────┐
  │    POINTS OF DEFENCE      │          │     POINTS OF CLAIM       │
  └──────────────────────────┘          └──────────────────────────┘
                                                  14 DAYS
            14 DAYS                     ┌──────────────────────────┐
                                        │    POINTS OF DEFENCE      │
                                        └──────────────────────────┘
  −12 WEEKS                                       14 DAYS

                        ┌─────────────────────────┐
                        │     POINTS OF REPLY      │
                        └─────────────────────────┘
                                 14 DAYS
                        ┌─────────────────────────┐
                        │    CLOSE OF PLEADINGS    │
                        └─────────────────────────┘
                                 14 DAYS
                        ┌─────────────────────────┐
                        │        DISCOVERY         │
                        └─────────────────────────┘
                                 14 DAYS
                        ┌─────────────────────────┐
                        │  SUMMONS FOR DIRECTIONS  │
                        └─────────────────────────┘
                        ┌─────────────────────────┐
                        │      SETTING DOWN        │
                        └─────────────────────────┘
                                 24 DAYS
                        ┌─────────────────────────┐
                        │          TRIAL           │
                        └─────────────────────────┘
```

Chapter 19

Hints for cross-examination

Introduction – Courtroom behaviour – Court courtesies – Dress in court – Attitude in court – Preparation for cross-examination – Proofs of evidence – The court file – Other witnesses' testimony – The examination – Devices of cross-examination – Breaks in the examination – Transcripts – Summary

INTRODUCTION

1901   When an expert witness is first briefed, he cannot be sure he will be called to give evidence; most cases are settled out of court and many that get to court settle before the trial is completed. So the chances are high that he will not be cross-examined on his written report. But he cannot be sure. The possibility of having to defend his opinions before a judge makes it all the more important to avoid expressing extreme or untenable viewpoints.

1902   Undergoing cross-examination is a daunting task, not to be entered into lightly. People who enjoy a verbal tussle are better suited to it than those who do not. Practice makes perfect; ideally an expert should have attended court to see how experienced people manage in the witness box.

1903   To make an effective expert witness, the accountant must be confident about the strength of his written testimony. He must also develop techniques for presenting himself and his opinions to the best advantage in what may seem a hostile environment. Finally, he needs to understand the etiquette of the courtroom. This chapter covers presentation. It also covers the preparation he should make for cross-examination and the type of questioning he is likely to face.

COURTROOM BEHAVIOUR

Court courtesies

1904   The tradition of courtesy within the legal profession is heightened when lawyers get to court, for example, barristers call each other 'my learned friend' when discussing points in front of a judge. An expert should know the etiquette to follow in his own examination.

1905   A barrister is usually addressed in court as 'Mr X' or 'Sir'. His questions are supposed to give rise to a response which is addressed to the court, ie to the judge, and not to the barrister. 'M'Lord' is the proper address for the judge in the

High Court; the judge is never referred to as 'you' but always as 'your Lordship'. 'Your Honour' is the address if the judge is sitting in the county court. In an arbitration, the arbitrator may be addressed as 'Sir' even though he may be a High Court judge.

1906 In other courts, for example, on the continent, the courtesies are not so easy to establish in advance. An expert witness cannot be expected to know all the rules but he cannot go far wrong if he calls people 'Sir' within the court.

1907 Of course it is possible to overdo the courtesies. There is nothing worse than listening to an expert peppering all his sentences with 'My Lord' or with 'Sir'. It simply breaks up the sense of what he is trying to say.

1908 Certain phrases which lawyers use in court are also useful for the expert witness. 'My Lord, can I look up my papers?' or 'I am grateful to your Lordship', or 'My Lord, is it possible to ask my colleagues to bring the file over?' or 'My Lord, this is not really within my own expertise'.

1909 The potential witness may ask, 'What does it matter how I look or how I behave as long as I know what I'm talking about?' All aspects of court behaviour are important in that they contribute to the overall impression received by the judge or the arbitrator. If the expert creates a bad first impression it cannot help his client, regardless of the subsequent quality of his evidence. A good first impression, of a relaxed, confident and knowledgeable expert can help the client enormously.

Dress in court

1910 Dress and personal appearance can be important. The expert should be soberly dressed and businesslike. If he is not sure about dress conventions, the expert should ask. Appearing at the High Court in the Bahamas on a very hot day, our team turned up at the opening of the court in lightweight tropical suits. Although the temperature was in the 90s, everyone else was wearing dark three piece suits. The next day we put on dark suits only to find that the barristers and clients had followed our example of the day before.

1911 An arbitration hearing may be held over a weekend and the barristers may turn up in less formal clothes. But if the expert is giving evidence we suggest he should not risk anything other than a grey or dark suit, or the equivalent for a woman.

Attitude in court

1912 Our purpose is to alert the expert witness to some of the potential pitfalls of cross-examination and to offer some advice as to how to avoid them. The advocate has some of the advantages in his 'contest' with the expert. He knows where he is going and what answer he expects before he puts the question. The question may not appear relevant to the expert but will certainly serve a purpose for the advocate. He may be setting an ambush, putting up a smoke screen, or preparing pegs on which to hang later arguments quite outside the expert's evidence.

1913 But the expert should not be overly concerned about the inequality of the contest. It is inevitable and the judge is aware of it. If the expert follows the guidelines in this chapter and knows his stuff, he should be able to put up a good showing. The key to success is good preparation.

1914 It is also important to feel confident and to act in a confident manner. The expert is not on trial and should try to be helpful. The expert witness should not show emotion. To show scorn or glee – for example, if the barrister on your side is scoring a point against the opposing expert – is unprofessional.

1915 A barrister may well use the cross-examination to try to make the expert change his mind. Barristers seem to divide professional witnesses into two types: the robust and those who dissolve under cross-examination. Before going into the box, the expert must be clear about the points he has made and about the limits to which he will go in accepting any reservations or variations on these points. He may well be pressed to the ultimate on this but must not depart from his prepared position. As one barrister said:

> 'I met Mr X in conference. He was clear and very convincing. But once he got into the witness box it was unbelievable how he came apart, changed his story, hedged his bets with all sorts of "buts" and detailed assumptions. What I wanted was a clear and firm view, not watered down by qualifications that left him an escape hatch if the going got rough.'

It is best to answer the question that is being asked without introducing supplementary matter. Many accountants have a tendency to say too much and to be too thorough in reply to a question on accounting matters.

1916 Often the most effective answer a witness can offer is 'yes' or 'no'. First, it gives the cross-examiner very little time to think ahead. Second, it is clear and brief, leaving little scope for a supplementary question on the same point. If the question cannot be answered so briefly it is often effective to answer with a 'yes' or 'no' followed by a qualification. It is important to keep answers brief and clear. A witness should if necessary insist on completing his answer before dealing with the next question. A common fault in cross-examination is for the expert to refuse to make concessions that ought reasonably to be made. This can have serious spin-off consequences on the rest of his evidence. An expert is permitted to refresh his memory by reference to documents where matters of fact are concerned. This may include reference to a textbook if it has been of significance to the expert in forming his opinion.

1917 When giving evidence, the expert should look at the judge or the advocate rather than look down all the time at the evidence bundles, or worse still, at his feet. He should not relax his guard or keep looking over into his own barrister's corner for help. An experienced barrister will sometimes come to the expert's help; if he does so, it is a good rule to stop and sit motionless while he has his say. The two faults most commonly committed by the witness, whether expert or not, are dropping his voice and not pacing his evidence to the speed of the judge's pen.

1918 A witness should not leave the witness stand until there is a clear indication that he can do so. Someone may want to put further points to him. Often the barrister will seek permission for the expert to leave; if not, it is normal to seek permission from the judge or the arbitrators to leave.

PREPARATION FOR CROSS-EXAMINATION

Proofs of evidence

1919   An important part of the expert's preparation is to think out well in advance all the topics likely to emerge during cross-examination and to work out the answers to each possible question. The witness and the team that have been helping him in the preparation of his written report may be too close to the job to see all the related points which could reasonably be raised. The expert witness should ask someone who has had no dealings with the case to read his or her affidavit in a constructively critical manner and raise any topics likely to assist the cross-examining barrister.

1920   After that, the expert witness should prepare 'proofs of evidence' for each main topic. A proof of evidence is merely a written statement of what a witness intends to say during his oral evidence. In these 'proofs' the witness should put down all the arguments (for and against his point of view) in a logical and easy-to-follow way. He should consider what outside authorities he can bring in to support his views; what outside authorities might be quoted against him; and how best to dispose of them.

1921   The proofs must be kept as simple as possible; if necessary a separate proof should be prepared for each main topic. Proofs of evidence normally follow a simple narrative or note style, but in some circumstances counsel may want them put in a question and answer form. This is so that he can use them to put evidence to the witness to elicit, without 'leading' the witness, the information that he is seeking during the examination-in-chief which does not always happen, but precedes cross-examination if it does.

1922   It is not unusual for solicitors to spend many days preparing proofs of evidence for witnesses of fact (who are not generally permitted to meet counsel prior to the trial) and then submit them in agreed form to counsel before trial. An expert on the other hand is permitted to meet counsel before trial when the key aspects of his expert testimony can be discussed. (See also Chapter 18.)

The court file

1923   The preparation of a good court file is for the expert to deal with himself. He may be able to take the court file with him into the witness box when he gives his oral evidence, but if he does so he must recognise that the other side will be entitled to ask to see it, so care must be exercised in what it contains in these circumstances. The most practical form of file is a lever arch file which, although bulky, allows papers to be taken off neatly and replaced. The written report (or the sworn affidavit) should be in front with a separate section behind for each main topic covered in the report. Ideally, the expert should include in the file any documents relating to key points and which may be queried later during cross-examination; but there is a limit to how much bulk should be carried around in court.

1924   The witness should do the final cross-referencing of his report himself, preferably just before the hearing, so that it is all fresh in his mind. Being able to find one's way around the papers is a lifeline when in the witness box. The cross-referencing will link the report to relevant evidence, whether in the material which supplements the expert's evidence or in the evidence of others which corroborates the expert's written evidence.

1925 Each person has his own way of annotating the report. We find it useful to put on the left-hand side, that is on the reverse pages, a few useful phrases or analogies which will help to clarify a complicated point. The phrases should be easily read, like notes for an informal speech.

Other witnesses' testimony

1926 Experts, but not witnesses of fact, are allowed to be present in court when other witnesses are giving evidence. It may have been many months since the written evidence was prepared. Attending for as much as possible of the hearing will serve to remind the expert of the detail of the case, to concentrate his mind and to get a feel for the style of the players. Before giving evidence, the expert witness must be familiar with the evidence given or to be given by other witnesses on his side in the case, including non-financial witnesses. Similarly, the other witnesses should be familiar with what the expert witness on financial matters is intending to say. Contradictions or inconsistencies between experts appearing on the same side can cause a lot of expensive delay and confusion, or worse.

THE EXAMINATION

1927 There are usually three stages of examination. The witness is examined first by counsel on his side so as to introduce any points not covered in the affidavit evidence and to bring to the attention of the court the main points on which the evidence has been given. This is known as the 'examination-in-chief'. It is becoming less common but remains the right time to cover any new points which have just arisen and to correct any recently detected errors in the expert's written evidence.

1928 The next stage is for the expert to be cross-examined by the other side. The objective of counsel for the other side is to challenge anything with which he disagrees and in particular to cast serious doubt on any points which go against the case that he is trying to make. This is the cross-examination. Finally there is the re-examination: the expert is re-examined by his counsel, who can clarify any matters which have been left in doubt or get the witness to put a different gloss on some evidence that he has given in cross-examination. During re-examination, counsel is not entitled to raise new points but simply to check that what has been said is utterly clear and not the subject of second thoughts. It can be very useful to have one of the expert's colleagues sitting near counsel at this stage to help with appropriate questions for re-examination.

1929 The judge or the arbitrator may take it upon himself to converse with the expert. Indeed, having the inherent right to resolve conflicting testimony, he may, in exceptional cases, appoint his own expert. Invariably he will be friendly, courteous and polite, but it is a mistake for the expert to relax his concentration. The judge is certainly not looking for small talk. Everything is on record. On one occasion a distinguished arbitrator, Sir John Megaw, said to one of us: 'Now, let's forget what everyone else has been saying and see whether you and I can make accounting theory and the law converge!' But what followed was an intense half hour of discussion.

1930 Some useful insights into the way in which expert testimony is perceived and assessed by the judge were given in *Loveday v Renton*,[1] a medical negligence case, where Stuart-Smith LJ said:

'The court has to evaluate the witness and soundness of his opinion. Most importantly this involves an examination of the reasons given for his opinions and the extent to which they are supported by evidence. The judge also has to decide what weight to attach to a witness's opinion by examining—

—the internal consistency and logic of his evidence;
—the care with which he has considered the subject and presented his evidence;
—his precision and accuracy of thought as demonstrated by his answers;
—how he responds to searching and informed cross-examination and in particular the extent to which a witness faces up to and accepts the logic of a proposition put in cross-examination or is prepared to concede points that are seen to be correct;
—the extent to which a witness has conceived an opinion and is reluctant to re-examine it in the light of later evidence, or demonstrates a flexibility of mind which may involve changing or modifying opinions previously held;
—whether or not a witness is biased or lacks independence.

. . . There is one further aspect of a witness's evidence that is often important; that is his demeanour in the witness box. As in most cases where the court is evaluating expert evidence, I have placed less weight on this factor in reaching my assessment. But it is not wholly unimportant; and in particular in those instances where criticisms have been made of a witness, on the grounds of bias or lack of independence, which in my view are not justified, the witness's demeanour has been a factor that I have taken into account . . .'

Devices of cross-examination

1931 We have found that counsel in cross-examination use standard ploys, presumably picked up at bar school and developed in court. Cross-examination is, as we have said, an unequal contest, and it will assist the expert if he can recognise some of the methods commonly used to try to discredit him.

(a) Narrowing the basis of the expert's testimony to assumptions of questionable validity, and then taking his position to its illogical extreme. The expert should be cautious therefore in answering questions in case they lead to an illogical conclusion.

(b) Demonstrating that the expert's client gave him inaccurate or incomplete information. From the mass of papers in front of him it is not difficult for the advocate to find a topic unfamiliar to the expert. The expert should not be thrown by this or attempt to bluff. If the point is a weighty one the expert can reply 'I believe I have seen it but would like to refresh my memory' or words to that effect.

(c) Showing that there are errors in the expert's computations – a technique especially effective against accountants. It is important to check the arithmetic beforehand and not leave it all to the assistant or to the client.

(d) Showing that the expert usually testifies for only one side in a case (for example, always against the contractor), has testified for this particular client many times in the past, and has been paid a lot for doing so. This approach seems to be more common in America than in England. The aim is to suggest that the expert is strongly biased in favour of his client. It is enough to keep one's calm and sense of humour.

(e) Suggesting that the expert is out of touch with the real world. Counsel may try by various means to suggest that the expert's experience is hardly relevant to the real issues being faced. It is important to show that this is not the case.

(f) Appearing to leave the point before he has finished with it only to return to it later when, he hopes, the expert has dropped his guard.

1932 Then there are hypothetical questions. One hardy annual is to tell the witness to assume something that the witness does not believe to be realistic or which conflicts with the facts of the case. Counsel then takes the witness through a whole series of 'on this basis' questions with a view to getting the answer he is seeking. If the point is important, the best way for the expert to counter this ploy is to say, as often as he reasonably can, something like: 'Well, I'll try to answer. Please bear in mind that your basic assumption is not realistic.' The expert should also try to explain why the hypothetical question is at odds with his written evidence. This usually makes the process very laborious, and the judge may well encourage counsel to drop that particular line of attack. Another, rather extreme, way of countering it is to decline to answer hypothetical questions; but this can seem uncivil in some circumstances and the judge may insist that the expert does answer.

1933 Another ruse in cross-examination is for counsel to make remarks that put the witness off his stride. A frequent example is: 'We shall come back to that later.' In practice counsel rarely does; indeed the remark often signals that he has given up that particular line of attack. Another standard device is for counsel to say something like: 'Just answer my question,' with the clear implication that all he wants is a simple answer such as 'yes' or 'no'. But many questions cannot reasonably be answered with a simple affirmative or negative. The expert should not allow himself to be bullied. He can ask the judge for permission to give a complete answer but must not turn an answer into a lecture.

1934 Sometimes the witness is asked two questions wrapped up in one. If he is uneasy about this, he can say: 'Which shall I answer first?' Certainly only one question should be answered at a time. At other times the advocate will formulate a series of sub-questions. Here a 'yes' or 'no' is by far the best reply to each sub-question. Precision is the name of the game. Prolific answers may bore the court and run the grave risk of seeming vague or contradictory.

1935 The witness should not be put out if counsel asks him something which is not in his specialised field and was not addressed in his written report. Counsel sometimes does so at the beginning of cross-examination either to shake the expert's confidence or to try to demonstrate that the expert is outside his field. If the expert does not know the answer he should say so without feeling that he is in some way at fault. Of course, a witness should not venture opinions on topics on which he is not well versed.

1936 The question and answer sessions can go on for a long time. Counsel may ask the same question again, possibly in a different form. It may be that the answer the first time was not to his liking and he is hoping that, with the passage of time, the expert has either changed his mind or forgotten what he said, or will answer less convincingly. The expert must do his best to remember his previous answers. The expert must resist the temptation to modify his opinion with such phrases as 'in many cases', 'usually', 'often' or 'of course there are others who would disagree'. Such reservations water down helpful direct testimony. The cross-examination lawyers will simply drop such modifiers. If counsel wants to waste his time on a repetitious trawl, that is his affair, not the expert's. In certain sorts of arbitration, the total time allocated to each party in any phase of the hearing is strictly limited; any time wasting by one side will be to the advantage of the other. There is no point in getting tetchy with counsel in such cases. At most it may be appropriate to say: 'As I have just said . . .', but it may be equally appropriate simply to answer the question in the same terms, however many times it is put.

1937 Expert witnesses have a tendency either to use too much jargon or be too concise in answers on difficult matters. The judge or the tribunal need a base of knowledge from which to build. The expert who tries to dazzle with his erudition, or confuse with technical words and complicated sentences, is wasting his time. The judge probably resents and discounts any expert who patronises him. The expert should use simple words and if he has to use technical phrases or technical approaches he should ensure that he defines what he means. He should watch the judge and if he looks dazed or puzzled, should help with an example, a metaphor, or even a story.

1938 In summary, the witness must be alert at all times, listen to the questions, and answer responsively. He should not be too casual; where half truths are concerned it is better to be too particular than too easy going. He should never argue or lose his temper, and he should never play the lawyer.

Breaks in the examination

1939 Once the witness has started to give evidence, he is not allowed to discuss the case with anyone during the lunch break, overnight, or during any recess that takes place. In our interpretation this does not stop him giving instructions for work to be carried out by people who are assisting him (particularly to enable the expert to reply to any new points arising in cross-examination) provided he clears this with the other side before doing so. But he should not discuss the case with his colleagues or client, since this might influence the evidence he is to give.

1940 Often matters arise during cross-examination that cannot be dealt with by the witness at once. In these circumstances it is not unusual for the witness to offer to look at the matter when the court rises and to be ready to give his response the following morning. Furthermore, points may occur to a witness, once he sees the direction that cross-examination has taken, on which research needs to be done in the lunch interval or overnight. He should make arrangements for resources to be available to him to get this done adequately.

Transcripts

1941 In a long trial it may be uneconomic for the expert to attend throughout the hearing. He should, however, be supplied with a transcript so that he can keep track of developments.

1942 Shorthand writers are very quick but cannot always keep up. Also they cannot record a nod or shake of the head; always say 'yes' or 'no'! Also they may not know how to spell unusual names or write unusual phrases with technical meanings. Sometimes a shorthand writer will ask the expert to elucidate something which he has not fully understood. The time is well spent in doing so.

1943 Seeing one's own oral contribution in print can be a little unnerving. Since most people talk in long sentences without punctuation and sometimes with a verb missing, that is how it comes out in the transcript. We strongly recommend looking through the transcript to see whether the shorthand writer has got anything fundamentally wrong, and if so, drawing it to the attention of the lawyers conducting the case.

1944 These hints are perhaps of more importance in an arbitration than in an English courtroom, where the trend has been to use recording tapes rather than writers. They are particularly relevant where the arbitration is in a foreign court with instant translation facility.

SUMMARY

1945 The role of an expert accounting witness is the more difficult because of a general misunderstanding of the nature of accounting and the lack of certainty in many of its aspects. People without an accounting background do not understand the degree to which judgment must enter into any accounting determination; consequently they may rely too heavily on published material of general application without fully appreciating its limitations in particular circumstances.

1946 A brief checklist of 'Do's and Don'ts' appears as Appendix H to this book.

NOTE

1 *Loveday v Renton* [1990] 1 Med LR 117.

Chapter 20

Arbitration and other forms of alternative dispute resolution

Introduction – Advantages and disadvantages of arbitration – The arbitration process: the main steps – Agreement to arbitrate – Choice of arbitrator – Definition of the issues – The preparation and the hearing – The award – The enforcement of the award – Procedures for large cases – Arbitration in international contract disputes – The accountant's role – Acting as an expert witness – Acting as an arbitrator – Dispute resolution by an expert – Acting as expert not arbitrator – Advising one of the parties – Assisting with private settlements – Acting as a conciliator – Acting as a negotiator

INTRODUCTION

2001 An accountant may be called upon to act as an expert witness in an arbitration or to act as an arbitrator himself. In this chapter we therefore describe in some detail the whole process of arbitration, whether it be for the simpler and more straightforward disputes, or for the really complex disputes which call for considerable litigation expertise on the part of the players. We also consider the role of the accountant in other forms of alternative dispute resolution or 'ADR'.

2002 Arbitration is popularly believed to be much less formal and complex than litigation in the courts. To the layman the apparent advantages of arbitration over litigation include lower costs, less formality and a more speedy outcome. In addition the outcome seems less of a gamble. In reality, however, these advantages are often insignificant or even non-existent. The popular misconceptions arise largely because of the difference between the theory of arbitration and the practice. This chapter explains the nature of and steps in the arbitration process, and suggests guidelines for someone invited to act as an arbitrator.

2003 An arbitration is defined as a consensual process for resolution of legal disputes in private, but with binding legal consequences, before a third party chosen by the parties to the dispute.

2004 The process of arbitration sprang out of a concern in the Middle Ages that the courts were inappropriately structured to deal with commercial disputes arising from the growing amount of trading between merchants. The basic problem was the cumbersome procedures of the court, which prevented quick and economical resolution of the disputes. Many commercial disputes are even more complex today and various specialist arbitral organisations have been established, offering methods of ADR. The most recent of these are the City Disputes Panel, serving the wholesale financial services industry, and the Centre for Dispute Resolution ('CEDR'). Whatever form ADR takes, its objective is the same – to resolve commercial disputes quickly and economically.

2005 To be effective, arbitration relies on the agreement of the disputing parties to subject their differences to the arbitration process. The law intervenes only to ensure that the process works and that its awards are effectively enforced. Arbitration in the UK is governed by the Arbitration Acts of 1950 and 1979. International arbitration is controlled by international legislation and treaties.

ADVANTAGES AND DISADVANTAGES OF ARBITRATION

2006 Arbitration is normally preferred to court proceedings when:

(a) the skill and personality of the arbitrator is deemed to be important to both sides. They may well agree on who is best suited to preside;
(b) there is clear scope for economy, for example, by limiting legal representation or even dispensing with it at times;
(c) convenience of timing or location is important. Clearly, if the court administration is involved, such things tend to be arranged rather inflexibly;
(d) the proceedings need to be held in private to minimise publicity for the dispute;
(e) the disputes relate mainly to fact, especially technical matters, rather than to legal liabilities;
(f) only two parties are involved in the contractual dispute. Disputes involving three or more parties tend to end up in the courts for all sorts of technical reasons and any money previously spent in bipartisan arbitration may well be wasted; and
(g) it is possible to limit the issues at stake to specific areas.

2007 Arbitration has one important cost disadvantage: namely, the work of the arbitrator and the rent of the arbitration room have to be paid for by the disputants. However, provided the arbitrator takes control of the process from the start and maintains control to the end, adhering to an agreed timetable, a speedy and cost effective conclusion should be reached. Furthermore, appeals from the arbitrator's decisions are rare, which can be an economy.

2008 One feature of an arbitration which is absent from court cases, is that the parties to the dispute may represent themselves or be represented by someone without legal qualifications. We have seen cases on the continent where this has been an inestimable advantage, although there are many risks in such a practice.

2009 It is generally held that a court of law is preferable to an arbitration if the dispute is over legal matters, for example, the true meaning of a phrase in a construction contract. However, an alternative course of action is to appoint as arbitrator a respected lawyer, say a retired High Court judge. (There will be cases where a judge of the Commercial Court or an Official Referee may be appointed as an arbitrator, if he is prepared to do so and the Lord Chief Justice agrees (see Mustill and Boyd *Commercial Arbitration* (2nd edn, 1989) Butterworths at p 238).)

THE ARBITRATION PROCESS: THE MAIN STEPS

2010   The principal steps in the arbitration process are:

- agreement to arbitrate;
- choice of arbitrator;
- definition of issues;
- the preparation and the hearing;
- the award; and
- the enforcement of the award.

Agreement to arbitrate

2011   The agreement of parties to arbitrate is often enshrined in an arbitration clause in their original contract. It is usually more difficult for parties to agree to arbitration once the dispute has arisen, if the contract is silent on the matter.

Choice of arbitrator

2012   The method of appointment of the arbitrator is usually laid down in the contract. Sometimes a specific person is mentioned, especially where the dispute has arisen before the appointment. A common practice is to provide that each side should nominate one arbitrator with these two appointing a third. The fact that two of the tribunal are appointed by the respective parties should not in theory affect their impartiality when it comes to making judgment; in practice, during the hearing itself, the two arbitrators tend to watch the interests of the people who nominated them.

2013   There is usually a provision for 'Presidential Appointments' in the arbitration clause of a contract. That is to say, if the parties are unable to agree on the identity of the arbitrator within a specified period, the matter is referred to the president of the appropriate professional body or institution. That body is likely to have a list of members with arbitral experience who are willing to be nominated. The Chartered Institute of Arbitrators maintains panels of members who are qualified in one or more disciplines as well as having arbitral experience.

2014   It is possible for the court to appoint arbitrators, but only with the consent of the parties to a dispute.

2015   The Arbitration Act 1950 rules that when an agreement leads to the appointment of two arbitrators they may appoint a third party to act as 'umpire' unless the agreement expressly precludes such a step. They are to do so forthwith if they cannot agree. An umpire may sit with the arbitrators but cannot take part in proceedings until the latter signify in writing that they cannot agree on a decision.

2016   The position of an umpire is quite different from that of the third arbitrator referred to in para **2012** above, where all three arbitrators have equal voice.

2017 On a less complex level, parties to a dispute may decide to appoint an independent person to arbitrate. For example, they may wish to appoint an accountant to rule on an accounting issue. In such cases, the parties in conjunction with the nominated arbitrator will agree on the way the arbitration is to proceed and this will be embodied in an arbitration agreement between the parties.

Definition of the issues

2018 One of the principal advantages of arbitration over litigation is that it is possible to set limits on the issues at stake and so reduce the time and cost of resolving the dispute. This sounds fine in theory; whether it works depends on the firmness of the arbitrator in setting the limits and the willingness of the parties to abide by them. All too often, points of principle and a desire to refer too regularly to the Rules of the Supreme Court turn the arbitration process into a conventional litigation battle. To combat this tendency, some arbitration agreements now specifically exclude the parties' right to legal representation.

The preparation and the hearing

2019 The preparatory steps and the hearing will vary in length and complexity according to the weight of the dispute itself. We describe later in this chapter (para **2025**) the sequence for a full scale arbitration. An effective arbitration should result in a quick decision at a low cost. The flexibility in the choice of arbitrators, and the limitation of points at issue as discussed above, are helpful here. When the hearing is under way, time is saved by putting much reliance on written submissions to the arbitrators, and by restriction on the time available for oral presentation and cross-examination. We have observed that failure to follow these guidelines can sometimes result in an arbitration that costs more in professional time than the amount in dispute.

The award

2020 The parties must decide at the outset whether they require a reasoned or unreasoned award. The reasoned award – one in which the arbitrator gives his reasons for arriving at the sum – is not only a prerequisite to a successful appeal, but reassures the parties that the arbitrator has reached a decision after proper consideration. It is, however, more expensive than an unreasoned award, in which the arbitrator does not justify his decision.

2021 The acceptance of an unreasoned award renders it very difficult to get leave from the court to appeal against that award. On the other hand, for many disputes of a commercial nature, a quick irreversible decision from an impartial third party is all that is needed.

2022 Every arbitration agreement is deemed to provide that the award of the arbitrator is final and binding. The arbitrator normally also decides on the apportionment of the costs of the hearing between the parties to the dispute. He can also award simple interest on the award up to the time of his decision.

2023 There are circumstances where a court can, on the application of one of the parties, set aside the award, for example, because the arbitrator has misconducted himself. Discussions of such applications are beyond the scope of this book.

The enforcement of the award

2024 Ultimately, the strength of the arbitration process depends on the enforcement of the arbitrator's award and the settlement of the parties' costs. The law will assist in such enforcement. The arbitrator's hand was strengthened by the Arbitration Act 1950 and more particularly by the 1979 Act, which severely limited the powers of the court to interfere in arbitration without the agreement of both sides. The legislation also gives the arbitrator the power to determine how the parties' costs will be dealt with if this is not prescribed in the arbitration agreement. The arbitrator may take the advice of a costs clerk regarding his award of costs.

PROCEDURES FOR LARGE CASES

2025 The procedures for larger and more complex arbitrations, such as arise in the construction field, generally follow those of the court.

(a) **The pleadings** Whether pleadings are the best way of clarifying issues is debatable. They tend to be rather negative in style and rarely distil the real issues which separate the parties. An alternative is for the arbitrator to invite the claimant to prepare a statement of his case and the evidence on which he relies, which is followed by the respondent's statement indicating which parts of the claimant's case he disputes and why. This procedure can cut down the ambit of discovery.

(b) **Discovery** Usually the arbitrator has the right to order discovery. However, the arbitrator may well decide that, in the interest of saving time and cost, discovery should be dispensed with, for example, where the decision mainly turns on expert evidence rather than on the production of documents.

(c) **Inspection** The arbitrator should usually visit the site to see the cause of complaint for himself. He is normally accompanied by representatives of both sides.

(d) **Timetable for hearings** It is clearly of importance to all participants that the arbitrator should fix the timetable early on and adhere to it as far as possible.

(e) **Directions** After hearing both sides, the arbitrator can issue written directions as to the timetable and preparation of the case for both sides.

(f) **The hearing** In the UK, the arbitrator will normally choose to follow High Court procedure. That is, the case is opened on the claimant's behalf followed by evidence from his witnesses; the respondent's counsel then opens his case and calls his witnesses. The hearing is closed by the respondent's counsel addressing the arbitrator, to which the claimant's counsel then replies. The arbitrator may well seek to short-circuit some of the more time-consuming procedures typical of High Court hearings such as inordinately long opening and closing speeches, the use of too many experts, and the reading out verbatim of innumerable documents. One effective way is for the arbitrator to ration the time, in advance, for each successive step in the advocacy process (the 'egg-timer' approach); this seems to be a popular method in some European countries.

2026 There can be situations where, with the agreement of both parties, a 'documents only' arbitration is conducted. But in the UK the adversarial system is so deeply engrained that absence of oral submission in an important case will probably leave the protagonists, or their advisers, feeling short-changed.

ARBITRATION IN INTERNATIONAL CONTRACT DISPUTES

2027 Arbitration suits international contract disputes because it provides the opportunity to find neutral territory in which to air grievances. Various bodies have been set up to co-ordinate and administer international arbitration, including:

- International Chamber of Commerce (ICC);
- International Centre for the Settlement of Investment Disputes (ICSID);
- London Court of International Arbitration; and
- special tribunals set up under various international treaties to resolve disputes between governments.

2028 These bodies have each established rules under which the arbitration is to be conducted and set a fee structure for the cost of hearings. A copy of the ICC rules is included at Appendix I to illustrate the way in which an international arbitration is structured.

2029 International treaties often provide for arbitration under the 1976 UNCITRAL Arbitration Rules (United Nations Commission for International Trade Law). These rules are considered especially appropriate for cases involving parties from different political or cultural backgrounds.

2030 The expert accountant, when appearing in international tribunals on the continent, will tend to experience some notable differences in the procedures followed as compared with those in the UK. The first is the emphasis which arbitrators on the continent give to the appointment of their own expert witnesses. Great reliance seems to be placed on those witnesses' conclusions, even though the parties produce experts of their own who may differ substantially with the tribunal's appointee. Indeed, on occasion, the tribunal's appointee will not even be subjected to full cross-examination. Secondly, there is no full discovery of the sort experienced in Britain and the USA. Lastly, the rules of cross-examination seem to be considerably looser. Someone who has previously only encountered the British method may find the experience rather rugged. (But it is up to him to adapt – when in Rome, or when litigating under Roman law, do as the Romans do!)

THE ACCOUNTANT'S ROLE

Acting as an expert witness

2031 The work involved for an expert witness in an arbitration is little different from that for a court hearing. If he comes to give evidence, the relative informality of an arbitration is a benefit to an expert. He will feel more relaxed and he has greater scope for presenting his conclusions in an imaginative way, such as with use of visual aids. In theory he is, with the judge's permission, able to do this in court also; in practice courtroom arrangements usually rule it out.

Acting as an arbitrator

2032   Because of his training and business experience an accountant has a role to play in an arbitral capacity. With the right basic knowledge on the subjects of the dispute, an experienced accountant is competent to adjudicate on them as an arbitrator or an expert, provided he observes a few basic 'do's and don'ts'.

(a)   Avoid conflict of interest. Find out which parties are behind the dispute and question them carefully to ensure they are not related in some way to a group or company in which your firm has an interest; the arbitrator must be seen to be fully independent if he is to succeed in his role.

(b)   Establish that you have sufficient knowledge of the subject matter, or access to that knowledge independent of the parties, to be able to assess the credibility of the evidence.

(c)   Question the issues in dispute. Make sure that there are clear and limited terms of reference. To do so will assist greatly in working towards a clear and proper award.

(d)   Establish before the battle starts how the campaign is to be fought.

2033   Item (d) is of critical importance if the arbitrator is to keep control of the timetable and reach a satisfactory outcome. We tabulate opposite the key questions which should be asked at the outset.

2034   Once decided, the answers to these questions should be set down in writing and formally agreed by all the parties in dispute.

2035   An arbitrator's right to receive fees, if there is no express arrangement for payment, is implied by his appointment. Such implied right would comprise an undertaking to remunerate him reasonably for his services. A specific arrangement as to fees, however, avoids uncertainty. It is not uncommon for an arbitrator to request payments on account from the parties before and during the proceedings. This helps to protect the arbitrator from circumstances where the progress of the arbitrator is delayed by one or both of the parties or in the event the parties settle and no arbitrator award is required. An arbitrator can find himself in much difficulty if he endeavours to renegotiate his fees after accepting appointment. In the case of *K/S Norjarl A/S v Hyundai Heavy Industries Co Ltd*[1] it was held that an arbitrator is entitled to seek to negotiate, though not to insist on, a commitment fee to safeguard his financial position in the event of settlement. He should not agree to receive payments from one party without the consent of the other party because to do so may leave him open to the imputation of bias constituting misconduct and justifying his removal.

2036   In all but the most simple of cases, it is sensible practice for the arbitrator to begin by calling the parties to a meeting either separately or together. The attendance of legal advisers at such meetings is a matter of choice; if one side is insisting on bringing his adviser then clearly the other side must be told of this beforehand. It is helpful to let the parties know what the agenda will be so that they can come prepared with views.

KEY QUESTIONS AT THE OUTSET

- Should the parties be represented by lawyers?
- Should submissions be in writing, oral or both?
- Should the parties present their case separately or with both parties in attendance?
- Should each party be allowed to comment on the other's submission?
- Should cross-examination of witnesses be permitted?
- Should evidence from expert witnesses be admitted?
- How many witnesses will be permitted for each side?
- How much time will each party be allowed for the various stages of the arbitration process? (A clear timetable must be fixed and adhered to.)
- Will there be a time limit on oral presentations?
- What steps, if any, should be taken to record the oral hearings, for example, transcripts?
- Should there be a reasoned or unreasoned award? (Generally the arbitrator should approach the work on the basis that a reasoned award will be required unless his written instructions state otherwise.)
- How will costs be met by the parties? (In equal shares? By the losing party? At the sole discretion of the arbitrator?)
- Should the parties deposit a sum with a third party, in advance, as security for the arbitrator's costs? (It is generally worthwhile to arrange for costs to be met before the award is issued.)

2037 If there are technical matters to be decided, it may be desirable for the arbitrator to have a preliminary meeting with the proposed technical experts; but usually this will only be done with the ready consent of the parties.

2038 The arbitrator should be firm in the way he conducts all meetings. He should prevent the parties or their legal advisers raising irrelevances as a tactic for delaying the case. Acting as arbitrator is an opportunity to assist in resolving a dispute in an efficient and economic manner. He must therefore prevent the process becoming bogged down in arguments over the way the arbitration is conducted. Discipline and direction will help achieve an effective outcome.

DISPUTE RESOLUTION BY AN EXPERT

Acting as expert not arbitrator

2039 A contract may provide that disputes arising under it are to be resolved by someone acting as an expert and not as an arbitrator. (There will also be contracts where an expert is chosen by each side, under the provisions of the contract, to decide any disputes thereunder; in the event that they cannot agree they will normally be given specific powers to select a third expert to work with them and to decide an issue by a majority vote.)

2040 An arbitrator is subject to the Arbitration Acts of 1950 and 1979. An arbitrator acts in a judicial, rather than an expert, capacity. In practical terms in the

UK this means that he must obey the rules of evidence and he must base his award on reasoned choice made between the evidence produced by the parties. This means that many of the procedural rules adopted in the High Court on matters such as disclosure should be observed in the conduct of the arbitration. Although the arbitrator has a limited amount of procedural flexibility in certain circumstances, he is ultimately subject to controls by the court under the Arbitration Acts. An expert, on the other hand, is not subject to these rules. His determination does not need pleadings, discovery, formal hearings, oral evidence or cross-examination of witnesses. He can base his decision upon the result of his own expertise and enquiry alone.

2041   An arbitrator cannot be sued in his capacity as arbitrator but his decisions can be subject to judicial review. Appeals from arbitrators' decisions are rare or, at least, rarely successful. But the disputing parties often resort to the courts for directions on matters of procedure if the arbitrator does not conduct the case in accordance with the proper procedure.

2042   Accountants who accept appointments as arbitrators should proceed with caution, particularly when matters of evidence, disclosure, privilege and so on are concerned. Consideration should be given to appointing an independent solicitor or barrister to advise the arbitrator directly on such matters.

2043   By contrast, the appointment as 'expert' to determine an issue in dispute is less burdensome in terms of following laid down procedure. The expert can decide how the evidence will be put before him and how he will go about his task. His determination is based on his own expertise and investigations.

2044   An expert can, however, be sued for negligence and his decision can be put before the court; but usually this will only succeed in circumstances of manifest error by the expert in his determination. The courts have recently made it clear that they will only allow an expert's decision to be set aside in exceptional circumstances.

2045   In accepting an appointment as expert, the letter of engagement is a very important document. It sets out the modus operandi of the engagement, covering procedure and timing as well as the form of the determination, which may be reasoned or unreasoned. It may be necessary from time to time for an expert to seek legal advice, for example, where there is a dispute as to the proper construction of a contract. The engagement letter should provide for this possibility.

2046   Finally, it is necessary to establish how fees should be dealt with. Almost without exception the engagement letter should provide for fees to be paid in full by all parties before the determination is handed down to anyone. As with other forms of engagement letter, reference to hourly rates, out-of-pocket expenses and VAT may also be appropriate.

2047   The allocation for fees between the parties to the dispute can be an issue. In arbitration there is usually no specific agreement prior to the dispute as to how costs are to be borne. Typically costs would follow the event, ie be borne by the losing party. However, when acting as expert, it is generally appropriate to include a term in the engagement letter giving the expert discretion in the allocation of his costs to the parties, if this is not already provided for in the underlying agreement between the disputing parties.

2048 The requirement to be paid in full prior to releasing the determination makes prior disclosure of fee allocation difficult. If, for example, the determination goes against one party entirely and the expert awards all costs against that party, so awarding costs will clearly point to the nature of his decision. In these circumstances there may be no incentive for the clearly losing party to pay. To overcome this impasse the expert may choose to ask both parties to pay in full, holding the sums in escrow and returning the relevant proportion not required to the respective parties when his determination is issued.

2049 The conduct of the engagement itself on a professional and technical level is a matter for the individual expert and his team. The following points are recommended as good practice:

- adherence to an agreed timetable;

- any variations to timetable to be confirmed in writing by the expert;

- each party or the expert to ensure the other party receives copies of each other's submissions;

- detailed notes to be taken at all meetings and at oral presentations of evidence; and

- a full memorandum of issues, arguments for and against and the expert's final decision on each issue to be prepared.

Advising one of the parties

2050 It is increasingly common for accountants to be asked to advise one party or the other in a dispute which has been referred to an independent expert accountant. Such advice may cover procedural aspects as well as technical matters.

2051 In complex commercial disputes, in particular where issues of construction of the agreement arise, it is likely that legal advice will also be required. In these situations, while the lawyer and accountant each have their part to play advising the client, it should not be forgotten that it is essentially an accounting matter that has been referred to the expert for determination. Attempts to circumvent the agreed process of expert determination and move the dispute into a legal forum are almost bound to fail.

2052 In our experience, the accountant's advice can be invaluable in disputes which have to be referred to an expert for determination. A common example is where a company or business changes hands and disagreements emerge over the consideration payable for the shares or assets acquired. Sale and purchase agreements are often signed in a rush and in a co-operative atmosphere, only to find later that the parties to the agreement are at loggerheads over the detailed implementation and calculation of the purchase price. Generally there is a formula for the calculation of the consideration payable, usually based on the net worth of the business or shares acquired, or on earnings by reference to completion accounts. The disputes might have arisen over the accounting conventions adopted in the past, or the adequacies of contingency provisions or a whole host of arguments about what was really intended by each side when they signed the agreement.

2053 The development of such disputes and the procedures for resolving them normally follow a similar pattern:

- preparation of the draft completion accounts;
- review of the draft completion accounts and the raising of objections thereon;
- discussion between parties of objections to identify matters in dispute;
- agreement and appointment of expert accountant;
- agreement of expert's terms of reference and procedure for arriving at determination; and
- written submissions to the expert.

2054 Accountants advising one of the parties may be involved in some or all of these stages. In the initial stages it is vitally important that the accountant understands the basis on which it was agreed the completion accounts would be drawn up. Often, special accounting policies will have been agreed which may vary from and override those policies followed in the past in preparing statutory accounts. It is important to appreciate the special purpose for which completion accounts are prepared.

2055 The expense, delay and uncertainty involved in referring a dispute to an independent expert may cause the parties to attempt to settle their differences. Indeed, the agreement will often require that the parties attempt in good faith to do this. The accountant's advice on the strengths and weaknesses of the various arguments will assist his client in deciding whether and for how much to settle the dispute.

2056 If there are matters which cannot be resolved, the accountant can assist in the process of engaging an independent expert accountant and ensuring that the expert understands the issues involved. The accountant may be asked to prepare submissions to the expert on behalf of his client or, alternatively, may assist in their preparation. This is an important task and involves explaining the background to the dispute, the requirements of the sale and purchase agreement, the accounting policies and practices adopted in the past, marshalling all relevant documentation and demonstrating in a persuasive manner why an adjustment is or is not required to the completion accounts. Rebuttal of the other party's arguments then follows before the expert accountant makes his determination.

ASSISTING WITH PRIVATE SETTLEMENTS

Acting as a conciliator

2057 The formal process of dispute resolution, whether by appointment of an expert or arbitrator(s) or through the courts, is expensive. Resolving the dispute can be more costly than the real differences which separate the disputing parties; there will be delays while discovery takes place, there will be delays while waiting for a trial, there will be substantial legal costs and, perhaps of greatest disadvantage, the time and energy of people who are better employed running their businesses will be consumed.

2058   Often the parties are better advised to settle their differences using much more informal and expeditious methods of ADR. This can be done on a 'without prejudice' basis, ie without prejudice to the rights which flow from the underlying agreement or contract which gave rise to the dispute; it can be done with or without the presence of lawyers and with or without the presence of experts.

2059   Handling such settlement negotiations is an art not a science. It should only be practised by people who by their training and experience are able to assess the strengths and weaknesses of the position of both parties and who, when they come to a decision, carry the weight to persuade both sides of their opinions on these matters.

2060   For the conciliator there are certain essential rules of conduct for successful resolution of such disputes.

(a) He must get a full grasp of the problems underlying the dispute. This is usually a matter of obtaining proper briefing through interviews with the parties and by studying the papers before such interviews.

(b) He must define for himself the goals which he is seeking to reach. In effect he must determine the range within which a fair result can lie.

(c) He must, in discussions with both sides, satisfy himself that both are willing to make a compromise and that both are empowered to accept or reject a decision made by the conciliator. There is nothing less effective than seeking to find a fair result only to find that one side is without the power to accept any decision.

(d) Once he has evaluated all the alternatives and come to a decision he must communicate his decisions orally (in outline) and then in a document (in detail). Whether the oral communication is done serially with the two parties, or with both present at the same point in time, is a matter of intuition.

2061   One thing which is essential is a high degree of patience on the part of the conciliator. It is sometimes helpful to break off discussion at a certain point, for example, to allow parties to think over what has transpired in discussion or to seek further information. In such an event it is of course desirable to fix the date and place of the next meeting before breaking off discussion.

Acting as a negotiator

2062   Sometimes the accountant will be asked to assist in negotiating a settlement of a dispute on behalf of one side. The tactics required here are rather different from those outlined above for the conciliator.

2063   The psychology needs to be considered. It is essential to know how far one can commit one's client to a certain course of action. Intuition plays its part, there is a time to be genial and a time to be unresponsive. It may be that deadlock is in fact the best outcome at this stage, ie as a tactic in the battle. Integrity must clearly be the negotiator's watchword; without this the necessary degree of mutual trust when it comes to making concessions and seeking compromise will be absent.

2064 The key points for someone undertaking negotiation are as follows.

(a) Know all the issues involved. While excessive detail is best avoided, it is equally fatal to be underbriefed.

(b) Keep control of the agenda.

(c) Do not assume that the opponent has all the weak cards and you have all the strong, nor that he is desperate to settle the dispute.

(d) Begin the discussions on the issues which are most easy to settle. If difficult points arise, it may be desirable to set them on one side for later discussion.

(e) Be patient. Never be boxed in by too tight a timetable. Be prepared to return to the negotiation at a later date, if necessary.

(f) Keep a scoresheet of exactly what has been conceded by both sides.

(g) Before breaking up, run through the decisions reached explicitly, so as to ensure mutual agreement.

(h) After the meeting write an impartial summary of what transpired and send a copy to the other side seeking their endorsement.

2065 At the root of too many negotiations is the bland assumption that if two extreme views exist in a claim or on a dispute there must be a reasonable degree of merit in both views and the truth lies somewhere near the middle. This is, of course, a nonsense. The same goes for the amount of paper generated. It is no guide to the weight of the argument. Beware of those who grossly exaggerate their case; their tactic might well be then to modify their overstated position, only to ask the other side to make a similar move so as to achieve settlement.

2066 Another common theory, which in our view is suspect, is that the first person to break the deadlock and concede in a negotiation will lose the battle. Keeping silent might suit those who are short of facts or short of merit; those who have a well documented case or a confidence in their final standpoint on the issues involved should not be afraid to make the first move towards settlement. A certain relentlessness is needed to pursue genuine issues, but not the excessive holding of cards to the chest.

NOTE

1 [1991] 1 Lloyds Rep 260.

Chapter 21

Day-to-day practice notes

Introduction – The new case – Conflict of interest? – Terms of reference – Choosing the team – Administration – The timetable – Fee arrangements – Paperwork – Discovery of expert's working papers – Privilege of expert's report until disclosure – Use of computers – The accountant's report – Compiling the information – Drafting the report – Reviewing the draft report – Rules of presentation – Meetings of experts – Conclusion

INTRODUCTION

2101 We are concerned in this chapter not with the technical side of being an effective expert, but with the day-to-day running of a litigation support practice. Such a practice is almost bound to be part of a much larger consultancy; we therefore restrict ourselves to points that arise on litigation work, ignoring other aspects of practice administration.

2102 In litigation work, it is important to be able to respond rapidly to requests for help. A well organised office, with standard routines and systems, enables the expert to provide a prompt service to instructing solicitors or other clients with the minimum of fuss.

THE NEW CASE

2103 The phone rings. It is the litigation partner of Belvedere Blenkinsop. 'We have been given your name by Hubert Harrison QC. He suggests that you might be able to help us in a rather complex case.'

2104 This is a compliment. Obviously the case is significant, or it would not have a silk involved. Original thinking will be needed and the task is almost bound to be an urgent one. The best response is to ask for the briefest outline of the dispute on the phone and to fix an early meeting, for fuller discussions. It is too early to offer advice or to suggest a fee. Terms of reference have to be established first.

2105 Alternatively the enquiry may come from quite a different source: as an extension of a task already under way, or from an old client, or a partner, or an acquaintance. The same rules apply: get to know the detail before plunging in. If it is a lawyer who is enquiring he will have usually been into the facts in some depth and lots of advice will already be on the table. In almost every case we have undertaken, the facts (and the merits of the case) have turned out to be quite different from the initial impressions formed.

Conflict of interest?

2106 The instructing solicitor will, or should, want an assurance that the accountant has no conflict of interest in accepting the case. There are two reasons for this. First, if there is conflict, the expert's independence will be called into question later in the proceedings. No one will thank him for backing out then if it should have been clear to him from the start that he was not really independent. Second, if, say, the expert's partner is already acting for the other side, even in an unrelated matter, it will cause considerable embarrassment if that is not revealed to all parties concerned with the case.

2107 To check for conflict the accountant must find out the names of the parties in dispute and, if these parties are part of larger groups (say, an international corporation), the names of related companies too. This information must then be checked against the firm's own client list. A good client database is useful here. Generally, the existence of a conflict of interest will be clear. If there is any uncertainty it should be disclosed to the instructing solicitor, who can then decide whether the possibility of conflict would prejudice the expert's role.

2108 One question which is often posed is whether the judge or arbitrator will regard a previous potential relationship of the expert, such as an auditing appointment, as casting doubt on his independence. If the opinion sought from the expert relates to his own work, he can hardly claim to be objective. If, on the other hand, the opinion which is sought relates to a topic not previously examined, then the auditor can reasonably claim to be acting independently on behalf of his client. No hard and fast rules apply but obviously, if in doubt, it is safer to look outside existing professional relationships for an independent opinion.

2109 In the USA it is sometimes suggested that conflict exists if the expert is in receipt of fees from his client. Contingency fee arrangements in the USA are perhaps the clue to this difference of attitude. We have not met this suggestion in English courts.

Terms of reference

2110 It is essential to have clear terms of reference (instructions) from the instructing solicitor from the outset. These do not have to cover every aspect of possible involvement in the case, but must at least set the scene for the initial phase. A typical letter of instruction is attached at Appendix J; we refer below to some of the points to be considered.

2111 In all but the most straightforward of cases, we prefer to discuss the terms of reference with the lawyers before they are finalised. The lawyers or their clients may not fully appreciate the range of expertise and investigatory skills that we can bring to bear on the case. Ideally this discussion should include counsel since misunderstanding can arise when counsel suggests a line of approach to the solicitors, who then fail to convey counsel's intention to the expert accountant. Since in the end it is counsel who has to advance the reasoning in court, he is the best judge of how the accountant's contribution can be brought into the case.

2112   The expert should keep a written record of how his terms of reference develop. He can always ask for his terms of reference to be widened at any stage as he learns more. If terms of reference are so narrow as to damage objectivity, he should refuse to act. If he feels he is being given false or biased explanations he should also withdraw, since his reputation for integrity and fair dealing will be at stake. But he should not withdraw simply because some area of the case which is not part of his expertise troubles him. Lastly, the expert should always look sceptically at any assertion that all the wrong is on one side and all the right is on the other. Life is not like that, least of all in commercial disputes.

Choosing the team

2113   The terms of reference enable the expert to decide who should be put into his team. In cases of substance, the expert rarely does all the research himself. Specialist knowledge, past experience and availability are decisive in the choice of team. If the expert is working in a large mixed consultancy practice, he can tap the experience of his colleagues. On occasion he will have to bring in expert help from outside his own firm, for example, from universities or from special sectors of commerce or consultancy; before finalising such an arrangement it will have to be cleared with the instructing solicitors.

ADMINISTRATION

The timetable

2114   The initial terms of reference usually include an outline timetable; this rarely turns out to be realistic. A litigation lawyer tends to use the court's timetable as part of his overall strategy. The service of writs, defences, requests for further and better particulars and summonses for directions are all opportunities to put pressure on the other side.

2115   The expert needs to know when his written evidence has to be supplied to the other side. He has to adhere to that programme since nothing is gained by being so thorough that he misses the boat. He should allow time for discussion, revision and cross-checking with other experts when planning his work.

2116   Lawyers rightly get irritated if their strategy is upset by a delay in an expert's report (deadlines are often set for exchange of experts' reports in the summons for directions) or his unavailability at a crucial time, for example, when the hearing comes up. The golden rule is to get clear instructions and then gear the team up to meet the deadlines. This requires good internal communication, regular contact with other experts, and probably a readiness to work far into the night when emergencies arise, as they will.

Fee arrangements

2117   Increasingly, solicitors are requesting from the outset information from experts as to their likely fees or scale rates. This is sound commercial practice. The level of fees is generally a function of the time spent on the case by the expert and his staff and the level of expertise being purchased.

2118 The best thing is to estimate the time needed to carry out the work, with an ample margin for contingencies. The following headings illustrate the principal steps in two typical assignments; the figures in the columns could be very wide of the mark.

	Assignment A		Assignment B	
	Estimated working weeks	*%*	*Estimated working weeks*	*%*
Preliminary analysis of issues	2	15	1	10
Discovery and investigation work	3	23	4	40
Research	2	15	½	5
Drafting report	3	23	3	30
Discussion of report with counsel and updating process	1	9	1	10
Preparation for cross-examination, oral evidence and attendance in court	2	15	½	5
TOTAL WORKING WEEKS	13	100	10	100

2119 The working week estimate can be used to derive an overall budget. Hourly charging rates can be applied for each person according to his skill; or average rates can be used for the preliminary fee estimates. Out-of-pocket expenses have to be added to the estimated fee, for instance: air fares, hotels, car expenses, telephone, telex and copying charges. If outside people are recruited into the team, their time and fee budgets will have to be incorporated into the total estimate.

2120 Problems arise if the work scope cannot be determined in advance. As we have said earlier, cost is a function of time; if the trial which is due to be heard in 12 months suddenly gets put back to say, 24 months, costs may well double; Parkinson's Law applies.

2121 Occasionally we are asked to work to a fixed fee. Whether this is acceptable or not depends on the terms of reference and the nature of the case. Where there is uncertainty over, for example, the extent of papers to be inspected or people to interview, a fixed fee is not acceptable and agreed rates per hour is the only practical course. No expert should be without a revision clause in his fee arrangements since the time ultimately required, for example, due to the length of the trial or hearing or the extent of the other side's reply evidence, is not of the expert's choosing.

2122 The timing of fee payments should be established at the outset. Litigation is notoriously lengthy, so progress payments should be billed for at monthly intervals or at the completion of phases in the work, for example, on production of the draft or final report and after giving oral evidence.

2123 It is important to know who is going to pay the fees. In theory, the instructing solicitor is an intermediary; the party to the action should pay the costs, hoping, of course, to recover a contribution from the other side on the successful conclusion of the case. In practice, the expert often has to rely on the solicitor who has introduced him to his client, and who alone knows whether the client can pay his costs. In the absence of any specific agreement to the contrary, it is the instructing solicitor who is responsible for the expert's fees. If the solicitor does not wish to assume responsibility, a payment by his client in advance of work may be desirable. A suggested format for such a fee agreement is set out in Appendix K.

2124 If a case has been funded publicly, for example, under legal aid, special rules apply. The fee estimates of the accounting expert have to be given prior approval and certified as necessary by counsel and cleared through the Law Society. In legal aid and other cases there is sometimes a reluctance or direct refusal to meet the full cost of satisfactory preparation by the expert. The expert may nevertheless be tempted to accept the brief in the hope that he can limit his involvement to match the fee offered. We strongly advise against such a course. We have a professional duty to do work to a proper standard; we also risk being made to look a fool in the witness box if there has been insufficient preparation.

2125 Lawyers in the UK are now permitted to use 'contingency fees', ie fees which depend on and reflect the outcome of the case. Contingency fees for expert witness work are still not permitted by the accounting bodies in England, and in any event the use of such fees by the expert accountant would conflict with his independent role.

2126 If a litigant's costs are to be met by the other side, under an award, the other side usually has the right to check them, so that the latter is safeguarded from the risk that a bigger fee will be charged if someone else is picking up the tab. Records of the work done, preferably in diary form, and in some detail can be essential here.

Paperwork

2127 Litigation invariably creates mountains of paper. The advent of the photo-copier has heightened these mountains. Haphazard filing adds hours to the job and could also result in vital points being overlooked. For an efficient job, the paper must be ordered and filed, to assist in quick reference to working papers, notes of meetings and letters of instruction. A centralised filing system should be set up to handle specific categories of documents from the outset, and it should be rigorously maintained.

2128 Internally generated working papers should be assembled in an orderly manner with separate sections for each issue. Each section should contain a lead schedule, ie one which codifies and explains the contents. Ultimately the files should be cross-referenced to each other and to the final proofs of evidence submitted.

2129 The source of all the facts and figures, for example, a table or a page of annual accounts, should be noted. The source should appear on the working papers file in full whenever possible. Each schedule should be signed and dated by the team member who prepared it in case follow-up is needed.

Discovery of expert's working papers

2130 In the USA, an expert's working papers are believed to be discoverable insofar as the expert is an impartial person whose task it is to establish the facts and sources on which his evidence is based.

2131   In the UK, discovery of an expert's papers is less freely given to the other side. Often his papers will be privileged. But occasionally a voluntary showing to the other side is offered to avoid time wasting discussion in court on matters of quantum. Privilege is a complex subject and if in doubt the expert should consult his instructing solicitors. A useful description of the general law of privilege is to be found in Hodgkinson T, *Expert Evidence Law and Practice* (1st edn, 1990) Sweet & Maxwell.

2132   The accountant should bear this in mind when preparing his papers, so that he leaves no unanswered questions in them. Working papers should be kept in a manner which reflects the possibility that the other side will sometimes wish to see certain sections. Extraneous information and irrelevant material should be avoided.

Privilege of expert's report until disclosure

2133   An expert's report prepared for the purpose of litigation is privileged until disclosed by the party, and if the expert declared an intention not to give evidence, then the party receiving the report is not obliged to disclose it. The report is privileged and a court cannot override that privilege by ordering disclosure.

2134   In the case of *Derby & Co Ltd v Weldon (No 10)*,[1] the parties were given leave to call expert witnesses in several categories, one of which was an accountant. It was the intention that the reports would be mutually disclosed. One of the parties decided not to call evidence on that subject. The other party sought an order for the first party to disclose the report, but the Court of Appeal ruled that it was not disclosable in the circumstances.

Use of computers

2135   Because of the volume of data involved, computers are becoming the workhorses for litigation disputes:

- to control and recover case papers;

- to provide specialist libraries of reference and to search published sources, eg, for newspaper and magazine articles relating to a particular topic;

- to review case precedents at home or overseas;

- to hold a database of legislation;

- to analyse a mass of figures and reveal the importance of each element, eg, the labour, overhead and materials costs of a building claim;

- to calculate the effect on quantum of varying certain assumptions about the claim;

- to create a database for negotiation and for establishing outcomes;

- to select advocates – with the emphasis on specialism and past performance; and

- to print reports and other court documents.

2136 Recording each piece of paper by electronically copying its contents onto a computer disc is often worthwhile for larger disputes; the adoption of realistic coding (preferably in co-operation with the other side if it is to be employed in court) is obviously important.

2137 In legal research, the use of computer packages, such as the Lexis system, to check relevant precedents is common. The accounting expert may find it useful to have access to one so that he can see if case law throws any light on issues relating to quantum.

2138 Word processors are revolutionising the text drafting process, enabling documents to be amended at the eleventh hour. Word processors can also check spelling and cross-references, re-calculate tables, and compile indexes.

2139 Improvements in electronic hardware and systems now enables the contents of documents to be stored electrically and, in the more advanced systems, to be searched and sorted by reference to key words. In complex cases, such systems can be an invaluable aid to sorting the evidence both before and during trial. In fraud cases, the linking of documents by common themes can be instrumental in proving the fraud.

THE ACCOUNTANT'S REPORT

2140 The expert accountant's report should be written so as to make the judge's task easier. It will be successful only if it is put together under the supervision of the client's lawyers, who can ensure that it is consistent with, but does not overlap, the other evidence.

2141 A good report will usually anticipate and deal with, as far as possible, the weak points in the client's case and any objections that are likely to be raised. If it does not do so, and if the other side puts in reply evidence, the credibility of the accounting witness may suffer irreparable damage. The initial planning to identify objectives should take account of such incipient problems in the client's case.

2142 An accounting expert's written evidence usually takes one of the following forms:

● proof of oral evidence;

● the personal report;

● the report of the firm; or

● the affidavit (or, sometimes, statutory declaration).

2143 For guidance in proof of oral evidence the reader should refer to Chapter 19. The personal report is written in the first person singular. 'I did this . . .', 'I conclude that . . .', 'In my opinion . . .'. It contains details of the expert's qualifications and experience. It may be addressed to the instructing solicitor or prepared as a statement with no addressee and be signed by the expert in his own name. Where the expert uses his staff to carry out part of the work, he makes this clear by using introductions such as: 'I, together with staff/colleagues under my direction . . .', 'In this context I refer hereafter to we/us'.

2144   The report of the firm is written in the first person plural: 'We were asked to . . .', 'In our opinion . . .'. This style is appropriate where the expertise in the report comes from the firm's collective knowledge and experience rather than from an individual. Britain's legal system still requires that evidence rests on an individual's opinion and expertise. If the case goes to court, the expert may have to issue a supplementary report in which he takes responsibility for, and concurs with, the conclusions in the main report of his firm.

2145   The affidavit, which is a sworn statement of fact, is usually sworn and placed before the court in written form, and is used where there is little expectation of personal appearance by the expert to give oral evidence. Oral evidence is, of course, given under oath; evidence in writing must also be given under oath, hence the swearing of an affidavit. The layout of an affidavit is laid down by the rules of court and must be observed if the evidence is to be properly admitted. An example of an affidavit is set out in Appendix G.

2146   If exhibits are to be enclosed, the affidavit should include a sentence along these lines: 'In the exhibit hereto is a bundle of documents the pages of which I shall refer to below'. The courts now prefer one single exhibit in paginated form rather than the old method of a series of exhibits, each one of which has to be separately initialled by the solicitor or commissioner for oaths.

Compiling the information

2147   The basic accounting information required for the accountant's report is often best compiled by the client who should be instructed carefully as to what is required. The client's involvement helps to avoid the danger that the expert's ignorance of the precise nature of the client's activities and/or accounting records will lead to errors. Once the client's staff have gathered the basic information, the expert accountant (or his staff) should verify, on a test basis, that basic information has been correctly extracted. (Data about the other side in the dispute is generally compiled by the expert.)

2148   The expert may be tempted to include in his report remarks about events he has heard from others. This is considered to be hearsay evidence and will not generally be admissible. The expert's evidence should be confined to information derived from documents he has seen, or from his professional expertise.

Drafting the report

2149   The format of the report must be tailored to the case and follow the terms of reference. Nevertheless, some general advice applies to most reports.

2150   Once he has the information he needs, the accountant should review it and present it in a way that is most helpful to consideration of the issues in the case. An expert's report must always explain:

(a) the nature of the financial evidence in the report and in the figures;
(b) the source of each of the figures, in detail, and any further analysis carried out by the accountant; and
(c) the accountant's conclusions.

2151   A useful structure for an expert's report is the following:

- introduction;
- the main issues;
- the contractual background;
- the quantum issues on each matter;
- records and technical data;
- summary and conclusions;
- appendices.

Examples of reports, necessarily rather selective in content, appear in Appendices L and M to this book.

2152   As far as possible, each section of the report should be written up as soon as work on it is completed. In this way, important information can be recorded while it is still fresh in the mind; any gaps can be followed up immediately so as not to delay the completion of the report.

2153   Where members of the team are engaged on drafting different sections of the report, they should follow a common approach to the structuring of their drafts. Otherwise time will be wasted in consolidating the different sections into a single report.

2154   Presenting findings for maximum effect needs considerable thought. Judges have a fairly short attention span and a keen desire to get on with the case; accountants tend to over-elaborate – too often they include lengthy explanations of accounting points and, in tables, too many decimal places and columns of figures. Detail which interferes with an understanding of the case should be relegated to an appendix. The perfect message is one that can be taken in at a glance by an intelligent and informed layman – namely, the judge. If in doubt, leave it out.

Reviewing the draft report

2155   When the report is complete, the expert accountant should review it as a whole to ensure that it concentrates on the most important themes in the case and reads coherently.

2156   In reviewing the report the expert should ask himself the following questions.

- (a) Plaintiff or defendant? A report written on behalf of the former should aim to record precisely what the claim is, how it has been accounted for, and what assumptions have entered into the calculation of quantum. The report for the defence should examine critically every item in the claim and pronounce on its reasonableness.
- (b) Limited or wide terms of reference? If the task is simply, say, one of valuation of a business, the format follows standard lines. But it may range over every aspect of quantum, and the format must then be adapted accordingly.

(c) Opinions or facts? Facts should be clearly identified and sources noted; opinions should be supported by reasons.
(d) Will the layman understand it? Experts too often assume that others share their intimate knowledge of, for example, an accounting standard.
(e) Is the report in a logical order? Not only is a logical flow to the report essential to assist the judge in understanding the arguments but it will also help the expert find his way around the report later, when under the pressure of cross-examination.

2157   In complex cases, counsel usually wishes to discuss an early draft of the report. He often recommends that matters are covered in the report in the order in which he wishes to argue the case in court. When the report reaches its final draft stage, counsel may wish to go through the report line by line, first, to ensure that he understands the expert's evidence, and second, to test the strength of the expert's opinion before counsel for the other side gets the chance in cross-examination. Barristers are permitted to make suggestions to the expert about the way in which his report is drafted. However, this permission only extends to improving the clarity and expression in the report and not to changing its meaning. The expert must ensure that the opinions expressed in his final report are his own.

2158   An 'executive summary' can be a powerful means of putting over a complex and lengthy document, but it needs skilful drafting if it is to serve its purpose properly. An executive summary should be produced only when the lawyers think it appropriate. It should be written for those who are not seeking detail but want to know what has influenced the findings and what the recommendations are. The first paragraph should state that the contents are selective and that no attempt is made to address all the issues in the main report. An executive summary is quite separate from the report itself and is no substitute for a conclusions section.

Rules of presentation

2159   We place great emphasis on the presentation of reports. Certain basic rules of presentation are suggested in the following paragraphs.

2160   At the front of the document, except in very short reports, a list of the section and paragraph headings should be included in a contents page. Paragraph headings and sub-headings should describe the subject matter involved.

2161   Paragraph numbering should normally make it easy to locate each section, for example, 101, 102 . . . 201, 202, etc. Only for very short reports should paragraphs be numbered from 1 on to the end. The report should be given page numbers. In our experience, lawyers, and especially judges, prefer to be referred initially to specific pages rather than paragraph numbers.

2162   Figures in the report should be presented in such a way that the reader will understand without difficulty how they have been calculated. Complicated calculations should be relegated to an appendix. Some guidance on the use of tables, charts and graphs is given in Appendix N to this book; perhaps the most important yet simple rules to observe are:

(a) tables of figures must be presented in a consistent manner, for example, always start with the most recent years on the right-hand side of the page throughout the report;

(b) trends must be capable of being discerned without too much effort, so for example, where appropriate, sterling amounts should be rounded to the nearest £000 or £ million, and/or graphs should be used to supplement the figures;

(c) any tables or figures should be clearly labelled as to their identity;

(d) where a substantial volume of information is being presented, appendices should be put into a separate cover thus limiting the size of the main report and making appendices easier to refer to; and

(e) use of printed dividers between the report and its appendices or between sections of the report and/or between each appendix, is often helpful.

2163 Co-ordinating arrangements for typing, printing and collating should, wherever possible, be made the responsibility of one member of the staff.

2164 Some aspects of report production have a long lead time and must be considered well before the report is required:

(a) the number of copies of the report required may dictate the printing method. Where only a small volume of copying is to be undertaken, high-grade photocopying may be preferable to printing;

(b) the early production of covers, appendices and sections of the report containing factual information of a non-contentious nature will save valuable time; and

(c) graphics can take some time to prepare if they involve special design or colour. There is no point in leaving this part to the last phase.

2165 In certain circumstances (for example, relating to intellectual property disputes) the expert will need to refer in his report to confidential financial information. Such information should be attached in a confidential appendix or exhibit. In this way, when the report is exchanged or referred to in court, it will be kept off the public record; when it is discussed at trial, that part of the hearing will be held in camera.

MEETINGS OF EXPERTS

2166 It is surprising how many cases could have been settled or settled earlier if only the experts had met and narrowed their differences. Meetings of experts have become a common feature of litigation support work. Such meetings are ordered by both the court and arbitrators as part of their interlocutory directions. The facility to order such meetings is provided under RSC Ord 38 r 38:

'In any cause or matter the Court may, if it thinks fit, direct that there be a meeting "without prejudice" of such experts within such periods before or after the disclosure of their reports as the Court may specify, for the purpose of identifying those parts of their evidence which are in issue. Where such a meeting takes place the experts may prepare a joint statement indicating those parts of their evidence on which they are, and those on which they are not, in agreement.'

The main purpose of such meetings is to increase the opportunities for pre-trial settlement of disputes. A secondary, but no less important, reason in many cases involving financial matters is to narrow the areas of dispute between the parties, and so avoid protracted and expensive hearings at which each party adduces much detailed and sometimes complex financial evidence before the judge or arbitrator.

2167   As the rule makes clear, meetings of experts are always held on a without prejudice basis. This approach conforms with the general public policy adopted by the court to encourage full and frank discussion of issues during pre-trial procedure.

2168   Meetings can be ordered to take place either before or after the expert reports have been exchanged. The choice of alternative may be influenced by the nature of the case. Where the expert is addressing many detailed issues it can help to have access to the other expert's report before the meeting, in order to provide focus to the discussions. Some would argue, however, that once experts have committed their views to paper in an exchanged report they may be less inclined to revise their opinions. In such cases meetings before exchange of reports may be preferable.

2169   Before attending a meeting of experts, some preparation is essential. It can be very helpful to produce a list of points for discussion, identifying those which are capable of agreement and those which are not. It is also important to obtain clear instructions as to the expert's authority at such a meeting. The expert should therefore clarify with his instructing solicitor and the lay client what his terms of reference are and whether, for example, he has any authority to bind the party by whom he has been retained. It would appear that he has no such implied authority. Indeed, it was held that at a meeting ordered under RSC Ord 38 r 38 it would be 'quite alien to the role of expert witnesses that they should have automatic powers to bind parties at the conclusion of "without prejudice" meetings'.[2] In order to avoid uncertainty and confusion arising, the expert should make clear at the outset of any meeting with other experts the general extent of his authority.

2170   The court's powers to order meetings of experts do not extend to requiring experts to prepare a joint written statement. The experts themselves can decide on this with or without reference to those instructing them. We find it pays to prepare a written note of any matters agreed at the meeting of experts to be signed by each expert. Ideally, this should be before any of the experts leave the meeting. It would appear that such written statements are open (ie not without prejudice).[3] In this way, there is less opportunity for subsequent misunderstandings about what was and what was not agreed. In any event, a detailed note of discussion should be made by the expert so that he can report back to those instructing him.

CONCLUSION

2171   It seems appropriate to end this book by quoting the passage in the Preface from the Report of the Committee on Legal Education (Cmnd 4594) which was prepared under the chairmanship of Ormrod J (later Lord Justice). Paragraph 91 at p 38 explained (with our emphasis):

'The raw material of every practising lawyer is *facts*, and a great deal of his time will be spent, whether he is a judge or barrister or solicitor, in *finding the facts*. The law cannot be properly applied until they are ascertained. If the facts are wrong, the advice of the most learned lawyers will be, at best, worthless – and may be dangerous. Facts therefore are of *crucial importance* to the practising lawyer at all levels, and his *ability to handle facts*, and then *investigate and scrutinise* them for accuracy. Analysis of all the available data, to *separate the relevant from the irrelevant* and to perceive the relation between one set of facts and another and so to *check reliability* or *expose errors*, is an essential process in every case. In every case, also, he must synthesise his facts in order to *present them lucidly and cogently*, whether as an advocate, or as a pleader, or even as a draftsman, or negotiator or even as a letter writer. All stages of these processes will of course be controlled by his knowledge of the relevant law, without which the exercise would be futile.'

Everyone concerned with administration of justice should have the same regard for finding the facts. Often the accountant is better placed to do this than any other.

NOTES

1 [1991] 1 WLR 660.
2 *Richard Roberts Holdings Ltd v Douglas Smith Simon Partnership* (1990) 6 Const LJ 71.
3 *Carnell Computer Technology Ltd v Unipart Group Ltd* (1988) 45 BLR 100.

A legal lexicon

A

Action	Formal exercise of a right of suing for that which is due. Usually commences by *writ* or other mode as prescribed by the rules of court.
Action, cause of	'A factual situation the existence of which entitles one person to obtain a remedy against another person.'
Affidavit	A written or printed declaration or statement of facts, made voluntarily and confirmed by *oath* or affirmation of the party making it (usually before a commissioner for oaths).
Agency, creation of	An agency can be created: by express agreement, verbally or in writing; by implication of conduct; and by necessity.
Agent	Generally one who is employed so as to bring his principal into contractual relationships with other persons.
Amiable compositeur	Term deriving from French law; in *arbitrations* one having ill-defined duties to arrive at an equitable decision, ie in a spirit of fairness and compromise rather than by reference to the letter of the law.
Ante litem motam	Before litigation commenced.
Anticipatory breach	Term referring to the repudiation of a *contract* before the time for performance. The other party may immediately treat the *contract* as though it were discharged and sue for *damages*.
Anton Piller order	High Court order to a *defendant* to permit the *plaintiff* to enter the *defendant's* premises to inspect, remove or make copies of the plaintiff's *documents*.
Arbitration	The submission for determination of a disputed matter to a neutral person (the arbitrator) chosen by the parties involved in a controversy, in a manner provided by law or agreement.

B

Breach	The infringing or violation of a right, duty or law.
Breach of contract	The refusal or failure by a party to a *contract* to fulfil an obligation imposed on him under that *contract*, resulting from, for example, *repudiation* of liability before completion, or conduct preventing proper performance.
Bullock order	Where the *plaintiff* joins two *defendants* in the alternative because he is unsure as to which one is liable, he may be able to obtain an order against the unsuccessful *defendant* to pay the

269

costs of the successful *defendant*. The *plaintiff* is not entitled to such an order as of right.

Burden of proof

The obligation to provide *evidence* that will convince the court of the truth of one's contention. The burden of proof may shift from one side to the other in certain situations.

C

Care, duty of

Reasonable care to avoid acts or omissions which you can reasonably foresee would be likely to injure persons who are so closely and directly affected by your act that you ought reasonably to have them in contemplation as being affected by your acts or omissions.

Case law

The rule whereby legal questions may not be determined differently by the court where the facts are the same.

Causation

The relationship of cause and effect. Where the causal link between an event and its alleged consequences has to be proved (see *proximity of cause*).

Caveat emptor

Let the buyer beware. In general, the buyer is expected to look to his own interests.

Common law

The chief cornerstone of the laws of England which is general and immemorial custom, or common law, from time to time declared in the decisions of the courts of justice (Blackstone).

Competition law

That part of the law dealing with matters such as those arising from monopolies and mergers, restrictive trading agreements, resale price maintenance, and agreements involving distortion of competition affected by EC rules.

Consideration

That which is actually given to be accepted in return for a promise. 'Some right, interest, profit or benefit accruing to one party, or some forbearance, detriment, loss or responsibility given, suffered or undertaken by the other.'

Contract

A legally binding agreement. 'Contracts when entered into freely and voluntarily shall be held sacred and shall be enforced by courts of justice.'

Contributory negligence

'A man's carelessness in looking after his own safety.' A defence established where it is proved that an injured party failed to take reasonable care of himself, thus contributing to his own injury or loss.

Costs

The expenses relating to an action, includes 'fees, charges, disbursement, expenses and remuneration.'

Counsel

A practising barrister.

Cross-examination

The witness's story is subjected to examination before the court by the opposing counsel (see *examination-in-chief*).

D

Damages

The court's estimated compensation in money for detriment or injury sustained by the *plaintiff* in *contract* or *tort*.

Defendant	Includes any person served with a *writ* of summons or process, or served with notice of, or entitled to attend, any proceedings.
Dictum	An observation by a judge on a matter arising during the hearing of a case.
Discovery and inspection of documents	Disclosure by a party of the relevant *documents* in the action which are in his custody or possession. A party may require inspection of any *document* referred to in the other party's *pleadings*. In an action commenced by *writ*, discovery without order must be made by exchanging lists of documents within 14 days of the close of proceedings. Discovery by order of the court follows where a party is not satisfied with the opponent's list, or where a party fails to comply with a rule of discovery without order.
Document	A paper which can be relied upon as proof, or in support, of something. A document can be in other than written form, ie any plan, map, graph or drawing; photograph; disc; tape; soundtrack; film; or negative.

E

Equity	Primarily fairness or natural justice. Equity is the body of rules formulated and administered by the court of Chancery to supplement the rules and procedure of *common law*.
Escrow	A deed or bond delivered to a person who is not party to it, to be held by that party until certain conditions are performed, after which it is delivered and becomes absolute.
Estoppel	A rule of *evidence* preventing a person from denying the truth of a statement he has made previously, or the existence of facts in which he has led another to believe.
Evidence	Testimony and production of *documents* and things relating to the facts into which the court enquires and the methods and rules relating to the establishing of those facts before the court. 'That which demonstrates, makes clear, or ascertains the truth of the very fact or point of issue.' The law of evidence comprises those rules which govern the presentation of facts and proof in proceedings before a court. Evidence may be classified as: direct and circumstantial; primary and secondary; conclusive and inconclusive.
Evidence, hearsay	The oral or written statements of one who is not called as a witness which are narrated to the court by a witness or through a *document* for the purpose of establishing the truth of what was asserted. Such evidence is generally inadmissible.
Examination-in-chief	The witness's story is put before the court by the witness and conducted by the witness's own *counsel*.
Ex parte	In the absence of one side to a dispute.
Expert opinion	Expert opinion is admissible *evidence* when the subject is one 'upon which competency to form an opinion can only be acquired by a course of special study or experience'. The expert's duty is to 'furnish the judge or jury with the necessary scientific criteria for testing the accuracy of their conclusions so as to enable the judge or jury to form their own independent judgment by the application of these criteria to the facts proved in *evidence*.'

F

Force majeure | An event that can generally be neither anticipated nor reduced to control, eg, an industrial strike which leads to loss of profits.

Forensic | Belonging or having application to courts of justice.

G H I

Implied term | A term which will be implied (eg, from statute or custom) where it is necessary to carry out the presumed intention of the parties to a *contract* and is so obvious that the parties must have intended it to apply. Such a term will not override an express term.

Indictment | A written accusation of one or more persons of a crime, at the suit of the Queen formerly presented on oath by the grand jury.

Intellectual property | A group of rights, for example, patents, registered designs, copyright, trade marks, know-how.

Interlocutory order | While a final order determines the rights of the parties, an interlocutory order leaves something further to be done to determine those rights.

Interlocutory proceedings | All steps taken for the purpose of assisting either party in the prosecution of his case. These steps are incidental to the principal object of the action, normally the judgment.

J K L M

Mareva injunction | Procedure based on foreign attachment whereby the court comes to a creditor's aid when the debtor (resident or non-resident) has absconded or is overseas but has assets in this country.

Misrepresentation | A statement, or conduct, which conveys a false or wrong impression.

Misrepresentation, fraudulent | A false representation made knowingly or without belief in its truth or recklessly, careless whether it be true or false.

Mitigation | It is the duty of the *plaintiff* to take all reasonable steps to mitigate the loss caused by a *breach of contract*.

Monopoly power | The power or ability of a single or dominant seller to fix or control prices or to exclude competition from a relevant market.

Monopsony | A condition of the market in which there is a single or dominant buyer of a particular commodity.

N

Negligence, tort of | The breach of a legal duty to take care, resulting in damage to the *plaintiff* which was not desired by the *defendant*. 'The omission to do something which a reasonable man, guided upon those considerations which ordinarily regulate the conduct of human affairs, would do, or doing something which a prudent and reasonable man would not do'.

O

Oath
A form of attestation by which a person affirms the truth of a statement, which renders one wilfully asserting untrue statements punishable for perjury.

Obiter dictum
An observation by a judge on a legal question suggested by a case before him, but not arising in such a manner as to require decision. It is therefore not binding as a precedent.

P

Plaintiff
One who brings an action into the court.

Plea
An answer to the *plaintiff's* declaration in a common law action; a defence; a *pleading*.

Pleadings
Written statements delivered alternatively by the parties to one another. Every pleading must state the material facts in summary form. Pleadings are deemed to be closed at the end of a period of 14 days after the service of reply or defence to counterclaim on the service of defence.

Pleadings, amendment of
Pleadings may be amended once without leave of court prior to the close of *pleadings*. An amended *pleading* must be served on the other party. After the close of pleadings, amendments may be made only with leave.

Pre-trial conference
An informal conference of *counsel* and pre-trial judge either in the courtroom or judge's chambers, for the purpose of determining the matters upon which the parties agree and the genuine issues. At the pre-trial conference or within five days thereafter, the judge makes a pre-trial order, which is a statement of the nature of the case, and the matters agreed on. The clerk serves the pre-trial order upon the attorneys and once filed, the pre-trial order becomes a part of the record in the case and, where inconsistent with the *pleadings*, controls the subsequent course of the case.

Privilege, claim of
Claim entitling a person to refuse, for example, the production of *documents* for inspection. It may apply to communications between solicitors and clients; opinions of *counsel*; incriminating *documents*; state papers.

Privity of contract
Relationship subsisting between parties to a *contract*. 'In the law of England certain principles are fundamental. One is that only a person who is a party to a *contract* may sue on it.'

Proximity of cause
That cause which, in natural and continuous sequence, unbroken by an efficient intervening cause, produced the injury or damage complained of, without which such injury or damage would not have occurred.

Q

Quantum
How much. A quantity, amount.

Quantum meruit
As much as is deserved. In the absence of contractual provisions a party may be entitled to a reasonable price for work done and services performed.

R

Ratio decidendi	The underlying principle of the case without which no judgment could have been given.
Rebuttal evidence	*Evidence* which tends to explain, contradict, or disprove *evidence* offered by the adverse party and also includes *evidence* given in opposition to a presumption of fact or a prima facie case.
Referee	A person appointed to exercise judicial powers, to take testimony, to hear parties, and to report the findings.
Remoteness of damage	Damage which results from an act of the *defendant* but which cannot be said to be caused by the *defendant*.
Repudiation	Refusal to be bound by, for example, a *contract*. It generally amounts to a breach of *contract*, as where a party states that he will not carry out a promise or does some act which disables him from performing his promise.
Rescission	Abrogation of a *contract* induced by innocent or fraudulent *misrepresentation*. A party intending to rescind must notify the other party. Right of rescission is lost: if restitutio in integrum is impossible; if the injured party takes a benefit under the *contract* with the knowledge of the *misrepresentation*; if a third party has acquired for value rights under the *contract*.
Respondent	One against whom a petition is presented or an appeal is brought.
Response	The *document* filed in reply to a complaint. The response either denies that certain allegations or parts of them are true, or denies other allegations for lack of information or belief, or admits those that are true.

S

SR & O	Statutory rules and orders.
Scott Schedules	Sometimes known as Official Referee's Schedules – a formal *document* used in litigation and *arbitration*, setting out the issues in dispute in tabular form with space for the contentions of the opposing parties to be set out against each other for easy reference. There is no standard form for a Scott Schedule.
Solicitor	A person employed to conduct legal proceedings or to advise on legal matters. They are officers of the court and are bound to use reasonable diligence and skill in transacting the business of their clients.
Standards of proof	In civil cases, generally proof on a preponderance of probabilities. In criminal cases, where the burden of proof rests on the prosecution, proof beyond reasonable doubt, but where the burden of proof is on the defence it is proof on a preponderance of probabilities. In matrimonial cases, it is, apparently, proof on a preponderance of probabilities.
Subpoena	An order of the court directing a witness to appear in court.
Sworn statement	A statement on *oath* of a witness written down before a magistrate and witness. It must be signed both by the witness and at least one of the committing magistrates.

T

Taxation of costs	Procedure of examining, and altering where necessary, amounts payable by a party in an action.
Taxing Masters	Salaried officials of the Supreme Court Taxing Office who consider taxation of *costs*.
Testimony	*Evidence* presented as oral statements made under *oath* during a trial.
Tort	A private or civil wrong or injury other than a breach of *contract* for which the court will provide a remedy in the form of an action for *damages*. There must be a violation of duty owing to the *plaintiff* which arises by operation of the law and not by agreement between the parties.

U V W X Y Z

Writ	The legal document which commences the lawsuit and in which are set forth the facts upon which the suit is brought and the grounds for the complaint.

An accounting lexicon

Terms which may be relevant to financial disputes

Accounting	A discipline which establishes rules, regulations, and techniques for recording, classifying and summarising the results of business transactions and presenting these data to the user in the form of financial reports.
Accounting evidence	Proof obtained by any of the devices employed by the public accountant in the examination or review of accounting records.
Accounting policies	'Specific accounting bases selected and consistently followed by a business enterprise as being, in the opinion of the management, appropriate to its circumstances and best suited to present fairly its results and financial position' (SSAP 2.16).
Accounting principles	The body of doctrine associated with accounting, serving as an explanation of current practices and used as a guide in the selection of conventions and procedures.
Accruals concept	An accounting concept in which revenue and costs are recognised in the accounts as they are earned or incurred, not as money is received or paid. Revenue and costs are 'matched with one another so far as their relationship can be established or justifiably assumed, and dealt with in the profit and loss account of the period to which they relate . . . The accruals concept implies that the profit and loss account reflects changes in the amount of net assets that arise out of transactions of the relevant period' (SSAP 2.14 (b)).
Acquisition	Purchase of one company by another which does not qualify as a *merger*; the acquired company's pre-acquisition reserves are not distributable.
Adjusting events	'*Post balance sheet events* which provide additional evidence of conditions existing at the balance sheet date. They include events which because of statutory or conventional requirements are reflected in financial statements' (SSAP 17.18).
Allocation	The process whereby costs, which are not directly identified with particular categories of income in the accounting records, are examined and so identified.

Apportionment
The process whereby costs which are not directly identified with particular categories of income in the accounting records are apportioned between such categories; the basis of apportionment may be highly sophisticated or relatively arbitrary depending on the circumstances.

Associated company
A company not being a subsidiary of the investing group or company in which the interest of the investing group or company is for the long term and, having regard to the disposition of the other shareholdings, the investing group or company is in a position to exercise significant influence over the company in which the investment is made (Interim Statement issued by the Accounting Standards Board).

Bills of quantities
A list of the materials, parts, and assemblies or sub-assemblies, and the quantity of each, required to make a product or to build the items specified by a particular order.

Brand
Name, symbol or design identifying a consumer product of which the rights to use may be of great value in terms of generating profitable future sales but the cost of which has not been reflected in accounts prepared under generally accepted accounting conventions. Such conventions are currently under review.

Breakeven chart
A chart showing the relationship of costs, prices, volumes and profits under varying conditions. Its purpose is to reveal the point at which the scale of operation will yield a profit to the businessman.

Budgeting
Using a financial plan to serve as an estimate of and a control over future operation.

Burden
See *indirect cost, overhead costs*; costs of manufacture or production not directly identifiable with specific products.

Cash flow statement
A financial statement showing for specific time periods the sources and amounts of cash receipts and the purpose and amounts of cash payments.

Consistency
A fundamental accounting concept that there should be 'consistency of accounting treatment of like items within each accounting period and from one period to the next' (SSAP 2.14 (c)).

Contingency
'A condition which exists at the balance sheet date, where the outcome will be confirmed only on the occurrence or non-occurrence of one or more uncertain events. A contingent gain or loss is a gain or loss dependent on a contingency' (SSAP 18.14).

Contribution
The amount available from sales of goods or services, which after deduction of direct costs is available to absorb fixed overheads and to cover dividends and retained profit.

Controllable cost
A cost which may be directly regulated at a particular level of management and authority. Such costs vary with volume, efficiency, choice of alternatives and management determinations.

277

Cost

An expenditure or an outlay of cash, other property, capital stock, services, or the incurring of a liability therefore, identified with goods or services acquired, or with any loss incurred and measured by the amount of cash paid or payable, or the market value of other property, capital stock, or services given in exchange.

Cost absorption

The expensing of a cost incurred, either at the time incurred and first given expression in the accounts, or at a subsequent point in time.

Cost of conversion

'Comprises:

(a) costs which are specifically attributable to units of production, ie direct labour, direct expenses and sub-contracted work;
(b) *production overheads*;
(c) other overheads, if any, attributable in the particular circumstances of the business to bringing the product or service to its present location and condition' (SSAP 9.19).

Cost – fixed assets

This may be either the purchase price or the cost of making it. 'The purchase price of an asset should be determined by adding to the actual price paid any expenses incidental to its acquisition' (Companies Act 1985 Sch 4.26(1)). The cost of a capital asset may include 'interest on capital borrowed to finance the production of that asset, to the extent that it accrues in respect of the period of production' (Companies Act 1985 Sch 4.26(3)).

Cost plus

A method of pricing goods or services by reference to actual cost incurred plus an agreed percentage for profit. It is to be contrasted with predetermined pricing methods which leave the producer with the risks and benefits if costs turn out to be more or less than expected.

Cost of purchase

'Comprises purchase price including import duties, transport and handling costs and any other directly attributable costs, less trade discounts, rebates and subsidies' (SSAP 9.18).

Cost – stocks and work in progress

'That expenditure which has been incurred in the normal course of business in bringing the product or service to its present location and condition. This expenditure should include, in addition to the *cost of purchase*, such *costs of conversion* as are appropriate to that location and condition' (SSAP 9.17).

Critical path

The route which if followed yields the greatest efficiency of operation, at any stage of which a possible obstruction in performance would delay the programmed time.

Deferred tax

'Tax attributable to *timing differences*' (SSAP 15.17).

Depreciation

'The measure of wearing out, consumption or other reduction in the *useful economic life* of a fixed asset whether arising from use, effluxion of time or obsolescence through technological or market changes' (SSAP 12.10).

Direct costs

Costs directly identified in the accounting records with particular categories of sales income (eg, individual contracts in a contracting company or individual products in a manufacturing company); often comprises direct labour costs, by reference to which indirect costs are *apportioned* or *allocated*, direct material costs and sub-contract costs. Usages vary from industry to industry and company to company.

Earnings per share	'The profit in pence attributable to each equity share, based on the consolidated profit of the period after tax and after deducting minority interests and preference dividends, but before taking into account extraordinary items, divided by the number of equity shares in issue and ranking for dividend in respect of the period' (SSAP 3.10).
Economic lot size	The number of units to be ordered in a single purchase, or to be produced in a single run before machines are reset for another item, and which will minimise costs.
Exceptional items	'*Material* items (in a set of accounts) which derive from events or transactions that fall within the ordinary activities of the reporting entity, and which individually or, if of a similar type, in aggregate, need to be disclosed by virtue of their size or incidence if the financial statements are to give a true and fair view' (FRS 3.5).
Exchange gain/loss	'This will result during an accounting period if a business transaction is settled at an exchange rate which differs from that used when the transaction was initially recorded, or, where appropriate, that used at the last balance sheet date. An exchange gain or loss will also arise on unsettled transactions if the rate of exchange used at the balance sheet date differs from that used previously' (SSAP 20.7).
Exposure draft	This is shortened to ED and is a draft *SSAP* exposed to public comment; it may represent authoritative guidance on best accountancy practice.
Extraordinary items	'*Material* items (in a set of accounts) possessing a high degree of abnormality which arise from events or transactions that fall outside the ordinary activities of the company and which are not expected to recur' (FRS 3.6).
Expired cost	An expenditure from which no further benefit is anticipated.
Fair value	'The amount for which an asset (or liability) could be exchanged in an arm's length transaction' (SSAP 22.30).
Fixed cost	Overhead expense incurred which does not vary in proportion to scale of activity.
FRSs	Financial Reporting Standards. See *SSAPs*.
GAAP	Generally accepted accounting principles contained, in the UK, in the Companies Act 1985 as amended (in particular by the Companies Act 1989), in FRSs, *SSAPs*, *SORPs*, the International Stock Exchange's Continuing Obligations (which apply to listed companies) and its General Undertaking (which applies to companies listed on the Unlisted Securities Market).
Going concern concept	'The enterprise will continue in operational existence for the foreseeable future. This means in particular that the profit and loss and balance sheet assume no intention or necessity to liquidate or curtail significantly the scale of operation' (SSAP 2.14 (a)).

279

Goodwill	'The difference between the value of a business as a whole and the aggregate of the fair value of its separable net assets' (SSAP 22.26).
Historical cost	The cost to the present owner at the time of acquisition.
Incremental cost	The change in aggregate cost that accompanies the addition or subtraction of a unit of output or a change in factors affecting cost, such as style, size, or area distribution. Also called marginal or differential cost.
Indirect cost	A cost which is not directly attributed to the production of a specified good or service, but can be identified with an activity associated with production, such as supervision, building depreciation, factory rent, and so forth.
Inflation adjusted costs	Costs that have taken into account the changes in the general price level, specific prices or both.
Joint costs	Costs incurred in the concurrent production and/or distribution of two or more closely related products.
Lump sum contract	A contract with a fixed fee.
Material	A matter is material 'if knowledge of the matter would be likely to influence the user of the financial or other statements under consideration. The use of the word "material" in relation to accounting matters is intended to allow scope for different interpretations according to the variety of circumstances which can arise. It is not possible or desirable therefore to give a definition of "material" in the sense of a formula which can be applied mechanically' (Accounting Recommendation No 2.1).
Merger	'A rare type of business combination in which two or more parties come together for the mutual sharing of benefits and risks arising from the combined businesses, in what is in substance an equal partnership, each sharing influence in the new entity' (FRS 6.44).
Non-adjusting events	'*Post balance sheet events* that concern conditions which did not exist at the balance sheet date' (SSAP 17.20).
Oligopoly prices	The price that prevails in a market of a few sellers and many buyers.
Opportunity cost	The opportunity cost of adopting a course of action is the value of what is foregone as a result.
Overhead costs	Costs other than *direct costs* (ie, which do not necessarily increase with increases in sales or production).
Post balance sheet events	'Events, both favourable and unfavourable, which occur between the balance sheet date and the date on which the financial statements are approved by the board of directors' (SSAP 17.18).
Priced bill of quantities	A measured account of work done and materials supplied on a construction contract evaluated at unit rates.

280

Prime cost — The cost of direct labour and direct materials associated with a particular product.

Production overheads — Overheads incurred in respect of materials, labour or services for production, based on the normal level of activity, taking one year with another.

Prudence — A fundamental accounting concept whereby 'revenue and profits are not anticipated, but are recognised by inclusion in the profit and loss account only when realised in the form either of cash or of other assets, the ultimate cash realisation of which can be assessed with reasonable certainty; provision is made for all known liabilities (expenses and losses) whether the amount of these is known with certainty or is a best estimate in the light of the information available' (SSAP 2.14 (d)).

SORPs — Statements of Recommended Practice; unlike *SSAPs* and *FRSs*, SORPs are not mandatory. SORPs provide guidance on best accounting practice in selected industries.

SSAPs — Statements of Standard Accounting Practice. Like *FRSs*, these are applicable to all financial statements whose purpose is to give a true and fair view of financial position and of profit or loss for the period.

Standard costing — A system of costing using predetermined measures of what costs should be under specified conditions.

Starred items — Items in a *priced bill of quantities* which represent variations from the contract specification and therefore require post-contractual agreement of appropriate 'star' rates.

Statistical inference — The use of a limited quantity of observed data as a basis for generalising on the characteristics of a larger, unknown universe or population.

Sunk cost — A past cost arising out of a decision that cannot be reversed.

Target costing — Equivalent to *standard costing*.

Timing differences — 'Differences between profits or losses as computed for tax purposes and results as stated in financial statements, which arise from the inclusion of items of income and expenditure in tax computations in periods different from those in which they are included in financial statements. Timing differences originate in one period and are capable of reversal in one or more subsequent periods' (SSAP 15.18).

Useful economic life — 'The period over which the present owner [of an asset] will derive economic benefits from its use' (SSAP 12.11).

Variable cost — An operating expense that varies directly with sales or production volumes, or with other measures of activity.

Variance — A deviation from a standard forecast.

Some examples of claims settled

Figures stated have been rounded

Type	Original claim (before interest) £000	Settlement (including interest) £000	Relationship to original claim %	Comment on the settlement or award
Construction	250,000	50,000	20	The settlement heavily discounted claimed rebuilding costs and loss of profit items.
Construction	23,000	8,000	35	The settlement recognised reasonable rebuilding costs but not loss of profits.
Construction	21,000	1,500	7	The settlement recognised loss of profits through poor design but not costs of rebuilding.
Construction	4,200	2,800	66	This result reflected that full litigation might have been risky to both sides.
Construction	2,400	1,100	46	The settlement included rebuilding costs together with a minimal allowance for loss of profits.
Business disruption	2,300	750	33	The award represented an allowance against cost of wasted plant. There was no evidence of lost sales.
Business disruption	1,200	750	63	The award was mainly for loss of profits from a fire. The court accepted that loss of assets and profits should be compensated.
Business disruption	500	75	15	Little causation was established between the alleged loss of profits and the event complained of.
Breach of contract	450	75	17	The loss of profits was shown to be minimal.
Business disruption	450	175	39	The settlement was mainly an allowance for wasted costs plus interest. There was little allowance for loss of profits claimed.

Type	Original claim (before interest) £000	Settlement (including interest) £000	Relationship to original claim %	Comment on the settlement or award
Business disruption	350	50	14	No causation was established between the event and the loss of profits claimed.
Breach of contract	320	18	6	No causation was established between the event and the loss of profits claimed.
Breach of warranty	1,400	400	29	The claim related to valuation of stock. The settlement reflected difficulty in proving when discrepancy in stock arose.
Breach of contract	1,700	400	24	The claim included substantial indirect costs and overheads. Settlement was based on direct losses only.
Compulsory purchase order compensation	300	50	16	Claim based on loss of goodwill based on profits capitalised at a factor of 5. Award based on a factor of 3 applied to adjusted profits.
Personal injury	500	240	48	The claim inflated income of surgeon from sessional work.
Personal injury	90	20	22	The original claim had not addressed the plaintiff's erratic career record.
Intellectual property	5,000	1,200	24	In a claim for damages for infringement, liability was, in the event, not admitted and the settlement avoided the risks inevitable in going to trial.

Note. Several of these cases were the result of arbitration action, where confidentiality about the proceedings has to be observed. Hence the rather cryptic comments in the last column.

Valuation of businesses

Capitalisation using the price/earnings method – The assessment of maintainable earnings – Review of accounting policies – Other types of adjustments that might be required – Determining the appropriate P/E ratio – The comparable company method – The investment method – Other factors affecting value – The size of the shareholding – Negotiability of the shares – Capitalisation using the DCF method – Forecasting cash flows – Choosing the discount rate – The residual value – Discounted earnings: a variation on DCF – DCF versus the P/E method: the pros and cons – Reference books

This appendix has been written to supplement the material in Chapter 4, dealing with the two principal methods of valuing a business, namely price/earnings and discounted cash flow methods. There are some excellent textbooks on valuation and these should be referred to as required. Our purpose here is to draw from our experience as forensic accountants and describe those matters which are of central importance when preparing for litigation.

CAPITALISATION USING THE PRICE/EARNINGS METHOD

We explain in Chapter 4 that there are two principal ways of calculating the earnings value of a business. First let us describe the method known as 'price/earnings'.

Here we are normally concerned with the valuation of an unquoted company, that is, where its shares have no day-to-day market price established by a stock exchange.

The capitalisation of future maintainable earnings is the most frequently used method of valuing a controlling interest in any entity, and the use of this method has generally been well supported by the courts. The method is particularly applicable to businesses with relatively steady growth histories and forecasts of future earnings and regular capital expenditure requirements.

This methodology multiplies expected future maintainable after tax accounting profits by a ratio called the price earnings ratio, and often referred to as the P/E ratio, in order to establish market value. The P/E ratio therefore represents the number of years' earnings (assuming a constant level of profitability) it would take the share to earn an amount equal in money terms to its current price. Thus, the application of this methodology involves two main tasks:

(a) assessing the future maintainable earnings; and
(b) determining an appropriate rate of capitalisation, or P/E ratio.

THE ASSESSMENT OF MAINTAINABLE EARNINGS

The assessment of future maintainable profits and their stability will normally involve reviewing budgets, isolating trends and results and, in appropriate cases, averaging those results.

The specific sources of profits and the nature of the income and expenses comprising them are important. The nature of the business from which profits flow and the relative risks associated with the business will influence the valuer's choice of a capitalisation rate (see later).

We emphasise that it is the future profit stream that the business can expect to maintain in real terms that is being valued, not the past results. The extent to which past profits are reviewed will depend upon circumstances; the objective of the review will be to establish whether the pattern is one of growth or decline. In practice, there is seldom need to review profits for more than the previous five years. Where there have been major changes in the way in which the business is conducted, dependence upon the most recent year, together with some reliable budgets, is often more useful than going back over the past.

A particular problem in the assessment of future maintainable profits arises with the valuation of 'early stage' investments. These vary enormously by industry. They usually have the following in common:

(a) a short period of earnings, or none at all;
(b) high uncertainty and variability in the levels of future earnings and sales predictions; and
(c) a plan projecting good growth 'if all goes well'.

The court is reluctant to make awards of damages based on speculative forecasts. Good presentation of arguments in support of such forecasts is therefore critical.

In assessing maintainable profit by reference to past performance, it is appropriate to adjust for extraordinary and non-recurring items of income and expenditure to provide a better guide to the future. But some businesses experience these items annually and in those cases it is questionable whether any adjustment should be made.

Review of accounting policies

Accounting policies are defined in SSAP 2.16 as:

'the specific accounting bases selected and consistently followed by a business enterprise as being, in the opinion of the management, appropriate to its circumstances and best suited to present fairly its results and financial position.'

The review and evaluation of accounting policies will be important when looking at past performance. Adjustments may be necessary for any unacceptable accounting policies, in particular:

(a) those which in the opinion of the valuer are unsound, misleading or inapplicable to the circumstances of the company under examination; or
(b) those which are inconsistent with the accounting policies adopted by the prospective purchaser for whom the valuation is being prepared.

Typical adjustments arising out of a review of accounting policies include those relating to inadequate or excessive depreciation charges, unacceptable treatment of deferred expenses and goodwill, and unacceptable methods for the valuation of stocks or work in progress.

There will be cases for the adjustment of abnormal tax charges also. The treatment of accumulated tax losses is contentious. On the assumption that the losses will be deductible against future assessable income, the practical solution is to calculate future maintainable profits and to give some credit for the tax relief which can be obtained against past losses. There can be no rules for this. It depends on the particular circumstances of each case.

Furthermore, the valuer should ensure that he understands the official pronouncements that specify how each asset is to be valued for financial reporting purposes.

In particular, the requirements of Financial Reporting Standard 7 (FRS 7), which deals with the valuation of assets being acquired, should be referred to. This standard requires that the acquired tangible assets be valued at 'fair values reflecting their condition at that date'. In these circumstances, the fair value is based on the market value of a comparable asset, or alternatively, the depreciated replacement cost of the asset being acquired.

Other types of adjustments that might be required

Other adjustments that might be required to be made to reported earnings in order to determine the future maintainable earnings of an entity include the following:

- the effect of foreign exchange gains and/or losses;

- the inclusion of income from, or expenses incurred in relation to, surplus assets;

- the amortisation of goodwill and other intangibles;

- non-arm's length transactions such as excessive (or inadequate) directors' remuneration and personal expenses;

- changes in the nature of the business including acquisitions, divestments, upgrade of plant and equipment or change in core activities;

- the existence of abnormal or extraordinary items;

- the current stage of the product cycle and outlook for the industry;

- external factors (that is, economic indicators);

- minority interests in subsidiary companies (where minorities exist, the controlling shareholder will not have complete access to the cash flows of subsidiaries and the assessment of the maintainable earnings must, therefore, adjust for the minorities' share in those earnings); and

- other non-recurring items such as fixed asset sales, penalties, trade union disputes and the like.

Consideration should also be given to making relevant adjustments to reflect expected industry developments and future economic conditions, anticipating changes in such areas as market regulation, technological change, the entrance of new competitors, the introduction of new products and services, interest rates and foreign exchange rates.

Based on any of the relevant factors listed above, and the valuer's assessment of their relative importance, a conclusion is then made as to the underlying profitability of the company or entity being valued. It should be evident that the process of determining maintainable earnings is not a mechanical exercise and requires commercial judgment.

DETERMINING THE APPROPRIATE P/E RATIO

The choice of an appropriate P/E ratio at which to capitalise profits is perhaps the single most subjective decision taken in the course of a valuation. There are basically two methods used in selecting an appropriate ratio. These are the comparable company method and the investment method.

The comparable company method

The objective in using this method is to find comparable share ratings in a relevant sector of the quoted securities market, on the basis that two companies in the same industry with broadly similar records, earnings prospects and risk would command similar stock market ratings as expressed in their P/E multiples. However, if their rates of growth are significantly different, then the P/E ratios will differ also.

The choice of the correct multiple is of course decisive. This is where the judgment of the valuer is required. He must look for a comparable business with a stock exchange listing to arrive at an objective result. The starting point is to see what sort of multiple the stock market accords to shares with similar characteristics. If valuing a bank, the obvious place to look for comparable ratios is in the banks' section of the stock market quoted prices. If valuing a brewery, guidance will be found in the breweries sector of the stock market listings.

The reliability of comparisons will vary considerably. Arriving at a sensible answer requires research into the history of the 'comparable' company; only then will the differences and similarities be appreciated. Differences will inevitably distort or destroy comparability. In valuation disputes, the research into comparable situations needs to be exhaustive and comprehensive. The valuer may have to defend himself against accusations of upward or downward bias. Obviously, the more unusual the company's activities, the harder it is to extract helpful criteria from published investment statistics.

The type of questions to consider about a suitable company to use as a comparison are listed below.

(a) Is it in the same sector?
(b) Is it of comparable size?
(c) Are the managements equally competent?
(d) Is the financial leverage, the capital structure, reasonably similar?
(e) Are parts of the business under-exploited?
(f) Do the companies have a similar or dissimilar history of earnings trends over the previous years?
(g) Have the shares been subject to recent special influences (for example, takeover or rumoured takeover)?
(h) What special factors (if any) make either company unique?

The sources of information to answer these questions will typically include:

- published accounts;
- extel cards;
- brokers' reports;
- the *Financial Times* market statistics;
- the Stock Exchange Daily Official List; and
- the *Investors' Chronicle*.

The capitalisation rates of listed companies result from sales of parcels of shares representing only a minute proportion of the total issued capital, a fact to bear in mind when valuing a controlling interest in an unquoted company.

The capitalisation rates of listed companies are calculated by comparing the prevailing market price to the profits of the most recently reported accounting period, that is, to a past period. Insofar as market prices normally anticipate the results of the current year, distortions can arise when the market expects an increase in reported profits or an imminent takeover. Thus, care is needed in the use of listed company P/E rates as a starting point for the selection of a P/E ratio for valuing a private company. For similar reasons, care needs to be exercised if using an industry sector average P/E ratio since there may be special factors affecting certain of the companies in the sector which might distort the sector average.

The investment method

With this method, reference is made to the rates of return on alternative forms of investment available in the marketplace, which are then adjusted to reflect the perceived degree of specific risk associated with the company or business being valued. Alternatively, in an acquisition, the required rate of return of the company making the offer may be appropriate. The mathematical techniques used to determine the appropriate rates of return include the widely used Capital Asset Pricing Model. An examination of the detailed calculations used in the Capital Asset Pricing Model are beyond the scope of this book.

OTHER FACTORS AFFECTING VALUE

The size of the shareholding

Most share transactions, in the absence of a takeover bid, take place in small parcels; they represent a minority stake and usually a very small minority where the shareholder has no individual influence over the company. For listed companies, this assumption is reflected in the price and thus in the P/E ratio given in stock market listings. If the valuer is trying to use the transactional price to value the whole company, he must add a premium for the control (or the majority stake) implicit in his calculations. That premium should be researched by reference to the level of premia being achieved in the marketplace, at or about the relevant time at which the valuation is to be carried out; a premium of between 25% to 50% or sometimes even more may be justified. One of the most important factors affecting the premium for control is the asset backing of the company.

Companies with underperforming assets often stand at a large discount below their asset value. Bidders seeking control will often have to pay a premium over the market price, raising their bid to much nearer full asset value. In private companies, restrictions on transfer of shares may affect the value of the shares. It is often important to look at the Articles of Association and also to consider how real the restrictions are.

Negotiability of the shares

The lack of negotiability of unlisted shares, through lack of a Stock Exchange quotation or restriction on share transfer, has to be recognised. People holding unlisted investments are normally considered to be there for the long term. This depresses the rate at which profits or dividends are capitalised by between 15% and 30%, at least, of the comparable listed companies. Of course, if the purchaser of the private company shares is going to hold 50% or more of the total issued share capital, then he is going to get control; for reasons mentioned above, a discount for lack of negotiability would then be inappropriate.

CAPITALISATION USING THE DCF METHOD

As we have mentioned in Chapter 4, the DCF method is the other principal method of calculating the earnings value or economic value of a business. This method of valuation is generally used to value projects with finite lives, typically in the mining industry or for capital infrastructure projects. Some people, especially in the academic world, would accord it pride of place; however, there are limitations to be borne in mind when valuing a company using DCF methodology (see later in this appendix).

(a) Forecasting cash flows

The estimation of future cash flows is a difficult process which requires reliable financial information and involves considerable professional judgment. There is no specific period over which future cash flows should be discounted, however, because of the practical difficulties in estimating cash flows over an extended period, it is often inappropriate to project cash flows any further than about ten years.

The following steps, which are typically followed in the early stages of a DCF valuation, serve as a guide to making forecasts and as a means of ensuring that the valuer identifies and highlights the assumptions underlying the valuation, in the process of making the forecasts.

Step 1: Examine past performance to determine clues to future performance. The pattern of profits will be of interest here.

Step 2: Compare the market environment in which the entity is now operating with that in which it is expected to operate in the future.

Step 3: Examine the macro-economic factors which have influenced past earnings and which might have an influence in the future.

Step 4: Examine recent business plans which will influence earnings in the future.

Step 5: Combine all the above with any other relevant company data available: plans, budgets, forecasts, information on pricing, margins, volumes and so forth.

In following this framework some steps will be more subject to uncertainty than others; the more uncertain, the higher the discount factor.

The skill of the valuer lies in minimising the risk of error in his forecast by obtaining as much information as possible about the outcome of the project or business venture being valued. There are two main ways of dealing with such risk. The first is to build the uncertainty into the cash flow projections, by adjusting costs and revenues. For example, in a building project, costs may be uplifted to allow for the risk that labour costs may increase because of delays in supplies or the effect of adverse weather. This route, which amounts to the inclusion of extra costs or the reduction of revenues for contingencies, is commonly used in preparing estimates for major construction projects. The risks of uncertainty can be built into the discount rate, though it is important to ensure that the same risk is not adjusted for twice.

(b) Choosing the discount rate

Some risk always attaches to commercial projects. War can break out; new inventions can render an existing line of production obsolete; management can falter; any of these or some lesser catastrophe can make nonsense of the hopes of an enterprise. There is a further risk inherent in any forecasting exercise: that the whole investment environment will be altered and that in general investors will look for a higher return on their investments than that envisaged by the forecasters.

The greater the risk that the investor bears, the greater the reward he expects. The return on any investment can therefore be regarded as the return on a risk-free asset plus some sort of risk premium.

The risk premium expected on an investment will be related to its risk by comparison with other investments. If the risk is the same, the risk premium will be the same; if the risk is less, or more, the premium will be less, or more. Studies have been carried out by economists to establish what is the average risk of all possible investments. This is known as the market risk. They have developed a model known as the Capital Asset Pricing Model, which seeks to relate an individual investment risk to the general market risk. Complex formulae are involved and it is not the purpose of this book to cover this other than to refer the reader to studies published by Jack Taylor, William Sharpe and John Lintner.

Finally, if the cash flows to be discounted incorporate an allowance for future inflation, then it will be necessary to include in the discount rate a percentage to reflect anticipated inflation.

It will be apparent from the foregoing discussion that the discount rate will represent an amalgam of two or three components:

- the risk-free rate of interest;
- the risk factor; and
- the inflation factor where appropriate.

The risk-free rate of interest is the rate of interest that can be earned on an investment on which there is no risk of loss. The nearest thing to a risk-free investment is a loan to a stable government. The rate of return on a government bond or Treasury Bill will be an acceptable approximation to a risk-free rate.

The impact of inflation on forecasting can be significantly reduced if the forecasts of costs and revenues exclude any allowance for inflation. By excluding inflation, the future costs and revenue will be shown in real monetary terms. However, there remains the risk that inflation rates will change in future. This can be important in cases where future revenues are fixed in money terms. In those circumstances, it is important to consider whether an allowance should be made in the risk component of the discount rate for a prospective change in the rate of inflation.

The rate to be applied in recognition of the specific and general risks faced by the business being valued must depend on the valuer's experience; the investor will wish to obtain a premium which is comparable to that obtainable on an identical investment elsewhere.

(c) The residual value

DCF analysis is a concept easier to understand where projects of finite length of life are being valued. For businesses which have an indefinite life span, the problem is overcome by including some sort of residual value in the analysis. In such cases, the terminal or residual value of the project or business at the end of a cash flow forecast period represents the value of the business or asset at that time, which, in turn, reflects the NPV of the cash flow beyond that period.

For example, it may be possible in a business project with indefinite length to forecast, with sufficient reliability, the cash flows for the next five years and for the remaining (indefinite) period to assume that the cash flows of the fifth year are then received in perpetuity. The value of the perpetuity, or the 'residual value', can form a significant part of the total DCF valuation, although it often turns out (if the discount rate is high) that the net present value of cash flows arising after, say, ten years is negligible. Indeed, it is usually unnecessary to consider any residual income beyond the ten-year period.

Discounted earnings: a variation on DCF

The discounted earnings method of valuation is a simplified version of the discounted cash flow method. Its usefulness in court valuations is, first, that the problems of precise timing of cash flows (for example, investment in new plant) are ignored and, second, that the table of earnings projections can be used in parallel to the price/earnings approach and thereby simplify the presentation of alternative valuations in the courtroom. Because it represents something of a simplification, it will not be as rigorous a method, mathematically, as DCF and will in particular be unreliable if a smooth progression of investment is not occurring in the business being appraised.

DCF versus the P/E method: the pros and cons

One of the attractions of the P/E approach is the opportunity it gives the valuer to see (and apply) what other people consider to be a suitable multiple for purposes of valuing between willing buyer and willing seller. Investment is very much influenced by mood and fashion. For all sorts of seemingly irrational reasons, a sector of the stock market can command high ratings. The underlying cause may be the personal ambitions of a major player in the market; or the search for synergy, for established trends, or for diversification; or the need for long-term security of raw material supply. The valuer will not be unduly concerned as to the cause; what concerns him is that businesses with similar characteristics are likely to command the same premium rating if sold.

Consider also the currency of the bid when a takeover takes place. The predator will take all sorts of factors into account. Can I use my own cheap paper to acquire the other's assets? Can I gear up my borrowing and achieve a similar result? Should I use cash? The resulting price will almost certainly be quite different from a DCF valuation.

In contrast, a DCF model is not responsive to fashion, mood, or the whims of the big players in the market; it tends to be a better tool for wise and considered investment decisions (for example, making choices between alternative courses of action) than for second-guessing the investment market itself. It certainly does not respond to sudden ebbs and flows in the stock market indices. A DCF valuation requires a forecast of future cash flows over a relevant period of time, the choice of an appropriate discount rate and the estimation of the terminal residual value at the end of the chosen time period.

Time is one factor that rules against using DCF in many litigation situations. Doing long-term projections and choosing the right inputs is a long process; if it is not done carefully the answer will be incorrect. Even minor changes, for example, to the discount rate, can swing the results by wide margins. So if, as is often the case, the accountant is under time pressure, the DCF option may well have to be discarded. Moreover, in many instances the court will find it easier to accept the price/earnings approach than the more thorough DCF method. The problem is that a projection of, say, ten years' anticipated profits looks to a judge or to an advocate to be too speculative for determining a business's value. They will prefer a valuation based on actual figures, even though the element of speculation then devolves on the choice of the multiple.

Having said this, we must note that we have been concerned with valuations in the International Court at The Hague where tribunals have used the DCF approach in preference to any other. Sometimes one is forced to use it in the absence of a history of earnings, for example, where the business being valued had not started trading. In addition, it can be a useful way of valuing a specific capital investment project.

Reference books

For a more comprehensive description of general valuation theory we recommend reference to the following:

Eastaway, N, Booth, H, and Eamer, K, *Practical Share Valuation* (3rd edn, 1994)
  Butterworths
Glover, C G, *Valuation of Unquoted Securities* (1986) Gee
Pratt, S, *Valuing a Business* (1981) Dow Jones-Irwin

Building contract disputes: overheads formulae

In Chapter 5 we refer to occasions when formulae might be used to evaluate overheads to be included in a building contract claim. In this Appendix we introduce four such formulae which are used from time to time in construction disputes. They are representative examples of formulae used to compute what proportion of overhead costs to include in a contract claim. We comment also on some of the pros and cons of the use of these formulae in practice.

The Hudson Formula
(Source: Hudson's *Building and Engineering Contracts* (11th edn, 1994) Sweet and Maxwell)

The formula takes the percentage allowance made by the contractor for head office overheads and profit in his original tender ('HO'), divides it by the original contract period and multiplies the result by the period of the contract extension:

$$\frac{\text{HO Profit percentage}}{100} \times \frac{\text{Contract sum}}{\text{Contract period}} \times \text{Period of delay (weeks)}$$

The formula is a very broad brush approach to dealing with claims for overheads. It is designed to deal only with overruns in contract time. It compensates for both overhead expenses and profits. It may not be appropriate to claim for loss of profit unless there is a clear indication that the contractor would have been able to earn profits on other contracts but for the overrun. Also it uses as its base, overhead and profit percentages taken from the original tender. These may not properly reflect the contractor's true overhead cost and profitability.

Emden's Formula
(Source: *Emden's Construction Law*, Butterworths)

Emden's formula applies the percentage that the contractor's total overheads and profit bear to total turnover ('h') to the proportion of the original contract sum ('c') represented by the period of delay ('pd') – (the original contract period is 'cp'):

$$\frac{h}{100} \times \frac{c}{cp} \times pd$$

The advantage of this formula is that it uses a head office overhead percentage based on the contractor's total business rather than on the specific contract in dispute. Again it does not necessarily reflect the real effect on overhead costs arising from the delay, but it may provide a reasonable approximation particularly if some simplistic approach is looked for to assist in negotiating an out of court settlement.

Direct cost allocation

The direct cost allocation method expresses the contractor's total overhead costs over a period as a rate per £ of direct costs. This 'average' rate of overheads per unit of direct cost is then applied to the total additional direct costs associated with the contract claim.

Although simple, this method implies that overheads vary proportionately with direct costs. This is not necessarily the case. Some contracts will consume very high levels of labour or valuable materials which should not have a corresponding effect on overheads and can distort the implicit average relationship between overheads and direct cost.

Furthermore, where delay is the subject of the claim, there may have been little additional direct cost incurred but that would not necessarily mean little extra overhead to be allocated.

Specific base allocation

The specific base allocation method relates, as far as possible, individual categories of overheads to specific categories of direct cost. For example, site preliminary costs may be related to direct labour hours. This method can overcome the problems associated with the broad brush total cost allocation methods. However it is dependent for its success on the existence of reliable detailed cost analyses.

Recent developments in accounting practice relating to overheads may also be relevant. As a result of cheaper computing power, it has been possible to introduce relatively complex systems of accounting for overheads costs which relate more precisely the costs incurred to the activities which generate these costs. Such systems include 'activity-based costing' systems. If a contractor employs such a system in his management accounts it may be that this will provide an alternative method of dealing with overheads preferable to any of the above bases.

Conclusion

It is important that the expert accountant is aware of the application of formulae in construction claims to compute the amount of overheads to be recovered. However, we would urge caution in the blind application of such formulae. Their individual suitability will depend on the circumstances of each case.

Auditing standards

EXTRACTS FROM SAS 100: OBJECTIVE AND GENERAL PRINCIPLES GOVERNING AN AUDIT OF FINANCIAL STATEMENTS

(Issued March 1995)

2   **In undertaking an audit of financial statements auditors should:**

  (a) **carry out procedures designed to obtain sufficient appropriate audit evidence, in accordance with Auditing Standards contained in SASs, to determine with reasonable confidence whether the financial statements are free of material misstatement;**

  (b) **evaluate the overall presentation of the financial statements, in order to ascertain whether they have been prepared in accordance with relevant legislation and accounting standards; and**

  (c) **issue a report containing a clear expression of their opinion on the financial statements. (SAS 100.1).**

Reasonable assurance

8   An audit carried out in accordance with Auditing Standards is designed to provide reasonable assurance that the financial statements taken as a whole are free from material misstatement. The term 'reasonable assurance' is therefore central to an audit undertaken in accordance with Auditing Standards. The view given in financial statements is itself based on a combination of fact and judgment and, consequently, cannot be characterised as either 'absolute' or 'correct'. When reporting on financial statements auditors provide a level of assurance which is reasonable in that context but, equally, cannot be absolute.

9   The work undertaken by auditors to form an opinion is permeated by the exercise of judgment, in particular regarding:

  (a)   the gathering of evidence: for example, in deciding the nature, timing and extent of audit procedures; and

  (b)   the drawing of conclusions based on the evidence gathered: for example, assessing the reasonableness of the estimates made by the directors in preparing the financial statements.

10   The extent to which audit risk (that auditors may give an inappropriate opinion on financial statements) can be reduced is restricted due to the inherent limitations of any audit. Such limitations include those resulting from:

  ● the impracticality of examining all items within an account balance or class of transactions;

- the inherent limitations of any accounting and control system;
- the possibility of collusion or misrepresentation for fraudulent purposes; and
- most audit evidence being persuasive rather than conclusive.

11   Auditors recognise the possibility that material misstatement may exist and plan and perform the audit with that possibility in mind. This involves examining critically and with professional scepticism the information and explanations provided and not assuming that they are necessarily correct.

Ethical principles

13   **In the conduct of any audit of financial statements auditors should comply with the ethical guidance issued by their relevant professional bodies. (SAS 100.2).**

SAS 600: AUDITORS' REPORTS ON FINANCIAL STATEMENTS

Statements of Auditing Standards ('SASs') are to be read in the light of 'The scope and authority of APB pronouncements.' In particular, they contain basic principles and essential procedures ('Auditing Standards'), indicated by paragraphs in bold type, with which auditors are required to comply in the conduct of any audit. SASs also include explanatory and other material which is designed to assist auditors in interpreting and applying Auditing Standards. The definitions in the Glossary of terms are to be applied in the interpretation of SASs.

INTRODUCTION

1   The purpose of this Statement of Auditing Standards is to establish standards and provide guidance on the form and content of auditors' reports issued as a result of an audit of the financial statements of an entity ('the reporting entity'). Much of the guidance provided can be adapted to auditors' reports on financial information other than financial statements.

2   **Auditors' reports on financial statements should contain a clear expression of opinion, based on review and assessment of the conclusions drawn from evidence obtained in the course of the audit. (SAS 600.1).**

3   An appreciation of the inter-relationship between the responsibilities of those who prepare financial statements and those who audit them is also necessary to achieve an understanding of the nature and context of the opinion expressed by the auditors. Readers need to be aware that it is the directors (or equivalent persons) of the reporting entity and not the auditors who determine the accounting policies followed. Auditors' reports therefore also set out the respective responsibilities of directors and auditors.

4   It will aid communication with the reader if the auditors' report is placed before the financial statements and, where the directors set out their responsibilities themselves, if this description is immediately before the auditors' report.

5   The requirements of the SAS are intended to achieve informative reporting by auditors within the reporting obligations current at its date of issue. Further developments may in the future alter the matters on which auditors are required to report or the manner in which they are required to report: such changes will be reflected in amendments to the requirements in this SAS when appropriate.

Nature of assurance provided

6   The view given in financial statements is derived from a combination of fact and judgment, and consequently cannot be characterised as either 'absolute' or 'correct'. When reporting on financial statements, therefore, auditors provide a level of assurance which is reasonable in that context but, equally, cannot be absolute. Consequently it is important that the reader of financial statements is made aware of the context in which the auditors' report is given.

Applicability

7   This SAS applies to all reports issued by auditors which express an opinion in terms of whether financial statements give a true and fair view, or where statutory or other specific requirements prescribe the use of a term such as 'presents fairly' or 'properly prepared in accordance with'.

DEFINITIONS

8   The following definitions apply in interpreting the requirements of this SAS.

9   *Financial statements*: the balance sheet, profit and loss account (or other form of income statement), statements of cash flows and total recognised gains and losses, notes and other statements and explanatory material, all of which are identified in the auditors' report as being the financial statements.

10   *Directors*: the directors of a company, the partners, proprietors or trustees of other forms of enterprise or equivalent persons responsible for the reporting entity's affairs, including the preparation of its financial statements.

11   *Material*: a matter is material if its omission or mis-statement would reasonably influence the decisions of a user of the financial statements.

     Materiality may be considered in the context of the financial statements as a whole, any individual primary statement within the financial statements or individual items included in them.

12   *Inherent uncertainty*: an uncertainty whose resolution is dependent upon uncertain future events outside the control of the reporting entity's directors at the date the financial statements are approved.

13   *Fundamental uncertainty*: an inherent uncertainty is fundamental when the magnitude of its potential impact is so great that, without clear disclosure of the nature and implications of the uncertainty, the view given by the financial statements would be seriously misleading.

     The magnitude of an inherent uncertainty's potential impact is judged by reference to:

- the risk that the estimate included in financial statements may be subject to change;

- the range of possible outcomes; and
- the consequences of those outcomes on the view shown in the financial statements.

BASIC ELEMENTS OF THE AUDITORS' REPORT

14 **Auditors' reports on financial statements should include the following matters:**

  (a) **a title identifying the person or persons to whom the report is addressed;**

  (b) **an introductory paragraph identifying the financial statements audited;**

  (c) **separate sections, appropriately headed, dealing with:**
   (i) **respective responsibilities of directors (or equivalent persons) and auditors,**
   (ii) **the basis of the auditors' opinion,**
   (iii) **the auditors' opinion on the financial statements;**

  (d) **the manuscript or printed signature of the auditors; and**

  (e) **the date of the auditors' report. (SAS 600.2).**

15 The use of a standard format for auditors' reports on financial statements assists the reader to follow the report's contents. The section headings indicate to the reader the nature of the matters contained in the section concerned: for example, where a qualified opinion is expressed, the heading 'Qualified opinion' may be used.

16 Auditors draft each section of their report on financial statements to reflect the requirements which apply to the particular audit engagement. However, the use of common language in auditors' reports assists the reader's understanding. Accordingly, Appendix 2 [not reproduced here] includes examples of auditors' reports on financial statements to illustrate wording which meets the Auditing Standards contained in this SAS.

Title and addressee

17 An appropriate title is used to distinguish clearly the auditors' reports from other information relating to the reporting entity with which it may be published.

18 The auditors' report on the financial statements of a company is addressed to its members (normally the shareholders) because the audit is undertaken on their behalf. The auditors' report on financial statements of other types of reporting entity is addressed to the appropriate person or persons, as defined by statute or by the terms of the individual engagement.

Identification of financial statements

19 The purpose of the introductory section of the auditors' report, identifying the financial statements that have been audited, is to ensure that there is no ambiguity regarding the information to which the auditors' opinion relates. The introductory section may refer to the accounting convention and accounting policies which have been followed in preparing the financial statements.

STATEMENTS OF RESPONSIBILITY AND BASIS OF OPINION

20 **(a) Auditors should distinguish between their responsibilities and those of the directors by including in their report:**
    (i) a statement that the financial statements are the responsibility of the reporting entity's directors;
    (ii) a reference to a description of those responsibilities when set out elsewhere in the financial statements or accompanying information; and
    (iii) a statement that the auditors' responsibility is to express an opinion on the financial statements.

    (b) Where the financial statements or accompanying information (for example the directors' report) do not include an adequate description of directors' relevant responsibilities, the auditors' report should include a description of those responsibilities. (SAS 600.3).

21 The matters to be included in the description of the directors' responsibilities reflects the specific requirements applicable to the reporting entity. A description of the responsibilities of a company's directors is normally considered adequate when it includes the following points:

    (a) company law requires directors to prepare financial statements for each financial year which give a true and fair view of the company's (or group's) state of affairs at the end of the year and profit or loss for the year then ended;

    (b) in preparing those financial statements, the directors are required to:
- select suitable accounting policies and then apply them on a consistent basis, making judgments and estimates that are prudent and reasonable;
- (*large companies only*[1]) state whether applicable accounting standards have been followed, subject to any material departures disclosed and explained in the financial statements;
- (*where no separate statement on going concern is made by the directors*) prepare the financial statements on the going concern basis unless it is not appropriate to presume that the company will continue in business;

    (c) the directors are responsible for keeping proper accounting records, for safeguarding the assets of the company (or group) and for taking reasonable steps for the prevention and detection of fraud and other irregularities.

    These points may be adapted for different requirements applicable to different categories of reporting entity, for example to reflect special legal requirements relating to small companies, insurance companies or banks, or specific requirements applicable to a non-corporate entity.

22 In the case of reporting entities other than companies, auditors assess the adequacy of the description by reference to statutory or any other specific requirements with which the reporting entity's directors are required to comply.

---

1 'Large' in this context means those companies which fall outside the categories of small and medium-sized companies as defined in the Companies Act 1985.

23 Illustrative wording of a description of the directors' responsibilities, which may be included in auditors' reports on company financial statements where the directors' statement is inadequate, is shown in Appendix 3 [not reproduced here]. Auditors' reports on the financial statements of other reporting entities provide equivalent details, reflecting appropriate legal and regulatory requirements when necessary to do so.

24 **Auditors should explain the basis of their opinion by including in their report:**

    (a) a statement as to their compliance or otherwise with Auditing Standards, together with the reasons for any departure therefrom;

    (b) a statement that the audit process includes:

        (i) examining, on a test basis, evidence relevant to the amounts and disclosures in the financial statements,

        (ii) assessing the significant estimates and judgments made by the reporting entity's directors in preparing the financial statements,

        (iii) considering whether the accounting policies are appropriate to the reporting entity's circumstances, consistently applied and adequately disclosed;

    (c) a statement that they planned and performed the audit so as to obtain reasonable assurance that the financial statements are free from material misstatement, whether caused by fraud or other irregularity or error, and that they have evaluated the overall presentation of the financial statements. (SAS 600.4).

25 A reference to compliance with Auditing Standards is necessary in order to provide assurance that the audit has been carried out in accordance with established standards.

26 In some exceptional circumstances, a departure from Auditing Standards may be appropriate to fulfil the objectives of a specific audit more effectively. If this is the case, the auditors explain the reasons for that departure in their report. Other than in such exceptional and justifiable circumstances, a departure from an Auditing Standard is a limitation on the scope of work undertaken by the auditors. In such circumstances the auditors assess whether a qualified opinion or disclaimer of opinion is required, as set out in SAS 600.7.

27 In certain circumstances, auditors are required by statute to follow other comparable standards, such as the Code of Audit Practice for Local Authorities and the National Health Service in England and Wales or the requirements of the Scottish Accounts Commission. Where this is the case, auditors refer to these standards.

28 In some circumstances, auditors may be required to report whether the financial statements have been properly prepared in accordance with regulations or other requirements, but are not required to report on whether they give a true and fair view. Where the special circumstances of the reporting entity require or permit the adoption of policies or accounting bases which would not normally permit a true and fair view to be given, auditors would refer to those circumstances in the paragraphs dealing with the respective responsibilities of directors and auditors (unless the matter is included in a separate statement given by the

directors) and may draw attention to them in the basis of opinion section of the report.

29 Auditors may wish to include additional comment in this part of their report to highlight matters which they regard as relevant to a proper understanding of the basis of their opinion.

EXPRESSION OF OPINION

30 **An auditors' report should contain a clear expression of opinion on the financial statements and on any further matters required by statute or other requirements applicable to the particular engagement. (SAS 600.5).**

31 An auditors' report may include an unqualified opinion or qualified opinion. The circumstances giving rise to each type of opinion are set out below and example reports illustrating each form of opinion are contained in Appendix 2 [not reproduced here].

Unqualified opinions

32 An unqualified opinion on financial statements is expressed when in the auditors' judgment they give a true and fair view (where relevant) and have been prepared in accordance with relevant accounting or other requirements. This judgment entails concluding whether *inter alia*:

- the financial statements have been prepared using appropriate accounting policies, which have been consistently applied;
- the financial statements have been prepared in accordance with relevant legislation, regulations or applicable accounting standards (and that any departures are justified and adequately explained in the financial statements); and
- there is adequate disclosure of all information relevant to the proper understanding of the financial statements.

Qualified opinions

33 A qualified opinion is issued when either of the following circumstances exist:

(a) there is a limitation on the scope of the auditor's examination (see SAS 600.7); or
(b) the auditors disagree with the treatment or disclosure of a matter in the financial statements (see SAS 600.8);

and, in the auditors' judgment, the effect of the matter is or may be material to the financial statements and therefore those statements may not or do not give a true and fair view of the matters on which the auditors are required to report or do not comply with relevant accounting or other requirements.

Adverse opinions

34 An adverse opinion is issued when the effect of a disagreement is so material or pervasive that the auditors conclude that the financial statements are

seriously misleading (see SAS 600.8). An adverse opinion is expressed by stating that the financial statements do not give a true and fair view.

35 When the auditors conclude that the effect of a disagreement is not so significant as to require an adverse opinion, they express an opinion that is qualified by stating that the financial statements give a true and fair view except for the effects of the matter giving rise to the disagreement.

Disclaimers of opinion

36 A disclaimer of opinion is expressed when the possible effect of a limitation on scope is so material or pervasive that the auditors have not been able to obtain sufficient evidence to support, and accordingly are unable to express, an opinion on the financial statements (see SAS 600.7).

37 Where the auditors conclude that the possible effect of the limitation is not so significant as to require a disclaimer, they issue an opinion that is qualified by stating that the financial statements give a true and fair view except for the effects of any adjustments that might have been found necessary had the limitation not affected the evidence available to them.

COMPLIANCE WITH RELEVANT ACCOUNTING REQUIREMENTS

38 The auditors' opinion is expressed in the context of the particular accounting requirements applicable to the financial statements concerned and normally includes, in addition to an opinion on the view given by the financial statements, an opinion on whether or not those requirements have been followed. For example, an auditors' report on the financial statements of a company incorporate in Great Britain includes the words '. . . and have been properly prepared in accordance with the Companies Act 1985'.

39 Save in exceptional circumstances, compliance with accounting standards is necessary to give a true and fair view.

40 Financial statements are normally required to contain particulars of any material departure from an accounting standard which applies to the reporting entity, together with the financial effects of the departure unless this would be impracticable or misleading in the context of giving a true and fair view.

Requirements of company law

41 In the context of financial reporting by companies, directors are required by law to prepare annual accounts which consist of a balance sheet and profit and loss account together with accompanying notes and which give a true and fair view of the state of affairs of the company (or group) at the end of the financial year and of the profit or loss of the company (or group) for that year. Company law requires the auditors to state whether in their opinion the company's annual accounts give such a view.

42 There is no specific legal requirement that companies should comply with accounting standards. However, legislation in the UK gives specific recognition to accounting standards and requires large companies to state in

their financial statements whether those statements have been prepared in accordance with such standards and to give particulars of any material departure and the reasons for it – para 36A of Sch 4 to the Companies Act 1985.

43 It is likely that a Court would infer from this requirement, taken together with other changes introduced into UK company law by the Companies Act 1989, that financial statements which meet the Act's requirements will follow rather than depart from accounting standards, and that any departure would be regarded as sufficiently abnormal to require justification. Therefore, in general, compliance with accounting standards is necessary to meet the requirement of company law that the directors prepare annual accounts which give a true and fair view of a company's (or group's) state of affairs and profit or loss.

Primary statements

44 Accounting standards contained in Financial Reporting Standards require, in certain circumstances, further 'primary statements' in addition to the balance sheet and profit and loss account. It follows from the principle stated in the last paragraph that, where required by an accounting standard, these further primary statements are normally necessary in order that the annual accounts give a true and fair view, as required in the United Kingdom by the Companies Act 1985 or the Companies (Northern Ireland) Order 1986 and, in the Republic of Ireland, the Companies Acts 1963 to 1990. The annual accounts, including the additional primary statements required by accounting standards, are referred to by the term 'financial statements'.

45 Accordingly, reference in an auditors' opinion on a company's financial statements to the primary statements required by accounting standards is unnecessary. It may also be misleading to the reader of the auditors' report, in that it may appear to detract from the role of the additional primary statements in supporting the information contained in company's balance sheet and profit or loss account so as to give a true and fair view as required by the law.

46 Auditors may be requested to report separately on one or more primary statements. When making such a separate report, they need to ensure that in doing so no impression is given that the primary statement(s) referred to is other than integral to the financial statements as a whole and that it is clear to a reader that the primary statement is necessary to give a true and fair view of the state of affairs and profit or loss for statutory purposes.

Non-compliance with accounting standards

47 When the auditors conclude that the financial statements of a company do not comply with accounting standards, they assess:

(a) whether there are sound reasons for the departure;
(b) whether adequate disclosure has been made concerning the departure from accounting standards;
(c) whether the departure is such that the financial statements do not give a true and fair view of the state of affairs and profit or loss.

In normal cases, a departure from accounting standards will result in the issue of a qualified or adverse opinion on the view given by the financial statements.

48   Where no explanation is given for a departure from accounting standards, its absence may of itself impair the ability of the financial statements to give a true and fair view of the company's state of affairs and profit or loss. When auditors conclude that this is so, a qualified or adverse opinion on the view given by the financial statements is appropriate, in addition to a reference (where appropriate) to the non-compliance with the specific requirement of company law referred to in paragraph 42 above.

Small companies – Great Britain and Northern Ireland

49   Directors of companies which fall within the category of small companies as defined by company legislation in the UK may draw up financial statements taking advantage of a number of exemptions from the full requirements of company law.[2] Financial statements prepared using these exemptions are nevertheless required to give a true and fair view, and the legislation further specifically provides that they shall not be deemed not to do so by reason only of the fact that advantage has been taken of the exemptions.

50   Auditors reporting on the financial statements of a small company prepared using these exemptions are permitted (but not required) to report in terms which omit reference to whether a true and fair view is given, referring only to the proper preparation of those statements in accordance with the requirements of company law applicable to small companies. However, their legal obligation to consider whether the financial statements give a true and fair view as required by company law remains unchanged. The requirement for a clear expression of opinion (contained in SAS 600.5) is therefore best met by referring to the true and fair view, except for particular circumstances in which the auditors consider it impossible to do so.

51   Illustrative wording for an auditors' report on financial statements of a small company taking advantage of the exemptions is given in Example 5 of Appendix 2 [not reproduced here].

FURTHER MATTERS REQUIRED BY STATUTE OR OTHER REGULATIONS

52   Further opinions or information to be included in the auditors' report may be determined by specific statutory requirements applicable to the reporting entity, or, in some circumstances, by the terms of the auditors' engagement. Such matters may be required to be dealt with by a positive statement in the auditors' report or only by exception. For example, in the Republic of Ireland auditors are required to state whether, in their opinion, proper books of account have been kept, whereas company legislation in the United Kingdom requires auditors to report only when a company has not maintained proper accounting records.

---

2   Set out in Sch 8 to the Companies Act 1985, as inserted by SI 1992/2452.

53   Where further opinions are required by statute or other regulation, matters which result in qualification of such an opinion may also result in a qualification of the auditors' opinion on the financial statements; for example, if proper accounting records have not been maintained and as a result it proves impracticable for the auditors to obtain sufficient evidence concerning material matters in the financial statements, their report indicates that the scope of their .examination was limited and includes a qualified opinion or disclaimer of opinion on the financial statements arising from that limitation, as required by SAS 600.7.

FUNDAMENTAL UNCERTAINTY

54   **(a) In forming their opinion on financial statements, auditors should consider whether the view given by the financial statements could be affected by inherent uncertainties which, in their opinion, are fundamental.**
      (b) When an inherent uncertainty exists which
        (i)   in the auditors' opinion is fundamental, and
        (ii) is adequately accounted for and disclosed in the financial statements
      the auditors should include an explanatory paragraph referring to the fundamental uncertainty in the section of their report setting out the basis of their opinion.
      (c) When adding an explanatory paragraph, auditors should use words which clearly indicate that their opinion on the financial statements is not qualified in respect of its contents. (SAS 600.6).

Inherent uncertainties

55   Inherent uncertainties about the outcome of future events frequently affect, to some degree, a wide range of components of the financial statements at the date they are approved. It is not possible for the directors to remove the uncertainties by obtaining more information at the date they approve the financial statements: the statements can reflect only the working assumptions of directors as to their financial outcome and, where material, describe the circumstances giving rise to the uncertainties and their potential financial effect.

56   In forming an opinion, auditors take into account the adequacy of the accounting treatment, estimates and disclosures of inherent uncertainties in the light of evidence available at the date they express that opinion.

57   Auditors recognise that, in preparing financial statements, directors are required to analyse relevant existing conditions, including uncertainties about future events and their effect on financial statements. An audit includes assessment of whether there is sufficient evidence to support the directors' analysis and resulting estimates and disclosures given in the financial statements. Usually auditors are able to obtain sufficient evidence concerning the directors' assessment of the outcome of inherent uncertainties by considering various types of evidence, including the historical experience of the reporting entity.

58   Forming an opinion on the adequacy of the accounting treatment of inherent uncertainties involves consideration of

the appropriateness of accounting policies dealing with uncertain matters;
the reasonableness of the estimates included in the financial statements in respect of inherent uncertainties; and
the adequacy of disclosure.

59   Auditors distinguish between circumstances in which an unqualified opinion is appropriate and those in which a qualification or disclaimer of opinion is required due to a limitation on the scope of their work. An inherent uncertainty can be expected to be resolved at a future date, at which time sufficient evidence concerning its outcome would be expected to become available. When evidence does or did exist (or reasonably could be expected to exist) but that evidence is not available to the auditors, the scope of their work is limited and a qualification or disclaimer of opinion is appropriate.

60   Where auditors conclude that the accounting policies followed lead to material misstatements in the financial statements, or that the estimates included in the financial statements are materially misstated, or that disclosures relating to the uncertainty are inadequate, a qualified or adverse opinion is required by SAS 600.8.

Fundamental uncertainties

61   In some circumstances, the degree of uncertainty about the outcome of a future event and its potential impact on the view given by the financial statements may be very great. Where resolution of an inherent uncertainty could affect the view given by the financial statements to the degree that the auditors conclude that it is to be regarded as fundamental, they include an explanatory paragraph when setting out the basis of their opinion describing the matter giving rise to the fundamental uncertainty and its possible effects on the financial statements, including (where practicable) quantification. Where it is not possible to quantify the potential effects of the resolution of the uncertainty, the auditors include a statement to that effect. Reference may be made to notes in the financial statements but such a reference is not a substitute for sufficient description of the fundamental uncertainty so that a reader can appreciate the principal points at issue and their implications.

62   Communication with the reader is enhanced by the use of an appropriate sub-heading differentiating the explanatory paragraph from other matters included in the section describing the basis of the auditors' opinion.

63   In determining whether an inherent uncertainty is fundamental, auditors consider:

(a)   the risk that the estimate included in financial statements may be subject to change;
(b)   the range of possible outcomes; and
(c)   the consequences of those outcomes on the view shown in the financial statements.

64   Inherent uncertainties are regarded as fundamental when they involve a significant level of concern about the validity of the going concern basis or other matter whose potential effect on the financial statements is unusually

great. A common example of a fundamental uncertainty is the outcome of major litigation.

Opinions expressed

65   An unqualified opinion indicates that the auditors consider that appropriate estimates and disclosures relating to fundamental uncertainties are made in the financial statements. It remains unqualified notwithstanding the inclusion of an explanatory paragraph describing a fundamental uncertainty. The explanatory paragraph is included as part of the basis for the auditors' opinion so as to make clear that it describes a matter which the auditors have taken into account in forming their opinion, but that it does not qualify that opinion.

66   When the auditors conclude that the estimate of the outcome of a fundamental uncertainty is materially misstated or that the disclosure relating to it inadequate, they issue a qualified opinion.

67   A disclaimer of opinion is issued by auditors as a result of an inherent uncertainty which in their opinion is fundamental only when a limitation of the scope of their work directly affects their assessment of the adequacy of its accounting treatment and disclosure.

LIMITATION OF AUDIT SCOPE

68   **When there has been a limitation on the scope of the auditors' work that prevents them from obtaining sufficient evidence to express an unqualified opinion:**

   (a)   the auditors' report should include a description of the factors leading to the limitation in the opinion section of their report;
   (b)   the auditors should issue a disclaimer of opinion when the possible effect of a limitation on scope is so material or pervasive that they are unable to express an opinion on the financial statements;
   (c)   a qualified opinion should be issued when the effect of the limitation is not so material or pervasive as to require a disclaimer, and the wording of the opinion should indicate that it is qualified as to the possible adjustments to the financial statements that might have been determined to be necessary had the limitation not existed. (SAS 600.7).

69   In considering whether a limitation results in a lack of evidence necessary to form an opinion, auditors assess:

   (a)   the quantity and type of evidence which may reasonably be expected to be available to support the particular figure or disclosure in the financial statements; and
   (b)   the possible effect on the financial statements of the matter for which insufficient evidence is available. When the possible effect is, in the opinion of the auditors, material to the financial statements, there will be insufficient evidence to support an unqualified opinion.

70   Inherent uncertainties do not arise from, or give rise to, a limitation on the auditors' work and are considered under SAS 600.6.

71   A description of the factors leading to a limitation enables the reader to understand the reasons for the limitation and to distinguish between:

(a)   limitations imposed on the auditors (for example, where not all the accounting records are made available to the auditors or where the directors prevent a particular procedure considered necessary by the auditors from being carried out); and

(b)   limitations outside the control of the auditors or the directors (for example, when the timing of the auditors' appointment is such that attendance at the entity's stock-take is not possible and there is no alternative form of evidence regarding the existence of stock).

72   When the proposed terms of an audit engagement include a limitation on the scope of the auditors' work such that they believe the need to issue a disclaimer exists, they would normally not accept such a limited engagement as an audit engagement, unless required by statute to do so.

73   Where a scope limitation is imposed by circumstances, auditors would normally attempt to carry out reasonable alternative procedures to obtain sufficient audit evidence to support an unqualified opinion.

DISAGREEMENT ON ACCOUNTING TREATMENT OR DISCLOSURE

74   **Where the auditors disagree with the accounting treatment or disclosure of a matter in the financial statements, and in the auditors' opinion the effect of that disagreement is material to the financial statements:**

(a)   **the auditors should include in the opinion section of their report**
   (i)   **a description of all substantive factors giving rise to the disagreement;**
   (ii) **their implications for the financial statements;**
   (iii) **whenever practicable, a quantification of the effect on the financial statements;**

(b)   **when the auditors conclude that the effect of the matter giving rise to disagreement is so material or pervasive that the financial statements are seriously misleading, they should issue an adverse opinion;**

(c)   **in the case of other material disagreements, the auditors should issue a qualified opinion indicating that it is expressed except for the effects of the matter giving rise to the disagreement. (SAS 600.8).**

75   An auditors' report including a qualified opinion arising from disagreement includes a description of the reasons for qualification and the effects on the financial statements. Whilst reference may be made to relevant notes in the financial statements, such reference is not a substitute for sufficient description of the circumstances in the auditors' report so that a reader can appreciate the principal points at issue and their implications for an understanding of the financial statements.

DATE AND SIGNATURE OF THE AUDITORS' REPORT

76 **(a) Auditors should not express an opinion on financial statements until those statements and all other financial information contained in a report of which the audited financial statements form a part have been approved by the directors, and the auditors have considered all necessary available evidence.**

   (b) The date of an auditors' report on a reporting entity's financial statements is the date on which the auditors signed their report expressing an opinion on those statements. (SAS 600.9)

77 The report may be signed in the name of the auditors' firm, the personal name of auditor, or both, as appropriate. The signature is normally that of the firm because the firm as a whole assumes responsibility for the audit. To assist identification, the report normally includes the location of the auditors' office. Where appropriate, their status as registered auditors is also stated.

Date of the auditors' report

78 Dating the auditors' report informs the reader that the auditors have considered the effect on the financial statements of events or transactions of which they are aware which occurred up to that date.

79 The auditors are not in a position to form their opinion until the financial statements (and any other financial information contained in a report of which the audited financial statements form a part) have been approved by the directors and the auditors have completed their assessment of all the evidence they consider necessary for the opinions to be given in their report. This assessment includes events occurring up to the date the opinion is expressed. Auditors therefore plan the conduct of audits to take account of the need to ensure, before expressing an opinion on financial statements, that the directors have approved the financial statements and any accompanying financial information and that the auditors have completed a sufficient review of post balance sheet events.

80 The date of the auditors' report is, therefore, the date on which, following:

   (a) receipt of the financial statements and accompanying documents in the form approved by the directors for release;

   (b) review of all documents which they are required to consider in addition to the financial statements (for example the directors' report, chairman's statement or other review of an entity's affairs which will accompany the financial statements); and

   (c) completion of all procedures necessary to form an opinion on the financial statements (and any other opinions required by law or regulation) including a review of post balance sheet events,

   the auditors sign (in manuscript) their report expressing an opinion on the financial statements for distribution with those statements.

81 The form of the financial statements and other financial information approved by the directors, and considered by the auditors when signing a report expressing their opinion, may be in the form of final drafts from which printed documents will be prepared. Subsequent production of printed

copies of the financial statements and auditors' report does not constitute the creation of a new document. Copies of the report produced for circulation to shareholders or others may therefore reproduce a printed version of the auditors' signature showing the date of actual signature.

82   Before signing a report expressing their opinion after consideration of final drafts of the financial statements and other accompanying documents, auditors will need to consider whether the form of draft documents is sufficiently clear for them to assess the overall financial statement presentation. When the auditors conclude that this is not the case, it will be necessary for them to defer signing their report until it is possible for them to do so.

83   If the date on which the auditors sign their report is later than that on which the directors approved the financial statements, the auditors take such steps as are appropriate:

(a)   to obtain assurance that the directors would have approved the financial statements on that later date (for example, by obtaining confirmation from specified individual members of the board to whom authority has been delegated for this purpose); and

(b)   to ensure that their procedures for reviewing subsequent events cover the period up to that date.

Registrar of companies

84   The copy of the auditors' report which is delivered to the registrar of companies is required to state the name of the auditors and be signed by them. Where the auditors sign their report in a form from which a final printed version is produced, they may sign copies for identification purposes in order to provide the registrar with appropriately signed copies. No further active procedures need be followed at that later date.

COMPLIANCE WITH INTERNATIONAL STANDARDS ON AUDITING

85   Compliance with this SAS ensures compliance in all material respects with International Accounting Standard on Auditing 700 'The Auditor's Report on Financial Statements'.

EFFECTIVE DATE

86   Auditors are required to comply with the requirements of this SAS in respect of audits of financial statements for financial periods ending on or after 30 September 1993. Adoption of the requirements when reporting on financial statements for accounting periods ending before that date is encouraged.

CCAB material has been reproduced by kind permission of the ICAS.

An example of an affidavit used in a security for costs application

Submitted on behalf of
the Defendant

IN THE HIGH COURT OF JUSTICE   *1993 T No 9999*

QUEEN'S BENCH DIVISION

BETWEEN:

IN-THE-RED LIMITED   Plaintiffs

-and-

SECURITY CONSCIOUS LIMITED   Defendants

AFFIDAVIT OF
ANDREW JAMES MEADOWS

I, ANDREW JAMES MEADOWS of Yew Court, London EC4A 6AZ, MAKE
OATH and say as follows:

I am a Fellow of the Institute of Chartered Accountants in England and Wales and
a partner in the firm of Smith & Jones, Chartered Accountants in the City of
London. I was articled to a partner in that firm in September 1968 and was
admitted a Member of the Institute of Chartered Accountants in England and
Wales in 1971. I became a partner in the firm in October 1976 and have continued
in this capacity up to the present time. In the main, I have been concerned during
that period with audits and special work of various kinds including financial
investigations.

I have been asked to comment on the affidavits sworn in these proceedings by
Ronald Rees and in so far as they refer to the accounts of the Plaintiffs, In-the-Red
Limited ('In-the-Red') and that company's ability to pay the costs of the

defendants if successful in their defence. According to the affidavit of Geoffrey Charles South these will not be less than £120,000.

I have read the affidavit of Mr R Rees. I have also examined the audited accounts of In-the-Red for the years 31 December 1990 and 1991, exhibited as 'RR1' to Mr R Rees' affidavit.

The latest accounts available for In-the-Red are those for the year ended 31 December 1991. Mr R Rees confirms in paragraph 5 of his affidavit that the accounts for the financial years ended 31 December 1992 and 1993 have not been prepared.

The first comment that I should like to make in relation to the task I have been asked to undertake is that, in the absence of more up-to-date financial information, I think it is impossible to form a definite view as to whether In-the-Red is able to meet any or all of its liabilities. This is essentially because the said accounts are too old for this purpose. I find it surprising that there are no more up-to-date accounts filed because, under s 242(2) of the Companies Act 1985, accounts of private companies must be filed with the Registrar of Companies within ten months of the company's accounting reference date. As the company has not changed its accounting reference date, this means that the accounts for the year to 31 December 1992 should have been filed by 31 October 1993 at the latest.

My second comment is that, in my experience, a delay in filing of accounts for a long period as indicated above is often a sign that the company is in financial or other difficulties.

There are a number of other matters that support such an inference.

(a) The profit and loss account of In-the-Red for the year ended 31 December 1991 shows that the company made an operating loss of £25,000. This was turned into a net profit for the year of £10,000 by extraordinary profit relating to the sale of a building of £35,000. This profit would not necessarily be recurring.

(b) The balance sheet of In-the-Red at 31 December 1991 shows an accumulated deficit on its profit and loss account of £40,000. Also the balance sheet shows that In-the-Red's current liabilities exceeded its current assets by £10,000. These measures are tests of solvency and in my opinion are indicative that In-the-Red was in a tight financial position at that time.

(c) At 31 December 1991 In-the-Red had no bank borrowings, but was financed in part by a director's current account of £20,000. This suggests to me that In-the-Red had no overdraft facilities at that time.

(d) Mr Rees, in paragraph 8 of his affidavit, states that 'further income has been received by the company in the course of 1992 and that these sums should also be taken into account when assessing the state of account of the Plaintiff'. I do not disagree that income subsequent to 31 December 1991 should be taken into account, but should like to point out that so too should expenditure incurred subsequent to that date. I note that In-the-Red's profit and loss account for the year ended 31 December 1991 discloses expenditure under two main headings: 'cost of sales' amounting to £50,000 and 'administration expenses' amounting to £31,000. In my opinion, it is reasonable to assume that In-the-Red has also incurred expenses since 31 December 1991, but I do not know how much they have been.

(e) Mr Rees also refers in paragraph 6 of his affidavit to his belief that In-the-Red's assets exceeded its liabilities as at 31 December 1992 and continue to do so. However, he has produced no financial evidence to substantiate this belief. Furthermore, he gives no indication of the extent by which he considers In-the-Red's assets exceed its liabilities; nor in my opinion does he provide the sort of financial evidence I would expect to see, for example, draft accounts, information on bank overdraft facilities or other available sources of finance to show that In-the-Red's financial position has improved to any significant extent since 31 December 1991.

In the absence of (a) more up-to-date audited accounts, and (b) further information as to In-the-Red's overdraft or borrowing limits and any other available sources of finance, none of the matters mentioned above can properly be regarded as conclusive. However, in my judgment, they are all indicative that In-the-Red has been, and probably still is, in a tight financial situation. On the basis of the limited amount of financial information available to me, I therefore conclude that there is reason to believe that In-the-Red will be unable to comply with an order to pay costs of £120,000, or indeed anything approaching that amount.

Sworn at

this   th day of   , 1995

Before me

A solicitor

1st Affidavit of

ANDREW JAMES MEADOWS

SWORN

Filed on behalf of the Defendants

1993 T No 9999

IN THE HIGH COURT OF JUSTICE

QUEEN'S BENCH DIVISION

BETWEEN:

IN-THE-RED LIMITED
                    Plaintiffs

and

SECURITY CONSCIOUS LIMITED
                    Defendants

AFFIDAVIT OF
ANDREW JAMES MEADOWS

Green, Ribbon & Co
Lincoln's Inn
London
EC2V 7XZ

Solicitors for the Defendants

Do's and don'ts in cross-examination

- Become *familiar with the layout* of the court room; in an arbitration, find out what facilities there are for showing tables, graphs, charts or other visual aids.

- Try to get a *'feel' for the whole trial* and attend other witnesses' cross-examination if this is permitted.

- Make certain you *understand the question* before answering it.

- Do not let the lawyer establish your *hypothesis*. If it is untenable, it is you that suffers in the witness box, not him.

- Do not be *aggressive* or biased.

- Do not give un*clear* testimony.

- Be *consistent*.

- Do not testify *ouside* the area of *your true expertise*.

- Answer the question as *directly, concisely*, honestly and courteously as you can.

- Use *layman's language*, rather than accounting jargon.

- Do not hesitate to *pause* and consult papers or even colleagues *before answering* a question. It is fatal to give a swift answer to a question which has many sides to it.

- *Avoid* the appearance of quibbling or *being evasive*.

- *Avoid* attempts at *humour*. They are almost always out of place and can be harmful to the testimony.

- Do not answer *ambiguous or equivocal questions* without obtaining clarification.

- Stay interested in what is being said and *do not show boredom* with the proceedings – for example, if there is a discussion between judge and counsel.

- *Speak loudly* at all times so that everyone in the court can hear every word.

- Never engage in personal exchanges with opposing counsel, however much there may be *provocation* to do so.

- Avoid taking too many papers into court. Collect together *the key papers* in one court file and leave everything else either with a colleague at the back of the court or, if you are confident, back at the office.

- *Be punctual* and make definite arrangements with the lawyers as to the time and place of the testimony and how you will meet them and where you will sit.

- *Be well prepared*. Thorough preparation is the essence of good evidence.

Rules for the ICC Court of Arbitration
(In force from January 1988, Appendix III in force from January 1993)

Article 1   Court of Arbitration

1.   The Court of Arbitration of the International Chamber of Commerce is the international arbitration body attached to the International Chamber of Commerce. Members of the Court are appointed by the Council of the International Chamber of Commerce. The function of the Court is to provide for the settlement by arbitration of business disputes of an international character in accordance with these Rules.

2.   In principle, the Court meets once a month. It draws up its own internal regulations.

3.   The Chairman of the Court of Arbitration or his deputy shall have power to take urgent decisions on behalf of the Court, provided that any such decision shall be reported to the Court at its next session.

4.   The Court may, in the manner provided for in its internal regulations, delegate to one or more groups of its members the power to take certain decisions provided that any such decision shall be reported to the Court at its next session.

5.   The Secretariat of the Court of Arbitration shall be at the Headquarters of the International Chamber of Commerce.

Article 2   The arbitral tribunal

1.   The Court of Arbitration does not itself settle disputes. Insofar as the parties shall not have provided otherwise, it appoints, or confirms the appointments of arbitrators in accordance with the provisions of this Article. In making or confirming such appointment, the Court shall have regard to the proposed arbitrator's nationality, residence and other relationships with the countries of which the parties or the other arbitrators are nationals.

2.   The disputes may be settled by a sole arbitrator or by three arbitrators. In the following Articles the word 'arbitrator' denotes a single arbitrator or three arbitrators as the case may be.

3.   Where the parties have agreed that the disputes shall be settled by a sole arbitrator, they may, by agreement, nominate him for confirmation by the Court. If the parties fail so to nominate a sole arbitrator within 30 days from the date when the Claimant's Request for Arbitration has been communicated to the other party, the sole arbitrator shall be appointed by the Court.

4.   Where the dispute is to be referred to three arbitrators, each party shall nominate in the Request for Arbitration and the Answer thereto respectively one arbitrator for confirmation by the Court. Such person shall be independent of the party nominating him. If a party fails to nominate an arbitrator, the appointment shall be made by the Court.

The third arbitrator, who will act as chairman of the arbitral tribunal, shall be appointed by the Court, unless the parties have provided that the arbitrators nominated by them shall agree on the third arbitrator within a fixed time limit. In such a case the Court shall confirm the appointment of such third arbitrator. Should the two arbitrators fail, within the time limit fixed by the parties or the Court, to reach agreement on the third arbitrator, he shall be appointed by the Court.

5.   Where the parties have not agreed upon the number of arbitrators, the Court shall appoint a sole arbitrator, save where it appears to the Court that the dispute is such as to warrant the appointment of three arbitrators. In such a case the parties shall each have a period of 30 days within which to nominate an arbitrator.

6.   Where the Court is to appoint a sole arbitrator or the chairman of an arbitral tribunal, it shall make the appointment after having requested a proposal from a National Committee of the ICC that it considers to be appropriate. If the Court does not accept the proposal made, or if said National Committee fails to make the proposal requested within the time-limit fixed by the Court, the Court may repeat its request or may request a proposal from another appropriate National Committee.

Where the Court considers that the circumstances so demand, it may choose the sole arbitrator or the chairman of the arbitral tribunal from a country where there is no National Committee, provided that neither of the parties objects within the time-limit fixed by the Court.

The sole arbitrator or the chairman of the arbitral tribunal shall be chosen from a country other than those of which the parties are nationals. However, in suitable circumstances and provided that neither of the parties objects within the time-limit fixed by the Court, the sole arbitrator or the chairman of the arbitral tribunal may be chosen from a country of which any of the parties is a national.

Where the Court is to appoint an arbitrator on behalf of a party which has failed to nominate one, it shall make the appointment after having requested a proposal from the National Committee of the country of which the said party is a national. If the Court does not accept the proposal made, or if said National Committee fails to make the proposal requested within the time-limit fixed by the Court, or if the country of which the said party is a national has no National Committee, the Court shall be at liberty to choose any person whom it regards as suitable, after having informed the National Committee of the country of which such person is a national, if one exists.

7.   Every arbitrator appointed or confirmed by the Court must be and remain independent of the parties involved in the arbitration.

Before appointment or confirmation by the Court, a prospective arbitrator shall disclose in writing to the Secretary General of the Court any facts or circumstances which might be of such a nature as to call into question the arbitrator's independence in the eyes of the parties. Upon receipt of such information, the Secretary General of the Court shall provide it to the parties in writing and fix a time-limit for any comments from them.

An arbitrator shall immediately disclose in writing to the Secretary General of the Court and the parties any facts or circumstances of a similar nature which may arise between the arbitrator's appointment or confirmation by the Court and the notification of the final award.

8.   A challenge of an arbitrator, whether for an alleged lack of independence or otherwise, is made by the submission to the Secretary General of the Court of a written statement specifying the facts and circumstances on which the challenge is based.

For a challenge to be admissible, it must be sent by a party either within 30 days from receipt by that party of the notification of the appointment or confirmation of the arbitrator by the Court; or within 30 days from the date when the party making the challenge was informed of the facts and circumstances on which the challenge is based, if such date is subsequent to the receipt of the aforementioned notification.

9. The Court shall decide on the admissibility, and at the same time if need be on the merits, of a challenge after the Secretary General of the Court has accorded an opportunity for the arbitrator concerned, the parties and any other members of the arbitral tribunal to comment in writing within a suitable period of time.

10. An arbitrator shall be replaced upon his death, upon the acceptance by the Court of a challenge, or upon the acceptance by the Court of the arbitrator's resignation.

11. An arbitrator shall also be replaced when the Court decides that he is prevented de jure or de facto from fulfilling his functions, or that he is not fulfilling his functions in accordance with the Rules or within the prescribed time-limits.

When, on the basis of information that has come to its attention, the Court considers applying the preceding subparagraph, it shall decide on the matter after the Secretary General of the Court has provided such information in writing to the arbitrator concerned, the parties and any other members of the arbitral tribunal, and accorded an opportunity to them to comment in writing within a suitable period of time.

12. In each instance where an arbitrator is to be replaced, the procedure indicated in the preceding paragraphs 3, 4, 5 and 6 shall be followed. Once reconstituted, and after having invited the parties to comment, the arbitral tribunal shall determine if and to what extent prior proceedings shall again take place.

13. Decisions of the Court as to the appointment, confirmation, challenge or replacement of an arbitrator shall be final.

The reasons for decisions by the Court as to the appointment, confirmation, challenge, or replacement of an arbitrator on the grounds that he is not fulfilling his functions in accordance with the Rules or within the prescribed time-limits, shall not be communicated.

Article 3　Request for Arbitration

1. A party wishing to have recourse to arbitration by the International Chamber of Commerce shall submit its Request for arbitration to the Secretariat of the Court, through its National Committee or directly. In this latter case the Secretariat shall bring the Request to the notice of the National Committee concerned.

The date when the Request is received by the Secretariat of the Court shall, for all purposes, be deemed to be the date of commencement of the arbitral proceedings.

2. The Request for Arbitration shall inter alia contain the following information:

(a) names in full, description, and addresses of the parties,
(b) a statement of the Claimant's case,
(c) the relevant agreements, and in particular the agreement to arbitrate, and such documentation or information as will serve clearly to establish the circumstances of the case,

(d) all relevant particulars concerning the number of arbitrators and their choice in accordance with the provisions of Article 2 above.

3. The Secretariat shall send a copy of the Request and the documents annexed thereto to the Defendant for his Answer.

Article 4   Answer to the Request

1. The Defendant shall within 30 days from the receipt of the documents referred to in paragraph 3 of Article 3 comment on the proposals made concerning the number of arbitrators and their choice and, where appropriate, nominate an arbitrator. He shall at the same time set out his defence and supply relevant documents. In exceptional circumstances the Defendant may apply to the Secretariat for an extension of time for the filing of his defence and his documents. The application must, however, include the Defendant's comments on the proposals made with regard to the number of arbitrators and their choice and also, where appropriate, the nomination of an arbitrator. If the Defendant fails so to do, the Secretariat shall report to the Court, which shall proceed with the arbitration in accordance with these Rules.

2. A copy of the Answer and of the documents annexed thereto, if any, shall be communicated to the Claimant for his information.

Article 5   Counter-claim

1. If the Defendant wishes to make a counter-claim, he shall file the same with the Secretariat, at the same time as his Answer as provided for in Article 4.

2. It shall be open to the Claimant to file a Reply with the Secretariat within 30 days from the date when the counter-claim was communicated to him.

Article 6   Pleadings and written statements, notifications or communications

1. All pleadings and written statements submitted by the parties, as well as all documents annexed thereto, shall be supplied in a number of copies sufficient to provide one copy for each party, plus one for each arbitrator, and one for the Secretariat.

2. All notifications or communications from the Secretariat and the arbitrator shall be validly made if they are delivered against receipt or forwarded by registered post to the address or last known address of the party for whom the same are intended as notified by the party in question or by the other party as appropriate.

3. Notification or communication shall be deemed to have been effected on the day when it was received, or should, if made in accordance with the preceding paragraph, have been received by the party itself or by its representative.

4. Periods of time specified in the present Rules or in the Internal Rules or set by the Court pursuant to its authority under any of these Rules shall start to run on the day following the date a notification or communication is deemed to have been effected in accordance with the preceding paragraph. When, in the country where the notification or communication is deemed to have been effected, the day next following such date is an official holiday or a non-business day, the period of time shall commence on the first following working day. Official holidays and non-working days are included in the calculation of the period of time. If the last day of the relevant period of time granted is an official holiday or a non-business day in the country where the notification or communication is deemed to have been effected, the period of time shall expire at the end of the first following working day.

Article 7   Absence of agreement to arbitrate

Where there is no prima facie agreement between the parties to arbitrate or where there is an agreement but it does not specify the International Chamber of Commerce, and if the Defendant does not file an Answer within the period of 30 days provided by paragraph 1 of Article 4 or refuses arbitration by the International Chamber of Commerce, the Claimant shall be informed that the arbitration cannot proceed.

Article 8   Effect the agreement to arbitrate

1.   Where the parties have agreed to submit to arbitration by the International Chamber of Commerce, they shall be deemed thereby to have submitted ipso facto to the present Rules.

· **2.**   If one of the parties refuses or fails to take part in the arbitration, the arbitration shall proceed notwithstanding such refusal or failure.

3.   Should one of the parties raise one or more pleas concerning the existence or validity of the agreement to arbitrate, and should the Court be satisfied of the prima facie existence of such an agreement, the Court may, without prejudice to the admissibility or merits of the plea or pleas, decide that the arbitration shall proceed. In such a case any decision as to the arbitrator's jurisdiction shall be taken by the arbitrator himself.

4.   Unless otherwise provided, the arbitrator shall not cease to have jurisdiction by reason of any claim that the contract is null and void or allegation that it is inexistent provided that he upholds the validity of the agreement to arbitrate. He shall continue to have jurisdiction, even though the contract itself may be inexistent or null and void, to determine the respective rights of the parties and to adjudicate upon their claims and pleas.

5.   Before the file is transmitted to the arbitrator, and in exceptional circumstances even thereafter, the parties shall be at liberty to apply to any competent judicial authority for interim or conservatory measures, and they shall not by so doing be held to infringe the agreement to arbitrate or to affect the relevant powers reserved to the arbitrator.

Any such application and any measures taken by the judicial authority must be notified without delay to the Secretariat of the Court of Arbitration. The Secretariat shall inform the arbitrator thereof.

Article 9   Advance to cover costs of arbitration

1.   The Court shall fix the amount of the advance on costs in a sum likely to cover the costs of arbitration of the claims which have been referred to it.

Where, apart from the principal claim, one or more counter-claims are submitted, the Court may fix separate advances on costs for the principal claim and the counter-claim or counter-claims.

2. The advance on costs shall be payable in equal shares by the Claimant or Claimants and the Defendant or Defendants. However, any one party shall be free to pay the whole of the advance on costs in respect of the claim or the counter-claim should the other party fail to pay its share.

3. The Secretariat may make the transmission of the file to the arbitrator conditional upon the payment by the parties or one of them of the whole or part of the advance on costs to the International Chamber of Commerce.

4. When the Terms of Reference are communicated to the Court in accordance with the provisions of Article 13, the Court shall verify whether the requests for the advance on costs have been complied with.

The Terms of Reference shall only become operative and the arbitrator shall only proceed in respect of those claims for which the advance on costs has been duly paid to the International Chamber of Commerce.

Article 10 Transmission of the file to the arbitrator

Subject to the provisions of Article 9, the Secretariat shall transmit the file to the arbitrator as soon as it has received the Defendant's Answer to the Request for Arbitration, at the latest upon the expiry of the time limits fixed in Articles 4 and 5 above for the filing of these documents.

Article 11 Rules governing the proceedings

The rules governing the proceedings before the arbitrator shall be those resulting from these Rules and, where these Rules are silent, any rules which the parties (or, failing them, the arbitrator) may settle, and whether or not reference is thereby made to a municipal procedural law to be applied to the arbitration.

Article 12 Place of arbitration

The place of arbitration shall be fixed by the Court unless agreed upon by the parties.

Article 13 Terms of Reference

1. Before proceeding with the preparation of the case, the arbitrator shall draw up, on the basis of the documents or in the presence of the parties and in the light of their most recent submissions, a document defining his Terms of Reference. This document shall include the following particulars:

(a) the full names and description of the parties,
(b) the addresses of the parties to which notifications or communications arising in the course of the arbitration may validly be made,
(c) a summary of the parties' respective claims,
(d) definition of the issues to be determined,
(e) the arbitrator's full name, description and address,
(f) the place of arbitration,
(g) particulars of the applicable procedural rules and, if such is the case, reference to the power conferred upon the arbitrator to act as amiable compositeur,

(h) such other particulars as may be required to make the arbitral award enforceable in law, or may be regarded as helpful by the Court of Arbitration or the arbitrator.

2. The document mentioned in paragraph 1 of this Article shall be signed by the parties and the arbitrator. Within two months of the date when the file has been transmitted to him, the arbitrator shall transmit to the Court the said document signed by himself and by the parties. The Court may, pursuant to a reasoned request from the arbitrator or if need be on its own initiative, extend this time-limit if it decides it is necessary to do so.

Should one of the parties refuse to take part in the drawing up of the said document or to sign the same, the Court, if it is satisfied that the case is one of those mentioned in paragraphs 2 and 3 of Article 8, shall take such action as is necessary for its approval. Thereafter the Court shall set a time limit for the signature of the statement by the defaulting party and on expiry of that time limit the arbitration shall proceed and the award shall be made.

3. The parties shall be free to determine the law to be applied by the arbitrator to the merits of the dispute. In the absence of any indication by the parties as to the applicable law, the arbitrator shall apply the law designated as the proper law by the rule of conflict which he deems appropriate.

4. The arbitrator shall assume the powers of an amiable compositeur if the parties are agreed to give him such powers.

5. In all cases the arbitrator shall take account of the provisions of the contract and the relevant trade usages.

Article 14   The arbitral proceedings

1. The arbitrator shall proceed within as short a time as possible to establish the facts of the case by all appropriate means. After study of the written submissions of the parties and of all documents relied upon, the arbitrator shall hear the parties together in person if one of them so requests; and failing such a request he may of his own motion decide to hear them.

In addition, the arbitrator may decide to hear any other person in the presence of the parties or in their absence provided they have been duly summoned.

2. The arbitrator may appoint one or more experts, define their Terms of Reference, receive their reports and/or hear them in person.

3. The arbitrator may decide the case on the relevant documents alone if the parties so request or agree.

Article 15

1. At the request of one of the parties or if necessary on his own initiative, the arbitrator, giving reasonable notice, shall summon the parties to appear before him on the day and at the place appointed by him and shall so inform the Secretariat of the Court.

2. If one of the parties, although duly summoned, fails to appear, the arbitrator, if he is satisfied that the summons was duly received and the party is absent without valid excuse, shall have power to proceed with the arbitration, and such proceedings shall be deemed to have been conducted in the presence of all parties.

3. The arbitrator shall determine the language or languages of the arbitration, due regard being paid to all the relevant circumstances and in particular to the language of the contract.

4. The arbitrator shall be in full charge of the hearings, at which all the parties shall be entitled to be present. Save with the approval of the arbitrator and of the parties, persons not involved in the proceedings shall not be admitted.

5. The parties may appear in person or through duly accredited agents. In addition, they may be assisted by advisers.

Article 16

The parties may make new claims or counter-claims before the arbitrator on condition that these remain within the limits fixed by the Terms of Reference provided for in Article 13 or that they are specified in a rider to that document, signed by the parties and communicated to the Court.

Article 17   Award by consent

If the parties reach a settlement after the file has been transmitted to the arbitrator in accordance with Article 10, the same shall be recorded in the form of an arbitral award made by consent of the parties.

Article 18   Time-limit for award

1. The time-limit within which the arbitrator must render his award is fixed at six months. Once the terms of Article 9(4) have been satisfied, such time-limit shall start to run from the date of the last signature by the arbitrator or of the parties of the document mentioned in Article 13, or from the expiry of the time-limit granted to a party by virtue of Article 13(2), or from the date that the Secretary General of the Court notifies the arbitrator that the advance on costs is paid in full, if such notification occurs later.

2. The Court may, pursuant to a reasoned request from the arbitrator or if need be on its own initiative, extend this time-limit if it decides it is necessary to do so.

3. Where no such extension is granted and, if appropriate, after application of the provisions of Article 2(11), the Court shall determine the manner in which the dispute is to be resolved.

Article 19   Award by three arbitrators

When three arbitrators have been appointed, the award is given by a majority decision. If there be no majority, the award shall be made by the Chairman of the arbitral tribunal alone.

Article 20   Decision as to costs of arbitration

1. The arbitrator's award shall, in addition to dealing with the merits of the case, fix the costs of the arbitration and decide which of the parties shall bear the costs or in what proportions the costs shall be borne by the parties.

2. The costs of the arbitration shall include the arbitrator's fees and the administrative costs fixed by the Court in accordance with the scale annexed to the present Rules, the expenses, if any, of the arbitrator, the fees and expenses of any experts, and the normal legal costs incurred by the parties.

3. The Court may fix the arbitrator's fees at a figure higher or lower than that which would result from the application of the annexed scale if in the exceptional circumstances of the case this appears to be necessary.

Article 21   Scrutiny of award by the Court

Before signing an award, whether partial or definitive, the arbitrator shall submit it in draft form to the Court. The Court may lay down modifications as to the form of the award and, without affecting the arbitrator's liberty of decision, may also draw his attention to points of substance. No award shall be signed until it has been approved by the Court as to its form.

Article 22   Making of award

The arbitral award shall be deemed to be made at the place of the arbitration proceedings and on the date when it is signed by the arbitrator.

Article 23   Notification of award to parties

1. Once an award has been made, the Secretariat shall notify to the parties the text signed by the arbitrator; provided always that the costs of the arbitration have been fully paid to the International Chamber of Commerce by the parties or by one of them.

2. Additional copies certified true by the Secretary-General of the Court shall be made available, on request and at any time, to the parties but to no one else.

3. By virtue of the notification made in accordance with paragraph 1 of this Article, the parties waive any other form of notification or deposit on the part of the arbitrator.

Article 24   Finality and enforceability of award

1. The arbitral award shall be final.

2. By submitting the dispute to arbitration by the International Chamber of Commerce, the parties shall be deemed to have undertaken to carry out the resulting award without delay and to have waived their right to any form of appeal insofar as such waiver can validly be made.

Article 25   Deposit of award

An original of each award made in accordance with the present Rules shall be deposited with the Secretariat of the Court.

The arbitrator and the Secretariat of the Court shall assist the parties in complying with whatever further formalities may be necessary.

Article 26   General rule

In all matters not expressly provided for in these Rules, the Court of Arbitration and the arbitrator shall act in the spirit of these Rules and shall make every effort to make sure that the award is enforceable at law.

APPENDICES

APPENDIX I – STATUTES OF THE COURT

Article 1   Appointment of members

The members of the Court of Arbitration of the International Chamber of Commerce are appointed for a term of three years by the Council of that Chamber pursuant to Article 5.3i of the Constitution, on the proposal of each National Committee.

Article 2   Composition

The Court of Arbitration shall be composed of a Chairman, of eight Vice-Chairmen, of a Secretary General and of one or several Technical Advisers chosen by the Council of the International Chamber of Commerce either from among the members of the Court or apart from them, and of one member for, and appointed by, each National Committee.

The chairmanship may be exercised by two Co-Chairmen; in this case, they shall have equal rights, and the expression 'the Chairman', used in the Rules of Conciliation and Arbitration, shall apply to either of them equally.

When a member of the Court does not reside in the city where the International Headquarters of the International Chamber of Commerce is situated, the Council may appoint an alternate member.

If the chairman is unable to attend a session of the court, he shall be replaced by one of the Vice-Chairmen.

Article 3   Function and powers

The function of the Court of Arbitration is to ensure the application of the Rules of Conciliation and Arbitration of the International Chamber of Commerce, and the Court has all the necessary powers for that purpose. It is further entrusted, if need be, with laying before the Commission on International Arbitration any proposals for modifying the Rules of Conciliation and Arbitration of the International Chamber of Commerce which it considers necessary.

Article 4   Deliberations and quorum

The decisions of the Court shall be taken by a majority vote, the Chairman having a casting vote in the event of a tie. The deliberations of the Court shall be valid when at least six members are present.

The Secretary General of the International Chamber of Commerce, the Secretary General of the Court and the Technical Adviser or Advisers shall attend in an advisory capacity only.

APPENDIX II – INTERNAL RULES OF THE COURT OF ARBITRATION

Role of the Court of Arbitration

1. The Court of Arbitration may accept jurisdiction over business disputes not of an international business nature, if it has jurisdiction by reason of an arbitration agreement.

Confidential character of the work of the Court of Arbitration

2. The work of the Court of Arbitration is of a confidential character which must be respected by everyone who participates in that work in whatever capacity.

3. The sessions of the Court of Arbitration, whether plenary or those of a Committee of the Court, are open only to its members and to the Secretariat.

However, in exceptional circumstances and, if need be, after obtaining the opinion of members of the Court, the Chairman of the Court of Arbitration may invite honorary members of the Court and authorize observers to attend. Such persons must respect the confidential character of the work of the Court.

4. The documents submitted to the Court of Arbitration or drawn up by it in the course of the proceedings it conducts are communicated only to the members of the Court and to the Secretariat.

The Chairman or the Secretary General of the Court may nevertheless authorize researchers undertaking work of a scientific nature on international trade law to acquaint themselves with certain documents of general interest, with the exception of memoranda, notes, statements and documents remitted by the parties within the framework of arbitration proceedings.

Such authorization shall not be given unless the beneficiary has undertaken to respect the confidential character of the documents made available and to refrain from any publication in their respect without having previously submitted the text for approval to the Secretary General of the Court.

Participation of members of the Court of Arbitration in ICC arbitration

5. Owing to the special responsibilities laid upon them by the ICC Rules of Arbitration, the Chairman, the Vice-Chairmen and the Secretariat of the Court of Arbitration may not personally act as arbitrators or as counsel in cases submitted to ICC arbitration.

The members of the Court of Arbitration may not be directly appointed as co-arbitrators, sole arbitrator or Chairman of an arbitral tribunal by the Court of Arbitration. They may however be proposed for such duties by one or more of the parties, subject to confirmation by the Court.

6. When the Chairman, a Vice-Chairman or a member of the Court of Arbitration is involved, in any capacity whatsoever, in proceedings pending before the Court, he must inform the Secretary General of the Court as soon as he becomes aware of such involvement.

He must refrain from participating in the discussions or in the decisions of the

Court concerning the proceedings and he must be absent from the courtroom whenever the matter is considered.

He will not receive documentation or information submitted to the Court of Arbitration during the proceedings.

Relations between the members of the Court and the ICC National Committees

7. By virtue of their capacity, the members of the Court are independent of the ICC National Committees which proposed them for nomination by the ICC Council.

Furthermore, they must regard as confidential, vis-à-vis the said National Committees, any information concerning individual disputes with which they have become acquainted in their capacity as members of the Court except when they have been requested, by the Chairman of the Court or by its Secretary General, to communicate that information to their respective National Committees.

Committee of the Court

8. In accordance with the provisions of Article 1(4) of the ICC Rules of Arbitration, the Court of Arbitration hereby establishes a Committee of the Court composed as follows, and with the following powers.

9. The Committee consists of a Chairman and two members. The Chairman of the Court of Arbitration acts as the Chairman of the Committee. He may nevertheless designate a Vice-Chairman of the Court to replace him during a session of the Committee.

The other two members of the Committee are appointed by the Court of Arbitration from among the Vice-Chairmen or the other members of the Court. At each meeting of the Court it appoints the members who are to attend the meeting of the Committee to be held before the next plenary session of the Court.

10. The Committee meets when convened by its Chairman, in principle twice a month.

11. (a) The Committee is empowered to take any decision within the jurisdiction of the Court of Arbitration, with the exception of decisions concerning challenges of arbitrators (Arts 2(8) and 2(9) of the ICC Rules of Arbitration), allegations that an arbitrator is not fulfilling his functions (Art 2(11) of the ICC Rules of Arbitration) and approval of draft awards other than awards made with the consent of the parties.

(b) The decisions of the Committee are taken unanimously.

(c) When the Committee cannot reach a decision or deems it preferable to abstain, it transfers the case to the next plenary session of the Court of Arbitration, making any suggestions it deems appropriate.

(d) The Committee's proceedings are brought to the notice of the Court of Arbitration at its next plenary session.

Absence of an arbitration agreement

12. Where there is no prima facie arbitration agreement between the parties or where there is an agreement but it does not specify the ICC, the Secretariat draws the attention of the Claimant to the provisions laid down in Article 7 of the

Rules of Arbitration. The Claimant is entitled to require the decision to be taken by the Court of Arbitration.

This decision is of an administrative nature. If the Court decides that the arbitration solicited by the Claimant cannot proceed, the parties retain the right to ask the competent jurisdiction whether or not they are bound by an arbitration agreement in the light of the law applicable.

If the Court of Arbitration considers prima facie that the proceedings may take place, the arbitrator appointed has the duty to decide as to his own jurisdiction and, where such jurisdiction exists, as to the merits of the dispute.

Joinder of claims in arbitration proceedings

13. When a party presents a Request for Arbitraton in connection with a legal relationship already submitted to arbitration proceedings by the same parties and pending before the Court of Arbitration, the Court may decide to include that claim in the existing proceedings, subject to the provisions of Article 16 of the ICC Rules of Arbitration.

Advances to cover costs of arbitration

14. When the Court of Arbitration has set separate advances on costs for a specific case in accordance with Article 9(1) (sub para 2) of the ICC Rules of Arbitration, the Secretariat requests each of the parties to pay the amount corresponding to its claims, without prejudice to the right of the parties to pay the said advances on costs in equal shares, if they deem it advisable.

15. When a request for an advance on costs has not been complied with, the Secretariat may set a time-limit, which must not be less than 30 days, on the expiry of which the relevant claim, whether principal claim or counter-claim, shall be considered as withdrawn. This does not prevent the party in question from lodging a new claim at a later date.

Should one of the parties wish to object to this measure, he must make a request, within the aforementioned period, for the matter to be decided by the Court of Arbitration.

16. If one of the parties claims a right to a set-off with regard to either a principal claim or counter-claim, such set-off is taken into account in determining the advance to cover the costs of arbitration, in the same way as a separate claim, insofar as it may require the arbitrators to consider additional matters.

Arbitral awards: form

17. When it scrutinizes draft arbitral awards in accordance with Article 21 of the ICC Rules of Arbitration, the Court of Arbitration pays particular attention to the respect of the formal requirements laid down by the law applicable to the proceedings and, where relevant, by the mandatory rules of the place of arbitration, notably with regard to the reasons for awards, their signature and the admissibility of dissenting opinions.

Arbitrators' fees

18. In setting the arbitrators' fees on the basis of the scale attached to the ICC Rules of Arbitration, the Court of Arbitration takes into consideration the time spent, the rapidity of the proceedings and the complexity of the dispute, so as to arrive at a figure within the limits specified or, when circumstances require, higher or lower than those limits (Art 20(3) of the ICC Rules of Arbitration).

APPENDIX III – SCHEDULE OF CONCILIATION AND ARBITRATION COSTS
(In force from January 1993)

Costs of conciliation

1. (a) The administrative expenses for a conciliation procedure shall be fixed at one-quarter of the amount calculated in accordance with the scale of administrative expenses hereinafter set out. Where the sum in dispute in a conciliation procedure is not stated, the Secretary General of the Court of Arbitration shall fix the administrative expenses at his discretion.
   (b) The fee of the conciliator to be paid by the parties shall be fixed by the Secretary General of the Court of Arbitration. Such fee shall be reasonable in amount, taking into consideration the time spent, the complexity of the dispute and any other relevant circumstances.

Costs of arbitration

2. (a) The advance on costs fixed by the Court of Arbitration comprises the fee(s) of the arbitrator(s), any personal expenses of the arbitrator(s) and the administrative expenses.
   (b) The submission of any claim or counter-claim to the arbitrator(s) shall be made only after at least half of the advance on costs fixed by the Court has been satisfied. Terms of Reference shall only become operative and the arbitrator(s) shall only proceed in respect of those claims and counter-claims for which the totality of the advance on costs fixed by the Court has been satisfied.
   (c) The Court shall fix the administrative expenses of each arbitration in accordance with the scale hereinafter set out or, where the sum in dispute is not stated, at its discretion. If exceptional circumstances so require, the Court may fix the administrative expenses at a lower figure than that which would result from application of said scale, provided that such expenses shall in no event exceed US$65,000. Further, the Court may require the payment of administrative expenses in addition to those provided for in the scale of administrative expenses as a condition to holding an arbitration in abeyance at the request of the parties or one of them with the acquiescence of the other(s).
   (d) Subject to Article 20(3) of the ICC Rules of Arbitration, the Court shall fix the fee(s) of the arbitrator(s) in accordance with the scale hereinafter set out or, where the sum in dispute is not stated, at its discretion.
   (e) When a case is submitted to more than one arbitrator, the Court, at its discretion, shall have the right to increase the total fees up to a maximum of three times the fee payable to one arbitrator.
   (f) When arbitration is preceded by attempted conciliation, one-half of the administrative expenses paid in respect of the said attempt shall be credited to the administrative expenses of the arbitration.

(g) Before any expertise can be commenced, the parties, or one of them, shall pay an advance on costs fixed by the arbitrator(s) sufficient to cover the expected fee and expenses of the expert as determined by the arbitrator(s).

Advance on administrative expenses

3. (a) Each party to a dispute submitted to conciliation under the Rules of Optional Conciliation of the ICC is required to make an advance payment of US $500 on the administrative expenses.
   (b) Each request to open an arbitration pursuant to the ICC Rules of Arbitration must be accompanied by an advance payment of US $2,000 on the administrative expenses.
   (c) No request for conciliation or arbitration will be entertained unless accompanied by the appropriate payment. This payment is not recoverable and becomes the property of the ICC. Such payment by a party shall be credited to its portion of the administrative expenses for the conciliation or arbitration, as the case may be.

Appointment of arbitrators

4. A registration fee of US $2,000 is payable by the requesting party in respect of each request made to the ICC to appoint an arbitrator for any arbitration not conducted under the ICC Rules of Arbitration. No request for appointment of an arbitrator will be entertained unless accompanied by said fee, which is not recoverable and becomes the property of the ICC.

Such fee shall cover any additional services rendered by the ICC regarding the appointment, such as decisions on a challenge of the arbitrator and the appointment of a substitute arbitrator.

Scales of administrative expenses and of arbitrator's fees

5. To calculate the administrative expenses and the arbitrator's fees, the amounts calculated for each successive slice of the sum in dispute must be added together, (*)(**) except that where the sum in dispute is over US $80 million, a flat amount of US $65,500 shall constitute the entirety of the administrative expenses.

(a) ADMINISTRATIVE EXPENSES

Sum in dispute (in US dollars)	Administrative expenses (*)
Up to 50,000	$2,000
From 50,001 to 100,000	3.00%
From 100,001 to 500,000	1.50%
From 500,001 to 1,000,000	1.00%
From 1,000,001 to 2,000,000	0.50%
From 2,000,001 to 5,000,000	0.20%
From 5,000,001 to 10,000,000	0.10%
From 10,000,001 to 80,000,000	0.05%
Over 80,000,000	$65,500

(*) (For illustrative purposes only, the table on the following page indicates the resulting administrative expenses in US $ when the proper calculations have been made.)

(b) ARBITRATOR'S FEES

Sum in dispute (in US dollars)				Fees (**) Minimum	Maximum
Up to	50,000			$2,000	15.00%
From	50,001	to	100,000	1.50%	10.00%
From	100,001	to	500,000	0.80%	5.00%
From	500,001	to	1,000,000	0.50%	3.00%
From	1,000,001	to	2,000,000	0.30%	2.50%
From	2,000,001	to	5,000,000	0.20%	0.30%
From	5,000,001	to	10,000,000	0.10%	0.50%
From	10,000,001	to	50,000,000	0.05%	0.15%
From	50,000,001	to	100,000,000	0.02%	0.10%
Over	100,000,000			0.01%	0.05%

(**) (For illustrative purposes only, the table on the following page indicates the resulting range of fees when the proper calculations have been made.)

A. ADMINISTRATIVE EXPENSES (*) (IN US DOLLARS) **B. ARBITRATOR'S FEES (**)** (IN US DOLLARS)

Sum in dispute (in US dollars)			Administrative expenses	Minimum	Maximum
Up to 50,000			2,000	2,000	15.00% of the sum in dispute
From	50,001 to	100,000	2,000 + 3.00% of amt. over 50,000	2,000 + 1.50% of amt. over 50,000	7,500 + 10.00% of amt. over 50,000
From	100,001 to	500,000	3,500 + 1.50% of amt. over 100,000	2,750 + 0.80% of amt. over 100,000	12,500 + 5.00% of amt. over 100,000
From	500,001 to	1,000,000	9,500 + 1.00% of amt. over 500,000	5,950 + 0.50% of amt. over 500,000	32,500 + 3.00% of amt. over 500,000
From	1,000,001 to	2,000,000	14,500 + 0.50% of amt. over 1,000,000	8,450 + 0.30% of amt. over 1,000,000	47,500 + 2.50% of amt. over 1,000,000
From	2,000,001 to	5,000,000	19,500 + 0.20% of amt. over 2,000,000	11,450 + 0.20% of amt. over 2,000,000	72,500 + 0.80% of amt. over 2,000,000
From	5,000,001 to	10,000,000	25,500 + 0.10% of amt. over 5,000,000	17,450 + 0.10% of amt. over 5,000,000	96,500 + 0.50% of amt. over 5,000,000
From	10,000,001 to	50,000,000	30,500 + 0.05% of amt. over 10,000,000	22,450 + 0.05% of amt. over 10,000,000	121,500 + 0.15% of amt. over 10,000,000
From	50,000,001 to	80,000,000	50,500 + 0.05% of amt. over 50,000,000	42,450 + 0.02% of amt. over 50,000,000	181,500 + 0.10% of amt. over 50,000,000
From	80,000,001 to	100,000,000	65,500	48,450 + 0.02% of amt. over 80,000,000	211,500 + 0.10% of amt. over 80,000,000
Over	100,000,000		65,500	52,450 + 0.01% of amt. over 100,000,000	231,500 + 0.05% of amt. over 100,000,000

(*) (**) See preceding page.

An example of a letter of instruction

Clear Case & Co
Claims House
Chancery Lane
London WC2

<u>STRICTLY PRIVATE & CONFIDENTIAL</u>

POS Hamilton
Abacus & Co
Rose Terrace
LONDON
EC4   10 February 1995

Dear Mr Hamilton

<u>JKL v WIZARD COMPUTERS LIMITED</u>

Further to our telephone conversation I confirm that we should like to instruct you on behalf of our clients as an independent expert in litigation which has arisen between our clients, Wizard Computers Limited, and JKL Limited. Our instructions are given on behalf of the clients and therefore you should look to our clients for payment of your fees rather than ourselves. In addition, our clients ask that both we and any professional firm whom we instruct should set out together with their bill details of the hours incurred and charging rates applied to them.

I enclose the following documentation:

1. Bundle of pleadings.
2. A List of Documents served by the Defendants.
3. Five bundles of discoverable documents as disclosed by JKL.

You are instructed as an accounting expert to advise on the quantum aspects of the claim. We have already instructed a computer expert, Mr Random Access, to advise on the questions of liability.

As you will see from the pleadings, the claim for damages arising from the alleged breach of contract and/or warranty is very generally pleaded at the moment. We have obtained an Order that Further and Better Particulars of this pleading be served by 24 February 1995. In addition, there is at present an Order that experts' reports on accounting evidence should be mutually exchanged within six months of 24 January 1995. Your report will have to be ready by the end of the week commencing 24 July 1995.

For the moment we should be grateful if you would review the discovery which is enclosed with this letter and write to us commenting on any deficiencies in it and any further documentation which you feel is required.

Upon service of the Further and Better Particulars by JKL, we shall also be passing these to you for your comments and consideration.

There are a further ten bundles of discovery supplied by JKL. The bundles which we enclose amount to section A which consists of the documentation specifically relating to the Wizard Computers contract. The other ten bundles relate to contracts between JKL and its customers. As their claim for loss includes claims in respect of loss of profit on sales to these customers, these further bundles will also need to be considered by you. However we have not sent them to you at this stage because it was felt they were somewhat peripheral. Rather than incur separate photocopying costs in respect of those bundles, we shall lend you our only copies of these documents when you are ready to review them. I trust that these arrangements will be in order and look forward to hearing from you with your initial comments on the discovery.

Yours sincerely

An example of terms of reference and fee arrangements

RDJ Mackenzie Esq
Clear Case & Co
Claims House
Chancery Lane
London   1 February 1995
WC2

Dear Mr Mackenzie

RAPID CONSTRUCTION PLC v HIGH STREET PROPERTIES LIMITED

We were very interested to hear what you and Mr Fisher of High Street Properties had to say on Monday about the dispute between your client and Rapid Construction. We have now had the opportunity to read the pleadings and other background papers which you gave to us, and are now able to comment on our perspective of the case and how we can assist you in defending the quantum of Rapid Construction's claim.

The Multistore development – background to the claim

We note that your client engaged Rapid Construction to act as main contractors in the Multistore shopping precinct development following the submission of competitive tenders and that Rapid Construction were awarded the contract on 3 May 1993. You have confirmed that the contract followed the JCT80 form.

Six months after the building commenced, the local authority ordered works to be suspended to allow them to carry out emergency repairs to an adjacent road. Rapid Construction have served on High Street Properties a claim for direct loss and expenses arising from the disruption amounting to £1,575,110. The claim can be divided into the following three principal categories:

		£
(a)	Additional direct costs	645,110
(b)	Additional overheads	530,000
(c)	Loss of profit	400,000
		£1,575,110

You require us to examine the claim and report to you as follows:

(a) What part of the claim for additional direct costs can be supported by adequate documentary evidence?

(b) Whether the claim for overheads is reasonable?

(c) Whether there are any grounds for the claim for loss of profits?

(d) What further documents of the plaintiff ought to be discoverable in this case?

You have indicated that the dispute may ultimately be argued over in court and that our report should therefore be prepared for the purpose of exhibiting in court.

Cost and fee arrangements

As we explained to you at our meeting, given the nature of this dispute it is not possible at the outset to give you an indication of what our total charges will be. Our fees will depend on the time necessarily incurred on the work and the grades of staff which are needed to carry out the work.

Our scale rate charges which will apply to this case for the period to 31 December 1995 are as follows:

	Scale rates per hour £
Partners	200
Managers	110
Senior assistants	75
Junior assistants	40

In addition, we would charge VAT and any out-of-pocket expenses. We would propose to submit bills to you for settlement on a monthly basis. We attach a copy of our standard terms for assignments charged on an hourly basis.

We hope this provides the information you require. We look forward to receiving your confirmation that our understanding of your requirements is correct and that the fee arrangements are in order.

Yours sincerely

ATTACHMENT TO FEE ARRANGEMENT LETTER

Standard terms for assignments charged on an hourly basis

1. Hourly fee rates are based upon the grade of staff to be used and the length of their experience. Unless specified to the contrary, fee rates do not cover the cost of travelling, accommodation and other out-of-pocket expenses incurred in connection with the client's business, or the costs of preparing reports. The actual costs incurred are therefore charged in addition to our fees.

2. Fee rates are varied from time to time. If the rates change during the term of an assignment we reserve the right to charge the amended rates.

3. It is assumed that the person accepting our proposal has the necessary authority to do so and has complied with any internal procedures before making the commitment. We normally expect to be instructed by our client and to be paid directly by him.

4. If our client is a company resident abroad, or is previously unknown to us, we expect to be paid by the solicitor instructing us, or in advance or by letter of credit drawn on a London bank. In any event, we always expect to be paid in sterling.

5. Prior to the start of the assignment, a monthly payment on account schedule may be agreed with the client. Invoices are payable on presentation. Any queries concerning an invoice must be raised within 30 days of the invoice date. In the event that invoices, whenever rendered, are not settled by the due date, we reserve the right to charge compound interest monthly at 3% above National Westminster Bank base rate until the debt is settled.

6. Subject to any legal requirements regarding evidence and discovery, we undertake to treat confidentially any information we may obtain regarding the business activities of the client. This obligation devolves upon all members of our staff individually and is a condition of their contract of service.

Expert accountant's report on consequential loss claim: example

TOTEM APPLIANCES LTD v VCM LTD

Evidence by
DONALD LEMAR COOPER FCA
February 1995

CONTENTS

Introduction

Section		Paragraphs
1	THE CLAIM	1–3
2	METHODOLOGY	4–10
3	INDIVIDUAL HEADS OF CLAIM	11–41
4	CONCLUSIONS	42–48

Appendix
I	The Report of Check & Chide	(Not attached)
II	Monthly Management Reports – extracts	(,, ,,)
III	Management Accounts and Budgets – extracts	(,, ,,)
IV	Graphs of Sales, Margins, Stock Levels and Output	(Attached)
V	Back Order Totals, 1990–92	(Attached)
VI	Canterbury Weekly Output, 1990–92	(Not attached)
VII	Stock Figures, 1990–92	(,, ,,)
VIII	Totem Published Accounts 1991/92	(,, ,,)
IX	Analysis of Intercompany Charges	(,, ,,)
X	Further Particulars Requested from the Plaintiffs and Their Advisers	(,, ,,)
XI	Plans of the Canterbury Factory	(,, ,,)

TOTEM APPLIANCES LTD v VCM LTD AND OTHERS

EVIDENCE OF DONALD LEMAR COOPER

I am a Fellow of the Institute of Chartered Accountants in England and Wales and also a Fellow of the Institute of Cost & Management Accountants. I graduated with an economics degree from London University in 1959. I am a partner in the firm of Value & Chance, Chartered Accountants, of 10 Cheapside, London EC2V 8AH; I became a partner in 1970. I am partner in charge of the Investigation Department of my firm. I advise the Electrical Trade Council on government contract negotiations and have held that appointment for five years. I have written the leading textbook on Costing for Widgets.

My experience has included the examination of claims for insurance compensation or government assistance in connection with interruptions to production caused by external or internal events. My experience also includes acting as independent expert witness in connection with such claims.

I first became conversant with the claim of Totem Appliances Limited (Totem) when, as an independent party, I was asked by Mr Charles Charles early in November 1993 to consider and advise on the basis and substance of the claim. Since that date, I and my staff have studied the papers relating to that claim; we have visited the site of the Canterbury factory of Totem, have spoken to the professional advisers of Totem and generally made every effort to become acquainted with the roof fall incident which occurred in March 1991 and from which the claim stems. We have reviewed the company's records for 1991/92 and also those of the preceding and subsequent years.

We have arranged the statement of evidence under four sections set out as follows:

Section 1 – describes the claim itself and the events leading to the claim.

Section 2 – examines critically the methodology followed in the claim.

Section 3 – deals with each item under the heads of claim and indicates our views on the validity of each main item.

Section 4 – gives our conclusions.

SECTION 1 – THE CLAIM

1 The event which caused the claim is well known to all participants and can usefully be summarised as follows:

(a) On Sunday 18 March 1991, following an exceptional snowfall and freezing weather conditions, one bay of the Canterbury factory suffered from the partial collapse of the roof ('the incident').

(b) Action was quickly taken to prop up the damaged sections of the roof and then to reorganise the production facilities and generally enable the factory to return to normal working. The warehouse was occupied by production departments, which necessitated the renting of outside storage space for both production stores and finished goods stores. See Appendix XI for plans of the factory. [Not attached.]

(c) Production was restarted one week later on 26 March 1991. Energetic steps were taken to raise output to its previous high level and then to maintain it during rebuilding. The manufacture of certain components was put out to sub-contractors. Other sub-assemblies were imported from Totem plants in Spain.

(d) Rebuilding work commenced in July 1991. The work was substantially completed by 21 December 1991 and the new building was fully re-occupied by the beginning of February 1992.

2 The heads of claim and sums claimed, amounting in total to £2.7m, are set out below. These are taken from a report prepared by Check & Chide, dated 5 January 1995, which we attach as Appendix I. [Not attached.]

Statement of claim schedule number	Summary of costs claimed	Amount £
1	Initial costs of clearing the damaged area, propping up the roof and relocating the affected operations to other parts of the factory	540,566
2	Cost of repairing the roof	874,609
3	Consequential loss of profit, calculated on the basis that an estimated 100,889 units failed to be manufactured and sold as a result of the incident	964,451
4	Inter-company support – additional cost of certain components bought from sister company in Spain in substitution for production lost through inefficient working in the period following the incident	288,629
	TOTAL CLAIM	£2,668,255

3 We have had the opportunity of talking with Mr Clive Debra, a partner in Check & Chide, and one of his colleagues who has been concerned with the verification work behind that report. We have reviewed their work in depth at the offices of the solicitors to the plaintiffs. Clearly Check & Chide have done a considerable amount of meticulous work in agreeing sums included in the claim with invoices from outside suppliers, and have also carefully checked the arithmetic accuracy of the various sections of the claim. We have ourselves carried out such checks on the claim, in terms of evidential support and arithmetic accuracy, as we considered necessary. There is third party documentation which corroborates a high proportion of the amount claimed under each heading. This observation does not in any way imply that the amounts claimed are properly claimed, but merely acknowledges that there is some evidence that most of the costs described have been incurred (apart from the labour transfer costs referred to elsewhere in this report, and the consequential loss of volume) and that their allocation to the various heads of claim is prima facie reasonable. The remainder of our report is therefore, to a large extent, a commentary on the justification, or otherwise, of claiming for costs actually incurred.

SECTION 2 – METHODOLOGY

4 The purpose in making any accounting calculations of his loss should be to put the plaintiff back into the position in which he would have been had the incident not taken place and not to leave him better off as a result of the incident. In making this observation we would like specifically to refer to some of the points of principle which appear to us to arise in the claim as presented by Totem.

(a) Firstly we disagree with the basic assumption on which the consequential loss portion of the claim, a substantial portion, is based. This assumption, which has not been substantiated in any meaningful way by Totem, is that lost production led directly to the loss of an equivalent volume of sales. Evidence so far available to us demonstrates that Totem's retail customers obtained all the goods they required during the crucial early summer months of 1991. This was due both to the ready availability of stocks of finished goods, in Totem's own warehouses (see Appendix VII) [not attached] and with their wholesalers, and to the remarkable speed with which production recovered to planned levels at Canterbury.

(b) For the purposes of the claim, supplies from an overseas affiliate should be costed in such a manner as to enable that affiliate to recover any costs which would not otherwise have been incurred, ie, marginal costs, but not to enable it to make even a normal overhead contribution on the increased volume occasioned by helping out the Canterbury factory.

(c) Totem have disregarded the betterment which has undoubtedly occurred in rebuilding the factory. The most striking example of this is the roof itself, where improvement has arisen from replacing a 20-year-old structure with one which is brand new.

(d) Totem is a manufacturing company without a fluctuating workforce. Looking at both manufacturing and general administrative overheads, we find that these follow a normal pattern for this type of manufacturing company, that is, they are not immediately affected by the volume of business being transacted. Given such a background, we cannot accept that extra claims should be made for such overheads where they have not increased as a result of the accident. Nor should there be claims for labour costs that were not due to an increase resulting from the incident. The plaintiff employed no more labour as a result of the roof fall, and it is only additional costs with which the claim should be concerned. There is clear evidence of duplication here.

The above is not a full list of the points of principle which have arisen. We come back to each of them when commenting on the relevant items of the claim in section 3, when their significance will become clearer.

5 An integral part of our review is the test of 'overall reasonableness'. There are certain steps which need to be taken in order to be satisfied that the claim falls within the likely maximum/minimum range of loss caused by the incident.

(a) The first step is to examine the company's historical performance and to establish whether the results, both before and after the inclusion of the revenue elements of the claim, look reasonable in relation to the year of loss.

(b) The second step is to examine the accounts and the budgets for the year of loss and to see how the actual results compared with the original budgets and any revisions to the budgets prior to the incident giving rise to the claim. It is also useful to examine here the experience of previous years, so as to establish the general reliability of the forecasting procedures.

(c) The third step is to examine the market environment in which the company has operated and is expected to operate in the future, to judge to what extent sales would be likely to be irretrievably lost (eg, through reduced market share) if factory supplies were temporarily interrupted and to identify the likely beneficiaries in the market place.

6 Let us take first an examination on the lines of (a) above. Totem's turnover and pre-tax profit for each of the four years to 30 September 1993 according to the UK published accounts of Totem can be summarised as follows:

	1989/90	*1990/91*	*1991/92*	*1992/93*
	£m	£m	£m	£m
Turnover	78.2	102.6	117.9	122.2
Pre-tax profit	8.8	14.0	13.1	12.4
Profit as % of turnover	11.3%	13.6%	11.1%	10.1%

7 It will be seen that, far from showing a profits setback for the year of the claim (1990/91), the company forged ahead, achieving peaks of both profits and margins that have not been reached before or since. The upward trend of profits and margins in the year of the incident becomes even more pronounced if the 'exceptional costs' which the company originally identified and charged in its management accounts as being caused by the incident, are added back:

	1989/90	*1990/91*	*1991/92*	*1992/93*
	£m	£m	£m	£m
Turnover	78.2	102.6	117.9	122.2
Pre-tax profit, restated to elimi-nate roof fall costs (b)	8.8	15.0	16.0	12.4
Restated profit as % of turnover	11.3%	14.6%	13.6%	10.1%

8 Let us now make a comparison on the lines of paragraph 5b above, ie, between original budgeted and actual profits and turnover in the year of the incident. In this instance the statistics are based on the more directly relevant management accounts of Totem.

Expert accountant's report on consequential loss claim: example

		1989/90	1990/91	1991/92	1992/93
	Sales Comparisons	£m	£m	£m	£m
1	Budgeted sales	70.0	78.0	111.0	115.0
2	Actual sales	78.2	102.6	117.9	122.2
	Pre-tax Profit				
3	Budgeted	8.0	8.8	12.9	13.5
4	Actual	8.8	14.0	13.1	12.4
5	Restated	8.8	15.0	16.0	12.4
	Marginal Comparisons				
6	Budgeted net income as % of budgeted sales	11.4%	11.3%	11.6%	11.7%
7	Actual net income as % of actual sales	11.3%	13.6%	11.1%	10.1%
8	Restated net income as % of actual sales	11.3%	14.6%	13.6%	10.1%

9   It will be observed that, with the exception of the year of the claim, budgets prepared by management for both sales and net income were sufficiently close to the actual results to lend credibility to the established forecasting procedures. For 1990/91, however, net income of £14.0m is 59.1% above that originally budgeted, and the margin on sales, 13.6%, is 20.4% higher than the margin originally budgeted. Eliminating 'exceptional costs' (ie, those roof fall costs identified in the management accounts for the period) raises the restated sales margin to 14.6%, some 29.2% higher than the previous year's actual margin of 11.3%. A graph comparing actual and budgeted sales in the period January to June 1991 is at Appendix IV.

10   Based on these tests and before examining any of the detailed financial evidence it is difficult to avoid the conclusion that exaggeration has entered into the formulation of the claim. In the next section we examine the individual heads of claim as best we can, although, given the time which has elapsed since the incident, and the recent origin of some aspects of the claim, no precision was achievable; nor was it possible to reconcile the conclusions we reached in our detailed examination with the overall impressions derived from the above exercises.

SECTION 3 – INDIVIDUAL HEADS OF CLAIM

Schedule 1.   Initial roof fall costs £540,566

11   Totem claim that the costs of propping up the damaged area of roof and of reorganising the manufacturing operations totalled £540,566. These are analysed below. The greater part of these costs was incurred in the brief period immediately following the incident.

	Paragraph	£	£
Propping up and making safe damaged area of roof	12		158,159
Movement of production sections from affected area	13		144,667
Labour costs	14		
First week's wages		175,089	
Overhead charges on above (estimated)		17,000	
Labour 'wasted'		52,185	
			244,274
Damage and scrap	15		5,511
			552,611
Deduct: Rate rebate			(12,045)
			£540,566

12   Roofbuild did the initial work involved in making the factory safe after the collapse. This part of the claim includes their costs, plus additional insurance premiums. We believe that the costs claimed are by and large relevant and that the total is not unreasonable in the circumstances.

13   Costs of moving the production sections include the amounts paid to outside contractors. Given the speed of the relocation, the costs may occasionally not have been kept to a minimum. They also include internal labour costs. We have seen no evidence to indicate that extra staff had been taken on by Totem nor that existing staff had to work overtime as a result of the incident. Indeed, we understand that many of the staff were sent home for the first week. Totem incurred no additional payroll costs. Instead continuing costs were allocated differently as a result of the incident. We take the view that those labour costs that were not an increase resulting from the incident should not be included in the claim.

14   Quite apart from this objection in principle, we noted that the charges for labour were not well evidenced. We have seen no formal documentation which records staff transfers and which would enable the accounts department to reallocate the labour costs as appropriate.

15   We have not checked the claim for damage and scrap or for the rate rebate. However, we do not believe any material misstatement is likely to have occurred here.

16   Our conclusions on this schedule of the claim are:

(a) external costs totalling approximately £300,000 are generally well-evidenced and appear valid; however,

(b) labour costs of approximately £244,000 are not relevant in principle and not well evidenced in practice.

Schedule 2.   Cost of roof repair £874,609

17   The cost of repairing the roof can be summarised as follows:

	Paragraph	£
Roofbuild – main contract	18	719,425
Electrical and plumbing services	18	42,481
Consulting engineers	18	93,906
Strengthening roof above general office	19	18,797
		874,609

18   The roof rebuild was put out to tender and Roofbuild Limited quoted the lowest price. We have seen the invoices and tenders. The electrical and plumbing services were reinstated using the existing piping and wiring wherever possible. The charges by the consulting engineers comprise those of Newey & Wilton and the other consultants who assisted them.

19   The strengthening of the roof above the former general office took place in September 1992, nine months after the reconstruction of the Phase 1 extension was completed. The long delay between completion of the main reconstruction and this further strengthening of the roof prompts us to doubt whether this additional cost was a direct result of the incident.

20   The claim at present includes the full cost of the expenditure on the new roof. It seems to us that this is excessive on three counts:

(a) The roof's useful life has been extended by at least a further ten years, by virtue of its reconstruction in 1992, 20 years after its original construction. The rate of depreciation adopted in the accounts was 2% per annum, on cost, which suggests a 40% reduction against the replacement cost claimed.

(b) There are areas where the new roof is an improvement on the old. We have noted:

  (i) the removal of the general office to the West side of the plant improved the flow of materials;

  (ii) the heat treatment area was walled in, which reduced heat loss to the rest of the factory. (This had been recommended by consultants in 1989.)

(c) Roofbuild erroneously submitted two invoices, each for £25,000, for Phase 3 of the repairs. Subsequently a credit note was issued to cancel the second invoice. Both invoices have been included in the amount claimed but no reduction has been made for the credit note. The cost of Phase 3 of the repairs is therefore overstated by £25,000.

21   We conclude that, while the evidence for this head of claim is good, a reduction of 40%, or £320,000, should be made to reflect the extended life of the new roof, with a further reduction of, say, £45,000 to allow for the improvements noted at para **20** above. £25,000, claimed twice, should be removed from the cost of Phase 3 of the repairs. This would leave the claim at £485,000 which we feel is reasonable, subject to the comments of the engineers.

Schedule 3.   Consequential loss claim £964,451

22   The consequential loss claim is based upon Totem's estimate of the shortfall of production attributable to the incident, in the 12 weeks from 19 March 1991 to 8 June 1991. This shortfall of 100,889 units has been allocated between products as follows:

Product	Units of production 'lost'	Contribution per unit	Consequential loss
		£	£
Electric Fires	40,075	11.19	448,439
Fan Heaters	20,775	8.72	181,158
Hair Dryers	2,238	6.34	14,189
Microwave Ovens	10,595	10.79	114,320
Transistors	15,803	7.49	118,364
Shavers	11,263	7.71	86,838
Miscellaneous	140	8.16	1,143
	100,889		£964,451

23   It is fundamental to any review of estimates such as these that the validity of the assumptions on which they are based should be subject to critical appraisal. We have also to be satisfied that the estimates are consistent with, and have been properly compiled on the footing of, those assumptions.

24   The detailed assumptions underlying the claim for loss of production and sales are set out in Appendix 3 of the Check & Chide report (see Appendix I). [Not attached.] The underlying concepts adopted are:

(a)   that lost production is equal to lost sales;
(b)   that planned and achievable production was at least 12,000 units per day;
(c)   that the products chosen to evaluate the lost production are representative of the products that would have been made and sold;
(d)   that the production mix, which occurred during the period of disruption and is being used to evaluate the claim, is similar to that expected, had the roof incident not taken place.

We deal below with each of these in turn [for illustration, only (a) and (b) are included below].

(a) Lost production is equal to lost sales

25   We discussed assumption (a) above at some length with Totem staff, but failed to be convinced that it was reasonable. Totem place much emphasis upon the increase in unsatisfied orders ('back orders') which, it is claimed, took place between the roof incident and the end of April; the general line of argument is that, if the number of unsatisfied orders increased during the relevant period, then the alleged lost production could easily have been turned into sales. It is noteworthy that no written evidence has been given to us or to Check & Chide, to support any of the foregoing. There are no records of instructions to the sales force that even hint at a reduced sales effort in the late spring and early summer of 1991. All the indirect evidence which we review below is either neutral or suggests that Totem recovered quickly from the production interruption and that they suffered no real setback in the market place. We think it would be useful to deal specifically with such indirect evidence as there is on the back orders argument.

26   We have examined the back order records of the company for the years 1990–92, as reported in monthly management reports for all the products made at Canterbury. An extract is shown in Appendix V attached to this report. The two most significant products in the plaintiff's claim are fires and fan heaters which account for approximately half the claim under this schedule, so we have set out below the record of back orders for these products:

	Back Orders	
	Fires	*Heaters*
1990/91	£'000	£'000
At month end		
October	638	223
November	799	117
December	361	118
January	281	252
February	195	428
March	538	372
April	693	192
May	282	83
June	122	110
July/August	703	121
September	298	82

27   Taking fires first, there was a rise in back orders towards the end of March 1991 which were then at an average level of £487,000 during the two following months of April and May 1991. A comparison with the back order position in October/November 1990 (£700,000) or with July/August 1991 (£700,000) reveals that this was a normal fluctuation, ie, within a normal range of seasonal experience. It demonstrates the typical capability of such a company to plan production and sales with a high degree of tolerance built in for the ups and downs in stock levels and in demand levels all through the pipeline from retail shelf stock back to the production line itself.

28   An examination of the statistics for heaters demonstrates a similar pattern. Back orders were at a seasonal high in February, a month before the roof incident,

and were brought down rapidly to 'normal' levels in March and April 1991.
Again, any interruption to production should have been easily accommodated in
the pipeline.

29 Looking back to the statistics of 1989/90 or forward to those of 1991/92 we
found a similar pattern of experience emerging. The following stock figures
demonstrate both the magnitude of stocks and the stability of the stock position at
this time:

	Finished Stocks	*Parts Stock*
1991	£m	£m
End of February	6.2	
March	6.9	·Information
April	6.9	not available
May	7.1	

30 We have not yet been able to get a breakdown of stocks by individual
product lines; neither have we been provided with the statistics revealing the
stock position of their wholesalers and retailers. However, discussions with
Totem personnel indicate that there is little written evidence to contradict the
conclusion we have reached that little if any permanent loss of sales followed the
interruption to production occasioned by the roof fall. Since Totem hold around
30% of the relevant markets, and since production was only interrupted for such
a short time, it seems likely that disappointed prospective customers, if any,
would merely have postponed their purchases rather than foregone them
altogether.

(b) Achievable production was 12,000 units per day

31 The assumed production of 12,000 units per day is in our view overstated.
We attach as Appendix IV production figures by week for the whole of 1983,
which show a production level during the 12 weeks before the roof incident
averaging 10,227 units per day compared with 11,194 units per day after it, an
increase of 9.5%.

32 Totem say that 12,000 units per day represents the 'planned level' of
production. Unfortunately, the crucial production plans for the months covering
the incident period are lost; in any case, it is more realistic to deal with the
actual production achieved on a continuing basis than with hypothetical
projections.

33 It is noteworthy that during the 12 weeks following the incident no weekend
or other overtime was worked; furthermore, the Canterbury factory was closed for
a total of eight days' holiday over this period. Clearly Totem at the time did not
feel it necessary, at relatively modest cost, to make an effort to offset the loss of
production by such measures. We think that the inventory on hand was sufficient
to tide them over the period of interruption.

Conclusion on the consequential item

34 In principle, this item of claim is not justified. To the extent that production losses did occur they led only to delayed, not lost, sales. We feel, therefore, that the claim should be reduced in full.

Schedule 4. Intercompany support: manufactured parts £288,629

35 In order to reach planned production levels at Canterbury through to February 1992, Totem imported assemblies from their associate in Spain. The full amount charged to Totem was £698,000, of which it is claimed that the cost, over and above normal cost, amounted to £288,629. Details appear in Appendix IX. [Not attached.]

36 We have been supplied with very little information about Spanish costs to support invoiced prices. Totem were able to tell us only that 'as far as they knew' Spanish prices excluded profit, and that they believed that costing structures were similar to those in the UK. Check & Chide have yet to complete their research into the prices charged. Since nearly four years have elapsed since the incident, we find this lack of information surprising.

37 In arriving at our conclusions on this section, we have therefore assumed that:

(a) Spanish charges represent full 'manufactured cost', and not simply direct variable cost or even marginal cost. That is, they recovered material, labour, variable overheads and fixed manufacturing overheads in the normal way.

(b) The charges exclude any contribution to administration, selling or financing costs, and, of course, any element of profit; this needs to be verified.

(c) The Spanish costing structure is broadly similar to that in the United Kingdom, albeit that costs are higher in absolute terms.

38 We have reviewed the costings of a sample of each of the UK major product lines and have noted a consistent cost-structure as follows:

	% of cost
Material	36
Labour	24
Variable overheads	10
Direct variable cost	70
Fixed manufacturing overheads	30
Manufactured cost	100

39 In arriving at the net claim, Totem have deducted United Kingdom *direct variable* costs from Spanish *manufactured* costs and to this extent the claim includes an unwarranted contribution to Spanish fixed manufacturing overheads. We consider the claim should be reduced in this respect by £209,000, being 30% of the total invoiced costs of £698,000 from Spain.

40   We now turn to the treatment of labour and material costs in the claim. We have established, following discussions with Señor Jerez, Totem's chief accountant in Spain, that no additional overtime was worked in the Spanish plant in order to satisfy the orders from Canterbury. On the basis that the Spanish company absorbed the UK demand without incurring additional labour costs, we consider that the Spanish labour content of the charge (24% × £698,000 = £168,000) should be excluded from the claim. For the same reason Totem need not then reduce the claim by their own Canterbury labour costs (24/70 × £426,000 = £146,000).

41   Our conclusions on this schedule can be summarised as follows:

		£'000	£'000
Claim			289
less:	fixed manufacturing overheads		(209)
add:	UK labour costs incorrectly deducted	146	
less:	Spanish labour costs	(168)	
			(22)
			58

SECTION 4 – CONCLUSIONS

42   Although the plaintiffs have produced extensive documentary information supporting the various detailed aspects of their claim, they have not, in our view, attempted to justify several of the fundamental assumptions used in formulating the claim. In particular:

(a)   Labour costs totalling some £261,000 have been included on various schedules. These are merely a re-allocation of costs from other cost-centres. They do not represent additional costs attributable to the roof fall incident, as they would have been incurred by Totem in any event.

(b)   As evidence that sales were lost as a result of reduced production we would normally expect to see board or departmental minutes recording concern at the company's threatened trading position, together with irate correspondence from customers or even cancelled orders or threatened litigation by customers. No such evidence has been produced. On the contrary, the public impression presented by the company was at the time, and continues to be, that, with the support of a co-operative work force, they overcame the problems with quite remarkable speed.

(c)   The roof re-build extends the useful life well beyond that originally envisaged.

43   We summarise below our comment on other aspects of the claim, and then in para **45**, evaluate the parts of the claim that we consider at this stage are justified, or unjustified.

(a)   Even without adjusting for the roof fall costs, Totem's reported profits before tax reached a peak in 1990/91 in absolute terms and as a percentage of sales. This achievement is particularly difficult to reconcile with a serious and permanent loss of sales.

(b)   Throughout the relevant period of the claim, production was at a very high level. The crucial evidence that it should have been even higher, the Canterbury production programme, has been lost.

(c)   If necessary to meet demand, production could easily have been stepped up by introducing overtime working and changing holiday arrangements. No overtime was worked.

(d)   We believe that import prices include a significant contribution to the Spanish associate's overheads and profits. The basis of the charges is currently being investigated by Check & Chide.

44   At this stage a considerable number of further particulars is required from Totem or their advisers. This is set out, in detail, in Appendix X [not attached].

45   In the table that follows we summarise, under each head of claim, those costs which we consider are properly included and those for which there is little or no satisfactory supporting evidence. It will be seen that we consider there are grounds for reducing the claim by up to £1,829,000.

Appendix L

Schedule of claim no	Description	Paragraph	Claim	Amount not justified	Amount justified
			£'000	£'000	£'000
1	Initial roof-fall costs	16	540	244	296
2	Cost of new roof	21	875	390	485
3	Consequential loss	34	964	964	NIL
4	Intercompany support	41	289	231	58
			2,668	1,829	839

Taxation aspects

46 We have not, at this stage, considered the taxation implications of any settlement. These could be of significance to the plaintiff and the defendants, and should be studied carefully at a later date.

Contributory negligence

47 The questions of contributory negligence and the division of alleged liability between plaintiff and defendants are outside our terms of reference and we have not considered them.

Finally

48 On behalf of my staff, and myself, I should like to express our thanks for the courteous and willing help we have received from the staff of Totem, and from their advisers at Lewin, Lagerberg & Co and Check & Chide.

DLC
1 February 1995

Appendix IV

TOTEM – A graph showing the daily production of units from 1 December 1990 to 8 June 1991

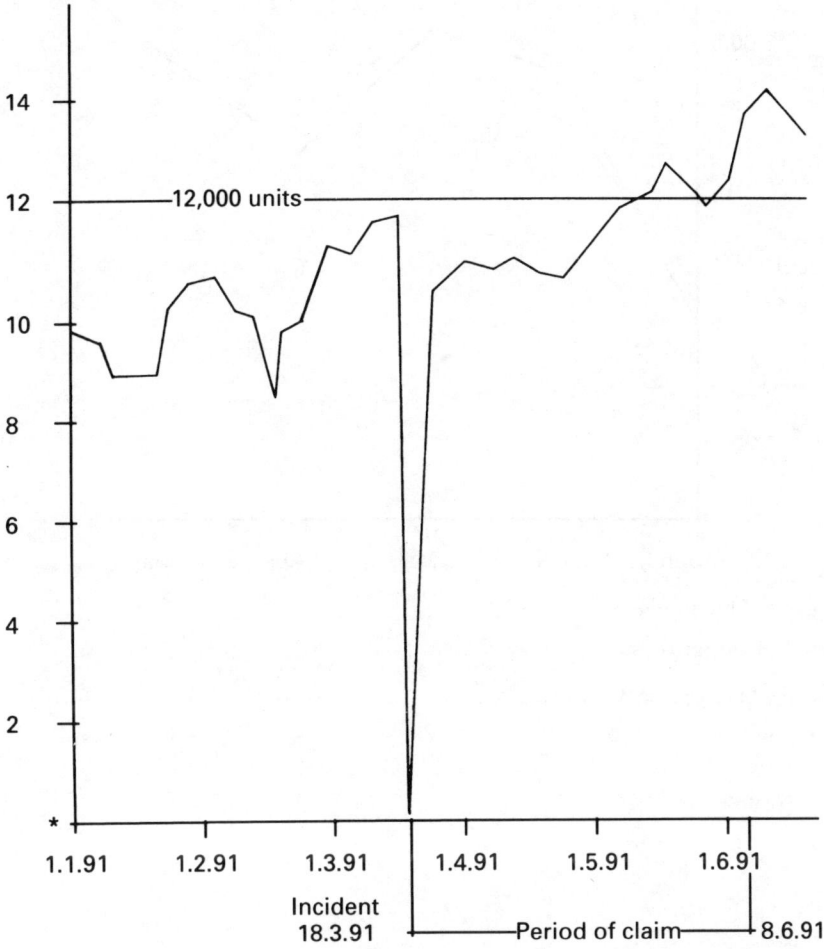

Source: Weekly production reports divided by the number of working days in each week.

TOTEM – A graph comparing actual and budgeted sales in the period January to June 1991 (see paragraph 9 of the main report)

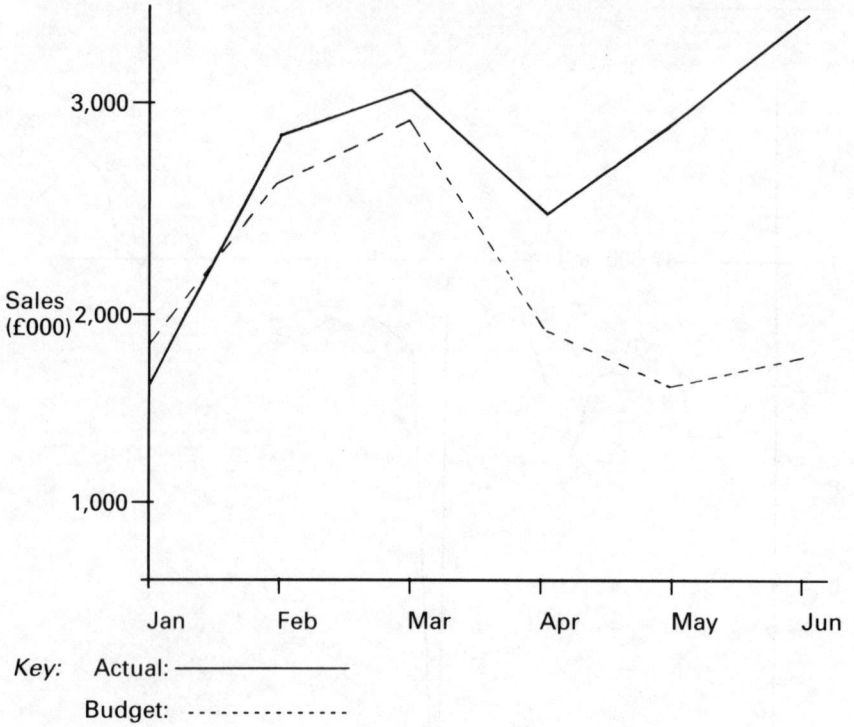

Key: Actual: ————————

         Budget: - - - - - - - - - - -

Source: Management Accounts.

Appendix V

TOTEM – A schedule of the value of monthly back orders from October 1990 to September 1991 (see paragraph 26 of the main report)

(a) for all Totem products, and

(b) for those products included in the claim

	Month	Total back orders	Back orders for products included in the claim
1990/91	October	1,677	1,048
	November	1,949	1,021
	December	1,198	654
	January	2,509	1,396
	February	2,644	1,844
	March	3,323	2,603
	April	3,520	2,876
	May	2,823	2,270
	June	2,170	1,938
	July	1,609	1,545
	August	907	844
	September	514	432
1991/92	October	3,224	2,465
	November	3,489	2,393
	December	3,031	2,087
	January	3,312	2,898
	February	3,314	3,102
	March	2,889	2,572
	April	1,876	1,805
	May	2,439	2,049
	June	225	188
	July	1,229	1,033
	August	988	926
	September	830	738

Source: Monthly back orders reports.

357

Expert accountant's report on compensation claim: example

RE CLARKE AND SMITH

V

BARSET COUNTY COUNCIL

REPORT TO BARSET COUNTY COUNCIL (DECEMBER 1994)

TAYLOR & TAMWORTH
Chartered Accountants

Peartree Court
London EC4

Telephone 0171 583 5000

County Solicitor
Barset County Council
County Hall
Top Lane
Barford
BR1 2DH

27 December 1994

Dear Sir

Clarke and Smith v Barset County Council

1 My name is Christopher Maltravers of Peartree Court, London EC4. I am a Fellow of the Institute of Chartered Accountants in England and Wales and a partner in the firm of Taylor & Tamworth, Chartered Accountants. I was admitted a member of the Institute of Chartered Accountants in England and Wales in 1977 and became a partner in Taylor & Tamworth in October 1986. I have been concerned with audits and special work including financial investigation. Since 1984 I have in the main specialised in examining and reporting on financial aspects of disputes of various kinds including claims for loss of profits from business disruption and valuations.

2 In accordance with your instructions and in connection with a claim for compensation under section 5 of the Land Compensation Act 1961 I have examined the financial information available to me in respect of the following businesses:

The Paper Shop (3 Barford Road);
The Pie Shop (4 Barford Road).

3 The purpose of my examination has been:

(a) to give a view on the business of the retail shops as drawn from the accounts provided;
(b) to comment on the net profitability of the businesses;
(c) to comment on the saleability of the businesses; and
(d) to assess the value of goodwill attaching to The Paper Shop and The Pie Shop.

4 I have not considered the affairs of the photocopier business at 6 Barford Road. I do not comment on the values of the freeholds.

Background to claim

5 The claims are made following a road widening scheme affecting Barford Road in which Barset County Council acquired under a compulsory purchase order part of the forecourts of the properties identified above.

6 I note that Section 5 of the Land Compensation Act lays down the rules for assessing compensation in respect of any compulsory action and I have taken these rules into account when considering the values to be attached to the relevant businesses in the remainder of my report.

Format of this report

7 This report is divided into two sections as follows:

	Paragraphs
Section I: The Paper Shop	101–129
Section II: The Pie Shop	201–221

Nature of financial information available

8 I describe in the individual sections of the report the nature of the financial information available to me for the purpose of my review. None of the financial accounts presented in this case has been audited and it is impossible to say what adjustments might have been made to the accounts had they been audited. I do however note some unusual features in the accounts that have been provided which might have given rise to audit adjustments had the accounts been subject to audit. Apart from those specific matters, I have taken the accounts at their face value for the purpose of my review and evaluation.

I THE PAPER SHOP (3 BARFORD ROAD)

101 The Paper Shop trades as a newspaper shop. It also sells confectionery and tobacco. It was formerly owned by Mr A Black and it should be noted that as at

August 1994 the name board over the shop still carried the names of Mr and Mrs Black.

102 The accounts of the business which are available to me are for the three years ended 30 June 1990, at which time it was owned by Mr Black and for the 13½ month period ended 31 July 1992.

103 I presume that the accounts for the period ending 31 July 1992 are the first accounts of The Paper Shop under the management of Mrs Clarke and Mrs Smith. I conclude from this that the business was acquired by Clarke and Smith from Black in mid-June 1991. I have seen no accounts for the period 1 July 1990 to mid-June 1991.

104 Other than the accounts referred to above, the only financial information available to me is an analysis of monthly turnover from July 1991 to December 1992 prepared by Tent & Co and a copy of the schedule of wholesale news charges rendered to the Blacks for the week ending 28 February 1991. The wholesaler charged £3,759.76 plus levies of £21.28. The charge sheet indicates that the retail value of newspapers and periodicals supplied amounted to £5,176.72. This information indicates to me that the gross margin on newspapers and periodicals could have been as high as 26%. However, in arriving at this figure, I have assumed that all stock purchased would have been sold. I accept that there may be some stock which could not be sold nor returned to the wholesaler. In such instances the proprietors would have to bear the wholesale cost themselves, and this would have a depressing effect on the gross margin.

105 If it is assumed that the newspaper and periodical purchases in the week ending 28 February 1991 were typical of the year as a whole, this would suggest that the potential annual sales of newspapers and periodicals by The Paper Shop in or around 1991 was of the order of £260,000 to £270,000 (£5,177 × 52 weeks = £269,204). It also suggests to me that such sales comprised about one-third of the business's total annual sales. (Total sales were £795,188 in the year to 30 June 1990.)

106 On pp 362–363 I set out the trading and profit and loss accounts for The Paper Shop for those periods where accounts are available to me. I have extracted the information directly from those accounts. As the final accounts are for a 13½ month period I have also shown what these accounts would have looked like if pro-rated for a 12 month period. For this purpose I have assumed that all revenue and costs vary directly with time. It is inevitably an approximation. I make the following comments about the results of the business as displayed by these accounts.

Sales turnover

107 The accounts for 1988, 1989 and 1990 show a steady growth in annual sales of between 5% and 7%, marginally ahead of retail price inflation in those years. Retail prices increased by about 6% between 1990 and 1991 and 4% between 1991 and 1992 (9.8% over the two years). If it is assumed that sales by The Paper Shop continued to increase marginally above the rate of inflation, say 11% between 1990 and 1992, then the sales for the 12 months to June 1992 might have been expected to be in the region of £883,000.

108 The annual rate of sales actually achieved in the year to 30 June 1992 I calculate to be in the order of £794,000. Thus it would appear, *prima facie*, that The Paper Shop sales in the year to 30 June 1992 were some £89,000 lower than the former trend, had it continued, might have been expected to achieve. There are several possible explanations, which I list in the order of priority, that I attach to the likely explanations:

(a) turnover may have been temporarily depressed in 1991/92 due to disruptions carried out by the road widening scheme;

(b) there may have been a downward trend in 1991 during the Blacks' last year of ownership, for which no accounts are available to me;

(c) there may have been a break or some discontinuity in trading between the Blacks' and Clarke's ownership which led customers to turn to other outlets;

(d) the business may have suffered from greater competition in 1992 perhaps due to the opening up of new outlets in the vicinity although I am not aware of any evidence of this.

Gross margins

109 The gross margins earned by The Paper Shop expressed in terms of gross profit as a percentage of sales were as follows for the years for which accounts are available:

Year	Gross profit margin
	%
1988	20.0
1989	14.8
1990	18.1
(average 1988 to 1990	17.6)
1992	16.6

110 It appears that gross margins varied from year to year when The Paper. Shop was owned by Mr Black. They ranged from 14.8% to 20.0% in the three years for which I have accounts for Black.

111 The weighted average gross margin in those years was 17.6%. The gross margin achieved by Mrs Clarke and Mrs Smith in 1992 (16.6%) was about 1% below the previous average, 1.5% below the most recent available year (1990), although 1.8% higher than the margin earned in 1989. On balance I would conclude that the margin of 16.6% achieved in 1992 was below that which, based on past performance, ought to have been achievable. I would put the achievable rate for this purpose at 18%.

Expenses

112 The level of overhead expenses incurred by The Paper Shop in the period ended 31 July 1992 was significantly greater than that incurred by the business in each of the three years to 30 June 1990 when the business was under its previous owners.

THE PAPER SHOP (FORMERLY A BLACK)
ANALYSIS OF TRADING AND PROFIT AND LOSS
ACCOUNTS 1989 TO 1992

Year ended 30 June

	1988		1989	
	£		£	
Sales	704,872		742,632	
Cost of sales	563,840		632,820	
Gross profit	141,032	(20%)	109,812	(14.8%)
Sundry income	7,732		7,400	
	148,764		117,212	
Expenses				
Wages	37,524		38,032	
Rates	3,856		3,932	
Motor expenses	5,020		5,160	
Repairs to premises	—		1,836	
Repairs and renewals	652		536	
Insurance	1,032		1,356	
Heat and light	1,432		2,792	
Telephone	976		1,108	
Professional fees	2,212		1,916	
Bank charges	3,448		3,180	
Loan interest	8,744		8,208	
Printing, stationery and advertising	572		596	
Sundry expenses	304		608	
Depreciation	4,328		6,224	
Special loan interest	—		—	
	70,100		75,484	
Net profit/(loss) for the period	£78,664		£41,728	

* No accounts available for the period 1 July 1990 to mid-June 1991

1990	1991*	13½ months ended 31 July 1992		1992 accounts pro-rated to a 12 months' equivalent period
£	£	£		£
795,188		893,164		793,924
651,368		745,192		662,392
143,820	(18.1%)	147,972	(16.6%)	131,532
7,400		—		—
151,220		147,972		131,532
42,196		102,884		91,452
3,984		3,056		2,716
4,888		4,780		4,248
112		—		—
1,200		512		456
1,972		2,432		2,160
2,460		4,436		3,944
1,188		1,376		1,224
2,932		5,200		4,624
3,212		—		—
6,808		7,992		7,104
528		2,260		2,008
692		8		8
9,416		8,448		7,508
—		42,412		37,700
81,588		185,796		165,152
£69,632		£(37,824)		£(33,620)

113 The two principal differences relate to loan interest charges and to wages. The 1992 accounts include loan interest of £42,412 where no such charge was included in the 1990 accounts. The charge for wages in the 1992 accounts was £102,884 compared with £42,196 in 1990. Even allowing for inflation and the 13½ month period in 1992, I estimate that in real terms wages paid in 1992 were double those paid in 1990. This suggests to me a change in the way the business was run between the two periods. The most likely explanation for the change is that in the years 1988 to 1990 the owners worked in the shop and remunerated themselves out of the profits of the business; whereas in 1992 the owners did not work in the shop but instead employed people to attend the premises.

114 In my opinion it is appropriate in the circumstances to adjust the 1990 figures for wages onto a consistent basis with 1992 because in examining the profitability and value of a business it is normal practice to include a charge to reflect wages or salaries of those who work in the business even if in practice they derive their income as proprietors by drawing from profits. The wages charged in 13½ months to 31 July 1992 are shown in the accounts as £102,884. On a pro-rata basis I calculate the 12 month equivalent to be £91,452. The index of retail prices rose by about 10% between 1990 and 1992. Discounting the 1992 wages bill of £91,452 to exclude this inflationary factor gives a 1990 equivalent of £83,138.

115 It is also appropriate, in my opinion, to exclude the loan interest charge of £42,412 (£37,700 – 12 month equivalent figure) from the 1992 results because this charge has arisen because the acquisition of the business was financed by an interest bearing bank loan of £344,000 rather than by proprietors' capital.

116 Finally, I note that in 1989 and 1990 the business under the ownership of the Blacks enjoyed sundry income of £7,400 per annum. This has not continued following the change of ownership. I believe the income may have been rental income for the living accommodation attached to the shop and as such is not income of the shop itself. Therefore it should be excluded in considering the profitability of the business.

117 I tabulate below the adjustments that I consider are necessary to the 1990 and 1992 accounts of the business in order properly to compare the two years' results:

	Year to 30 June 1990 £	13½ months to 31 July 1992 £	12 months equivalent 1992 £
Net profit/(loss) as contained in the accounts	69,632	(37,824)	(33,620)
Less			
Uplift to wages in 1990 (£83,138 – £42,196)	(40,942)	—	—
Sundry income in 1990	(7,400)	—	—
Add back			
Loan account interest in 1992	—	42,412	37,700
Adjusted net profit	£21,290	£4,588	£4,080

118   The adjusted results indicate that the profit for the business in 1990 was about £21,000 compared with a profit of about £4,000 in 1992. The reduction of about £17,000 is largely attributable to a reduction in gross margin between 1990 and 1992 of 1½% and an apparant shortfall in turnover in 1992 of about £89,000, offset by a net saving in certain business overheads.

119   I now consider the monthly turnover analysis for The Paper Shop prepared by Tent & Co. This analysis shows actual monthly turnover from July 1991 to December 1992 and certain projections of turnover. The analysis indicates that the road scheme works commenced with effect from September 1991 and ceased by the end of July 1992. Barset County Council have informed me that the works indeed commenced on 7 September 1991 and were completed on 4 August 1992. Furthermore, although there was general disruption throughout the whole of the period of the works there was severe disruption between 9 November 1991 and 1 February 1992. Coincidentally with the scheme, the Water Board laid new pipes along Barford Road. I understand that this work did not finish until after Easter 1992. I have seen a day-by-day account of the work in the vicinity of 3–5 Barford Road extracted from the Resident Engineer's diary which seems to support these comments.

120   On p 366 is a bar chart plotting the net actual monthly turnover for The Paper Shop from July 1991 to December 1992 taken from the figures in Tent & Co's schedule. The graph indicates a reduction in the monthly sales figure from November 1991. This coincides with the commencement of the severe disruption. It would be reasonable to assume that after the disruption ceased there would be an increase in the monthly turnover. However, on the contrary, the graph indicates that having been fairly steady during the scheme, the general trend of turnover became downwards on completion of the scheme. This suggests to me that the post scheme turnover was influenced by other factors in addition to the effect of the road widening.

Saleability of business

121   I have been asked to consider the saleability of the business. In order to assess this I have examined *The Newsagents and General Store Business Guide* published by the specialist business agents Christie & Co for the period June/July 1993. I have had regard to three particular features or financial indicators of a newsagent's business:

(a)   the weekly takings;
(b)   the average gross profit margin;
(c)   the weekly news bill.

122   These three factors are commonly stated by Christie & Co in its business guide on business for sale. I have compared the respective financial indicators for The Paper Shop with the range of indicators extracted from Christie & Co's guide for business which appear to be similar in character, and in particular with similar accommodation.

123   The population of my sample was derived from properties with the following characteristics:

Weekly turnover in range £13,800–£17,000
Accommodation included (on average 3 bedrooms)

	The Paper Shop	My sample of business for sale (average)
Weekly takings	£17,200	£15,256
Weekly news bill	£4,000	£4,580
Gross margin	18%	20%

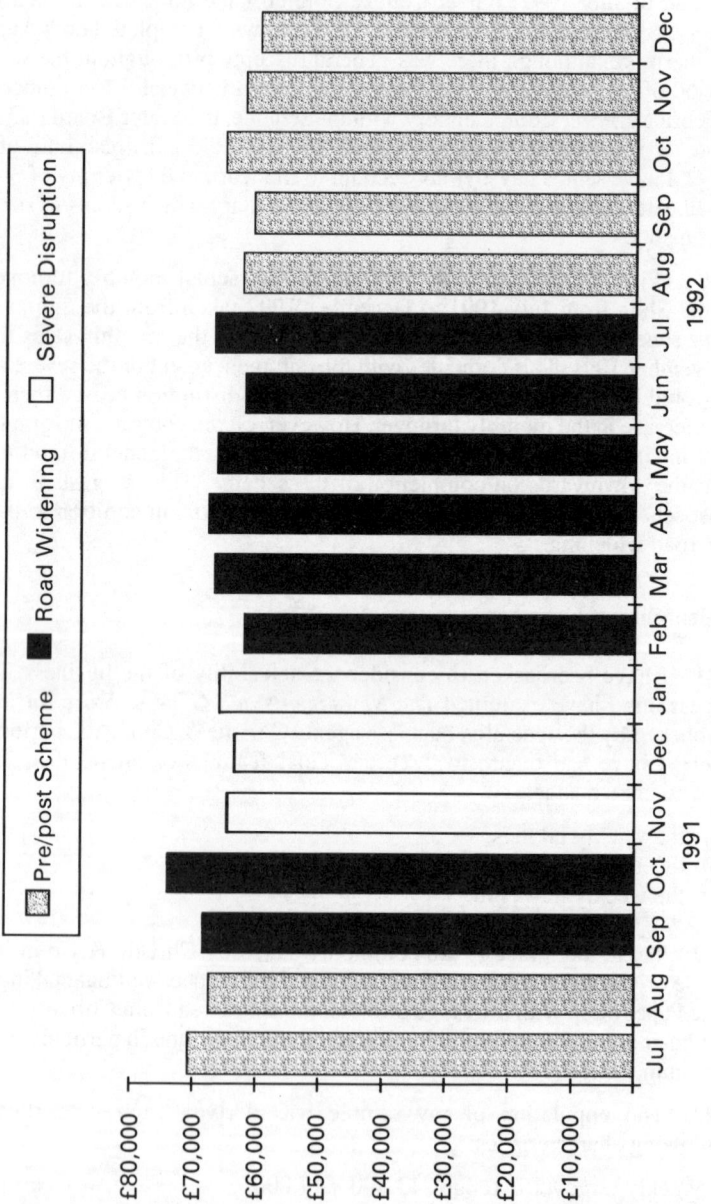

The Paper Shop – Monthly Turnover

Pre/post Scheme   Road Widening   Severe Disruption

124 It is of course not possible to draw precise conclusions about the specific value of The Paper Shop from this analysis. However, I conclude that The Paper Shop as a business does display financial indicators which, although lower, are not substantially out of line with similar businesses on the market. Furthermore, it would appear that the business was capable of producing sufficient gross profits to provide a reasonable remuneration for those working in the shop either as proprietors or staff. As a result I conclude that it was and is a saleable business.

Valuation of goodwill

125 In paragraph 117 I computed that in 1990, prior to the scheme, the business was profitable and, after making certain specific adjustments, concluded that this amounted to an annual profit of approximately £21,000.

126 For the purpose of considering the value of goodwill I believe it is reasonable to inflate this figure to allow for inflation between 1990 and 1993. The increase in the retail price index between January 1990 and January 1993 was 15.4%. Applying this uplift to the 1990 profit of £21,000 gives approximately £24,000 as the 1993 equivalent.

127 Goodwill in a business is traditionally valued as the difference between the total purchase price of the business and the fair value of its tangible assets. In the case of the Paper Shop the tangible assets comprise principally the freehold premises from which the trade is carried on. In this case I do not have a total purchase price from which to derive a figure for goodwill. Therefore, in the absence of such a price, to establish whether the profits are such that there exists goodwill in this business it is necessary to deduct from profits a notional charge relating to a fair return on the freehold premises. I am not qualified to determine such a return, so for the purposes of this report I have considered the result of using the annual rentals put forward by O Kaye & Sons (for Mr Clarke) and Mr R Rich (for Barset County Council). I make no adjustment for interest on working capital because I consider the amounts for bank charges and interest actually appearing in the accounts are the most appropriate indicators of the true cost of financing the business assets.

The adjustments therefore are as follows:

	Per Clarke and Smith £	Per Barset County Council £
Adjusted 1990 net profit per paragraph 117	21,000	21,000
Inflation adjustment (15.4% – approx)	3,000	3,000
	24,000	24,000
Less:		
Net annual income per O Kaye & Sons Document ABC/2	24,472	
Net rack rental value per Barset County Council		12,060
Adjusted result for goodwill valuation purposes	(472)	(11,940)

367

128   If the rental charge of O Kaye & Sons is taken as the correct one, this more than accounts for the net profit of the business. I conclude on this basis that the profits do not provide a full return on tangible assets and so in a sale between a willing buyer and willing seller I would not attribute any value to goodwill in these circumstances.

129   If, on the other hand, the Barset County Council rental value is the correct one then profits do remain after allowance is made for this notional charge.

II   THE PIE SHOP (4 BARFORD ROAD)

201   The Pie Shop trades as a fast-food takeaway. From the information made available to me it appears that Mr A Clarke acquired an interest in the shop in 1989 with 75% of the profits and losses being appropriated to Mr J Lamb.

202   Sometime before or during September 1990, part of the shop which had until then been used as a sit-in facility at The Pie Shop was converted into a self-contained car radio shop. According to Document ABC/1 of O Kaye & Sons, for the claimants, the selling areas are as follows:

	Sq feet
The Pie Shop	1,428
The Car Radio Shop	1,636
	3,064

203   Clearly a significant proportion of the selling area of the original Pie Shop was taken over by The Car Radio Shop. I do not know how long the conversion took, although it would be reasonable to assume this to have had some depressing effect on sales of The Pie Shop. However the monthly Pie Shop sales analysis prepared by Tent & Co appears to show no adverse change immediately prior to or after the commencement of trade at The Car Radio Shop. In fact September, October and November 1990 were the three best months' sales achieved by The Pie Shop since August 1989. It is not clear from the information at my disposal why this should have been.

204   Set out below are the trading profit and loss accounts of The Pie Shop for the three years ended 31 July 1990, 1991 and 1992 respectively. I have extracted the information directly from the annual accounts. I make the following comments about the results of the business as shown by these accounts.

Sales turnover

205   After a substantial increase in sales turnover of pies between 1990 and 1991, turnover fell back somewhat in 1992. I have reviewed the schedule of monthly turnover prepared by Tent & Co which indicates that turnover was particularly depressed in the months November 1991 to March 1992. I note that this is the period during which the road works caused the most disruption to the area. I also note that after some recovery in sales between April and September 1992 sales were again depressed for the months of October 1992 to January 1993 (the latest month for which I have figures). As the road widening scheme was completed in July 1992 there would not appear to be a direct link between the effect of the

THE PIE SHOP

TRADING AND PROFIT AND LOSS ACCOUNTS FOR THE YEARS ENDED 31 JULY

	1990		1991		1992	
	£	£	£	£	£	£
Sales						
Sausages and sand-						
wiches		89,964		89,744		67,904
Pies		363,244		501,000		456,152
		453,208		590,744		524,056
Cost of sales						
Opening stock	—		1,800		26,000	
Purchases	247,632		358,236		314,972	
Closing stock	(1,800)		(26,000)		(4,000)	
		245,832		334,036		336,972
Gross profit		207,376		256,708		187,084
Expenses						
Employment	110,968		95,896		116,852	
Establishment	34,140		32,420		29,916	
Administration	17,228		14,132		18,832	
Selling	2,872		2,632		3,540	
Financial	30,284		38,752		42,412	
Depreciation	3,548		9,208		9,512	
		199,040		193,040		221,064
NET PROFIT/						
(LOSS)		£8,336		£63,668		£(33,980)

scheme and the sudden drop in turnover from October 1992 onwards. It may be that this change was caused by some other factors, for example a general decline in spending power following the closure of a local factory (Shore Industries).

Gross profit and margins

206 The accounts disclose gross profit margins in the years 1990 to 1992 as follows:

	%
1990	45.76
1991	43.46
1992	35.70

207 I note that in arriving at these margins, particularly those for 1991 and 1992, there are some rather unusual fluctuations in the levels of closing stock. For the three years in question closing stock is shown as:

	£
1990	1,800
1991	26,000
1992	4,000

208   In each of the three years the value attributed to stock appears to be a round sum figure and was probably an estimated value.

209   I am particularly concerned by the value of stock disclosed in the 1991 accounts. Whereas the closing stock in 1990 and 1992 represented only 3 or 4 days worth of sales the closing stock in 1991 was sufficient for about one month's sales, which I consider to be high for a business of this kind. Neither the accounts nor the other financial information available to me for this business provide any explanation for this unusual fluctuation in stock levels.

210   For the purpose of considering the profitability of the business from year to year, in the absence of any explanation, I consider it appropriate to adjust the 1991 and 1992 figures for closing and opening stock respectively, substituting £4,000 as a reasonable level of stock for this purpose.

Expenses

211   Generally, the levels of overhead expense incurred by the business in each of the three years 1990 to 1992 are similar from one year to the next. There is however an important exception, the charge for employment (wages). The amounts disclosed are as follows:

	Wages
	£
1990	110,968
1991	95,896
1992	116,852

212   The relatively low figure disclosed in 1991 is all the more surprising since turnover was highest in that year and therefore, presumably the shop was busier in 1991 than the other two years. It may be that the proprietors or their families assisted in the shop to a greater extent in 1991 than the other years and did not draw wages for this. For the purposes of considering the underlying profitability of the business, it is appropriate in my opinion to substitute the actual charge for wages in 1991 with one of a similar level to 1990 and 1992. I propose to use the average of the charge for those two years, namely £113,910.

213   The effect on the net profit/(loss) of the pie shop of making these adjustments is as follows:

	1990	**1991**	**1992**
	£	£	£
Net profit/(loss) per accounts	8,336	63,668	(33,980)
Adjustment to closing stock (£26,000 – £4,000)	—	(22,000)	22,000
Adjustment to wages (£113,910 – £95,896)	—	(18,014)	—
Add back-loan interest	28,052	30,600	30,600
Adjusted net profit	36,388	54,254	18,620
Adjusted gross margin	45.76%	39.73%	39.90%

214 The adjusted results indicate that the profit for the business in 1991 was around £54,000 compared with about £18,500 in 1992. The reduction in profits of about £35,500 in total between 1991 and 1992 is largely attributable to the shortfall in turnover. This can be seen as follows:

	£
Actual turnover for 1991	590,744
Allowance for growth in 1992 in line with inflation in retail price index (say 4%)	23,630
Projected turnover for 1992	614,374
Less actual turnover	524,056
Shortfall in turnover	90,318
Gross margin on shortfall in turnover (39.90%)	36,037

Saleability of business

215 In summary, it appears to me that the business prior to the scheme was profitable, albeit not substantially so. Nevertheless, the premises do include living accommodation and the business does appear capable of providing proprietors who work in the shop a reasonable remuneration. For these reasons I conclude that the business was saleable prior to the scheme. I also note that the shortfall in profit in 1992 was largely due to a reduction in turnover which coincided with the period of severe disruption. 1 regard much if not all of that loss as temporary and therefore am satisfied that the loss recorded in 1992 should not be recurring. For these reasons I also consider the business to be currently saleable.

Valuation of goodwill

216 In paragraph **213** I computed that in 1991, prior to the scheme, the business was profitable and, after making certain specific adjustments, concluded that this amounted to an annual profit of approximately £54,000.

217 For the purpose of considering the value of goodwill I believe it is reasonable to inflate this figure to allow for inflation between 1991 and 1993. The increase in the retail price index between January 1991 and January 1993 was 6%. Applying this uplift, the 1991 profit of £54,000 gives approximately £57,000 as the 1993 equivalent.

218 Goodwill in a business is traditionally valued as the difference between the total purchase price of the business and the fair value of its tangible assets. In the case of The Pie Shop the tangible assets comprise principally the freehold premises from which the trade is carried on. Since there is no total purchase price available to me in these circumstances to establish whether the profits are such that there exists goodwill in this business, it is necessary to deduct from profits a notional charge relating to a fair return on the freehold premises. Again, I have considered the result of using the annual rentals put forward by O Kaye & Sons (for Mr Clarke) and Mr R Rich (for Barset County Council). I make no adjustment for interest on working capital because I consider the amounts for bank charges and interest actually appearing in the accounts are the most appropriate indicators of the true cost of financing the business assets.

219   The adjustments therefore are as follows:

	Per Clarke and Smith £	Per Barset County Council £
Adjusted 1991 net profit per paragraph **213**	54,000	54,000
Inflation adjustment (6% - approx)	3,000	3,000
	57,000	57,000
Less:		
Net annual income per O Kaye & Sons Document ABC/2	59,932	—
Net rack rental per Barset County Council (Note 1)	—	26,148
Adjusted result for goodwill valuation purposes	(2,932)	30,852

(Note 1) Barset County Council valued The Pie Shop and The Car Radio Shop as one unit. The net rack rental values have therefore been apportioned using the split of square footage as detailed in the valuation performed by O Kaye & Sons.

220   If the rental charge of O Kaye & Sons is taken as the correct one, then no profits remain. I conclude that in these circumstances the profits do not provide a full return on tangible assets and so no goodwill would be attributable.

221   If the Barset County Council rental value is the correct one then some profits do remain after allowance is made for this notional charge.

SUMMARY

222   Based on my review of the financial data available to me, I conclude that both The Paper Shop and The Pie Shop were trading profitably immediately before the road widening scheme. The level of profit was, in my opinion, sufficient to provide reasonable remuneration for those working in the shops either as proprietors or staff. For this reason I conclude that the businesses were saleable.

223   I have considered whether the level of profit was sufficient for a goodwill value to be attributed to the businesses. It was necessary to deduct from the profits an amount representing the notional rent on the freehold premises. For this purpose I used the claimant's expert's figures. Once this had been done, little or no profit remained. I therefore conclude, in these circumstances, that no goodwill can be attributed to either The Paper Shop or The Pie Shop.

Yours faithfully

Christopher Maltravers

Visual presentation of evidence

Clear communication is of the essence in expert witness work. Even the most penetrating investigation or analysis has little value if the court cannot readily grasp its message and significance. Of course, a clear and lucid prose style is a great help, but there are times when any number of words, however carefully chosen, will not manage to convey an important point quite as efficiently or powerfully as a well designed graph or table. This is true particularly often for accountancy-related issues where so much can depend on the interpretation of numerical and financial data.

When deciding how to present data, it is important never to lose sight of the exact point one is seeking to communicate and to be conscious throughout that the needs of the reader are paramount. Sometimes it is helpful to gauge 'the buyer's perspective' by asking a colleague who is not directly involved in the case to say which (if any) of various alternative presentational formats conveys the desired message most persuasively.

Apart from the text itself, three main kinds of visual presentation are potentially relevant in presenting expert accounting evidence:

- charts or graphs;
- tables of figures; and
- more generalised computer graphics, including animated displays.

The last category is, at least for now, outside the scope of this work because so few opportunities arise for using such techniques in trials in British courts. In the United States, for instance, most trials are heard before juries; it is probably not altogether coincidental that highly powered graphics and computerised slide shows are used relatively often there. In the United Kingdom, by contrast, almost all non-criminal trials are conducted by judges alone and the use of sophisticated computer equipment in court is quite rare. No doubt, this reflects the reasonable view that judges are experienced professional people, well able to master complex ideas without the greater pedagogical effort required to impart the same understanding to 12 lay jurors coming from a fairly random assortment of backgrounds and experience. Equally to the point, few British courts are yet physically equipped for the holding of live computer presentations. Times are changing, though, and some recent trials of complex criminal frauds have indeed involved the use of animated computer graphics: these can be used especially effectively to illustrate such topics as webs of cross-border flows of funds and the workings of complicated financial instruments.

A wide choice of computer software is now available to assist in presenting information effectively and attractively. Recent versions of many spreadsheet and word processing packages incorporate powerful presentational capabilities;

several varieties of specialised graphics software are also in common use. These programs have evolved considerably in recent years and, no doubt, will go on doing so. As the technology develops, methods which had been open only to those with access to expensive and specialised equipment are becoming more readily available to others. For all that, the essential aim of the expert can be expected to remain the same as ever: to assist and inform, and to persuade the court and opponents alike that his view is both correct and relevant and should be given due weight in the decision of the court. Thus, the basic presentational considerations can be regarded for practical purposes as constant.

The ideas presented in this appendix do not rely on any particular configuration of equipment or software. In principle, most of them might be implemented without a computer at all. In practice, a capable spreadsheet package will be helpful. However, it is essential to remember throughout that the use of any technology is no more than a means to that fundamental aim of getting the message across with maximum effectiveness.

CHARTS

Three main types of chart are generally appropriate for presenting data in expert accountants' reports:

- line graphs;

- bar charts; and

- pie charts.

Although some computer spreadsheets and graphics programs do offer further options, those are frequently variations on one or more of these three themes. Those graph types to which this remark does not apply are usually intended for the applications of scientists, statisticians or engineers; they are seldom (note that we do not say never) suitable for use in accountancy evidence. Fortunately, the three basic flavours are themselves quite diverse and can be applied, alone or in combination, to present many different types of data in ways that are clear and interesting, while also capable of being tailored to the needs of specific situations.

The names of the three basic types of chart are self-explanatory and most readers will already be familiar with them, but it can do no harm to illustrate the terminology by means of a simple example (Exhibit 1) which presents the same data in three alternative basic formats.

Line graphs

Line graphs are probably what the layman thinks of first upon coming across the word graph. In the contexts arising most commonly in expert accountants' exercises, line graphs typically illustrate movements in some variable quantity (plotted against the 'y axis') with time (shown as the 'x axis'). This type of graph tends to be suitable particularly where the variations with time are fairly continuous (as with daily movements in share prices). If the changes are more discrete so that a single point on the chart corresponds to a more extended period of time (as when charting annual data such as sales or profit figures), a bar chart will generally give a clearer message. Line graphs are often useful for illustrating

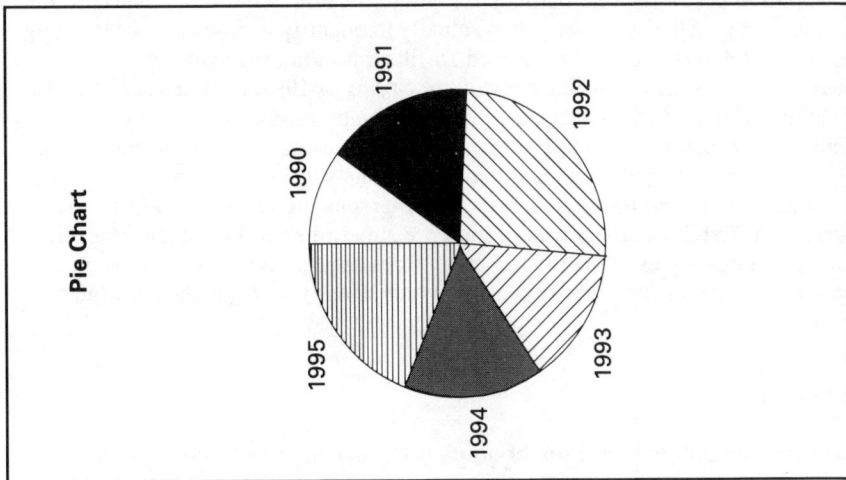

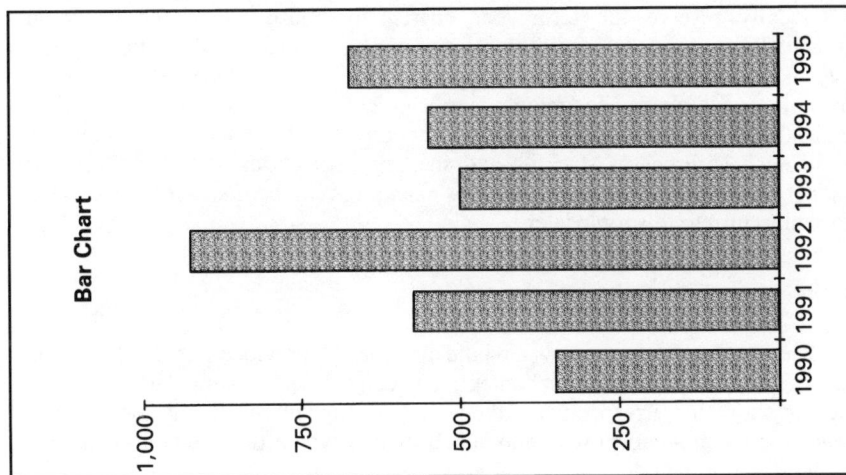

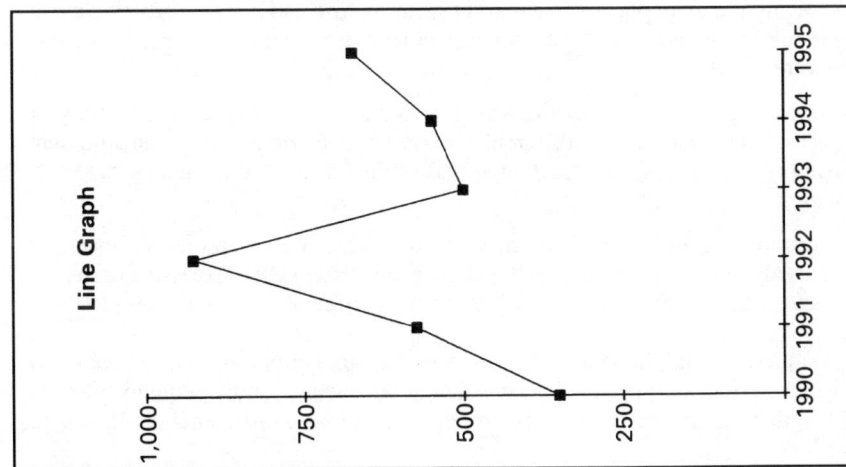

Exhibit 1

375

comparative performances, particularly where the aim is more to emphasise the existence of a disparity or trend than actually to quantify its impact. A chart along the lines of Exhibit 2 might be used to illustrate that, prior to some business interruption or other actionable event in the Spring of 1991, the sales performance of Injured Party Ltd outstripped an appropriate market index but declined thereafter. Of course, it would remain to be established by other means that the comparison was a proper one and that the decline was not attributable to factors completely unrelated to those in issue! Line graphs are probably most powerful when, as in Exhibit 2, two or more lines are superimposed in a single chart. It is important not to overdo this: if too many lines appear and/or they are too close together it becomes difficult to make out which line is which and the message may be lost.

Bar charts

The most commonly used form of graph is the bar chart or 'histogram' in which the counterpart of the points appearing in a line graph is a series of bars, the height of each corresponding to the value in question. Some computer programs rather pedantically reserve the term 'bar charts' for those where the bars run horizontally, calling the more common arrays of vertical bars 'column charts' instead. No such distinction tends to be made in common parlance. Bar charts are more often suitable in accountancy applications because, as noted earlier, they emphasise the discrete nature of yearly and quarterly data. Moreover, by judicious use of such facilities as stacking and shading, projections of lost income and 'budget versus actual' comparisons, for example, may be displayed effectively. We shall return to this topic later.

Pie charts

Pie charts are used to show how a whole amount is subdivided into the sum of its component parts. In a litigation context, they can be used to particularly powerful effect to show that, irrespective of the actual amounts involved, one part is much bigger (or much smaller) than another. Instances where this method of display might be useful include:

- showing the main players in a market sector before and after a disruptive event (as might be relevant if a major participant sustained a significant business interruption);

- illustrating the relative importance to an organisation's overall profitability of each of the organisation's different activities (this might be used in an argument over the significance of a particular part of the business to its overall success); and

- illustrating, as in Exhibit 3, the make-up of costs of various projects (this might be used to illustrate an argument that the profit element was excessive or that an undue amount of administrative overhead had been allotted to the project).

A similar aim might be achieved by means of an appropriate stacked bar chart in which all the columns are the same height but each is subdivided into sub-bars of length proportional to the size of the individual constituents as shown in Exhibit 4.

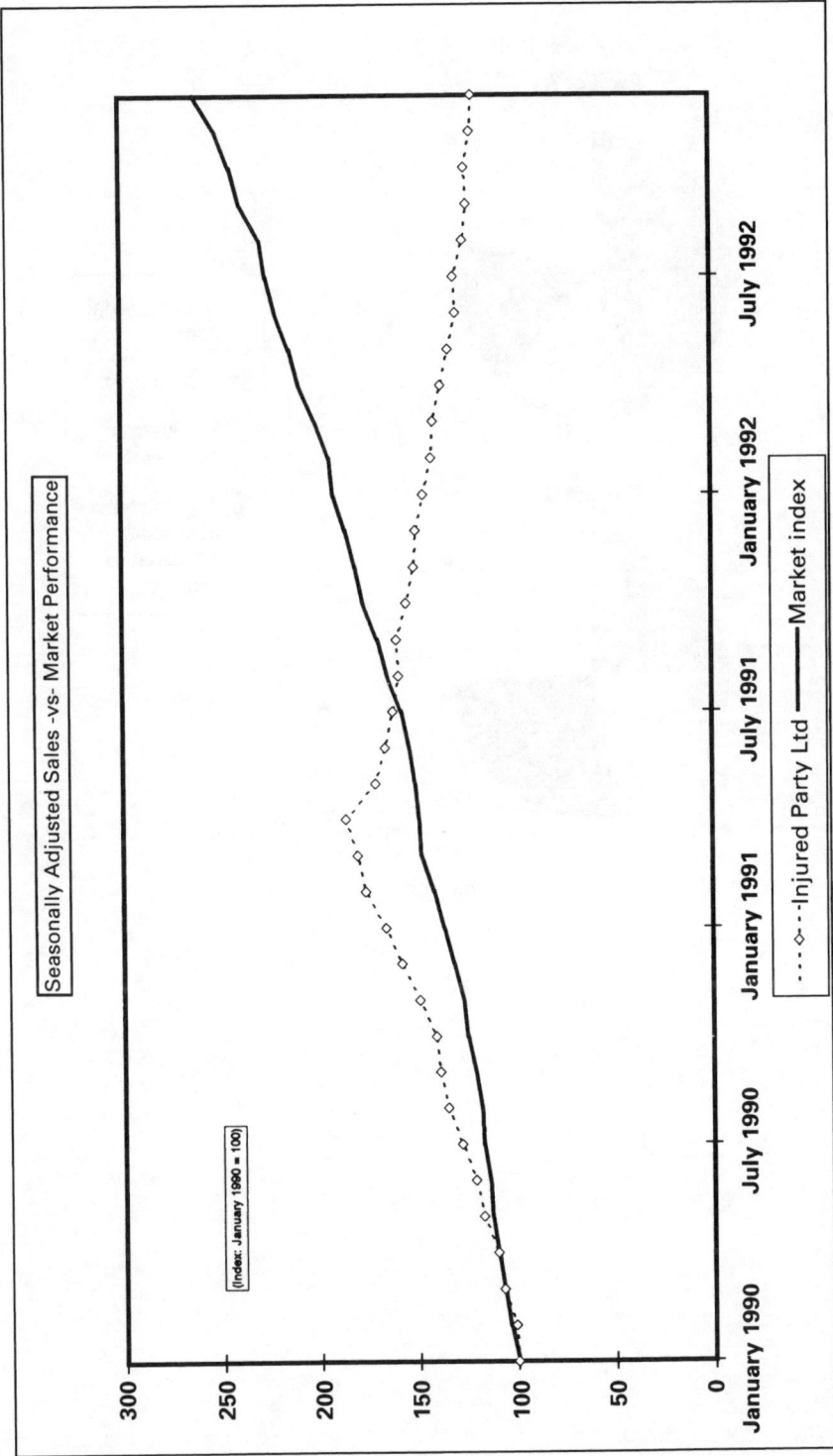

Seasonally Adjusted Sales -vs- Market Performance

(Index: January 1990 = 100)

- - -◇- - - Injured Party Ltd ——— Market index

Exhibit 2

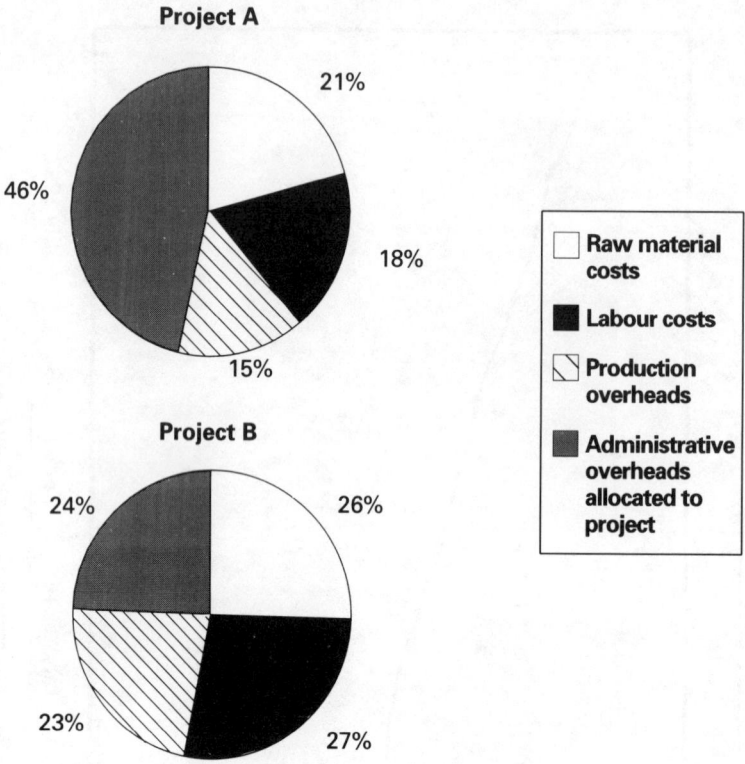

Project A

21%

46%

18%

15%

Raw material costs

Labour costs

Production overheads

Administrative overheads allocated to project

Project B

24%

26%

23%

27%

Exhibit 3

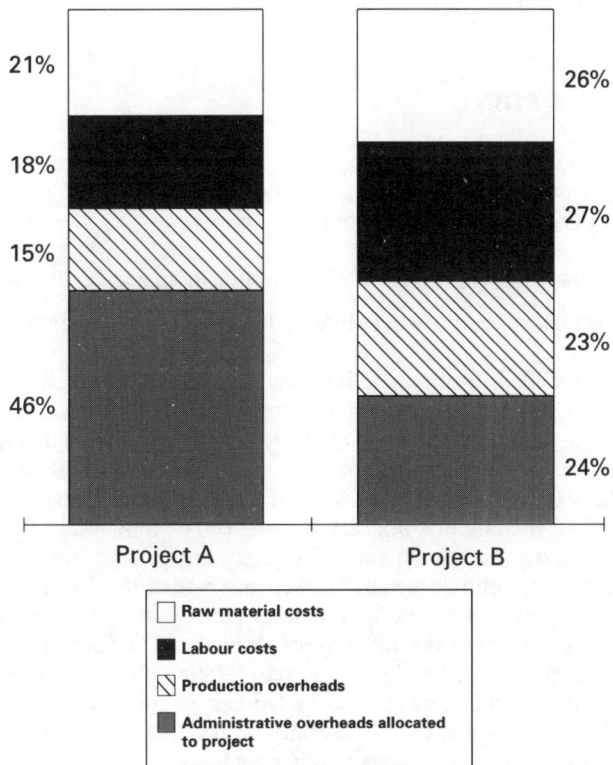

Exhibit 4

When using pie charts (or, for that matter, bar charts) it is well to remember that the slices of pie corresponding to minor components may be too small to be properly visible. It will often be worth considering the possibility of combining two or more of the lesser items into a single segment.

MAKING THE POINT

The basic purpose of using graphics when presenting numerical data in expert accountancy work is very often to draw the reader's attention to variations or differences of one kind or another, for example:

- losses of sales following a business interruption or an accident to an individual;

- failure to achieve sales growth in line with an appropriate market index.

Frequently, the identification and interpretation of such differences lie close to the heart of the evidence on quantum. For crucial points like these, it is especially worthwhile to make use of whatever tools are available to ensure that the message is driven home effectively. Presentational devices involving variation in typefaces or 'fonts' (for example, by changes of size, boldness, underlining, use of italics and so forth) and shading or colour have long been commonplace both in graphs and for showing data in tabular form. But there are other, more distinctive and impressive ways of highlighting such effects and one or more of these will often be worth considering when seeking to make a particularly powerful comparison. It is neither practicable nor desirable to prescribe detailed rules in this area, save that clarity must always be the dominant consideration. Some of the possibilities, however, may be illustrated by means of a worked example. This is intended as a source for ideas – imagination can usefully be brought to bear in applying and developing these or similar features in other contexts.

Imagine a company's main factory has been badly damaged by fire. The accountant is called upon to consider, among other things, the loss of sales flowing from the fire. For the present purpose, attention will be confined to one of the first tasks: to show that sales have indeed been depressed following the fire. It will probably be necessary to build upon this work in order, for example, to estimate a measure of the lost turnover and translate it into a loss of profits; such exercises are not really addressed here, but the presentational considerations involved would be very similar.

The following raw sales figures (on p 381) are available in respect of sales by calendar quarter for 18 months either side of the fire, which occurred on 30 June 1993.

At the simplest level, one might chart this information as a line graph or bar chart as shown in Exhibit 5.

This chart does show the sales and it does exhibit a dip, but the reader may have to work hard to make the connection between the depression in turnover and the fire. How might we make his life easier so that he feels more sympathetic to what we have to say? A first step might be to mark the graph so as to show explicitly where the fire fits into the chronology. This could be done with a strategically placed arrow as shown in Exhibit 6.

An alternative approach is to label the appropriate parts of the chart as shown in Exhibit 7.

The position can be made clearer still by using distinct patterns for the sales

	Quarterly Sales
1992:	
January–March	£500,715
April–June	£487,500
July–September	£578,090
October–December	£634,565
1993:	
January–March	£698,376
April–June	£662,737
July–September	£525,678
October–December	£445,676
1994:	
January–March	£479,084
April–June	£467,531
July–September	£590,245
October–December	£678,978

figures before and after the fire as illustrated in Exhibit 8. In this case it is important to have a clear legend so that the significance of the pattern change is not lost on the reader.

A parallel approach might then be used, later on in the report, when the projection of lost sales is presented, to apply the same graph for expected, actual and lost sales. As is clearly shown in Exhibit 9, the lost sales bar is stacked on top of the actual post-fire column so that the overall height of the stack represents the expert's estimate of what the sales would have been if there had not been a fire.

TABLES

Similar considerations apply to the presentation of the numbers underlying a chart, as to the chart itself. It is usually expedient for an expert accountant's report to show the figures underlying any chart it presents and clarity is no less important here. The table in Exhibit 10 presents the data graphed in Exhibits 5 to 9.

This fairly comprehensive example uses a variety of techniques for illustrative purposes: it is not obligatory, nor even necessarily recommended, to use all of them at the same time. Exhibit 10 uses separate columns to distinguish the data before and after the disruption. It also employs shading and distinctive borders.

A CAUTIONARY NOTE

Benjamin Disraeli said: 'There are three kinds of lies: lies, damned lies and statistics'. Had he lived a hundred years later, he might have considered extending that dictum to include deception by graphical means.

It ought to go without saying that graphics should never be used in an effort to mislead. And, yet, because such things do sometimes happen, it is important to be alert to the possibility that the visual impression given by a chart or other graphical representation is not actually supported by the underlying figures; some examples of the kind of abuse to watch out for will be shown later on. Two practical points follow from this:

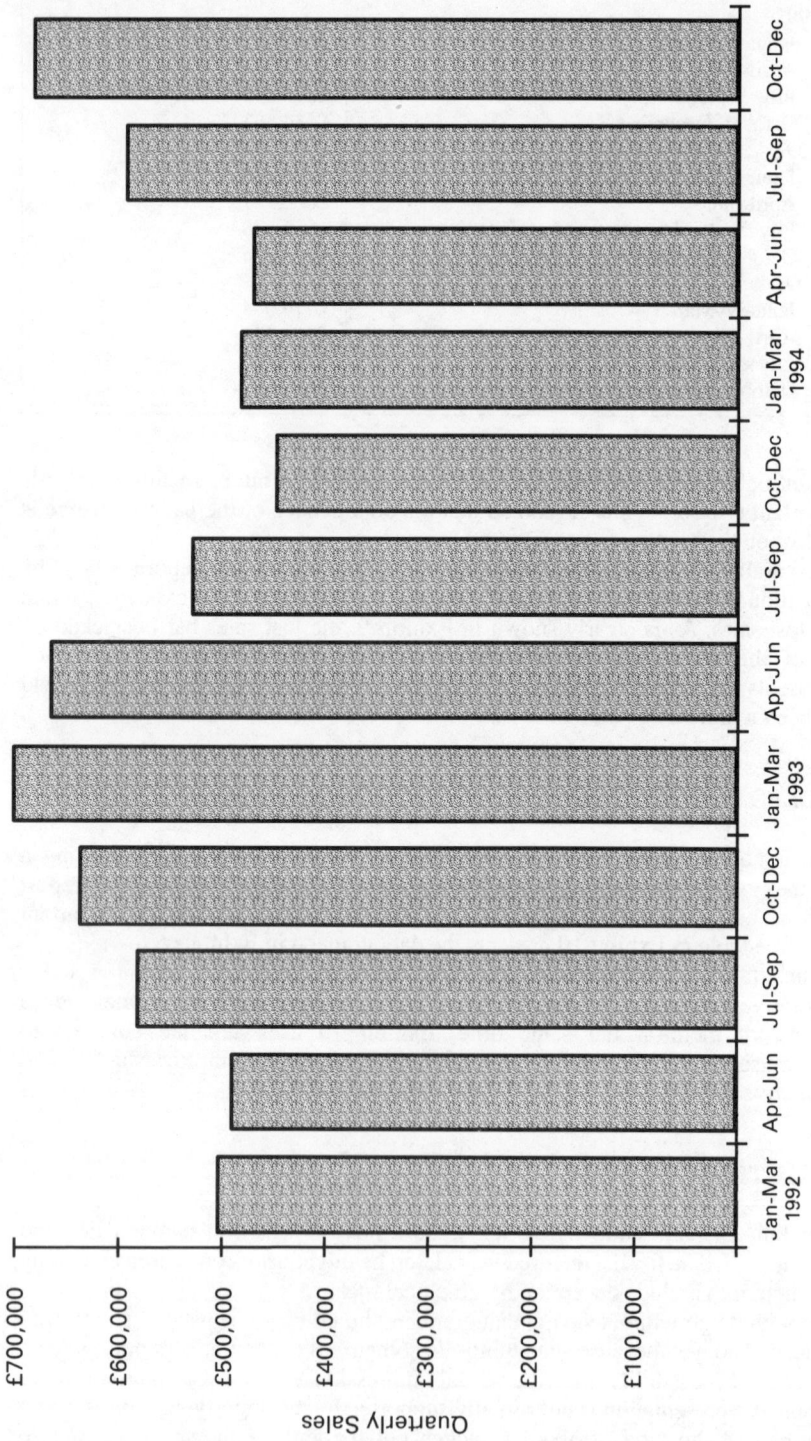

Exhibit 5

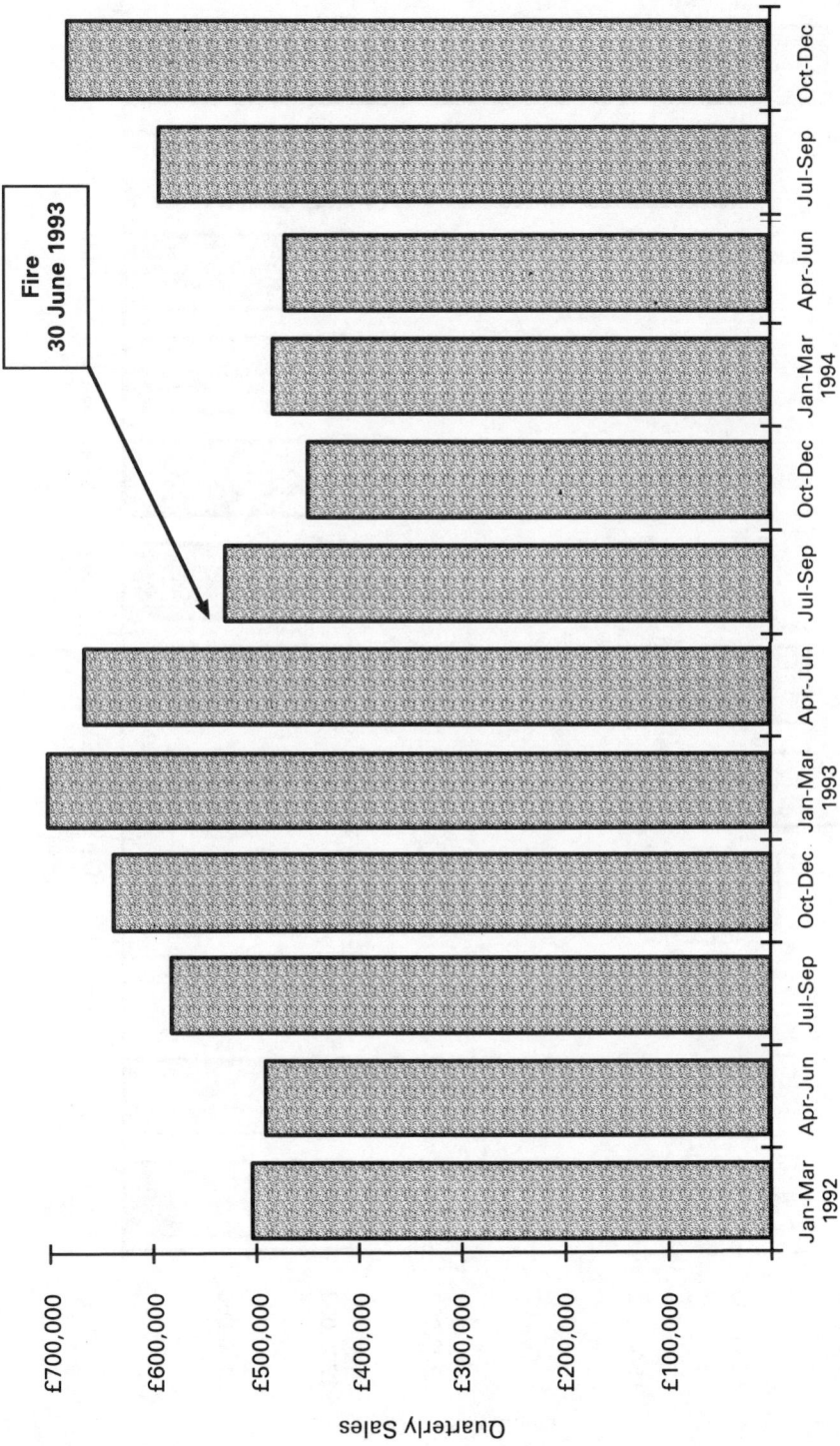

Exhibit 6

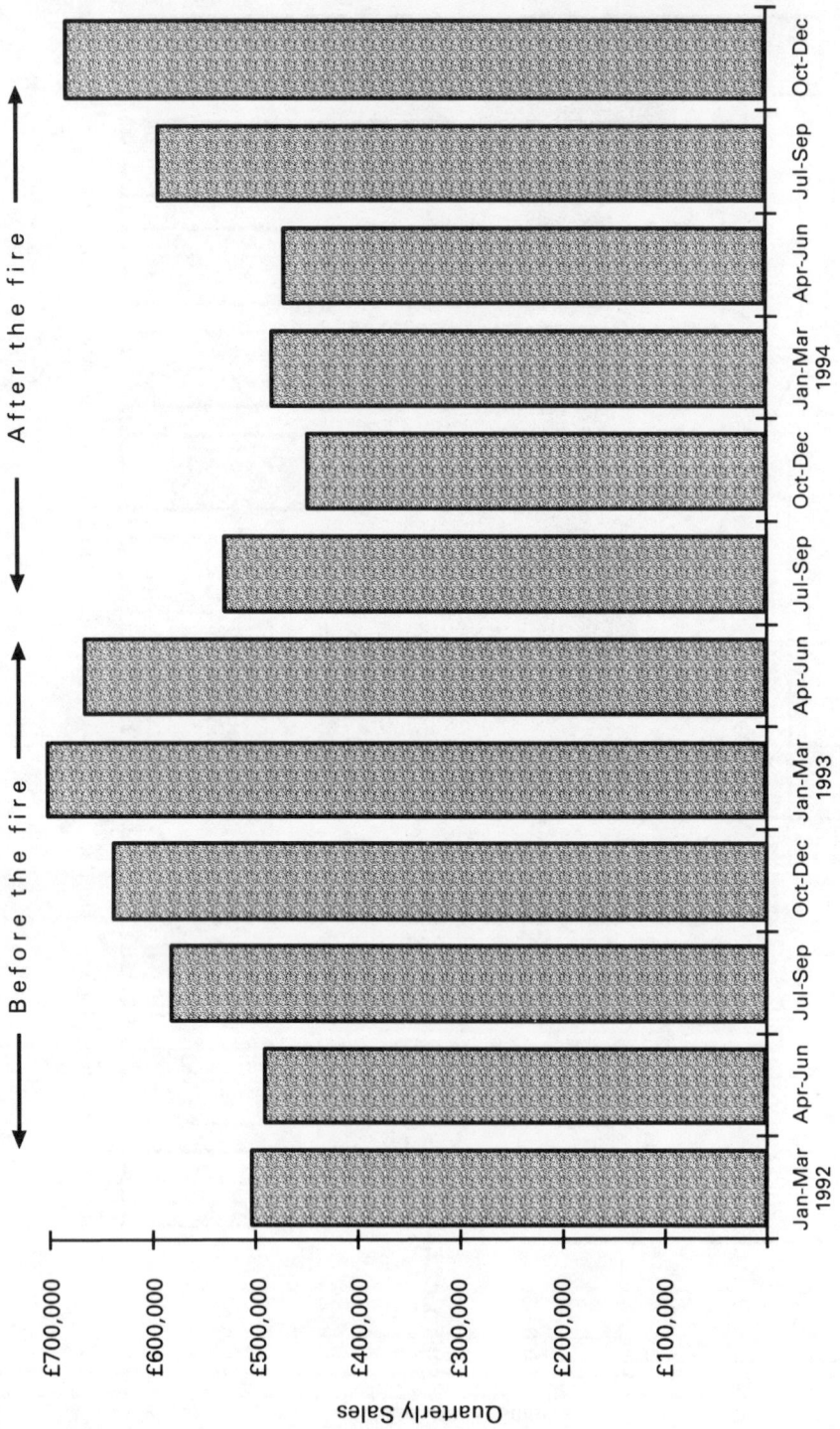

Exhibit 7

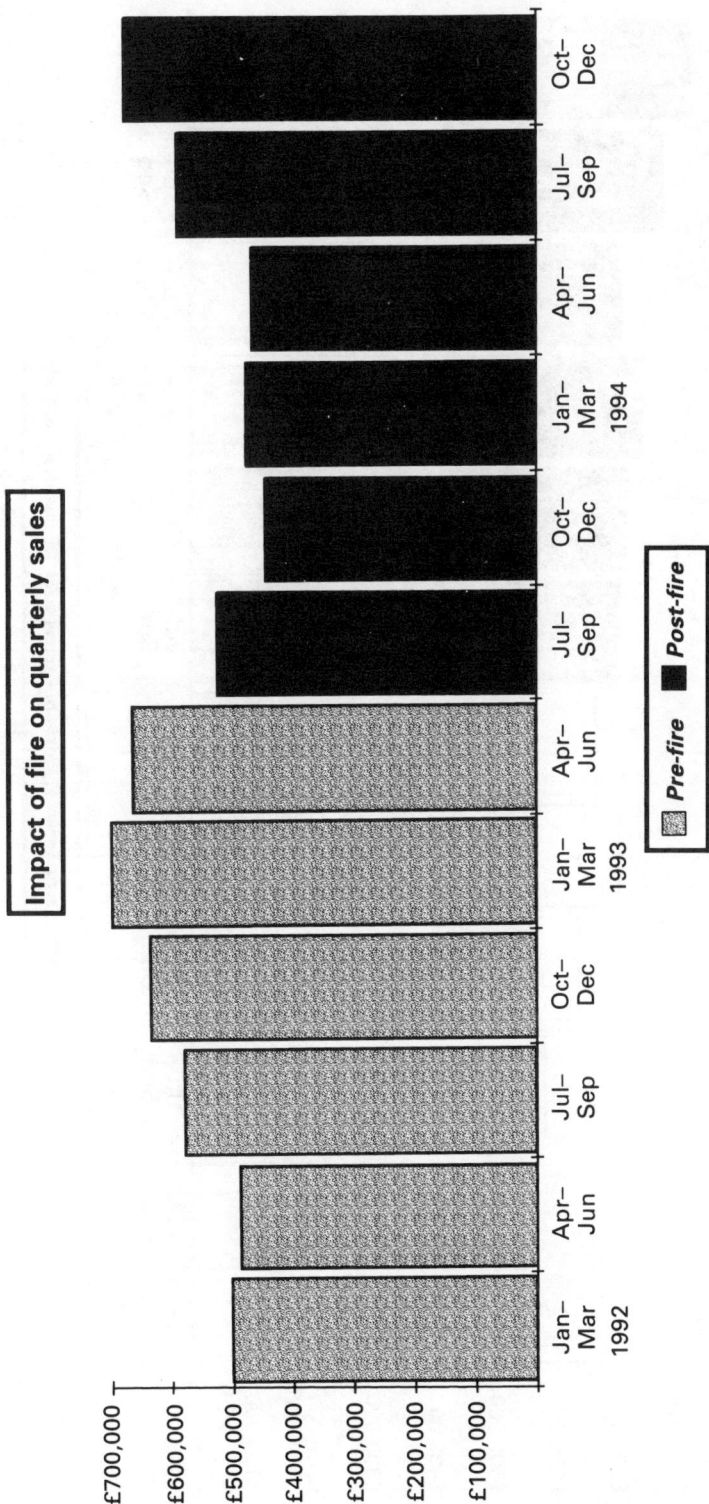

Impact of fire on quarterly sales

Exhibit 8

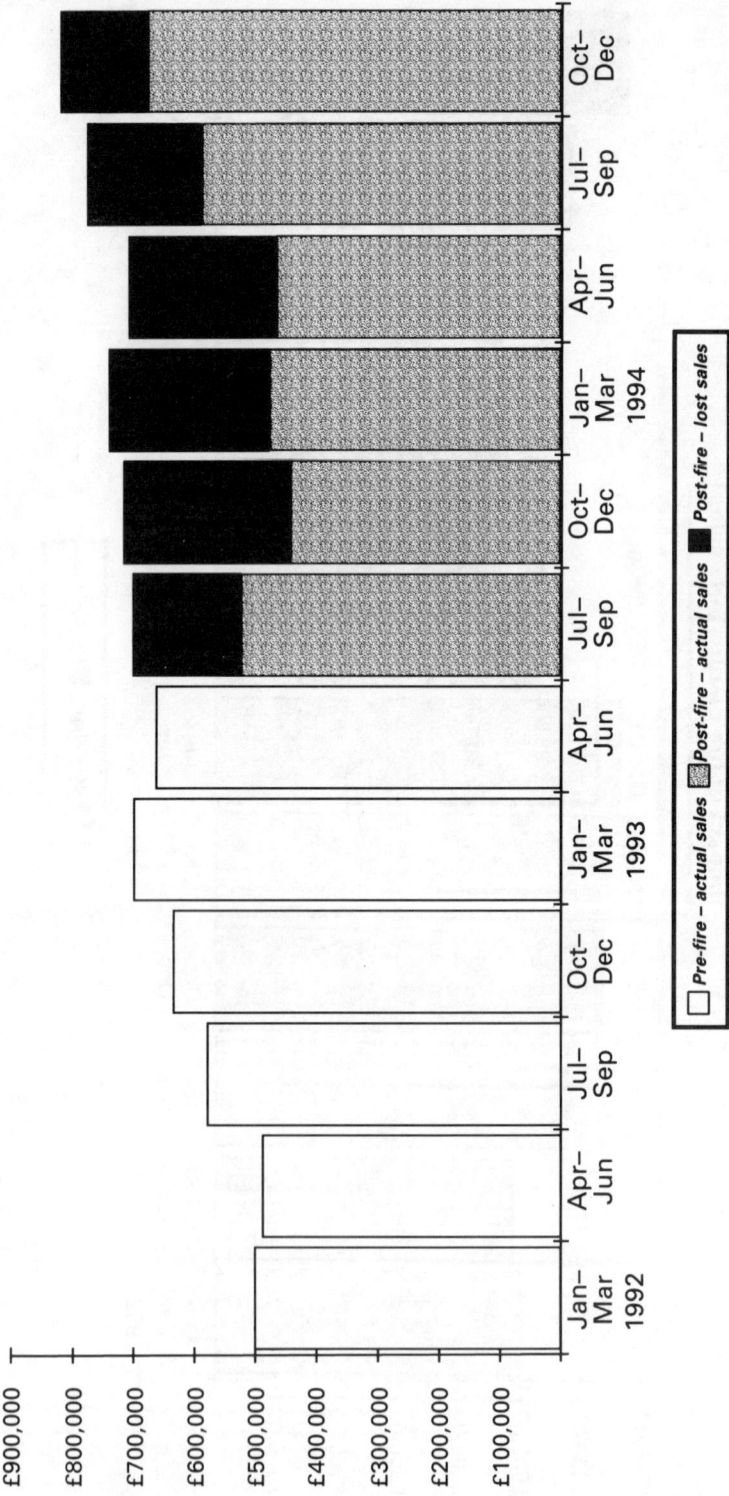

Loss of quarterly sales due to fire

Exhibit 9

Legend:
- Pre-fire – actual sales
- Post-fire – actual sales
- Post-fire – lost sales

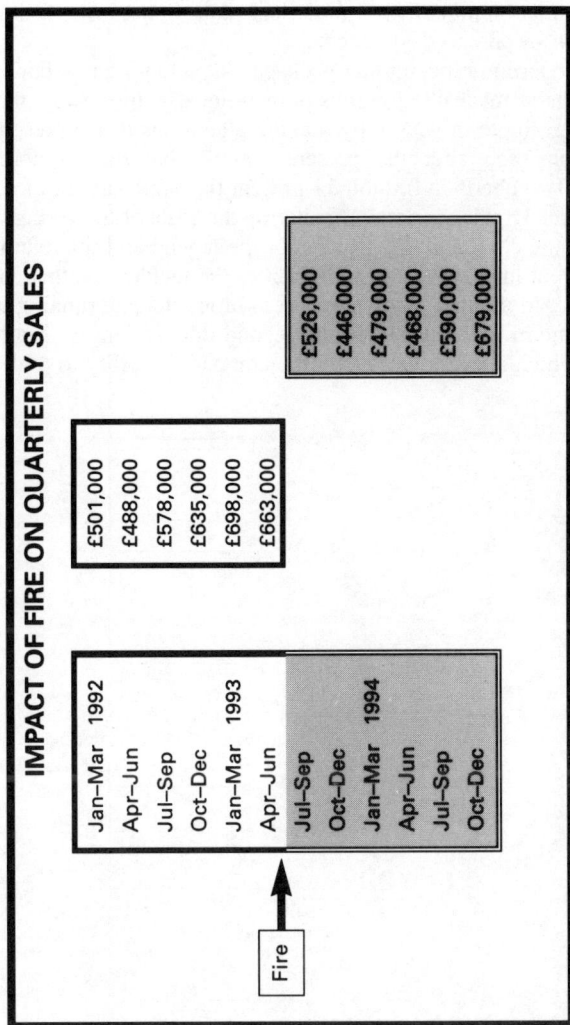

IMPACT OF FIRE ON QUARTERLY SALES

Jan–Mar 1992	£501,000
Apr–Jun	£488,000
Jul–Sep	£578,000
Oct–Dec	£635,000
Jan–Mar 1993	£698,000
Apr–Jun	£663,000
Jul–Sep	£526,000
Oct–Dec	£446,000
Jan–Mar 1994	£479,000
Apr–Jun	£468,000
Jul–Sep	£590,000
Oct–Dec	£679,000

Fire

Exhibit 10

387

- when critically appraising the report of an opponent, it is important to be alert to the possibility that the visual impression may not be borne out by the underlying figures;

- conversely, it is essential to ensure that one's own work is properly supported and so presented as not to fall prey to similar criticism.

Considerations like these are, of course, fundamental in expert witness work and are not peculiar to the visual aspects: equally valid points could be made about, for example, summarising numerical data (*pace* Mr Disraeli) and presenting extracts or précis of documents.

When using modern microcomputer packages in particular, it is fairly difficult to produce materially misleading graphs unintentionally. In closing, though, we give an extreme example in which, by making alterations to the presentation of identical data, one can alter the presentation of that data almost beyond recognition. The two charts in Exhibit 11 present the same pattern of actual and budgeted sales over 16 sales periods. By altering the scale of the vertical axis, the overall height of the chart and the position of the legend and title one is able to give a very different impression of the impact of the incident on that company's sales performance. In the first graph sales seem little affected, running under but in a consistent pattern with budget. In the second the incident is seen to have a dramatic effect which appears to destroy the company's ability to trade. Let the reader beware.

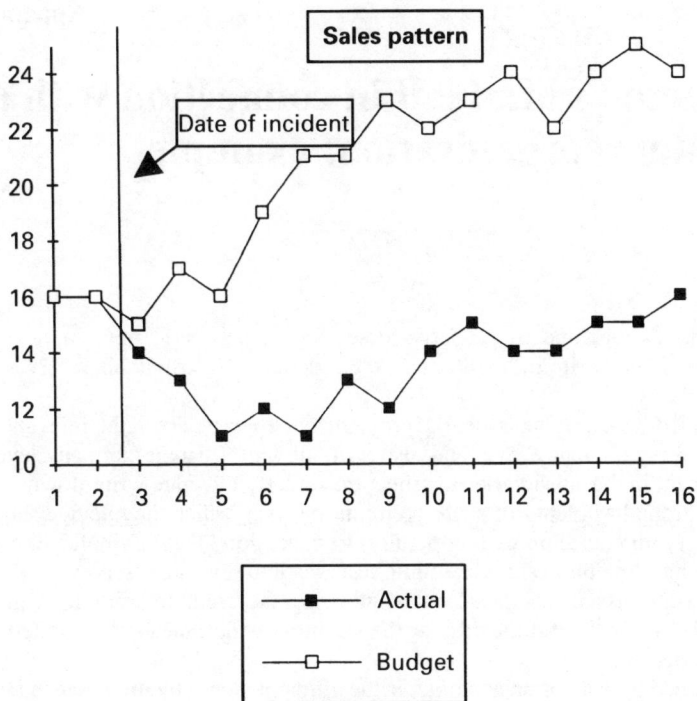

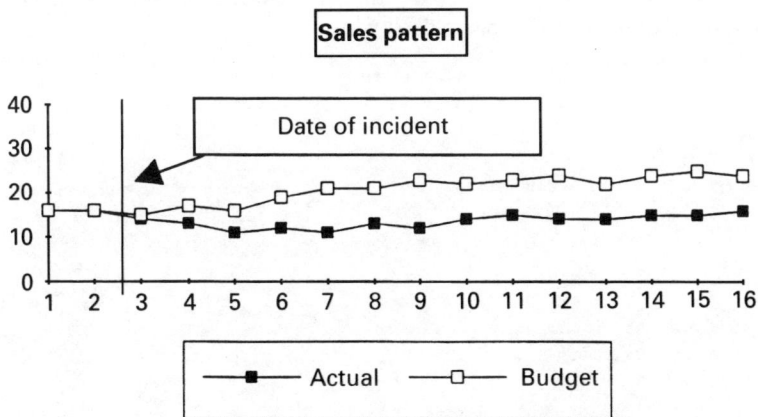

Exhibit 11

Director's affidavit in connection with a capital reorganisation: example

Heaveho Group, due to property losses and a non-performing mine, face a situation where write-offs will create a big deficit in distributable reserves in the top company.

Coupled with a rights issue, the group decide to write down the relevant assets at subsidiary company level and also write down (at parent company level) the investment in the subsidiaries to reflect the underlying value write-downs.

The group has plenty of share premium reserves which they decide should be utilised (with court approval hopefully) to make good the distributable reserves, ie by converting these share premium reserves into revenue reserves.

The rights issue receipts, by strengthening the creditors' situation, give the court the necessary safeguards for the creditors which means few undertakings have to be given.

Attached by way of an example, is the affidavit sworn by the Finance Director of Heaveho Group to accompany the petition for the capital reorganisation.

Note

In this affidavit we have reproduced an affidavit which includes some typical steps to redress a capital deficit problem. It should be possible to obtain from the legal advisers' database a sample affidavit which fits more exactly the requirements of the situation being dealt with.

<u>IN THE HIGH COURT OF JUSTICE</u>　　　　　　　　　1st Affidavit

C SMITH

<u>CHANCERY DIVISION</u>　　　　　　　　　　　　　Sworn 26 May 1994

On behalf of the Petitioner

No. 0004 of 1994

IN THE MATTER OF HEAVEHO PLC

and

IN THE MATTER OF THE COMPANIES ACT 1985

AFFIDAVIT

I, CHARLES SMITH of The Rectory, Guildford, MAKE OATH and say as follows:

1　I am and have been since 1 February 1980 the Finance Director of Heaveho PLC (the 'Company') and I am fully acquainted with the financial affairs of the Company. I am duly authorised by the Board of Directors to make this Affidavit on behalf of the Company. I have read the Petition in this matter now produced and shown to me marked 'CS 1' (the 'Petition') and I believe that all the statements therein contained are true and that belief is founded on the knowledge I have obtained as Finance Director as aforesaid and as a result of the enquiries and investigations I have made in connection with this application.

2　The documents now produced and shown to me marked 'CS 2' are copies of the original Memorandum and original Articles of Association of the Company. The bundle marked 'CS 3' contains copies of all resolutions required by law to be annexed thereto or embodied therein including, inter alia, the special resolution set out in the Petition. The Extraordinary General Meeting of the Company held on 1 April 1994 mentioned therein was duly convened by notice in the terms of the notice set out at page 26 of the document now produced and shown to me marked 'CS 4'. That notice together with the circular to the shareholders dated 22 March 1994 (the 'Circular') which comprises the rest of the document exhibited as 'CS 4' to this Affidavit was duly sent out to members of the Company in accordance with the Articles of Association of the Company and was also delivered to the auditors of the company.

3　As set out in the letter from Mr Heaveho, Chairman of the Company (set out on pages 4 to 8 inclusive of the Circular exhibited as 'CS 4' to this Affidavit), the proposed reduction of share premium account is one of two proposals which were submitted to shareholders. The rights issue, being the other proposal described in the Circular, has been completed and raised approximately £55,830,000 (net of expenses).

4　There is now produced and shown to me marked 'CS 5' a bundle containing true copies of the statutory audited accounts of the Company and its subsidiaries for the financial years ended 31 December 1991, 31 December 1992 and 31 December 1993.

5   The Company recorded a profit of £12,325,300 for the financial year ended 31 December 1991 arising out of dividend income of £66,350,650 less administrative expenses of £7,558,100, a provision in respect of its subsidiary, Heaveho Property Ltd, of £20,210,000, a tax charge of £4,532,050 and £21,725,200 paid out as dividends. This increased the balance on the Company's profit and loss account to £13,132,030.

6   For the financial year ended 31 December 1992, the Company incurred a loss of £5,865,400 arising out of dividend income of £13,953,900 less £4,325,200 paid out as dividends, administrative expenses of £2,348,110, a provision of £13,145,990 made against its subsidiary, Heaveho Property Ltd (which provision had to be made to reflect the permanent diminution in the Company's investment in Heaveho Property Ltd which itself arose due to the loss in value of the investment in its property-owning associated companies resulting from the continued decline in the commercial property market). This reduced the Company's balance on its profit and loss account to £7,266,630.

7   For the financial year ended 31 December 1993 the Company incurred a loss of £79,866,600 arising out of dividend income of £8,500,070 less £2,162,600 paid out as an interim dividend in respect of the six months ended 30 June 1993 (which interim dividend was declared and paid at a time when there were distributable reserves prior to the following provisions being made), a provision in aggregate of £74,477,470 made against its subsidiary, Heaveho Mines Ltd, (resulting from the decision to recognise the permanence of the losses in that subsidiary caused by the decline in the yield of minerals), a provision of £5,671,110 made against Heaveho Property Ltd, a direct subsidiary of the Company, (arising from an investment writedown of £7,000,000 (which writedown was made to reflect a permanent diminution in the value of a property in an associated company) less a tax credit of £1,328,890), other administrative expenses of £2,927,640 and a taxation charge of £3,127,850. This resulted in an adverse balance on the Company's profit and loss account of £72,599,970.

8   The Directors are satisfied that the Company's investments in its subsidiaries are fairly and accurately stated in the Company's audited accounts. The Directors of the Company have also considered carefully the values attributed to the other assets and liabilities contained in the Company's balance sheet as at 31 December 1993 and are satisfied that they are fairly and accurately stated in accordance with current accounting principles and practice. There has been a negligible loss made by the Company since 31 December 1993.

9   If the proposed reduction of share premium account is confirmed by the Court and becomes effective, a reserve amounting to £116,519,250 will arise in the books of account of the Company. The Directors propose that this reserve shall be applied in the following manner. The Directors wish to eliminate the whole of the deficit on the Company's profit and loss account as at 31 December 1993 amounting to £72,599,970 against part of the reserve arising on the reduction of share premium account being confirmed by the Court which will leave a balance on the said reserve amounting to £43,919,280.

10   I refer to paragraph **3** of this Affidavit. In that paragraph, I refer to the fact that the Company has made a rights issue which raised approximately

£55,830,000 (net of expenses). The gross amount of that rights issue amounted to £59,687,760 of which £25,951,200 was credited to share capital and £33,736,560 to share premium account. Whilst after the elimination of the deficit on the Company's profit and loss account, there will remain a reserve arising on the proposed reduction becoming effective of £43,919,280, it is submitted that, in view of the rights issue and accretions to the capital of the Company, no undertaking need be given to the Court in relation to the reserve arising.

11 Whilst it is not proposed to give undertakings in respect of the reserve arising of £43,919,280, the Company will offer to the Court an undertaking, should the Court consider the same necessary for the protection of creditors:

THAT the Company will credit to a special reserve in its books of account the following sums over and above £11,910,720 (being the net accretion to capital after the rights issue) and subject to a maximum of £60,689,250 (being the deficit on the company's profit and loss account less the net accretion to capital after the rights issue):

    (i) a sum equal to the release of any provisions included in the statutory accounts of the Company for the year ended 31 December 1993;

   (ii) a sum equal to the receipt by the Company of any dividends declared by any of its subsidiaries out of profits or reserves appearing in the books of the relevant subsidiary before the date upon which the proposed reduction of share premium account becomes effective (the 'effective date'); and

  (iii) a sum equal to the amount by which the value of any asset of the Company at the effective date shall, upon any realisation of such asset, appear to have been understated; and

THAT in respect of any sums standing to the credit of the special reserve that they:

    (i) shall not be treated as realised profits of the Company; and

   (ii) shall be treated as a non-distributable reserve of the Company for the purposes of the Companies Act 1985 s 264,

for so long as there shall remain outstanding any debt or claim against the Company which, if the date on which such reduction becomes effective were the date of the commencement of the winding-up of the Company, would be admissible to proof in such winding-up and the creditors entitled to the benefit of such debts or claims shall not have agreed otherwise, provided that:

(a) the Company shall be at liberty to apply the special reserve for any purpose for which a share premium account may be applied; and

(b) the amount standing to the credit of the special reserve may be reduced by the amount of any increase in the paid-up share capital or in the share premium account which occurs after the date on which the proposed reduction takes effect as a result of the payment up of any shares by the receipt of new consideration or by capitalisation of distributable reserves.

12 I respectfully submit that this is an appropriate case in which to dispense with the settlement of a list of creditors.

13 The Directors of the Company are satisfied that it is for the benefit of the Company that the relief sought in the Petition is granted.

Sworn at

this   th day of   , 1994

Before me

A solicitor

HEAVEHO PLC

UNDERTAKING

	£
Reduction of capital	116,519,250
Deficit on P&L	72,599,970
Balance of reserve arising on reduction	43,919,280
Giving credit for rights issue of	55,830,000

(a) No undertaking in respect of balance arising on reduction (para 10)

(b) As to the sums to be credited to the special reserve:

    (i) The company will take credit for the balance of the rights issue, being a net accretion to capital after deducting the surplus balance on the reduction (£55,830,000 − £43,919,280) (para **11**)

        11,910,720

    (ii) The maximum potential prejudice to creditors from the reduction is the amount by which the capital has been reduced   116,519,250

        That prejudice has been alleviated to the extent of the new capital raised under the rights issue   55,830,000

        Accordingly the maximum prejudice that creditors could suffer is   60,689,250

Index

References in this index are to paragraph numbers.

Accountant's report
  compensation claim, on, example,
      App M
  compiling the information, 2147, 2148
  consequential loss claim, on, example,
      App L
  content of, 2150, 2151
  divorce proceedings, establishing
      financial resources for, 703,
      704–706
  drafting, 2149–2154
  example of, 2151, App L, App M
  executive summary, 2158
  format of, 2149, 2150
  reviewing the draft report, 2155–2158
  rules of presentation, 2159–2165
  value of, 2140, 2141
  written evidence, forms of, 2142–2146
Accounting
  completion accounts, breach of warranty
      claims, 332
  post-balance sheet events, 314–316
  terms, meanings of, App B
Advance fee fraud. *See also* COMMERCIAL
      FRAUD
  nature of, 915
Affidavit
  content of, 2146
  director's, in connection with capital
      reorganisation, example, App O
  example of, used in security for costs
      application, App G
  meaning of, App A
  nature of, 2145
  swearing, 2145
Allowances
  state, deductions for, in personal injuries
      claims, 622–627
Anton Piller order
  commercial fraud, 937, 939, 940
  meaning of, App A
Appeal
  Court of
      position in hierarchy of courts, 1804
      role of, 1805

Appeal – *cont*
  High Court proceedings, from, 1836
Arbitration. *See also* DISPUTE RESOLUTION
      BY AN EXPERT
  accountant acting as arbitrator, 2001,
      2032–2038
  acting as expert witness, 2031
  advantages and disadvantages of,
      2006–2009
  agreement to arbitrate, 2011
  apportionment of costs of hearing,
      2022
  award
      enforcement of, 2024
      final and binding, 2022
      interest on, 2022
      reasoned or unreasoned, 2020, 2021
      set aside, where, 2023
  choice of arbitrator, 2012–2017
  costs, 2002, 2007, 2022
  definition of the issues, 2018
  directions, 2025
  discovery, 2025
  dispute settlement by an expert and,
      compared, 2039–2044
  fees, 2035
  generally, 2001, 2005
  hearing, 2019, 2025
  history of, 2004
  inspection, 2025
  international contract disputes, in,
      2027–2030
  judicial review, 2041
  key questions at the outset, 2033
  large cases, procedures for, 2025, 2026
  letter of engagement, 2045
  meaning of, 2003, App A
  nature of, 2003–2005
  pleadings, 2025
  preparation, 2019
  principal steps in the process of, 2010
  process, 2010–2024
  representation at, 2008
  role of the accountant in, 2001,
      2031–2033

Index

Arbitration – *cont*
Rules for the ICC Court of Arbitration,
App I
timetable for hearings, 2025
umpires, 2016
Assets
valuation of net tangible. *See* VALUATION
FOR COURT PURPOSES
Audit
Lloyd's syndicates. *See* LLOYD'S
DISPUTES
negligence in. *See* PROFESSIONAL
NEGLIGENCE
statements of auditing standards,
827–831
objective and general principles, App F
reports on financial statements, App F

Balance sheet
post-balance sheet events, 314–316
Banking fraud. *See also* COMMERCIAL
FRAUD
nature of, 915
Barristers
barrister's clerk, role of, 1821
chambers, 1815, 1816, 1817
company investigations, role in, 1620
debate on respective roles of solicitors
and, 1818–1820
how addressed in court, 1904, 1905
junior, 1813
Queen's Counsel, 1813
role of, 1811
self-employed individuals, 1814
solicitor's presence at expert's meeting
with, 1817
Benefits
lost, consideration in personal injuries
claim, 619
state, deductions for, in personal injuries
claims, 622–627
Betterment. *See* DAMAGES, new for old
Breach of contract
damages for. *See* CONTRACTUAL
DAMAGES; DAMAGES
meaning of, App A
Breach of duty of care. *See* PROFESSIONAL
NEGLIGENCE
Breach of warranty claims
completion accounts, 332
consistency, concept of
definitions, 318
importance of, 319–325
issue of consistent accounting, 317
damages arising from breach
double counting, 345
general rule, 336

Breach of warranty claims – *cont*
damages arising from breach – *cont*
method of calculation, 335
role of the expert, 333–335
value as warranted, 337, 338
value as was, opposing arguments,
338–344
de minimis clauses, 311, 312
debts, old, collection of, 329–331
financial warranties, examples of,
305–307
generally, 301–303
hindsight, issue of, 313–316
identification of possible causes of
dispute, 346
legal status of warranties, 304
materiality, meaning of, 309, 310
post-balance sheet events, 314–316
proving breach of warranty, 308
reinsurance contract disputes, in, 1133
stock provisions, 326–328
Building contracts. *See* CONSTRUCTION
CONTRACT CLAIMS

Calderbank letter, 1840
Caparo case
duty of care, establishing existence of
background to case, 813–819
extending principle to takeover
situations, 820–822
Capital gains tax
damages, effect on, 156, 1517–1525
divorce cases, 733, 734
sale and purchase dispute, revision of
consideration following settlement,
1526
Capital reorganisation
Companies Act 1985, under, 1705–1709
creditors' agreement, seeking,
1714–1716
director's affidavit in connection with,
App O
generally, 1701–1704, 1726
group of companies, 1710–1713
programme for, 1717
purpose of, 1702–1703
reduction in share premium account
consent for, 1703
group of companies, 1713
powers, 1705
rights issue, in conjunction with,
1723–1725
share capital reduction
grounds for, 1706, 1707
nature of, 1708
powers, 1705
preparation, 1704

398

Capital reorganisation – *cont*
steps to be taken on accounting side,
1717–1719
taxation and, 1722
timetable, 1720, 1721
Charts
visual presentation of evidence by using,
App L
Child
dependent, fatal accident award for, 611,
670, 671
personal injuries claim
assessments, 639, 640
case study, 674–678
Civil proceedings
commercial fraud, inter-relationship
with criminal proceedings,
950–953
Claims. *See also* DAMAGES
breach of warranty. *See* BREACH OF
WARRANTY CLAIMS
construction contract. *See*
CONSTRUCTION CONTRACT CLAIMS
costs of preparing, 174
personal injuries. *See* PERSONAL INJURIES
CLAIMS
settled, examples of, App C
Commercial fraud
advance fee fraud, 915
Anton Piller orders, 937, 939, 940
auditing standards, 962
auditor and
causation issues, 972–975
inherent risk factors, 964, 965
overview, 954–956
responsibilities
detect fraud, to, court's view,
966–971
directors' responsibilities and,
distinguished, 962
report fraud to regulators, 963
uncover fraud, to, 957–962
banking fraud, 915
causation issues, 972–975
commodity fraud, 915
computer fraud, 915
contrived insolvencies, 915
customs fraud, 915
cyclical nature of, 903–906
directors' responsibilities, 962
EEC fraud, 915
employee fraud, 909, 914
enquiries into
civil and criminal proceedings, inter-
relationship, 950–953
conditions conducive to, 911–915
criminal investigation, 919–923

Commercial fraud – *cont*
enquiries into – *cont*
documentary control systems,
932–935
documents, safeguarding, 930, 931
information
disclosure to third parties, 943, 944
powers to obtain, 924–928
interlocutory reliefs, 936–940
police procedures, 929
prosecution process, 919–923
reports, 945–949
role of the accountant, 916–918
tracing funds, 941, 942
generally, 901, 902
infinite variety, 907–910
inherent risk of, conditions increasing,
964, 965
insurance claims, false, 915
investment fraud, 915
management fraud, 909, 911–915
Mareva injunctions, 937, 938
methodology for, 915
Commodity frauds. *See also* COMMERCIAL
FRAUD
nature of, 915
Companies
group of, capital reorganisation,
1710–1713
Company investigations
accountant's role in, 1601, 1638–1640
announcements about setting up, policy
on, 1613
conclusions, 1638, 1639
conduct of, 1604
criminal offences, where, 1622
delegation of investigatory powers,
1606
DTI liaison with other regulatory
bodies, 1621
DTI officials, by, 1604
generally, 1601, 1602
initial arranagements, 1620
inspectors
act in fair and reasonable manner, to,
1617
availability of, need for, 1620
conflict, need for avoidance of, 1620
fees, 1620
indemnity, 1620
interviewing by, 1616
powers of, 1604, 1614, 1615
role of, 1607, 1608
Securities & Investment Board
appointments, 1608
statutory powers for appointing,
1603–1609

Company investigations – *cont*
interviewing
informally, 1616, 1620
oath, witnesses on, 1616
procedure, 1620
rules for good, 1618
key stages of an enquiry, 1620
practical aspects, 1610, 1611
progressing, 1620
purpose of, 1603, 1612
records, access to and review of, 1620
report, preparation and publication of,
1620
scope of, 1612–1617
stages of, 1619–1622
witnesses. *See* inverviewing, *above*
Computer
disputes relating to, 1025. *See also*
INTELLECTUAL PROPERTY DISPUTES
fraud, 915. *See also* COMMERCIAL FRAUD
software disputes, 1024, 1025
use of, by accounting expert, 2135–2139
Construction contract claims
analysis of, 577
construction industry, relating to. *See*
CONSTRUCTION CONTRACT CLAIMS
construction litigation team, 518, 519
delays, 506, 512, 523, 538, 555, 561,
567, 577
direct loss and/or expense
generally, 547–551, 577
overheads. *See* overheads, *below*
disputes generally, 501, 502, 578, 579
finance charges and interest, 568, 569
increased cost of working, 564–567
inflation, effect of, 576
loss of profit, 561–563
nature of construction industry,
tendering generally, 503
original specifications, disputes
concerning, 572
overheads
analysis, 578
computing the amount of, 560, App E
formulae in relation to disputes, 560,
App E
generally, 552
off-site costs and, 555, 556
project costs, disclosure of, 557–559
relevant jurisdiction, 554
tender rates, reference to, 553
provisional sums, 545–549
standard form contracts, 535–538
summary, 501, 502, 578, 579
types of contract
bills of quantity or unit price, 521,
525–527

Construction contract claims – *cont*
types of contract – *cont*
cost-plus, 521, 523, 524
fixed price, 521, 522
generally, 520, 521
time and materials, 521, 528
turnkey, 521, 529–534
typical project, 504–517
under-tendering, 503, 570–575
variation, 503, 539–544, 577
Contingency fees, 2125
Contractual damages. *See also* DAMAGES
construction industry, relating to. *See*
CONSTRUCTION CONTRACT CLAIMS
generally, 108
object of, 109
quantum of, principles in relation to,
110–115
scope of protection, remoteness as to,
133–136
Contributory negligence
limitation to damages where, 127, 128
meaning, App A
personal injuries claims, in, 656
Corporation tax
income, on, damages subject to
income or capital, whether,
1508–1510
treatment of interest, 1514–1516
wrongful dismissal, where,
1511–1513
Costs. *See also* FEE ARRANGEMENTS
arbitration hearing, of, 2002, 2007,
2022
contingency fees, 2125
expense involved by litigation, 1803,
1844–1847
interest on, 1424
meaning, App A
payment of, 1839–1842
preparing claims for damages, of, 174
security for. *See* SECURITY FOR COSTS
taxation of, 1841, 1842, App A
County courts
cases heard in, 1805
solicitors' rights of audience in, 1819
Courts. *See also* ARBITRATION
address, modes of, in, 1904–1909
Appeal, Court of
position in hierarchy of courts, 1804
role of, 1805
attitude in, 1912–1918
barristers
chambers, 1815, 1816, 1817
debate on respective roles of
solicitors and, 1818–1820
how addressed, 1904, 1905

Courts – *cont*
  barristers – *cont*
    juniors, 1813
    Queen's Counsel, 1813
    role of, 1811
    self-employed individuals, 1814
    solicitor's presence at expert's
      meeting with, 1817
  barrister's clerk, role of, 1821
  behaviour in, 1904–1918
  costs. *See* COSTS
  county
    cases heard in, 1805
    solicitors' rights of audience, 1819
  courtesies, 1904–1909
  cross-examination in. *See* CROSS-
    EXAMINATION
  Crown, solicitors' rights of audience,
    1819
  dress in, 1910, 1911
  hierarchy of courts in England and
    Wales, 1804, 1805
  High Court. *See* HIGH COURT
    PROCEDURES
  House of Lords
    position in hierarchy of courts, 1804
    role of, 1805
  judges
    appointment of, 1806
    role of, 1807–1810
  juries, role of, 1822
  legal system generally, 1801–1803
  magistrates' courts
    cases heard in, 1805
    position in hierarchy of courts, 1804
  solicitors
    debate on respective roles of
      barristers and, 1818–1820
    definition of, App A
    presence of, at expert's meeting with
      barrister, 1817
    rights of audience of, 1819
    role of, 1811, 1812
  view of
    auditor's responsibiliity to detect
      fraud, 966–971
    professions, in relation to professional
      negligence, 803–806
Creditors
  agreement to capital reorganisation,
    1714–1716
Criminal offences
  commercial fraud. *See* COMMERCIAL
    FRAUD
Cross-examination
  attitude in court, 1912–1918
  behaviour in courtroom, 1904–1918

Cross-examination – *cont*
  breaks in, 1939, 1940
  checklist for expert accounting witness,
    1946, App H
  court courtesies, 1904–1909
  devices of, 1931–1938
  dress in court, 1910, 1911
  expert testimony, perception of, 1930
  expert witness, of
    answers given by, 1915–1917
    generally, 1901–1903
  meaning of, App A
  preparation for
    court file, 1923–1925
    other witnesses' testimony, 1926
    proofs of evidence, 1919–1922
  role of expert accounting witness, 1945
  stages of, 1927–1929
  transcripts, 1939–1942
Crown Court
  solicitors' rights of audience in, 1819
Customs
  fraud, 915. *See also* COMMERCIAL FRAUD

Damages
  advice on law relating to, 101–103, 175
  breach of warranty claims, arising from.
    See BREACH OF WARRANTY CLAIMS
  certainty in relation to, 127, 141–144
  compensatory, valuations for, 403
  contractual
    generally, 108
    object of, 109
    quantum of damages, principles in
      relation to, 110–115
    scope of protection, remoteness as to,
      133–136
  contributory negligence, 127, 128,
    App A
  costs of preparing claims, 174
  expropriation
    lawful, 167–169, 172
    measure of compensation for,
      171–173
    unlawful, 167, 170, 171
  fatal accidents claims, 667–672
  foreign currency, effect on. *See* FOREIGN
    CURRENCY
  intellectual property rights, for
    infringement of. *See* INTELLECTUAL
    PROPERTY DISPUTES
  interest, effect on. *See* INTEREST
  limitation to
    cause, remoteness as to, 127, 129,
      130
    certainty, 127, 141–144
    contributory, negligence, 127, 128

Damages – *cont*
limitation to – *cont*
example, 145–150
generally, 127
mitigation, 127, 137–140
scope of protection, remoteness as to,
127, 131–136
Lloyd's disputes. *See* LLOYD'S DISPUTES
loss of profits, for. *See* LOSS OF PROFITS
meaning of, 104–108, App A
measure of. *See* quantum of, *below*
misrepresentation, arising from,
118–120
mitigation, 127, 137–140
'most favoured customer' clause, breach
of, 465, 466
new for old
betterment resulting, 122, 123, 125
diminution in value of property, 124,
125
example of, 149
special cases, 126
non-pecuniary losses, 121
personal injuries, for. *See* PERSONAL
INJURIES CLAIMS
professional negligence, for. *See*
PROFESSIONAL NEGLIGENCE
quantum of
contractual damages, 109–115
definition of, 106, 107
foreign currency, based on, 166
inflation, effect of, 158–160
insurance, effect of, 161–165
interest, award of, 157
meaning of, App A
negligence cases. *See* PROFESSIONAL
NEGLIGENCE
taxation, effect of, 151–156
tort, in, 116
reasonable foreseeability, 132
remoteness
cause, as to, 127, 129, 130
meaning of, App A
scope of protection, as to, 127,
131–136
tax, effect on. *See* TAXATION
tort, in
causes of action, 117
distinguished from contractual
damages, 116
foreign currencies, can be awarded in,
1435
generally, 108
valuations for assessment of. *See*
VALUATIONS FOR COURT PURPOSES
warranty claims, for breach of. *See*
BREACH OF WARRANTY CLAIMS

De minimis clauses
warranty schedules, in, 311, 312
Debts
collecting old, breach of warranty
claims and, 329–331
Directions
arbitration proceedings, in, 2025
summons for, in High Court
proceedings, 1834
Director
affidavit in connection with capital
reorganisation, example, App O
duties as to valuations, 409
**Disciplinary enquiries under Chartered
Accountants' and Certified
Accountants' Disciplinary Scheme**
accountant's role in, 1601, 1638, 1640
administration of, 1625
Appeal Committee
approach in relation to, 1632
composition of, 1631
role of, 1625
Committee of Inquiry
approach in relation to, 1632
composition of, 1625, 1630
extent of investigations, establishment
of, 1636
findings of, 1627, 1628
hearing, 1636
issues, identification of, 1636
key stages, 1636
people involved, 1637
preliminary steps, 1634
procedures to be followed, 1636
provisional criticisms, 1636
reports, 1636
stages of investigation, 1634–1637
complaint, origins of, 1625, 1626
generally, 1601, 1602
investigation committee
approach in relation to, 1632
composition of, 1623, 1629
nature of, 1623, 1629–1633
objectives of, 1624
procedures, 1625
stages of, 1623–1628
Discovery
arbitration cases, in, 2025
expert's working papers, of, 2130–2132
High Court proceedings, in, 1831–1833
meaning of, App A
privileged documents, examples of,
1832
Dispute resolution by an expert. *See also*
ARBITRATION
acting as expert not arbitrator,
2039–2049

Dispute resolution by an expert – *cont*
advising one of the parties, 2050–2056
company or business changing hands, 2052
completion accounts, 2053, 2054
conduct of the engagement, 2049
fees, 2046–2048
letter of engagement, 2045
private settlements, assisting with
conciliator, acting as, 2057–2061
negotiator, acting as, 2052–2066
procedures, 2053
role of the accountant in, 2050–2056
sued for negligence, possibility of being, 2044

Divorce
capital sum
computing, 742–745
raising, 738, 739
family trusts, 731, 732
financial resources, establishing
accountant's report, 703, 704–706
credit card statements, value of, 711
generally, 702
questionnaires, developing, 707–713
financial settlement
capital sum
computing, 742–746
raising, 738, 739
quantifying 'reasonable requirements', 740, 741
tax aspects, 733–736
valuations, family company, of shares in, farming businesses, 721, 722
role of the accountant, 737
pension arrangements, 728–730
role of the accountant
expert witness, as, 747
financial settlement, in relation to, 737
importance of, 701, 703, 748
valuations
family company, of shares in. *See also* VALUATIONS FOR COURT PURPOSES
farming business, 721, 722
importance of, 407, 714–720
Lloyd's underwriter, where husband or wife is, 723–727
pension arrangements, 728–730

DIY activities
personal injuries claims, value in, 647

Duty of care. *See* PROFESSIONAL NEGLIGENCE

Earnings
date of accident, to, 611, 612
personal injuries claims, consideration in
future loss, calculation of, 629–640
loss to date of trial, calculation of, 613–628

Economic loss. *See* LOSS OF PROFITS

EEC
fraud, 915. *See also* COMMERCIAL FRAUD

Employment
benefits, 619
future disadvantage in labour market, 645
income
future loss, calculation of, 629–640
loss to date of trial, calculation of, 613–628
job satisfaction, loss of, 646

Enquiries. *See* COMPANY INVESTIGATIONS; DISCIPLINARY ENQUIRIES UNDER CHARTERED ACCOUNTANTS' AND CERTIFIED ACCOUNTANTS' DISCIPLINARY SCHEME

Estate of deceased person
valuations where disputes, 406

European Union
import and export fraud, 915. *See also* COMMERCIAL FRAUD
intellectual property rights, 1028

Evidence. *See also* CROSS-EXAMINATION
professional negligence cases, in. *See* PROFESSIONAL NEGLIGENCE
visual presentation of, App N

Exchange rate. *See also* FOREIGN CURRENCY
movements, effect on reinsurance settlements, 1113

Expropriation
companies, of, 408
lawful, 168
nature of, 167–173
unlawful, 171

Family trusts
divorce disputes and, 731, 732

Farming businesses
divorce cases, value in, 721, 722

Fatal accidents
claims for damages, 667–672

Fee arrangements. *See also* COSTS
arbitrators, for, 2035
award, where met under an, 2126
contingency fees, 2125
dispute resolution by an expert, for, 2046–2048
estimates, 2117–2120

Fee arrangements – *cont*
example, App K
fixed fee, 2121
legal aid cases, in, 2124
timing of fee payments, 2122
who will pay the fees, 2123
Foreign currency
damages awards made in
appropriate conversions,
establishment of, 1439
associated foreign exchange losses,
1435
damages and foreign exchange
generally, 166, 1401, 1425,
1429, 1438
indirect losses, for, 1432
interest on, 1436, 1437
liquidated damages, 1430–1437
tort cases, 1433
unliquidated damages for breaches of
contract, 1431
international disputes, in, 173
reinsurance settlements, choice of
currency for, 1113
tax on awards made in, 1549
Fraud
commercial. *See* COMMERCIAL FRAUD
fraudulent misrepresentation, 119, 120

High Court procedures. *See also*
COURTS
appeals, 1836
costs. *See* COSTS
discovery, 1831–1833
divisions of High Court, 1805
joining third parties, 1830
judgments, 1835
pleadings, 1827–1829
position of High Court in hierarchy of
courts, 1804, 1805
privileged documents, 1832
Rules of the Supreme Court, governed
by, 1823
Scotland, equivalent procedures in,
1824
settling the case, 1837, 1838
solicitor's rights of audience in High
Court, 1819
summons for directions, 1834
writ, 1825, 1826
House of Lords
position in hierarchy of courts, 1804
role of, 1805

Income
income and corporation tax on, damages
subject to, 1508–1516

Income – *cont*
personal injuries claims, consideration
in
future loss, calculation of, 629–640
loss to date of trial, calculation of,
613–628
Income tax
income, on, damages subject to
income or capital, whether,
1508–1510
treatment of interest, 1514–1516
wrongful dismissal, where,
1511–1513
Inflation
construction contract claims, effect on,
576
personal injuries claims and, 634–636
quantum of damages, effect on,
158–160
Information
commercial fraud cases
disclosure, 943, 944
powers to obtain, 924–928
Inheritance tax
liability to, on damages, 1527
Inquiries. *See* COMPANY INVESTIGATIONS;
DISCIPLINARY ENQUIRIES UNDER
CHARTERED ACCOUNTANTS' AND
CERTIFIED ACCOUNTANTS'
DISCIPLINARY SCHEME
Insolvency
contrived, 915. *See also* COMMERCIAL
FRAUD
Instruction from client. *See also*
PRACTICE NOTES
example of letter of instruction, App J
fee arrangements, example, App K. *See
also* FEE ARRANGEMENTS
letter of instruction, example, App J
terms of reference, example, App K. *See
also* PRACTICE NOTES
Insurance. *See also* REINSURANCE
CONTRACT DISPUTES
false claims, 915. *See also* COMMERCIAL
FRAUD
national insurance contributions, 620,
621, 634
personal injuries claims, importance in,
603
quantum of damages, effect on,
161–165
reinsurance settlements, choice of
currency for, 1113
Intellectual property disputes, 1023
account of profits, 1008, 1011
adequate remuneration for rights in
question, issue of, 1020

Intellectual property disputes – *cont*
  compulsory licensing, 1027
  computer software disputes, 1024, 1025
  confidentiality, maintaining, 1021, 1022
  current developments in relation to,
      1023–1028
  damages, preparation of financial report
      on
    consistency with past legal precedents
        and statutes, 1009
    general principles, 1010
    objectives of, 1011
    relevant sales, identification of,
        1016–1018
    remedy sought, 1012, 1013
    royalty rate, choice of, 1014, 1015
  employee inventions, 1023
  European intervention, 1028
  generally, 1001–1003, 1029
  infringement, damages for. *See also*
      damages, preparation of financial
      report on, *above*
    account of profits as alternative, 1008,
        1012
    burden of proof, 1006
    liability and quantum dealt with
        separately, 1004
    purpose of, 1005, 1006
    quantum issues, 1009
  loss of reputation, damages for, 1007
  meaning of 'intellectual property', 1001,
      App A
  Patents Court, 1026
  quantum issues, purpose of, 1005, 1006
  royalty rate, choice of, 1014, 1015
  special considerations for the expert,
      1019–1022
Interest
  arbitration award, on, 2022
  compound interest, 1420–1424
  costs, on, 1424
  damages, effect on
    common law, interest as damages at,
        1404–1406
    foreign currency, awarded in, 1436,
        1437
    generally, 1401, 1402, 1403, 1438,
        1439
    interest on damages, 1407–1412
    interest on interest, 1420–1424
    period for which awarded, 1416–1419
    rates to apply, 1413–1415
  personal injuries claims, 613, 649–651
    eligibility for interest, 613
    possibility of high interest rates and,
        634–636
    rates to apply, 1414, 1415

Interest – *cont*
  quantum of damages, effect on, 157
  tax on, 1542–1548
International contract disputes
  arbitration, in, 2027–2030
Inventions. *See also* INTELLECTUAL
    PROPERTY DISPUTES
  employee, 1023
Investigations. *See* COMPANY
    INVESTIGATIONS; DISCIPLINARY
    ENQUIRIES UNDER CHARTERED
    ACCOUNTANTS' AND CERTIFIED
    ACCOUNTANTS' DISCIPLINARY SCHEME
Investment
  fraud, 915. *See also* COMMERCIAL FRAUD
  valuations. *See* VALUATIONS FOR COURT
    PURPOSES

Judges
  appointment of, 1806
  how addressed in court, 1905
  role of, 1807–1810
Juries
  role of, 1822

Legal aid
  accountant's fee arrangements in cases
      funded publicly, 2124
Legal terms
  meanings of, App A
Lloyd's disputes
  auditor's role and responsibility,
      1236–1239
  damages, issues concerning
    alleged negligence, proof of, 1246,
        1247
    categories of defendants, 1255–1258
    court's approach, 1253, 1254
    detailed analysis, need for, 1249
    future losses, calculation of, 1250
    generally, 1222, 1246–1254
    Names action groups, 1255–1258
    new Names, position of, 1248
    year that should have been left open,
        effect on Names, 1251, 1252
  economic matters, 1209–1211
  generally, 1201–1203
  global profit/loss, 1241, 1242
  Gooda Walker judgment, 1223
  liability issues
    account properly, failure to,
        1240–1243
    causation of loss, 1244, 1245
    claims against auditors, 1235–1239,
        1262
    claims against underwriters,
        1225–1229

Lloyd's disputes – *cont*
liability issues – *cont*
competent underwriting, failure to do,
1230–1234, 1260
generally, 1222, 1224
long tail problems, 1240
report properly, failure to, 1240–1243
limitation of claims: potential extension,
1204–1208
LMX spiral
example, 1218–1220
key issues, 1221
LMX, meaning of, 1215
major catastrophes, effect, 1218
reduction in premium rates, 1216
reinsurance with other syndicates,
1216
London Market excess of loss
reinsurance. *See* LMX spiral,
above
members'agents' duties to individual
name, 1243
negligence claims. *See* liability issues,
above
reinsurance to close (RITC),
1212–1214, 1227–1229, 1259,
1261, 1262
role of the expert accountant, 1222
Lloyd's underwriter. *See also* LLOYD'S
DISPUTES
divorce cases, in, where husband or wife
is, 723–727
Loss of opportunity
valuations in connection with. *See*
VALUATIONS FOR COURT PURPOSES
Loss of profits
calculation of
cost of management time, 237
double counting, 239–242
generally, 227, 243
gross profit, 235, 236
lost sales, 228–234
value added tax, 238
wasted expenses, 241
claims for damages
aide-memoire, 243
collection and interpretation of data,
generally, 207–211
documents relating to. *See* documents
relevant to claims, *below*
external evidence, 222, 223
generally, 201–206, 243
internal evidence, 216–221
statutory accounts, 212–215
visits to sites, need for, 224–226
construction contracts, claims in,
561–563

Loss of profits – *cont*
documents relevant to claims
financial documents, 216–219, 221
marketing documents, 216–219, 221
production documents, 216–221
statutory accounts, 212–215
economic loss, 201, 337–341
insurance protection for, 201
loss of opportunity and, distinction
between, 456

Magistrates' courts
cases heard in, 1805
position in hierarchy of courts, 1804
Mareva injunction
commercial fraud, 937, 938
meaning, App A
Meetings of experts
power to order, 2166, 2170
preparation for, 2169
purpose of, 2166
time for, 2168
without prejudice basis, on, 2167
Merger. *See also* BREACH OF WARRANTY
CLAIMS
meaning of, App B
Misrepresentation. *See also* COMMERCIAL
FRAUD
damages arising from, 118–120
reinsurance contracts, in relation to,
1134–1136

National insurance contributions
personal injuries claims, in, 620, 621,
634
Negligence
contributory, limitation to damages
where, 127, 128
meaning of, App A
meaning of 'tort of negligence',
App A
professional. *See* PROFESSIONAL
NEGLIGENCE

Opportunity, loss of
valuations in connection with. *See*
VALUATIONS FOR COURT PURPOSES

Patents. *See also* INTELLECTUAL PROPERTY
DISPUTES
employee inventions, 1023
Patents Court
role of, 1026
Payment into court, 1840
Pension
divorce cases, effect on arrangements,
728–730

Pension – *cont*
personal injuries claims and
    consideration of, 642
    employed person, 643
    self-employed person, 644
Personal injuries claims
case examples, 673–690
child, assessments for, 611, 639, 640
contributory negligence, 656
discovery of documents, plaintiff's
    entitlement to, 606
DIY activities, value of, 647
expenses, assembly of evidence on, 648
expert evidence, 607
fatal accidents
    assessment of damages, 667–672
    dependency, 670, 671
future disadvantage in the labour
    market, 645
future loss, calculation of
    actuarial evidence, 637, 638
    general damages, as, 613
    multiplicand and multiplier, 632, 633,
        635, 636
    pension, loss of or reduction in,
        642–644
    time value of money, 634–636
    uncertainty, 629–631
generally, 601–610, 691, 692
information gathering, 611, 612
insurance cover, importance of, 602
interest rates to apply, 1414, 1415
job satisfaction, 646
loss to date of trial
    benefits, 619
    deductions
        actual net income, 621
        national insurance contributions,
            620, 621
        non-deductible items, 628
        state and other benefits, 622–627
    delays before hearing, effect of, 614
    employed plaintiff, 611, 615
    income, 615–618
    interest on damage claims, 613,
        649–651, 1414, 1415
    'past loss', meaning, 613
    period covered, 613
    self-employed plaintiff, 611, 616, 620
    special damages, 613, 614
    taxation, 620
national insurance contributions
    future loss, in calculations of, 634
    loss to date of trial, in calculations of,
        620, 621
negotiations between parties, 652–655
past loss of earnings, 620

Personal injuries claims – *cont*
past loss. *See* loss to date of trial, *above*
pension loss or reduction, 642–644
preparation of claim, 608–610
quantum
    assessment factors, 668, 699
    objective of, 609
relevant factors, calculation of,
    641–656. *See also* future loss,
    calculation of; loss to date of trial,
    above
role of the accountant in, generally, 601,
    608
self-employed plaintiff, 611, 616, 620,
    644, 687–689
structured settlements, 657–666
taxation, future loss of earnings, 634
Pharmaceutical industry
compulsory licensing, royalties in, 1027
Pleadings
amendment of, App A
arbitration proceedings, in, 2025
High Court proceedings, in, 1827–1829
meaning of, App A
Police
commercial fraud, procedures as to, 929
Practice notes
accountant's report. *See* ACCOUNTANT'S
    REPORT
administration, 2114–2139
computers, use of, 2135–2139
discovery of expert's working papers,
    2130–2132
fee arrangements. *See* FEE
    ARRANGEMENTS
generally, 2101, 2102
meetings of experts, 2166–2170
new case. *See also* INSTRUCTION FROM
    CLIENT
    choice of team, 2113
    conflict of interest, checking for,
        2106–2109
    initial approach, 2103–2105
    terms of reference, 2110–2112,
        App K
paperwork, 2127–2129
privilege of expert's report, 2131, 2133,
    2134
timetable, 2114–2116
Privilege
examples of privileged documents, 1832
expert's report until disclosure, of, 2131,
    2133, 2134
Professional negligence
breach of duty of care
    ascertainment of accounting system,
        inadequate, 829

Professional negligence – *cont*
breach of duty of care – *cont*
audit evidence, failure to obtain
relevant and reliable, 830
audits, inadequate planning,
controlling and recording, 828
competence, general standards of,
833–838
financial statements, errors in
reviewing, 831
foreseeable damage resulting from,
807, 839–846
generally, 807, 823–827
internal controls, improper reliance
on, 829
reporting, errors in, 832
causes of trouble for accountants, 805,
806
court's view of professions, 803–806
duty of care
breach of. *See* breach of duty of care,
above
existence
Caparo case, 813–819
establishing, 807, 808–812
extending *Caparo* principle to
takeover situations, 820–822
meaning of, App A
reasonable practice, what is, 825–827,
App F
error of judgment and, distinction
between, 857
essential constituents of successful
claim, 807
expert resolving dispute, by, 2044
foreseeable damage
causation, 842–846
constituent of negligence claim, 807
foreseeability, establishing, 840,
841
tests for, 839
generally, 801, 802
Lloyd's disputes, in. *See* LLOYD'S
DISPUTES
practice manuals, 833
quantification of damage
cost of fresh audit and investigation,
854
defalcations by directors or
employees of audited
enterprises, 853
expert's approach
defendant's perspective, from,
863–868
plaintiff's perspective, from,
855–862
generally, 847–849

Professional negligence – *cont*
quantification of damage – *cont*
initial reviews on behalf of litigants,
869–872
lost investment, 850
monies wrongly paid out, 852
over-payment, 851
report to the court, 1319
security for costs, 1308
standards
accounting, 826
auditing, 827–831, App F
summary, 873–877
Profits
loss of, damages for. *See* LOSS OF
PROFITS

Quantity surveyor
role of, 514
Quantum of damages. *See* DAMAGES

Reinsurance contract disputes
accounting information, confirming
accuracy etc of, 1121
breach of warranty, 1133
cause of, 1108–1113
central accounting systems, 1131
collection and interpretation of data,
1129, 1130
compliance with contract, checking,
1119, 1120
currency for settlement, choice of,
1113
examples of matters affecting
allocation of claims, 1127
classes of business, confusion over,
1123, 1124
generally, 1122
period of cover, 1125
reallocation of risks, 1126
exchange rate differences, 1113
generally, 1101–1103, 1137, 1138
insurance cycle, 1109, 1110
language of reinsurance, 1104–1107
long tail liability claims, 1111
misrepresentation, 1134–1136
nature of reinsurance, 1105
net accounting, 1112
placing files, review of, 1118
placing slip, relevance of, 1115
policies, types of, 1106
role of the accountant in, 1114–1121,
1137, 1138
sampling approach, 1132
scheduling process, 1128–1136
types which frequently cause, 1107
Reinsurance to close, 1212–1214

Report
accountant's. *See* ACCOUNTANT'S REPORT
court, to the, in relation to security for
costs, 1319
Royalties
choice of rate, 1014, 1015
compulsory licensing, in, 1027

Sale
company, of, breach of warranty claims.
See BREACH OF WARRANTY CLAIMS
dispute over sale and purchase
agreement, revision of
consideration following settlement,
1526
lost, determination of, 228–234
Search and seizure powers
commercial fraud, 936–940
Security for costs
application for
affidavit used in, example, App G
company in liquidation, 1305
essential, need to be, 1308–1312
financial evidence. *See* financial
evidence, *below*
granting of discretionary, 1308
principal circumstances for, 1304
purpose of, 1304–1312
counterclaim, 1306
financial evidence
accountant's review of the financial
position, 1317, 1318
information obtained, nature of, 1315,
1316
problems associated with, 1314
requirements vary, 1313
generally, 1301–1303, 1320, 1321, 1843
methods of giving, 1307
professional negligence cases, 1308
report to the court, 1319, App G
Shares
investment fraud, 915. *See also*
COMMERCIAL FRAUD
over-payment for, 851
share capital reduction. *See* CAPITAL
REORGANISATION
valuations
circumstances where disputes may
arise, 404
court purposes, for. *See* VALUATIONS
FOR COURT PURPOSES
family business, of, in divorce cases,
407, 714–722
valuations for court purposes. See
VALUATIONS FOR COURT PURPOSES
Solicitors
company investigations, role in, 1620

Solicitors – *cont*
debate on respective roles of barristers
and, 1818–1820
meaning of, App A
presence of, at expert's meeting with,
1817
rights of audience in courts of, 1819
role of, 1811, 1812
State benefits and allowances
deductions for, in personal injuries
claims, 622–627
Statutory accounts
loss of profits, in claims for, 212–215
Stock
obsolete, breach of warranty claims and,
326–328
Structured settlements
personal injuries actions, of, 657–666

Tables
visual presentation of evidence by using,
App N
Takeover
breach of warranty claims. *See* BREACH
OF WARRANTY CLAIMS
duty of care, establishing
Caparo case
background to, 813–819
extending principle to takeover
situations, 820–822
Taxation
capital gains tax
damages, effect on, 156, 1517–1525
divorce cases and, 733, 734
capital reorganisation and, 1722
damages, of
capital gains tax, 156, 1517–1525
corporation tax
income or capital, whether,
1508–1510
treatment of interest, 1514–1516
wrongful dismissal, where,
1511–1513
deductibility of damages for tax
purposes, 1536–1538
effect of, generally, 151–156,
1501–1507
extent of, considerations, 1504–
1507
foreign currency, of awards made in,
1549
generally, 1501–1507, 1550
Gourley Principle, 1529–1533
income tax
income or capital, whether,
1508–1510
treatment of interest, 1514–1516

Taxation – *cont*
damages, of – *cont*
income tax – *cont*
wrongful dismissal, where,
1511–1513
inheritance tax, 1527
interest on, 1542–1548
period of deduction for the defendant,
1539–1541
reduction for tax effects, subject to,
1529–1533
tax period, 1534, 1535
value added tax, 1528
divorce cases, in, 733–736
personal injuries claims, in, 620, 634
sale and purchase dispute, revision of
consideration following settlement,
1526
value added tax
damages subject to, 1528
loss of profits claims, relevance in,
238
Tort
damages in. *See also* DAMAGES
causes of action, 117
distinguished from contractual
damages, 116
generally, 108
quantum of, 116
definition of, App A
negligence, of, meaning, App A
Trusts
divorce cases, family trusts in, 731,
732
valuations where disputes, 406

Valuations for court purposes
assumptions, importance of, 463–467
break up value, 460
businesses, of, App D
choice of concepts for litigation
purposes, 442–448
compensatory damages, 403
defining the entity to be valued,
413–417
director, duties of, 409
discounted cash flow method of
analysis requirements and effect, 426,
427
capitalising using, App D
computation, 424–426
concept, 423
divorces where partners running a
business, 407
estate and trust cases, 406
expropriation of companies, 408

Valuations for court purposes – *cont*
generally, 401, 471, 472
high multiples and capitalisation rates,
449, 451
information gathering for, 452–454
loss of investment opportunity, in
connection with
economic loss, 456
loss of profits and, distinction
between, 456
methods of measuring, 460–462
proof of, 457, 458
rules for, 455, 456
lost opportunity, 405
market capitalisation and asset values,
449, 450
methods of valuing business entity
discounted cash flow, 424–427
dividend yield valuations, 428–430
generally, 418–421
price/earnings method, 422, App D
special purpose valuations, 431
minority interests, 429
'net finance benefit' concept of, 465,
466
net tangible assets, of
choice of concepts for litigation
purposes, 442–448
economic value, 438, 447
going concern value, 437
liquidation basis, 439, 440
measurement by reference to costs,
433, 434
measurement by reference to current
'value', 433, 435
methods of measurement, generally,
432
premium payable, 436
realisable value, 435, 447
replacement cost, 435, 441, 447
preparation of, 472
price/earnings method of, 422, App D
reasonableness of claims, using
valuation theory to test, 411,
412
role of, in disputes, 402–412
share valuations, 404
techniques to apply in valuing
businesses, 401, App D
Value added tax
loss of profits claims, relevance in,
238

Warranty
breach of. *See* BREACH OF WARRANTY
CLAIMS

Warranty – *cont*
  de minimis clause in, 311, 312
  financial, examples of, 305–307
  legal status of, 304
Witness. *See* COURTS; CROSS-EXAMINATION;
    EVIDENCE; HIGH COURT PROCEDURES

Writ
  High Court proceedings, in, 1825, 1826
  meaning of, App A
Wrongful dismissal
  income and corporation tax liability,
    1511–1513